Grounding Global Justice

Grounding Global Justice

RACE, CLASS, AND GRASSROOTS
GLOBALISM IN THE UNITED STATES
AND MEXICO

Eric D. Larson

UNIVERSITY OF CALIFORNIA PRESS

University of California Press
Oakland, California

© 2023 by Eric D. Larson

A version of chapter 3 appeared as "Ode to the American Century: Ambivalent Americanism and the Founding of the Jobs with Justice Coalition," *Labor: Studies in Working-Class History* 12, no. 3 (September 1, 2015): 53–74, https://doi.org/10.1215/15476715-2920364.

A version of chapter 4 appeared as "Tradition and Transition: Neoliberal Multiculturalism and the Containment of Indigenous Insurgency in Southern Mexico in the 1990s," *Latin American and Caribbean Ethnic Studies* 13, no. 1 (January 2, 2018): 22–46, https://doi.org/10.1080/17442222.2018.1416895.

Library of Congress Cataloging-in-Publication Data

Names: Larson, Eric David, 1977– author.
Title: Grounding global justice : race, class, and grassroots globalism in the United States and Mexico / Eric D. Larson.
Description: Oakland, California : University of California Press, [2023] | Includes bibliographical references and index.
Identifiers: LCCN 2023002318 | ISBN 9780520388567 (hardback) | ISBN 9780520388574 (paperback) | ISBN 9780520388581 (ebook)
Subjects: LCSH: Anti-globalization movement—United States. | Anti-globalization movement—Mexico. | Social classes. | Race.
Classification: LCC JZ1318 .L366 2023 | DDC 303.48/40972—dc23/eng/20230302
LC record available at https://lccn.loc.gov/2023002318

32 31 30 29 28 27 26 25 24 23
10 9 8 7 6 5 4 3 2 1

Contents

	List of Illustrations	vii
	Acknowledgments	ix
	List of Abbreviations	xiii
	Introduction	1
PART I	(IN)VISIBILIZING EMPIRE: AMBIVALENT NATIONALISM AND THE ORIGINS OF GLOBAL JUSTICE	
1.	Food Sovereignty: The Origins of an Idea	15
2.	Ambivalent Nationalism: Food Sovereignty in Mexico's Age of NAFTA	30
3.	The Specter of US Decline: Ambivalent Americanism and the Jobs with Justice Coalition in the 1980s	50
PART II	RACISM AND GLOBAL JUSTICE IN A MULTICULTURAL AGE	
4.	Against Coca-Colonization: Neoliberal Multiculturalism and Indigenous Insurgency in Southern Mexico	73

5. Obscuring Empire: Color-Blind Anticorporatism and the 1999 World Trade Organization Protests in Seattle ... 97

6. Invisibilizing Immigration: Color-Blind Anticorporatism and the 1999 World Trade Organization Protests in Seattle ... 113

PART III TWO PROTESTS: GROUNDING GLOBAL JUSTICE IN THE TWENTY-FIRST CENTURY

7. "Localizing" Global Justice: Class, Nation, and the Jobs with Justice Coalition after Seattle ... 135

8. The WTO Is Back: UNORCA, the Vía Campesina, and the Struggle over Agriculture in Cancún ... 156

9. The Radical Road to Cancún: Anarchism and Autonomy for the Popular Indigenous Council of Oaxaca—Ricardo Flores Magón ... 176

Epilogue ... 197

Notes ... 207
Bibliography ... 281
Index ... 319

Illustrations

MAPS

1. United States: cities and global justice events featured in this book xvii
2. Mexico: cities and global justice events featured in this book xvi

FIGURES

1. Jobs with Justice march in Montgomery, Alabama (circa late 1980s/early 1990s) 67
2. CIPO-RFM member at the organization's first street protest in November 1997 in Oaxaca City, Oaxaca 86
3. Jobs with Justice activists and staff members during the week of protests against the International Monetary Fund and World Bank in Washington, D.C. 153
4. Mexican farmers affiliated with Vía Campesina at the 2003 protests outside the World Trade Organization meetings in Cancún, Mexico 170
5. Protester carrying a CIPO-RFM banner at the 2003 protests outside the World Trade Organization meetings in Cancún, Mexico 193

Acknowledgments

Writing a book can be a solitary experience. Academic institutions increasingly make research and writing competitive and acquisitive endeavors. This context makes me especially grateful for all the help, generosity, and companionship I've enjoyed over the years from students, peers, and scholars.

While I was an undergraduate at the University of Minnesota in 1998, a graduate assistant in the Spanish department first introduced me to the disproportionate power of the World Bank, the International Monetary Fund, and the World Trade Organization. While I was attending graduate school at the University of Colorado, my advisers helped shape the thinking that went into this book, especially in terms of nationalism and labor. Camille Guérin-Gonzales worked with me from the beginning, granting me unique opportunities for intellectual development. Julie Greene introduced me to the field of labor history and shepherded me through my early years as a graduate student. I thank her for her patience and rigor. Eric Rekeda introduced me (and others, I think) to the social importance and political potential of punk rock and hardcore music. I also met Evelyn Hu-DeHart at the University of Colorado, and for the first of many times she supported me when she really didn't have to. She agreed to sit on my master's thesis committee, though we were in different departments and we had never properly met. Later, when I was at Brown University, Evelyn stepped in again, various times, including, ultimately, as my dissertation director. This book wouldn't have happened without her support.

I am grateful for other support I received at Brown. Anthony Bogues offered inspiring seminars and went out of his way to support my project, offering me the kind of direct suggestions and criticisms I needed. I thank him for that. Paul Buhle agreed to work with me and helped me think through the history of the US left. Patrick Heller helped me generate a framework to understand international trade and investment. María Josefina Saldaña-Portillo helped guide me through important theoretical considerations. Phil Rosen allowed me to define and pursue my intellectual interests in my comprehensive exams.

Ani Mukherji, Margaret Stevens, and Sarah Wald were friends in American studies whose scholarship and ethical commitments helped keep me focused. I also thank Natalia Matta, Michael Seigel, and Teresa Villa-Ignacio for their interest in me and my work. Yvette Koch, as the first person I met at Brown, helped me find my place in graduate school. Rhacel Parreñas and José Itzigsohn offered support and commentary at different junctures. I thank Hilda Lloréns and Claire Andrade-Watkins for the conversations and insights, and Bob Lee for supporting the Solidarity School project. Richard Snyder supported my efforts long after I left Brown, as did the Center for Latin American and Caribbean Studies more generally. At Harvard, I thank Jeanne Follansbee for offering me an opportunity to work in the History and Literature program, and to my colleagues and students there for a lively and wide-ranging intellectual experience. Thanks in particular to Alba Aragón.

At the University of Massachusetts Dartmouth, I would like to thank my departmental colleagues for generating a bold intellectual environment. I thank Viviane Saleh-Hanna in particular for her mentorship and support. Thanks to Tammi Arford for making my pathway into the university easier as we entered together. I also thank the late José Soler and Ricardo Rosa for their friendship. Carlos Benevides has helped support efforts to create study abroad programming in Oaxaca. Thanks to the Provost's Office and CAS Dean's office for their support in the final years of the research for this book.

Scholars and activists outside of my academic workplaces also provided me with key channels to develop this work. Kathryn Brownell offered me the chance to present parts of chapters 5 and 6 at Purdue University. Maria Hwang has been a constant source of support and friendship and has read material on short notice. Kim Nolan-García provided helpful and critical comments as well. In Oaxaca, Jorge Hernández-Díaz and Martha Rees opened spaces for me to present my research. I appreciated Lynn Stephen's willingness to connect and allow me to work with Otros Saberes.

Others who deserve mention are Benjamín Maldonado Alvarado, Avi Chomsky, Roberto Ramírez, Michael Woo, Christina Heatherton, Joe Lowndes, Kate Goldman, Rebecca Leverett, Ligia Tavera Fenollosa, Juan José Bocanegra, Joe Uehlein, Rand Wilson, Alicia Rusoja, Manisha Desai, Luis Hernández Navarro, Jonathan Fox, Ricardo Ortega, Aunt Donna, and Uncle Cliff. Greetings and thanks to friends in Oaxaca, and in particular Sali, Beto, Hena, Tlahui, Luis, and Celia. I am forever grateful to Cindy Domingo and the late Garry Owens for opening their home to me. I would like to thank Tommaso Gravante and Alice Poma for opening the doors to the LACAB for me. Steve Striffler has created a range of opportunities for me over the years, and I thank him and David Roediger for their support and careful reading of my manuscript. Thank you to Niels Hooper and Naja Pulliam Collins for their constant support, to Elisabeth Magnus for the astute and thorough copyediting, and to Jessica Moll, who helped with other components of the project.

I would like to offer a heartfelt thank-you to the activists and organizers who allowed me to speak and work with them over the last fifteen years. Those from the Popular Indigenous Council of Oaxaca—Ricardo Flores Magón (CIPO-RFM), the National Union of Autonomous Regional Peasant Organizations (UNORCA), Jobs with Justice, and the Legacy of Equality, Leadership, and Organizing (LELO) deserve special mention. Thank you. I am forever grateful for my friendship with Alfonso Perez.

Working on this book took me away from River and Rui Rui too often. I can only hope to make it up to them some day. I dedicate this to Elena, who met me on deadline day and gave me a chance—even when I couldn't text back.

Abbreviations

A16	April 16, 2000, protests in Washington, D.C., against IMF/World Bank meetings
ACTWU	Amalgamated Clothing and Textile Workers Union
AFA-TWU	Association of Flight Attendants–Transport Workers Union
AFL-CIO	American Federation of Labor and Congress of Industrial Organizations
CAP	Consejo Agrario Permanente / Permanent Agrarian Council
CECVYM	Coalición de Ejidos Colectivos Valle del Yaqui and Mayo / Coalition of Ejido Collectives of the Yaqui and Mayo Valleys
CIPO-RFM	Consejo Indígena Popular de Oaxaca—Ricardo Flores Magón / Popular Indigenous Council of Oaxaca—Ricardo Flores Magón
CNC	Confederación Nacional Campesina / National Peasant Confederation

CNI	Congreso Nacional Indígena / National Indigenous Congress
CNMI	Coordinadora Nacional de Mujeres Indígenas / National Coordinating Committee of Indigenous Women
CODECI	Committee for Citizen Defense / Comité de Defensa Ciudadana
CODEP	Comité de Defensa de los Derechos del Pueblo / Committee of Defense of the Rights of the People
CWA	Communication Workers of America
ENR	European New Right
EPR	Ejército Popular Revolucionario / Popular Revolutionary Army
EZLN	Ejército Zapatista de Liberación Nacional / Zapatista Army of National Liberation
GATT	General Agreement on Trade and Tariffs
GGJ	Grassroots Global Justice
IAM	International Association of Machinists and Aerospace Workers
IFG	International Forum on Globalization
IMF	International Monetary Fund
LELO	Legacy of Equality, Leadership, and Organizing
LIMEDDH	Liga Mexicana por la Defensa de los Derechos Humanos / Mexican League for the Defense of Human Rights
MAI	Multilateral Agreement on Investment
MPR	Movimiento Popular Revolucionario / Popular Revolutionary Movement
MST	Movimiento de los Trabajadores Rurales Sin Tierra / Landless Workers' Movement
NAFTA	North American Free Trade Agreement
NFFC	National Family Farm Coalition
NIEO	New International Economic Order

NOW	National Organization for Women
OIDHO	Organizaciones Indias por los Derechos Humanos en Oaxaca / Indian Organizations for Human Rights in Oaxaca
PAN	Partido Acción Nacional / National Action Party
PNTR	Permanent Normal Trade Relations
PRD	Partido de la Revolución Democrática / Party of the Democratic Revolution
PRI	Partido Revolucionario Institucional / Institutional Revolutionary Party
PRONAL	Programa Nacional de Alimentación / National Food Program
RAN	Rainforest Action Network
REDGE	Red de Género y Economía / Gender and Economy Network
RMALC	Red Mexicana ante Libre Comercio / Mexican Network in the Face of Free Trade
SAGAR	Secretaría de Agricultura, Ganadería y Desarrollo Rural / Ministry of Agriculture, Livestock, and Rural Development
SAM	Sistema Alimentaria Mexicana / Mexican Food System
SCLC	Southern Christian Leadership Conference
SEIU	Service Employees International Union
SER-Mixe	SERvicios del Pueblo Mixe / Services of the Mixe People
SNTE	Sindicato Nacional de Trabajadores de la Educación / National Education Workers Union
TSEU	Texas State Employees Union
UAW	United Auto Workers
UCFW	United Food and Commercial Workers International Union
UCIZONI	Unión of Indigenous Communities in the Northern Zone of the Isthmus / Union de Comunidades Indígenas de la Zona Norte del Istmo

UMWA	United Mine Workers of America
UNORCA	Unión Nacional de Organizaciones Regionales Campesinas Autónomas / National Union of Autonomous Regional Peasant Organizations
UNOSJO	Unión de Organizaciones de la Sierra Juarez de Oaxaca / Union of Organizations of the Sierra Juarez of Oaxaca
UNT	Unión Nacional de Trabajadores / National Union of Workers
UPIU	United Paperworkers' International Union
WFO	World Food Organization

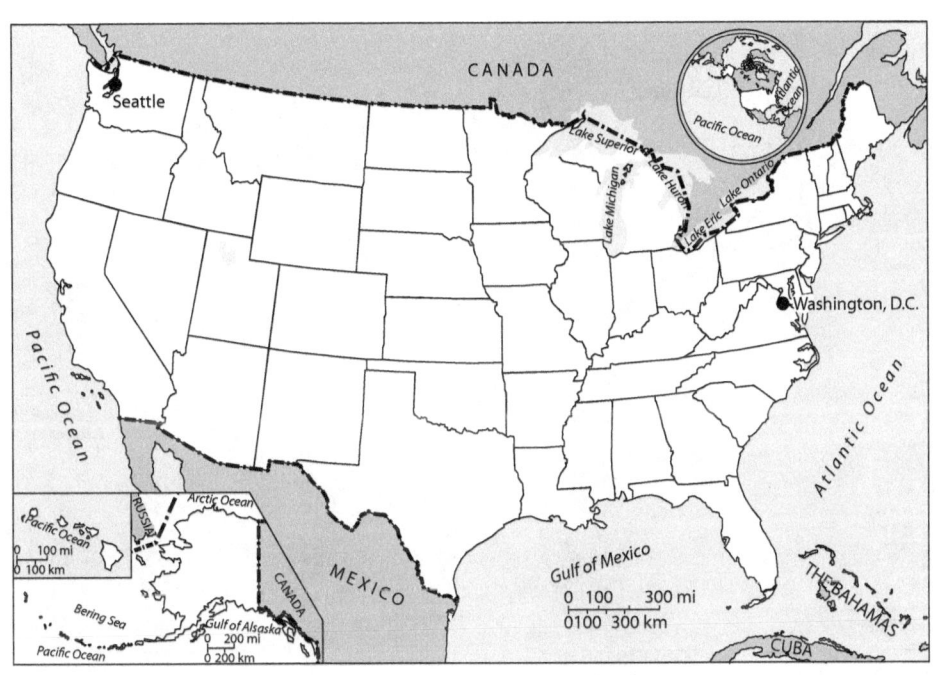

Map 1. United States map: cities and global justice events featured in this book.

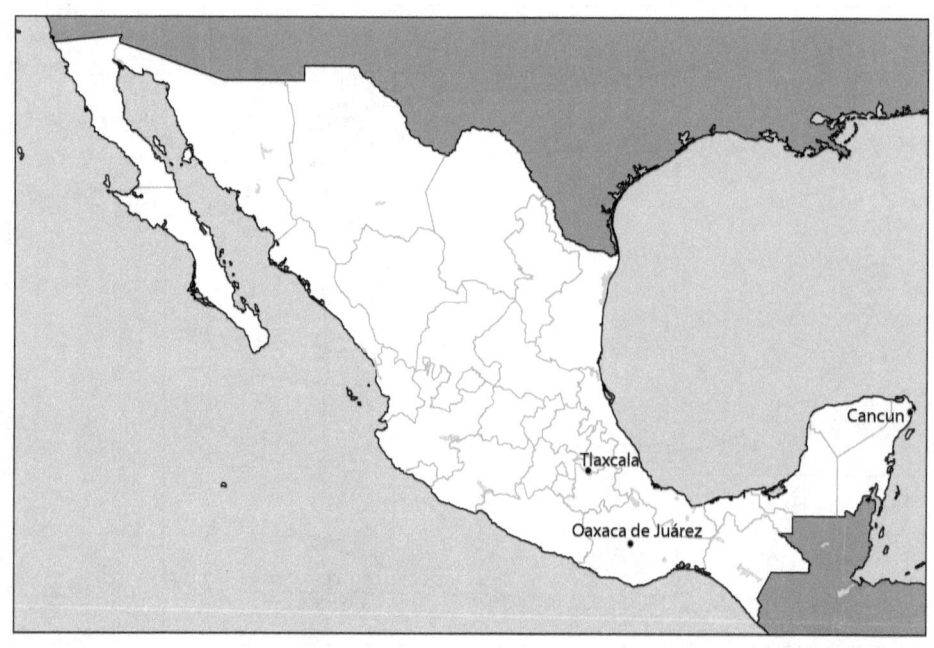

Map 2. Mexico map: cities and global justice events featured in this book.

Introduction

My great-uncle Cliff was unlike me in so many ways. I, the progressive college student with upper-middle-class credentials. He, the conservative wheat farmer, struggling in the face of drought and economic decline. I, the veteran of the student activism of the 1990s. He, the veteran of World War II. I, a young journalist, working at my university's daily newspaper. He, a member of the rural white working class, a demographic group that generated considerable hand-wringing from the big-city journalists who mentored me, particularly in later years, as Donald Trump rose to power. Trump's "America First" vision struck a chord with Cliff and his neighbors along County Road 1806, in rural western North Dakota.

Cliff told lots of stories. He respected the past. He was a sensitive person, whose gentle care for his cattle garnered him the respect of other family members. He was also unpredictable. I never knew quite what to expect, including when our family gathered for the annual Christmas visit to his farm in 1999.

I certainly didn't think we would end up talking about the protests outside the World Trade Organization meeting in Seattle. Yes, the November 30 demonstrations were still in the news, and yes, reports of their magnitude "shook the world."[1] Images of masked protesters, tear gas, and enormous puppets of endangered sea turtles circulated internationally, and the protests had temporarily shut down the meetings of the massive institution.

But national news wasn't plentiful around Zap, the nearby small town with two bars, one church, and fewer stoplights. Before the age of cell phones and satellite TV, the rural farmers in the area got their news through AM radio or staticky Channel 5, the NBC affiliate in Bismarck. While the protests may have caught the public's eye, the World Trade Organization itself probably didn't. The WTO emanated an air of uncontroversial technocracy, at least for people in the Global North. If the evening news started talking about it, you probably turned the channel.

Imagine my surprise, then, to see those same images of masks and tear gas on my great-uncle's couch, on the cover of one of his farming newsletters. Cliff not only approved of the protests but supported the direct-action methods the protesters used to blockade the ministerial. The WTO was bad for small farmers like him. He didn't know all the details why, and neither did I. But we both knew we didn't like what was going on.

If "WTO" ever became a household word in the US or in Mexico, it was for a few years in the 1990s and early 2000s. Trade and globalization became prominent topics of public debate.[2] Public demonstrations outside the meetings of the WTO and international financial institutions were nothing new, but Seattle initiated a new cycle of summit protests. Some marveled at how Seattle helped bring together the unlikely alliances of "Teamsters and Turtles," unionists and environmentalists, and human rights advocates and anarchists. It even brought together my great-uncle and me.

Most people reacted positively to the abstract idea of "opening" nations to trade, and to the exchange of ideas and products. The WTO proponents called it "free trade," and who didn't like freedom? But activists argued that the deceptive new rules were written for the multinationals. This trade wasn't free—it was private and managed. It wasn't even about countries; it was about corporations. WTO rules removed protections for social goods like health care and water. They prevented organizing or collective bargaining. These policies would ratchet up debt and dependency for the Global South.

I didn't know I would ever write a book on how people—including people like my great-uncle—came to oppose the WTO. I also didn't know that

I would be completing it as issues of trade and globalization returned to prominence in profound, and destabilizing, ways.

The rise of Covid-19 in 2020 galvanized a new wave of appeals to confront dangerous and unknowable forms of globalization, as I discuss in this book's epilogue. But anxieties about national independence in the face of a hostile world had already spiked with the election of Donald Trump as US president in 2016. Trump's campaign of "America First" was built around scapegoating China and slandering immigrants, and even on attacking longtime trading partners. Around the same time, the United Kingdom abruptly left the European Union, huffing about protecting traditional ways of life in the face of immigration and imports. Twenty years after the "Battle of Seattle," the WTO is once again an object of attack, but more for the former president than for left-wing protesters.

To be clear, I don't tell the story of this fleeting moment of agreement between my great-uncle and me simply to celebrate the political connections that Seattle made possible. This book, in fact, seeks to explore the tensions and limits of that moment and of these social movements, particularly around questions of race. Cliff, like Donald Trump today, saw trade through the lens of US greatness—and the threat the nation faced from foreign competition. Other perspectives, especially from the Global South, saw trade through the lens of a history of contending with US empire. Free trade was another example of US aggression. One central aim of this book is to think about how these issues of unequal and disproportionate US power are made visible (or not) when people talk about globalization.

What, then, can the movements that debated, discussed, and defied globalization in the 1980s and 1990s tell us about today? That's the central question of this book. It traces the history of the global justice movement through three organizations. The first is a national peasant organization in Mexico, the National Union of Autonomous Regional Peasant Organizations (Unión Nacional de Organizaciones Regionales Campesinas Autónomas, UNORCA). The second is a US-based national labor alliance named Jobs with Justice. The third is a radical Indigenous organization from southern Mexico, the Popular Indigenous Council of Oaxaca—Ricardo Flores Magón (Consejo Indígena Popular de Oaxaca—Ricardo Flores Magón, CIPO-RFM).[3]

In doing so, this volume juxtaposes a range of stories. It highlights the Mexican origins of the idea of food sovereignty. It asks us to think through the Seattle protests in the context of whiteness and immigration. It explores the politics of anarchism and autonomy in Mexico. Its interpretation of the April 2000 protests against the International Monetary Fund and World Bank is based on interviews, news clippings, and organizational documents, and is seen partly through the eyes of a protester who was there—me. That said, while I wrote the book, I didn't write it alone. It was only possible because of the intellectual labor of scholars and activists before me.

RACISM, EMPIRE, AND GLOBAL JUSTICE

Globalization was a big deal in the 1990s. People began using the term more and more in the late 1980s, but its use really skyrocketed between 1993 and 2000. It didn't have a single definition, and in the early 1990s left-leaning intellectuals published books that helped define the problem of globalization for a new generation of activists. These early accounts stressed that it was a new problem—and that was what made it so urgent. According to one account, the problems of globalization stemmed from shifting manufacturing work to the Global South.[4] In another, they stemmed from recent technological advances in fields like satellites and lasers.[5] In another, they arose from recent policy decisions by international financial institutions. These works shared the idea, though to varying degrees, that solutions must also be global. Activists, one writer argued, must create their own kind of "globalization from below" to oppose this new, corporate-led "globalization from above."[6]

The global justice movement's globe-spanning use of the internet, its international gatherings, and its targeting of supranational financial institutions (like the WTO) inspired many observers. For Marxists, the global reach of this new political enthusiasm signaled the coming of a truly international proletarian movement. For anarchists, it meant the prospect of interconnected local communities delinked from the troublesome nation-state. For liberals, it meant the chance for a new "global civil society" unbound by irrational nationalisms and populisms, particularly of the working classes. Some argued that "globalization" and global flows were overpowering the sovereignties of individual nation-states. Liberals and even some conservatives argued that these all-encompassing forces had shorn people of the certainties of home, community, or the guarantees of the welfare state. Liberals especially saw popular reactions to globalization as likely to veer toward dangerous extremism, whether white nationalism, violent leftism, or Islamic fundamentalism. The will to find liberal, secular alternatives informed a wave of studies that emphasized how global justice movements could be birthing new forms of postnational democracy.[7]

But the language of the "global" was also vexed and contradictory, opening up new possibilities but sometimes foreclosing others. In the months leading up to the 1999 Battle of Seattle, the most prominent direct-action organization of the protests sent information packets to activists around the country. The packets attested that because world trade and inequality was a "global" issue not tied to any "single-issue identity," activists could finally move beyond the "identity politics" that had "plagued" radical social movements.[8] The packet never went on to define "identity politics," but in the wake of the protests, activists of color like Elizabeth "Betita" Martínez published essays arguing that strategies and assumptions based in white experiences were creating exclusion and oppression in the movement, ultimately weakening its impact and harming communities of color.[9]

The essays generated important conversations within the emerging global justice movements. In addition, some of the recent movement scholarship has examined the questions of racism, representation, and empire that Martínez and others raised.[10] Yet other scholarship has treated racism as a secondary consideration. For some analysts, since the movement's brand of transnational organizing was multinational or anti-imperial, it didn't matter as much if it was multiracial or not.[11] While Jeremy Brecher and colleagues' widely cited work makes general statements about the need for social movements to struggle against racism and inequality within their organizations as well as outside, it also suggests the whiteness of Seattle was not of particular importance, partly since African Americans had their own global justice expressions in other venues. Citing the Martínez essay but misreading its spirit, Brecher et al. suggest that "it would be patronizing to assume that the African American community should simply show up at events like the Battle of Seattle and participate on terms set by other groups."[12] Some works emphasize the diversity of the global justice movement but leave out the Global South.[13] One positions the movement in a lineage of urban-based internationalism, yet that lineage is composed of distinctly white efforts, among them a movement that explicitly excluded Blacks.[14] Some scholars suggests that considerations of race are secondary, or even divisive and troublesome, to movements that seek to become transnational.[15] One analysis of the impact of global anticorporate movements warned that waging battles against corporate environmental racism was bound to create particularistic racial "identity politics." Talking about racism would threaten the new global connectivities.[16]

While the perspectives above are only one thread in a larger literature, the majority of the English-language scholarship on global justice movements continues to feature predominantly white movements from the US and Europe.[17] As political theorist Anthony Bogues noted in 2003, political engagement with questions of globalization at the time had mostly failed to consider Black histories of struggle against global inequalities. Those struggles helped create things like the program for a New International Economic Order (NIEO), a set of proposals for concrete reforms to narrow the gap between the Global South and the North in the 1970s.[18] Global South activists and officials, often drawing on the work of (Latin American) dependency theorists and others, noted how the South was trapped in an unfair trading relationship with the North. It was selling away at low prices their nonrenewable natural resources and raw materials—like lumber and corn—to buy refined products from the North at high prices. These activists proposed measures to stabilize the prices of raw materials and agricultural commodities. They advocated for transfers of needed technology to reduce the South's dependency on the North. As Adom Getachew has shown, intellectuals and revolutionaries in Africa and the Caribbean in the twentieth century defined empire not simply as the "alien rule" of a particular colony but also as an "international racial hierarchy." They understood decolonization as being not only about creating their own sovereign states but also about "worldmaking," about undoing inequality on a global level.[19]

INTRODUCTION   7

To be clear, this book is not about governments and intellectuals, it's not about the NIEO, and it's not only about the Global South. But the dissonance traced here—between pronouncements of "global" social movements at the 1999 WTO protests and the simultaneous fretting about "identity politics"—has guided my interpretations of what the book *is* about: the ways that popular organizations helped build the global justice movements, and how the politics of race, class, and empire shaped them. Drawing inspiration from work in transnational American studies and cultural histories of empire and resistance, I explore multiple origin stories in different countries—in this case the US and Mexico.[20]

GRASSROOTS GLOBALISM

You probably wouldn't think that a national peasant and farmer organization in Mexico, a US-based union alliance, and a radical Indigenous organization in Mexico's far south would have much in common. Yet comparing the three—UNORCA, the Jobs with Justice coalition, and CIPO-RFM, respectively—has shown me that they all developed a set of practices that *grounded* their opposition to seemingly distant, global economic forces in local, front-lines struggles.[21] The existing literature on global justice tends to focus on middle-class NGOs and intellectuals, on the one hand, or radical direct-action protesters, on the other. It focuses on the flexible and deterritorialized "networks" these groups created or the international gatherings and "spaces" that they helped build.[22] In focusing on working-class and poor people's responses to neoliberal economic restructuring, this book seeks to think about organizations that inhabited particular places and represented specific constituencies but also interacted with these broader networks.[23]

The book argues that, despite the massive differences between these three organizations, they each developed a form of what I call "grassroots globalism." Rather than an ahistorical theoretical concept, grassroots globalism is a distinct kind of politics that these organizations developed between the 1980s and the early 2000s. It emerged in the late twentieth century to respond to conditions distinct to that moment. While the term *grassroots* connotes a kind of romantic authenticity, I don't intend to suggest that this approach to global justice is more radical or pure than other kinds. It's a multifaceted, contradictory, and overlooked political orientation. This book seeks to capture the dynamism, tensions, and cultures of the broader movement by focusing on both the lived experience and the lively ideological debates and cultures of constituency-based groups as they built struggles to change globalization.

As a work of history, the book proceeds chronologically.[24] The early chapters focus on how the organizations came to understand globalization, and the latter chapters focus on how these groups participated in the wave of international protests after 1999. Two chapters in the middle momentarily step back from the organizations to analyze the iconic 1999 Battle of Seattle. The book hopes to offer breadth and comparative scope but simultaneously attend to historical detail and cultural nuance. My hope is that this detail and nuance allow the book to shed new light on the dynamics of race, class, and nation operating in and around these movements.[25]

Grassroots globalism consisted of three main characteristics. First, grassroots globalism was about grounding global justice politics in poor and working-class communities directly affected by neoliberal structural changes like the North American Free Trade Agreement (NAFTA). During the policy campaigns of the 1980s and early 1990s, just as amid the efflorescence of global justice organizing in the later 1990s, organizations from directly affected communities criticized how NGOs, political officials, and other activists tended to exclude their voices. Organizations with a grassroots globalist vision tried to center these marginalized perspectives. They set forth a classed vision of the impacts of neoliberal structural reforms, often through highly gendered and racialized notions of class. Sometimes those class ideologies disrupted racial and gender hierarchies, and sometimes they reinforced them. Grassroots globalism was about territorializing a movement sometimes considered deterritorialized. It was about "localizing the movement for global justice" to examine the local impacts on working-class communities.[26]

Second, the working-class organizations here were mainly dedicated to organizing sectors defined by their structural place in a political-economic system. The literature on global justice movements, however, tends to highlight groups brought together by ideological affinities, like anarchism.

The organizations at the center of this history organized directly affected people to build power and secure material gains. Amplifying or creating particular ideological currents was important but often secondary. Like other global justice activists, they maintained radical, even utopian visions of global justice. Grounding global justice, though, meant engaging with the local, regional, and national institutions that governed or controlled communities on the front lines of globalization's impacts. Much of their work was dedicated to engaging with governmental institutions and seeking out piecemeal changes within existing structures. The fact that much of their work entailed dealing with local people and regional politics shouldn't cast them as insufficiently "global." Instead, it highlights a distinct brand of global justice, a working-class brand of politics contesting larger forces of neoliberal power on the front lines of their implementation.[27]

The third characteristic is organizational, and it set them apart from both NGOs and global justice networks or affinity groups. Years before the "networked" organizational models of the later global justice movement, grassroots globalists created early, hybrid forms of network organizations out of their formal, membership-based organizations. They did so to offer a democratic and plural alternative to the bureaucratic organizations that had ordered working-class politics for most of the century in both countries. Their early models of networks reflected the strategic value they placed in forming expansive and innovative coalitions and alliances, including but not limited to transnational alliances.

ORGANIZATION OF THIS BOOK

The chapters of Part I, "(In)visibilizing Empire: Ambivalent Nationalism and the Origins of Global Justice," look at the early moments of grassroots globalism in the 1980s and show how Mexican activists visibilized empire as they confronted the trade and investment liberalization in Latin America's "Lost Decade." In contrast, early activist efforts in the US often invisibilized empire. Drawing from studies of empire and nationalism, these chapters note the subtle ways in which ideas of protecting national identity and national sovereignty textured progressive grassroots globalism at particular moments.[28] Chapter 1 shows how UNORCA mobilized a version of food sovereignty more than a decade earlier than the 1996 second world meeting of the international peasant confederation Vía Campesina.[29] Chapter 2 shows how UNORCA organizers expressed an ambivalent Mexican nationalism as they steered the organization into the Vía Campesina peasant confederation. As UNORCA grew, women members challenged its male leadership in seeking to balance power relationships. Chapter 3 documents the ways white progressives who founded the Jobs with Justice coalition in the US articulated their own kind of ambivalent nationalism as they attempted to organize US workers in a context of deep-seated and racialized suspicion about foreign imports.

Part II, titled "Racism and Global Justice in a Multicultural Age," examines the way organizers in the US and Mexico dealt with not only the politics of sovereignty but also racialized notions of who belonged in the nation in the first place. Chapter 4 shows how some Global North intellectuals characterized globalization as a "coca-colonization" of cultural differences. Yet Indigenous radicals tied to the Popular Indigenous Council of Oaxaca—Ricardo Flores Magón were confronted not so much with homogenization as with the Mexican state's brand of neoliberal multiculturalism, which sought control not by eliminating difference but by creating, defining, and patrolling it.

Chapters 5 and 6 momentarily step away to analyze the pivotal WTO protests in Seattle. The events influenced our three organizations to adopt the tactic of mass protest, even if they mostly watched Seattle from afar. That none of them played significant roles in Seattle, in fact, speaks to the central point of the chapters: distinct forms of exclusion accompanied the new alliances and broad-reaching impact of the protests. Chapter 5, taking up activist-intellectual Elizabeth "Betita" Martínez's essay "Where Was the Color in Seattle?," argues that the whiteness of the 1999 Seattle World Trade Organization protests was partly due to the framing of the problem of globalization by white progressives in the 1990s—a framing defined by what I call "color-blind anticorporatism."[30] Chapter 6, building on chapter 5, shows how color-blind anticorporatist perspectives helped isolate the issue of immigration from the larger debate about international trade in Seattle.

Part III, "Two Protests: Grounding Global Justice in the Twenty-First Century," considers the development of grassroots globalism in mass demonstrations outside economic summits after 1999.[31] Chapter 6 considers how Jobs with Justice "localized the movement for global justice" in protests outside the International Monetary Fund and World Bank just months after the Battle of Seattle. In doing so they contested the AFL-CIO's version of color-blind anticorporatism in its xenophobic targeting of Chinese trade practices. Chapter 7 examines how UNORCA, with the Vía Campesina, took on an important leadership role in the 2003 WTO protests in Cancún. It mobilized thousands of its members, many of them Indigenous Mayan farmers from nearby states, to protest the WTO's attempts to liberalize agriculture and privatize Global South forms of community-based knowledge and biodiversity. Chapter 8 discusses the grassroots globalism of CIPO-RFM as it prepared for the 2003 Cancún WTO protests and focuses on how their *Magonista* brand of autonomy and anarchism differed from the anarchism in the wider global justice movement.

PART I (In)visibilizing Empire
AMBIVALENT NATIONALISM AND
THE ORIGINS OF GLOBAL JUSTICE

1 Food Sovereignty

THE ORIGINS OF AN IDEA

Food Sovereignty! Few demands that circulated in the global justice movements of the 1990s and 2000s generated as much impact as the demand for a people's right to control its food. And no organizations have pushed the claim as far and fast as the Vía Campesina (Peasant Way), a worldwide coalition of peasant organizations from dozens of countries and five continents. While the Vía Campesina is often credited with coining *food sovereignty* at its 1996 world conference, the rallying cry actually has a deeper history.[1] That history is tied directly to a Mexican peasant organization that emerged in the 1980s to confront the economic crisis of Mexico's "Lost Decade," when the International Monetary Fund's loan-repayment conditions led the government to impose harsh austerity measures.[2] The history of this organization, the National Union of Autonomous Regional Peasant Organizations (Unión Nacional de Organizaciones Regionales Campesinas Autónomas, UNORCA), is an integral part of the broader history of food sovereignty and global justice.

As food sovereignty ultimately went on to shape major tendencies in global justice movements, activists and scholars have also discussed its limitations, and particularly the ways articulations of sovereignty could promote forms of "defensive localism" through invocations of territorial possession and parochial loyalty.³ As feminists have shown, expressions of national sovereignty in general have been used to justify masculinist militarism and Enlightenment-bound notions of dominance and ownership. They have been used to validate the annihilation of Indigenous peoples.⁴ Marxist theorists have noted how economic elites have masked class divisions by emphasizing national community and shared fate in national sovereignty. Contemporary food movements themselves, sometimes using explicit food sovereignty frameworks, have mobilized the politics of food and place to justify highly exclusive models of food politics. Shaped by orientations to individualistic consumption and leisure politics, or to romanticized ideas of the local as a kind of "ecological eden," these movements downplay race and class hierarchies. Their efforts foreground access to "artisanal" goods, private nature reserves, or other specialty consumption opportunities for the rich and light-skinned.⁵

This chapter suggests, though, that UNORCA's early vision of food sovereignty can be understood only as situated in long-established currents of Mexican nationalism and anti-imperialism. These views valorized national sovereignty, but specifically in terms of economic independence and national self-defense in the face of imperial aggression.⁶ While UNORCA's vision could be exclusionary in certain ways—ways that are discussed in the following chapter—this chapter shows how the organization's vision was far from defensive, individualistic localism. It wasn't based on middle-class consumption; it was based on a multiregional and national kind of economic development founded on rights for poor Mexican producers. It wasn't about a narrow nationalism; it was about national self-determination in the face of predatory imperial elites, and especially transnational corporations. It wasn't even about valorizing individual "family farmers" in the face of agribusiness or greedy banks; it was about refurbishing forms of collective agriculture developed in the Mexican Revolution.

SOVEREIGNTY: ORIGINS OF FOOD POLITICS IN NEOLIBERAL MEXICO

Mexico was in trouble. Its national debt was the highest in the world. Like other Global South nations, it had made massive public investments to industrialize, often pushed by Global North development agencies. But commodity prices tanked in the early 1980s, and Mexico's Global North trading partners slipped into recession. Private banks would extend credit only at astronomical interest rates—if at all.

After much debate, Mexico's political leaders turned to the lender of last resort—the International Monetary Fund. The fund agreed to give the country money. It gave Mexico more than it had given any other country in its forty-year history. But the funds came at great cost. The IMF loans forced Mexico to introduce austerity measures, and it had to slash public spending. The country had to import less and export more, thereby acquiring cash to pay off loans. The policies would likely spur a recession and if nothing else would severely damage the living standards of Mexico's working classes.

Peru. Jamaica. Egypt. The list goes on of countries that encountered similar circumstances and even more similar loan conditions. Many of these nations had only recently gained independence from colonial powers. Now they found themselves once again controlled by Euro-American nations. They were "sovereign" nations in only the most limited meanings of the term.

The story of the 1982 debt crisis, as it happens, is also the story of food sovereignty in Mexico. Like other Latin American countries, Mexico had been conquered by European powers. The Spaniards controlled it for nearly three hundred years. The US stormed the country and took nearly half its land mass in the 1840s. The French invaded shortly after. With good reason, Mexicans were sensitive about their sovereignty. Unlike other Latin American nations, though, Mexico was home to a massive social revolution in the twentieth century. Led by peasants, poor Mexicans successfully battled against big landlords, foreign interests, and liberal reformers, demanding, among other things, "land for those who work it." Mexico protected domestic industries, particularly steel and automotive, through nationalist policies meant to substitute domestic products for imports.[7] Working-class Mexicans wanted land to work for themselves, grow their own goods, and provide for themselves. Achieving food self-sufficiency in basic food crops had long been important for everyday Mexicans and for presidents themselves.[8] In other words, the idea of popular control over food and agricultural production—food sovereignty—had a long history in the country, even if not phrased as such.

FOOD SELF-SUFFICIENCY: PREDECESSOR TO FOOD SOVEREIGNTY

The immediate predecessor to food sovereignty in Mexico was the idea of "food self-sufficiency," and the latter was the guiding light of Mexico's food policy in the years before the 1982 crisis.[9] As the country was overrun with petroleum dollars and gained access to foreign credit, progressive and nationalist Mexican officials in 1980 created the Mexican Food System (Sistema Alimentaria Mexicana, SAM). In doing so they vowed to fundamentally alter a growing problem in Mexico: its agricultural subsidies tended to end up in the hands of agribusiness, usually geared to exporting food, while hunger was widespread at home. The program's implementation was plagued by top-down planning, unfriendly agricultural laws, and hurried implementation, but the basic vision was this: to tackle the twin problems of the poverty of small farmers and the malnourishment of the poor in both the cities and the countryside, the SAM affixed price guarantees for farmers of staple products and created a network of subsidized food stores. More farmers would produce more because of the (high) prices, so the increased supply would keep food prices low. And the subsidized food stores (and other reforms) would keep food affordable for even the country's poorest.[10] Small producers and working-class consumers would win. Middlemen who had long profited off of peasants' isolation would lose.

President José López Portillo's (1976–82) highly popular program was laid out in explicitly nationalist terms that defended the country's sovereignty through the idea of economic independence and food self-sufficiency.[11] The SAM's program of food self-sufficiency was announced on the anniversary of the 1938 Mexican expropriation of US and British oil companies—a point of pride for many Mexicans and a widely shared symbol of Mexican national independence.[12] Only six months earlier, López Portillo had withdrawn from efforts to enter a global trade agreement, the General Agreement on Trade and Tariffs (GATT). He had earned widespread praise for the move, which he explained was meant to protect Mexico's national autonomy. In terms of food, the recent US embargo of grain to the Soviet Union had raised the prospect that the US could weaponize food to negotiate with other countries as well. It was a nationalist moment, and the US was regarded with suspicion. Even "the generally conservative Agriculture Ministry ... [came to suggest] that U.S. government weather manipulation may have caused the [1979] drought" in Mexico.[13]

The president who took power in 1982 knew all this. President Miguel de la Madrid's (1982–88) party, the Institutional Revolutionary Party (Partido Revolucionario Institucional, PRI), had ruled the country for more than sixty years. It had long articulated an ideology of "revolutionary nationalism," a set of thoughts reflected in the patriotic impulse of López Portillo's late-term policies. The ideology, which grew out of the institutionalization of the revolution, dictated that Mexico was still a united, revolutionary republic and that the PRI was the only legitimate steward of the revolution's ideals. It was the benefactor of justice and social goods for all Mexicans and the defender of the nation, especially the popular classes, from external foes and internal hazards.[14] Many Mexicans had long ago given up the idea that the PRI was much more than an authoritarian party that repressed popular movements with a combination of bribes, manipulation, and force. But the party's nationalistic discourse, and especially its skillful method of incorporating peasants and urban workers into its own "official" organizations, helped the PRI to maintain its dominant status. De la Madrid's challenge was to continue the incorporation of those classes and to maintain the legitimacy of the order even as he became the enforcer and implementer of the new external power threatening Mexican sovereignty—the IMF.

The SAM, though, was everything the IMF advocated against. The IMF needed cuts to public spending, particularly the funding of peasant forms of agriculture, which it saw as inefficient and backward—far too unproductive to ever generate surpluses to export, or to profit and tax. In 1986, IMF and international pressure pushed Mexico into the GATT. Signing onto the agreement of over fifty countries worldwide meant the government would need to cut the tariffs that had long protected Mexican farmers from imports of cheap, factory-produced food in rich countries.

The early neoliberal philosophies that undergirded the GATT held that food should be distributed, not by concerns about peasants or national pride, but by price. Food was a commodity that should be produced by whoever could produce it cheapest. Countries should find the products for which they enjoyed a comparative advantage and should devote as much land as possible to those products' cultivation to maximize export earnings. For instance, Mexico's climate allowed for pineapple production, so it could produce pineapples easier—and cheaper—than could the US or Finland. Mexico could import potatoes or wheat with the money generated from its international pineapple sales. Small-scale peasants who grew a diversity of products, partly for self-consumption, were anathema to an arrangement that prized cheaply priced, mass-produced foods.

The term *food sovereignty* emerged in Mexico in an unlikely place—as a goal for the national food program that replaced the SAM. It emerged from an even more unlikely person—the very president whose implementations of IMF mandates meant less food for Mexicans and less sovereignty for Mexico. De la Madrid's replacement of *food self-sufficiency* with *food sovereignty* first appeared in the public pronouncement of his National Food Program (Programa Nacional de Alimentación, PRONAL).[15] De la Madrid, a longtime PRI functionary, sought to blend revolutionary nationalism with neoliberalism. For de la Madrid, "food self-determination, a fundamental aspect within the concept of national sovereignty," was just as much about consumption as production, commercialization, or distribution. Moving away from food self-sufficiency, with its singular focus on production, allowed de la Madrid to open the door to food imports. While this was not a direct challenge to food self-sufficiency, the president signaled the importance of protecting sovereignty even as he suggested that producers and production weren't the central focus. Besides, there are limits to what we can produce, the president said.[16] Reflecting the austerity dictates of this post-1982 moment, he said the country's food management system had to be reformed to cut costs. The new president argued that it was "not sufficient just to produce enough basic foods," because the country needed to target "existing deviations and waste" in the food system. Ultimately, sovereignty was more about the nation preserving the right to choose its food supply than about self-sufficiency itself.[17]

Though the term *food sovereignty* didn't take hold immediately, its basic components were discussed and promoted in the PRI government's left-leaning agrarian circles, as specialists noted how food self-sufficiency was no longer the central or only goal but rather part of a broader project of "food sovereignty" and "food independence."[18] In one 1984 convention in Mexico City dedicated to food sovereignty, one scholar affiliated with the PRI argued that "the achievement of obtaining food sovereignty" would allow Mexico "to no longer depend on the powerful industrialized countries and be easy prey to their foreign policy designs."[19] In short, the anti-imperialist tendencies in the PRI's revolutionary nationalism continued even in the aftermath of the SAM and coexisted uncomfortably with Mexico's continuing indebtedness to international financiers.[20]

Switching away from the goal of self-sufficiency—with its focus on producing more—seemed a move that could also challenge the peasant organizations who wanted to shift investment into agricultural production. UNORCA was one of a range of peasant organizations whose beginnings were based in struggles for land in the 1970s. As de la Madrid took power, the smaller, regional peasant organizations that would soon unite to form UNORCA gathered to develop their response—and food sovereignty would play a major role. UNORCA's early appeals regarding food and national sovereignty weren't simply about nationalism. They expressed a distinctly classed vision of national sovereignty, one based in the peasantry and rooted in a context of opposition to a new imperial incursion into Mexico through the IMF.

UNORCA: FOOD SOVEREIGNTY AND PEASANT SELF-MANAGEMENT

Some of the student radicals from the 1960s departed for peasant and Indigenous areas in Mexico's south in the 1970s to, in their words, organize the countryside. Luis Meneses, who would later help found UNORCA, was one of them. After experiencing the power of Mexican state repression as a student organizer in Mexico City in the 1960s, when the Mexican army massacred hundreds in Tlatelolco Plaza in 1968, Meneses went to the northern state of Sonora to work in the fields in an agricultural landscape dotted with ejidos.[21] One of those ejidos helped spur the creation of UNORCA.

In response to peasant demands for land in the Mexican Revolution, the Mexican government had granted land to landless farmers through the creation of ejidos. Ejidos are peasant communities tied to plots of state-owned land that peasants manage collectively. Some ejidos were born in the radical expropriation of large-scale haciendas, in which the former peons were granted the land to work together.[22] In most cases, though, individual peasants received land to work on their own, though as members of a larger ejido. Ejidos not only granted land to the landless but also provided them with a state-recognized local structure for electing representatives, making decisions about land use, and seeking credit together. The ejido, though, was also an apparatus of control. State officials could influence, bribe, or intimidate local elected leaders. State agencies could engage in corrupt lending or control production strategies.[23] Despite these contradictions, the ejido was one of the main ways the Mexican Revolution transformed the daily lives of multitudes of Mexicans.

UNORCA's early articulation of food sovereignty wasn't about defending the individual family farm against corporate agriculture. It was about defending the social and collective farming of Mexican peasants against corporate agribusiness and the development models of the Global North. It was about defending the ejido.

When ejidos found ways to work together democratically, they created the potential to achieve the important benefits of collective agriculture—pooling risk, establishing scale, obtaining credit—without the centralized state planning that had failed peasants in other societies. This is precisely what the Coalition of Ejido Collectives of the Yaqui and Mayo Valleys (Coalición de Ejidos Colectivos Valle del Yaqui y Mayo, CECVYM) in Sonora was able to do. CECVYM created a credit union for ejidatarios. They created their own insurance programs. They pushed the state to give them land. They defied conservative claims that corporate streamlining was the only path to efficient production. Their efforts led them to grow wheat, soybeans, and other crops in this fertile northern region at the same productivity as private business.[24]

Then they started to tell peasant organizations elsewhere about their success. They had yet to discuss the idea of food sovereignty, but their early demands reflected a core commitment to the sovereignty of the small producers through what they were beginning to call peasant "self-management" (*autogestión*). Through state support, the peasants themselves, they argued, should control their own credit, production, marketing, and storage. That way, they would avoid corrupt or paternalistic state agencies. And in an age when producers stayed poor but the marketers and distributors who bought their crops got rich, the farmers could develop, manage, and pocket the many potential forms of value added. They and other peasant organizations had won their battle to get land in the 1970s; now, they argued, peasants needed to "appropriate the productive process" for themselves.[25] It was a claim that became a central demand of many peasant organizations in the 1980s.

The coalition's efforts led to a series of national meetings in the early 1980s, and those meetings formed the basis of the creation of UNORCA in 1985. UNORCA's strength was partly in the range of groups it could convene.[26] The coalition's work helped inspire the collective work of a group of ejidos in Chiapas, a southern state with a highly Indigenous population. Producers from the central state of Guanajuato joined. Women in Sonora who wanted access to credit—for everything from cattle to sesame seed production—were involved, though early UNORCA was dominated by men. (More on that in the following chapter.)[27] Groups like the CECVYM also realized that peasants throughout the country were fighting the same struggles, but often doing so alone and isolated.[28] By 1989, UNORCA consisted of seventy-three member organizations from twenty-one different Mexican states.[29]

As Meneses recalled, food sovereignty "wasn't an idea that came out of someone's head, or from an academic discussion—but rather in the discussion with peasant leaders in these meetings. I remember, I participated actively in the [1985] meeting in Ahuacatlán, I was coming from Sonora, from producing wheat and some soybeans, and then with some corn producers from there and from other parts of the country, we talked about [food sovereignty]. And I remember in that meeting was when the theme of food sovereignty emerged."

UNORCA's first attempts to mobilize around "food sovereignty" emerged in a context where de la Madrid's commitment to paying the IMF seemed more important than his commitment to peasants. For UNORCA, supporting Mexican peasants was central to achieving food sovereignty. In an effort to have the administration sign a massive agreement with regional peasant organizations, ideally to establish new public policy, they argued that failing to capitalize peasant production would damage national production, and therefore the country's control over food. To "sustain the search for food sovereignty," the proposed agreement stated, the three crucial pillars were "strengthening the capitalization of the agricultural sector, supporting the organizations of ejidos and *comuneros*, and supporting peasant self-management." Peasants had to be central to food politics, they argued.[30]

The broad notion of food sovereignty also helped UNORCA bring together producer groups with seemingly conflicting priorities. According to Meneses, "[Organizations of medium-sized farms] from Nayarit could initiate a struggle for a higher price for their corn, and those from [poor, southern Mexican states] could initiate a struggle for cheaper corn [for consumption]. Notice that some asked for more money for their corn, and others asked for cheaper corn, and both were right [in our organization]."[31] Just as the designers of the SAM had recognized years earlier, small and medium-sized producers needed decent prices for their crops, but the rural working class also needed cheap corn to avoid malnourishment. "This carried us to the conclusion," Meneses said, "that we should defend food sovereignty along two lines: to have enough available food, to produce enough staple foods, [and also] to produce within the country, above all on the land of the small producers."[32]

THE ANTI-IMPERIAL ORIGINS OF FOOD SOVEREIGNTY

While "food sovereignty" for de la Madrid may have been "purely words," as Meneses told me in 2018, the idea of national sovereignty gained newfound importance as the country's economic crisis deepened. The effect on agriculture was clear. Government spending on the sector was cut in half in the 1980s, and budgets for agricultural agencies were cut nearly by two-thirds. The price the government would pay for corn increased, but not nearly as much as the prices of oil, tractors, and other necessary supplies. In 1988, farmers had to sell double the tons of beans or corn to buy the same tractor that they had in 1980.[33]

Equally importantly, Mexico's left was framing this economic scenario as one about sovereignty. Anti-imperial thought in Latin America had long denounced the ways powerful countries continued to exert control over the Third World by making them dependent on the First for everything from food to technology. As UNORCA was beginning to articulate its demand for food sovereignty, the biggest left-wing movement in recent history was making questions of sovereignty and dependency central to Mexico's political culture.

While Mexico staged presidential elections every six years, the PRI had never permitted real electoral challenges to its candidates. But that changed in 1987, when a progressive named Cuauhtemoc Cárdenas left the PRI and launched an independent bid against the candidate of the party's forceful neoliberal wing. Cárdenas made the election a dispute over the very fate of the nation. Elites had imposed austerity to pay off the foreign debt; in doing so, he argued, they had betrayed the nation by allowing the IMF, the US, and imperial powers to sack its resources. They had led the nation into an abject state of dependency. That dependency included what Cárdenas called "food dependency"—the subjection of the country to depending on imported food to survive.[34]

Cárdenas's message drew the PRI into arguments about the legacies of the revolution. For him, elites had betrayed the values of that massive social upheaval, including the sovereignty of Mexico in the face of imperial greed. Cárdenas himself represented the lineage of the revolution in Mexico. His father, as president in the 1930s, had redistributed far more land than any other president to Mexico's peasants. He had led the expropriation of US and British oil. For its part, the PRI in the 1980s could still effectively argue that it represented the principles of the revolution and that Cárdenas's repudiation of the party was itself an act of treason to revolutionary values.[35] But Cárdenas's momentum was unstoppable, and he very likely won the election. However, a mysterious blackout during ballot counting was followed by the government declaring Salinas the winner.

While not everyone on the left subscribed to Cárdenas's vision of sovereignty, it highlighted the importance of the theme in Mexico.[36] Amid the era's nationalist defenses of sovereignty, UNORCA became the voice of the specific claim of *food* sovereignty.[37] It wasn't a defensive localism. It was a classed vision of national sovereignty that situated the local in a larger structure of empire. It did so by tying food sovereignty to the Mexican Revolution, by defending the collective agriculture that the revolution had helped establish, and by situating it in a context of a Third World threatened by emerging transnational corporations,

In its "Manifesto to the Nation" (1988), for instance, UNORCA made it clear that peasants had to be crucial to any vision of sovereignty and dependency.[38] Published as a five-page spread in a leading progressive daily newspaper, the manifesto argued that the nation needed to inaugurate a "new period of the Mexican Revolution."[39] "We believe," UNORCA affirmed, "in a State that arose from the Mexican Revolution. And we know that in this moment food sovereignty is of the greatest national interest."[40] "Anyone who is fighting for an independent, sovereign, and just country," they concluded in an open letter to the public, should join UNORCA.[41]

UNORCA's food sovereignty in the 1980s also built on emerging understandings in the Latin American left of the threat of the transnational corporation.[42] Meneses, then the general coordinator of UNORCA, led the way. Arguing in 1988 at a national forum about rural reform, he declared that the post–World War II trade regime consolidated in the IMF and the GATT had penetrated the world production of everything from tomatoes to corn.[43] The "Green Revolution" technological packages that the US and these new imperial powers had pushed into the Third World, he declared, had rendered poor countries servile to the US and the biggest transnational corporations. "Defending food sovereignty is fundamental to our nationalist development," Meneses affirmed, and would help Mexico resist "the mechanisms of control and dependency and subjection of our country to those of the north."[44]

FOOD SOVEREIGNTY AND GLOBALIZATION

While scholars of global justice movements often trace movement origins to the major trade agreements of the 1990s (or possibly the GATT in the 1980s), UNORCA's work leading up to the 1988 presidential election presaged several of the themes of the global justice movements of the 1990s, and especially its anticorporate ideologies. The early 1990s marked preliminary discussions to create a "free trade area" among Mexico, the US, and Canada. That is, the liberalization that the GATT introduced would now be intensified in North America. The organization's adoption of food sovereignty ran counter to the rising levels of resistance to national-level policies that protected the working classes from international competition. Using the seemingly benign and cooperativistic language of "integration" with other countries, "opening" to the world, and "free" trade, Latin American leaders increasingly welcomed not only the liberalization of trade with their direct neighbors but also the creation of a hemispheric free trade area.[45]

UNORCA released its most detailed discussion of food sovereignty in 1992. Its *Proposal to the Peasant Movement* (1992) crafted a broad vision of food sovereignty, a vision that would carry it into an important role in the Vía Campesina, as the next chapter will discuss. The eighty-two-page work was published by the Friedrich Ebert Foundation in Mexico, a German foundation promoting democracy and associated with Germany's Social Democratic Party. The publication's contents stemmed from discussions held in UNORCA's National Assembly, and it was authored by Meneses and several other leaders in UNORCA.[46] UNORCA's fundamental argument in the document was that trade liberalization had to be tied to a patriotic form of national development that attended to national sovereignty and independence, partly through supporting its small producers.[47]

Two central claims shaped UNORCA's idea of food sovereignty in the proposal. The first was controlling the national food supply in the face of liberalization. Agricultural sovereignty was framed as a matter of national security in a hypercompetitive and insecure world.[48] An extreme approach tied to comparative advantage, they argued, would take the nation's focus off producing basic staples and leave its people vulnerable. If nothing else, it would lead to dependency. To integrate with North America, it argued, Mexico needed to do exactly what the Global North countries were doing: protecting and heavily subsidizing their agriculture and considering food a question of national security.

The second claim was directly related to the first. Producing enough basic staples for food sovereignty could and should be done by the small producers.[49] If not, Mexico faced ruin in the countryside and mass migration to the cities. More broadly, peasant agriculture "plays an important integrating role in [Indigenous] villages and communities and strengthens national identity." Peasants on socially held land constituted nearly half the total number of food producers in Mexico. Without the peasants, Mexico could lose its "existence as a nation," UNORCA argued.

The PRI's neoliberals wanted Mexican agriculture to "modernize" by forcing it to compete with US farming. For UNORCA, the party's expectation that the "North American model" of individual and factory farms could be developed in Mexico was both unrealistic and unwanted: it could destroy the country's national identity and sovereignty. Building on its work from the 1980s, UNORCA understood trade liberalization, not as a matter of trade between independent nation-states, but in a context of empire. What threatened food sovereignty were the corporate interests embracing the "agro-exporting model."[50] "National and foreign investors," UNORCA wrote, "have an—almost explicit—objective of ending the social sector and de-peasantizing agriculture." Their "transnational companies [sought] to control" the production of basic staples, not to meet the population's nutritional needs, but to use the grain as feed for hogs and cattle they could export.[51]

UNORCA's 1992 vision of food sovereignty wasn't a screed against globalization. UNORCA wanted a globalization *with* the peasants. Planned and sustainable rural development could accompany trade liberalization, they argued, but only if commercial opening was gradual, peasant agriculture was respected, and transnational corporate interests were defeated.[52] As the following chapter will make clear, documents such as UNORCA's 1992 treatise were important because the organization's power granted it influence in the highest rungs of Mexico's federal agricultural planners.

· · · · ·

Food sovereignty emerged in the 1980s as a malleable notion and would be just as malleable in the following decades. In later years it was used to campaign for everything from exclusive farmers' markets in the Global North to national production standards in Mexico and Mozambique. As Meneses recollected, "We saw that the theme of food sovereignty encompassed a large part of our proposal" for agriculture's future, from its petitions for rural financing to its focus on basic grains.[53]

While it may have led to forms of defensive localism in some contexts, UNORCA's early vision of food sovereignty was tied to upholding the commitments of the Mexican Revolution. Embracing and articulating an anti-imperialist sense of national sovereignty, the notion emerged from a long-standing valorization of food self-sufficiency in Mexico. The nationalist sentiments deployed in UNORCA's version of food sovereignty circulated in what the next chapter will examine as an ambivalent form of nationalism. UNORCA's anti-imperial idea of food sovereignty, we will see, helps explain not only the origins of food sovereignty but the origins of the global justice movements of the 1990s and beyond.

2 Ambivalent Nationalism

FOOD SOVEREIGNTY IN MEXICO'S AGE OF NAFTA

When Luis Meneses walked to the stage in a convention center in the central Mexican city of Tlaxcala in 1996, he must have felt a sense of satisfaction. UNORCA had come a long way, from sporadic gatherings of local peasant organizations in the 1980s to the hosting of a groundbreaking international conference with peasant representatives from around the world.[1] And Meneses, now UNORCA's executive coordinator, had been there from the beginning, as had the organization's vision of food sovereignty. As he addressed the gathering of more than one hundred delegates from the international peasant confederation called the Vía Campesina, he affirmed a simple vision: food sovereignty in Mexico was about the peasants.[2]

The Vía Campesina didn't invent food sovereignty. But it did make it famous. The idea's growing resonance in the 1990s was partly due to the Tlaxcala meeting, the alliance's second international conference, which UNORCA hosted. The term *food sovereignty* could mean a lot of things among the dozens of Vía Campesina affiliate organizations. It could mean providing land for the landless. It could mean fortifying ecologically sustainable agriculture. It could mean protecting culturally significant food products, like French cheese, from cheaper, mass-produced products with dangerous genetic modifications. In the US, food sovereignty mostly meant protecting individual "family farmers" from giant agribusiness.

For UNORCA, it meant all those things. But it mainly meant controlling the national food supply by creating a peasant-centered food system that would live up to the guarantees established by the Mexican Revolution, including its support of social landownership. While different organizations mobilized distinct ideas of food sovereignty, Vía Campesina's power was partly based in how it helped its affiliates target a common enemy: the multinational food corporations and the global food system they were creating.

Scholars today continue to claim that food sovereignty emerged in the 1996 conference. In doing so, they overlook how UNORCA articulated the idea as early as 1985, and how UNORCA played an important role in ensuring that the Tlaxcala conference could even happen. The historic Vía Campesina meeting in Tlaxcala was international in its composition and global in its impact, but the conference was possible only because a national organization like UNORCA hosted it.

The organization's prior work on food sovereignty paved the way for UNORCA's entrance into the Vía Campesina, as did the broader political approach it had developed to challenge corporate globalization. That approach, which I call "grassroots globalism," is the subject of much of the remainder of this book. As the following chapters show, grassroots globalism wasn't limited to a single organization, in a single country, in a single year; it defined how many popular organizations in both the US and Mexico challenged neoliberal trade policies in the late twentieth century.

Documenting this approach helps us look at the origins of the global justice movements from a new perspective. From its work to define food sovereignty in the 1980s to its efforts to build a local presence of the Vía Campesina in the 1990s, UNORCA's history shows us that in the Global South, the later global justice movements originated not just in spectacular moments of civil unrest or in narrow protectionism or nationalism but in steady organizing based on a complex mix of radical dreaming and highly institutional moderation. If global justice movements were later mostly recognized for efforts to upend long-standing social hierarchies and to launch massive street protests, UNORCA's history shows how their origins also lay in more traditional kinds of engagement with government officials and in a hesitation to challenge traditional gender roles. UNORCA focused on regional and national (rather than only international) political change, an approach guided by a discourse of sovereignty shaped by a distinctly ambivalent kind of nationalism.

FOOD SOVEREIGNTY IN THE AGE OF NAFTA

They depend on themselves for their hamburgers. They depend on us for their pickles.

That's how the agricultural trade between the US and Mexico was described by a leading Mexican critic after the new president of Mexico—Harvard-educated Carlos Salinas de Gotarí—made a dramatic move.[3] He ushered Mexico into a permanent trade and investment deal with the United States, the country Mexican foreign policy officials had so often described as untrustworthy at best, and greedy and imperialist at worst. As the previous chapter showed, Mexican food policy had long been dominated by the discourse of food self-sufficiency: only a Mexico that could feed itself could avoid humiliating forms of agricultural and economic dependency. Now, in signing the North American Free Trade Agreement of 1992, the president struck down long-standing measures that had protected Mexican agriculture. The country would almost certainly come to depend on the US for basic staple foods. The US, in contrast, would maintain its food self-determination. It would continue to provide the meat and bread for its hamburgers and would depend on Mexico for little more than its condiments.

Corn was at the heart of the matter. It was a spiritually significant product for the country's Indigenous peoples. It was a fundamental food source for the population. But now the corn supply, especially for the varieties used to feed livestock, would likely come from farmers in Iowa named Johnson or Smith, selling the corn first to distributors with names like Cargill and Monsanto. Technically, Mexican producers could still grow corn and try to sell to the Mexican or the US market. But now they would have to compete against US farmers, whose hefty subsidies from the US government, latest tractors and technology, and expansive acreage allowed them to sell corn for cheap. Mexican small producers, walking miles to their small plots of land and using mules to carry seeds, tools, and harvests, would face insurmountable challenges.[4]

Yet Salinas de Gotarí, knowing the power of the idea of sovereignty and the fear of dependency in Mexico, promoted his agricultural plans as a form of food sovereignty. In his National Development Plan he stated that "food sovereignty is a central purpose of the agricultural strategy." "Increased food sufficiency will be sought," he argued, "through priority actions aimed at increasing [production] . . . [and] all those export products that have comparative advantages will be promoted to permit us to strengthen our agricultural balance of trade."[5] His goal of guaranteeing enough food appealed to nationalist sentiments of self-determination. His secretary of budget programming—and future presidential successor—argued that foreign investment alone would not "undermine sovereignty." The president's secretary of agriculture and hydraulic resources stressed how "modernization" and getting a chance to sell into the US market would be the best way to seek food self-sufficiency.[6] Yet they usually failed to mention who should get the food, who should grow it, and who should get the profit. What's more, Mexico could reasonably expect to compete in the US market only for a few fruits and vegetables. And to do so they would need to emulate the factory-farm, agribusiness model that would likely push peasants off their land.

But UNORCA already had developed its own version of food sovereignty to address neoliberal trade reforms. As discussed in the previous chapter, UNORCA argued that any commercial opening like NAFTA must be tied to a patriotic form of national development centered on small producers and attendant to national sovereignty. In late 1990, UNORCA convened a series of marches to demand changes to state agricultural policies. Over a period of three weeks, and with the help of other peasant organizations, around ten thousand peasants marched from rural areas to Mexico City to make sure their demands were heard.[7]

Some Mexican farmers may have responded with resentment toward the producers to their north. Yet UNORCA, building on its vision of food sovereignty in the 1980s, helped recast the political enemy as the transnational corporations and the factory-farm model they were trying to internationalize. Food sovereignty in the age of NAFTA, in fact, featured new kinds of collaboration between farmers on different sides of the US/

Mexico border. In addition, targeting the predatory food corporation partly revolved around a series of cross-border dialogues between small farmers and activists in the early 1990s. To be clear, UNORCA already helped establish the corporate food model as the problem in Mexico the 1980s. But now it was less alone.

The gatherings bolstered activists' efforts to create a common message as the NAFTA discussions were still in their early days. They helped create "the vision of the corporations versus 'the rest of us,'" which became "shared across borders."[8] One Mexican farm representative who worked closely with UNORCA recounted that "'before, those from the United States were perceived simply as the enemy; all Americans are bad, the enemy.... And this has changed as we discovered allies, friends, *compañeros*, real brothers and sisters on [the other] side." In one of the gatherings, a Mexican farmer attested that "in Mexico they would tell us that U.S. agriculture was our future, and when we visit here, we found that you are busted, bankrupt, that the big corporations are making you pay." "We have discovered," he said, "that we share a nightmare. Now, together, we must build our dream from the future."[9]

Ultimately, UNORCA's vision was about food; Salinas de Gotari's was about figures. The president wanted production numbers to make agriculture a positive balance of trade, regardless of the kind of food produced and who would produce it.[10] UNORCA knew that simply boosting production wasn't enough. Without simultaneously considering the well-being of the peasantry, production support would most likely end up in the hands of the biggest Mexican agribusinesses. UNORCA wanted national, peasant production of staples like corn and beans—the crops that fed the poor.

The stage had been set for a momentous showdown between one of Mexico's most important national peasant organizations and a president who wanted to upend Mexican agriculture.

THE MODERATE ORIGINS OF GRASSROOTS GLOBALISM

Yet things were not as black and white as they might seem. UNORCA's approach to the moment was through a political viewpoint less about open confrontation or ideological purity than about policy proposals and negotiations. While the most radical organizations would soon reject NAFTA, UNORCA took a moderate and incrementalist stance. UNORCA's vision of food sovereignty, indeed, wasn't built on simply denouncing NAFTA; it was built on economically democratizing the world NAFTA created. UNORCA practiced an early kind of grassroots globalism in how its approaches to peasant organizing were framed by a changing analysis of global macroeconomic convulsions. It was in this period that UNORCA gained its greatest influence.[11] The 1982 debt crisis, for them, wasn't the kind of crisis moment that warranted polarizing the class struggle, as some Marxists had argued. It was, rather, a moment that signaled the demise of the often-generous spending by a state flush with money from oil sales.[12]

Simultaneously, the repression peasants faced in local and regional struggles seemed to be intensifying, and the potential benefits to win were smaller. What's more, there were new and stronger enemies. Mexican agribusiness began to organize itself as well, in order to push to liberalize Mexican farming in ways that would ruin small farmers.[13] UNORCA leaders claimed that there was less to fight over, so Mexicans needed to find a new way to fight. Building on the experiences of UNORCA-affiliated farmers and peasants joining forces to collectively seek credit or pool risks, the organization opted for a "proposal-based" politics oriented to generating plans for "complete rural development" and influencing public policy.[14] "UNORCA," one member said, "is not an anti-establishment organization, it is principally proposal-based."[15]

Like other grassroots globalists, UNORCA embraced early forms of network organization. It wanted to represent a democratic alternative to the hierarchical sectoral groups affiliated to the Revolutionary Institutional Party (PRI), which had ruled the country for more than fifty years. The PRI (Salinas's party) had long created peasant and worker organizations to co-opt and contain dissent. The National Peasant Confederation (Confederación Nacional Campesina, CNC) was the most prominent. According to Meneses, "The big peasant organizations were steered by governments from state capitals so that [independent] organizations wouldn't enter the countryside."[16] UNORCA decided to name itself a "union" rather than a confederation or a *central*, terms that implied hierarchical PRI organizations.[17] UNORCA's early bylaws and public pronouncements repeatedly emphasized how national leadership should be a rotating, coordinating body and should in no case have the power to override the wishes of a member regional organization.

They knew well the threat of simply being absorbed into the state. Member organizations were "autonomous," as the organizational name suggests, from both official political parties and UNORCA itself. As stated in the bylaws, "mobilization" and "political autonomy" needed to be UNORCA's "motors," since becoming "a new interlocutor of the state" could create "confusion and opportunism" and it would be a mistake to "underestimate how regional or national leadership could be absorbed." Elected leaders had to be peasants, not politicians, advisers, or technicians from agricultural colleges.[18]

Yet UNORCA's grassroots globalism was shaped by moderation and pragmatism, not revolutionary ardor. For one thing, its social base helped shape its political outlook. UNORCA organized the directly affected agriculturalists struggling to make a living, but it was never an organization of the most downtrodden. UNORCA's members at least had land to work, even if not very much. Its base was diverse, but a substantial segment of its membership was located in the ejidos of the relatively fertile areas in northern and central Mexico, where peasants were often running medium-sized operations.[19]

In a decade of perhaps unprecedented political polarization and new challenges to the PRI, UNORCA's policy of political autonomy spurred a range of reactions. One staff member discussed her first impressions: "Frankly, the organization seemed very interesting to me, because it was an organization in which different political currents participated, and that for me, in truth, was something new. . . . Honestly, I had some doubts, and I thought, 'How can this work?'" But, she concluded, it usually did.[20]

For others, though, what UNORCA called "autonomy" and "pluralism" could simply mean that anyone could participate—including leaders tied to the authoritarian PRI.[21] Ultimately, its central organizing goal of spurring peasant forms of production and commercialization was "questioned, in the best of cases, as economistic" and narrow. "In the worst [of cases]," the organization was viewed "as an agent of the neo-corporatization of the peasant movement." That is, some viewed its moderation as evidence of its being co-opted into the PRI's own world of agricultural politics.[22]

Its entrance into the Permanent Agrarian Council (CAP), an agricultural advisory group created by Salinas, is one way to look at the tensions around UNORCA's aim of political autonomy. While autonomy for UNORCA meant not being directed by any particular political party, it didn't mean lack of engagement with the state or with the PRI.[23]

Not only did UNORCA participate in the CAP, but between 1989 and 1992 it became "the privileged independent interlocutor of the government." Some UNORCA leaders were hired into the agricultural agencies of the Salinas government. Representatives of both the government and UNORCA began talking about creating new, "modern" kinds of producer organizations fit for what Salinas called the necessary "modernization" of Mexican agriculture.[24] UNORCA now spent less time in the streets and more time trying to mitigate the aspects of Salinas's proposals that were most damaging to the peasantry.[25]

Perhaps more importantly, its entrance into the CAP meant a temporary pause to pushing the issue of food sovereignty. UNORCA had included food sovereignty and other urgent demands during its participation with an independent coalition of peasant organizations in 1988. Yet food sovereignty and questions of the foreign debt and political democracy were left off the demands when UNORCA and others opted into the government-sponsored CAP.[26]

The tension between moderation and transformative change also emerged around UNORCA's most important project: protecting the ejido. Ejidos were socially owned plots of land distributed to the landless as part of the claims for justice during the Mexican Revolution (1910–17). As the previous chapter has shown, stimulating peasant forms of agriculture on ejidos was central to UNORCA's early vision of food sovereignty. Many peasant organizations launched a full-fledged campaign of resistance to Salinas's plans to allow for the privatization of ejido farming.

UNORCA, though, adopted an "ambiguous" position.[27] Partially accepting the presidential administration's claim that the ejido could be competitive only if it "modernized" itself by allowing for privatization, UNORCA's leadership signed an early 1991 statement supporting a proposed reform to the ejido. Yet the position drew deep criticism from some of its own affiliates.[28] Some leaders, and particularly Javier Gil, believed the reform could benefit small producers and argued "that the end of agrarian reform [of the Revolution] was inevitable." Many others thought the reform would simply allow major landowners and corporations to buy up ejido land for agribusiness.[29]

UNORCA's leadership, upon seeing the final language of the ejido reform, realized that they had less influence on the Salinas administration than they had thought. UNORCA had recommended that some controls over the concentration of land be maintained, but those were minimized in the final version. A host of peasant organizations, including UNORCA, had "let down their guard" in a moment when Salinas was promising funded projects and positions in his administration.[30] The intensive cycle of debate and conflict led many long-standing leaders of UNORCA, such as Gil, to leave its ranks.[31] By 1992, progressives in UNORCA gained more power, and the organization took steps to reprioritize the work of its regional affiliates.

WOMEN AND FOOD SOVEREIGNTY

Rural Mexican women had deep connections to food, but less to sovereignty. The women whose husbands or fathers participated in UNORCA were expected to prepare food for children and men. They had to carry water to the home and gather firewood. They managed food purchases and often helped tend or process small crops—especially gardens or animals near the home.[32] They conducted the labor-intensive preparation and making of corn tortillas, often on a daily basis. But they weren't sovereign producers of food—patriarchal gender roles confined them to be auxiliaries to their spouses, fathers, or brothers. The economic crisis of the era made their unpaid work even more vital. As the prices of commodity crops like coffee declined, peasant families were likely to break even—at best. Women's gardens and small-scale home livestock provided for key basic nutrition.

Yet women had been organizing in UNORCA's midst. Several groups of women in Sonora and other northern states had been attempting to launch cooperative productive projects, and they affiliated with the organization.[33] In 1989 at the UNORCA national meeting, women demanded the creation of an internal committee to advance women's economic empowerment. The women who ultimately worked in UNORCA's "Women's Area," as it was called, dared to enter the man's world of agricultural production, not just the reproductive labor of the household. Like UNORCA more broadly, the Women's Area was clear about blaming the state for failing to attend to "food sovereignty and social well-being," as well as for failing to maintain and promote food self-sufficiency.[34]

While the Women's Area would later become a "Women's Network" and be led by many peasant women, its early coordinating work was partly conducted by college-educated, city-based women who nevertheless were deeply tied to peasants' rights, women's rights, or both. Nancy Roman, an early coordinator of the Women's Area, had recently graduated with a degree in agricultural development. She was highly interested in agriculture but commented that even during her attendance at a well-known (and generally left-wing) public agricultural college in central Mexico, "In my four years I never learned anything about women in agriculture." That was new to her when she got to UNORCA, she said.[35]

One of the primary tasks of the coordinators was to lead the production of educational workshops and pamphlets for peasant women. As part of UNORCA's early grassroots globalism, these educational efforts attempted to discuss matters like food sovereignty or neoliberal reforms by centering the experience of peasants. Some were about practical agricultural knowledge, but others took on broader themes.[36] Some dealt with women's self-esteem. Some dealt with the analysis of the current political moment in Mexico.[37] While the Women's Area coordinators often gave workshops themselves, they also worked with Ana de Ita, who worked closely with UNORCA's leadership and help write its main statements on food sovereignty and issues of trade and globalization.[38] After I asked Women's Area staff member Erna Mergruen about Salinas's reform of ejidos and land distribution, she recalled, "I remember that there were many people talking about [it]. In the case of women not as much, but we did have workshops, talking a lot with peasant groups, with groups of women, in terms of the information about the reform, the implications it could have, [and] a lot too about the Free Trade Agreement."[39]

While UNORCA had faced criticism from the left for adopting a narrowly economic focus, the same emphasis on matters of agricultural production was evident in the Women's Area. Yet that emphasis generated a distinctly gendered set of impacts. When women in UNORCA had clamored for the creation of a Women's Area, men had defined its scope as advancing the general cause of the organization. That general cause was defined by the (male) membership and leadership, and it was defined as production.

Commenting on the early work of the Women's Area, Roman noted that while there was some freedom for the Women's Area to work, UNORCA ultimately "was an organization of men. There maybe were some women like Ana de Ita, [but] even Ana de Ita said that she would go to do a workshop [for UNORCA] and it would be all men." "In addition," Roman said, "in UNORCA we had the rule that we wouldn't do any work on gender." Roman went on to explain the origins of this "rule." "Gender," she said, "was very tied to feminism, and they didn't want anything about that. It was okay to work with women, but the major focus of the organization is productive. They said, 'Okay, you're going to work with women and you all are going to do productive projects.' Don't put anything else in there."

The UNORCA approach, then, was "Women, yes, but gender? No."

Yet even if the women agreed to steer clear of gender questions, their productive projects were not seen as carrying equal weight to men's productive work in the organization. According to Martha Romero, "There was a joke that when we would say, 'We need to put a women's roundtable into our congresses, into our meetings, [and] they would joke..., 'There's your table over there in the kitchen.'... [Or] they would reply, 'There's your table over there,' if there had been like a handicrafts table, for example. 'Put yourself over there and sell some clothes,' the things you're bringing, your handicrafts. But it wasn't really a space and a treatment for the necessities of women."[40]

In addition, women's production was seen as minor or reproductive, while men's was big and worthy of massive investment and training. This assumption locked women out of technology, enhanced productivity, and new forms of adding value to products. Men got trained in new technologies and techniques, but women were granted small productive projects that were seen as unskilled.[41] The idea that women's production possibilities were of minor importance was also clear as they sought credit or government agency support. For Martha Romero, "They were considered that way, as minor, secondary projects. 'Yes, let's manage this project, but she already knows how to do that.' If it would be a garden [*traspatio*] project you didn't need training because it's already known how to do it. But the men would propose [training] for wet processing of coffee—'They [Men] need this kind of training.'"

Romero said that peasant women, and especially Indigenous peasant women, would be ignored at government agencies that were mandated to attend to their requests. The receptionists wouldn't allow them to speak with the appropriate agent. The women would call her, Romero said, and say, "'Hey, Martha, . . . they don't want me to go to such-and-such person to ask for an appointment.' It was like [an UNORCA official] had to call for them to get an appointment." Even if agency staff would meet with women, they wouldn't spend much time or try to understand the local complexities, and certainly wouldn't go visit to see the conditions there. The same thing would happen if these Indigenous peasant women would go into a store. "They would go there and they [the salespeople] didn't want to attend to them there either. Because they think, 'You all aren't going to buy a mill,' or 'You all aren't going to by this equipment. . . .'" "If [salespeople] did attend to them," Romero added, "it would be like, 'Well, I'm doing you all a favor,'" as if they should be owed something in return.

Ultimately, pressure from institutions, including inside UNORCA, limited women's work to the narrow domain of "small" economic projects. In its major publication from the era, the Women's Area leadership described its projects in terms the UNORCA leadership would have commended. The book was dedicated to discussing options for women for agricultural production, and women's economic projects were described in terms, not so much of women's gaining economic independence, but rather of their supplementing the family income. Though the Women's Area coordination team were not longtime, avowed feminists, the group sometimes discussed whether the productive projects they were helping peasant women take on were ultimately extending their daily workload rather than empowering them. It was unlikely that men would pick up the daily reproductive tasks as women attended to their productive projects.[42] Ultimately, the productive focus of the Women's Area reflected the economistic focus of the entire organization. The Women's Area pushed UNORCA to address questions like gender inequality and gender roles. Yet like the rest of the organization, they stayed safely away from highly contentious matters like advocating political democracy in the country. Such an orientation allowed them to work with people of all political stripes, including rural PRIistas.

TLAXCALA 1996: FOOD SOVEREIGNTY AND THE VÍA CAMPESINA

It wasn't every day that peasants from dozens of countries could hold meetings together, given the financial limitations of the world's rural poor and the communication difficulties in an age when few rural habitants had access to the internet. Those who arrived in Mexico City in April 1996 were whisked to Tlaxcala, a regional hub about two hours away. Some may have found time for tourist excursions after the conference ended, but the Vía Campesina and UNORCA, the host of the meeting, planned for the event to be work-intensive. Once in Tlaxcala, participants arrived at an isolated conference center. UNORCA had selected the site, which was actually a vacation center for the workers of the Mexican Institute of Social Security, to prevent distractions given the importance of the work at hand. Everything the participants would need was available right there. "We could be together," Meneses said, "without even having to go into Tlaxcala."[43]

UNORCA's connection to the Vía Campesina was largely the work of Meneses. He had helped UNORCA forge international connections since at least the early 1990s.[44] As he recounts it, he was invited to several food and agriculture events in Europe, the US, and South America in those years, some of them sponsored by the World Food Organization (WFO). He first met peasant representatives who would soon be part of Vía Campesina in Rome at one such event. Meneses and other Mexican peasant representatives attended a WFO gathering in Quebec City in late 1995, and there Meneses and UNORCA decided to take on the task of hosting the Tlaxcala event the following year.[45]

The 1996 Tlaxaca meeting was historic for many reasons. The groups that founded the Vía Campesina in early 1990s were mostly from Europe or Latin America, but the organization had grown rapidly since then. The

Tlaxcala meeting had a range of themes and objectives, but one of the long-term plans was to articulate an organizational position on food and agriculture for the WFO meeting later that year. The WFO's position, guided by its idea of "food security," was one that understood hunger and malnutrition more as a problem of *quantity* of food than as a problem of distribution of food. If the problem was insufficient food for a growing world population, the answer was to focus on how the poor could buy food cheaply, not grow it. It was to support the most "efficient" producers of food (agribusiness, particularly in the Global North) so that the world food supply could also be cheap.

The Vía Campesina's effort to create another vision of food and agriculture validated the work UNORCA had long been developing and underscored UNORCA's claim that the problems in Mexico were urgent. The Vía Campesina decided to locate the conference in Mexico partly because the Zapatista Army of National Liberation (Ejército Zapatista de Liberación Nacional, EZLN), which opposed many of the developments UNORCA also criticized, particularly NAFTA and the emerging neoliberal global economy, had recently launched an armed insurgency in the country's poor, Indigenous South. For the Vía Campesina, choosing Mexico as the site acknowledged the deeply dangerous kind of neoliberal agricultural policy shaping the country—precisely the kind of policy UNORCA had long critiqued. The "misery" that NAFTA caused for Mexico's small producers, one Brazilian leader argued, made clear the danger of neoliberal agricultural policy for the rest of the Global South.[46] "We denounce trying to copy the Mexican model," he declared. Mexico was, as another international attendee said, "'in the eye of the hurricane'" because of NAFTA and the Zapatista uprising.[47]

In addition, the Vía Campesina's early work on food sovereignty validated UNORCA's own work on the idea and its emphasis on peasant self-determination. Meneses said that after Tlaxcala, the concept of food sovereignty was everywhere: "All of us [affiliates of the Vía Campesina] had it as a theme."[48] The "Declaration of Tlaxcala," which the invitees finished on the final day of the conference, affirmed that "fair trade" and agriculture must be based in food sovereignty. Peasants must push for "national and self-sufficient rural development" in the face of debt and structural adjustment. They had lost any self-determination they once had: "Big landowners and transnational corporations unjustly deny peasant and small producers the possibility to control their own destiny." From self-sufficiency to the evils of the corporations, the Vía Campesina's statement reflected themes that UNORCA's idea of food sovereignty had included since the 1980s.

While this was called an international conference, UNORCA's grassroots globalism meant that it tied its international work to the current political realities of Mexican peasant organizations. When Meneses took the stage in Tlaxcala, he stood in front of not only international representatives but a range of special local guests, introduced by name by a leader of Brazil's Landless Workers' Movement (Movimiento de los Trabajadores Rurales Sin Tierra, MST). Those included the Tlaxcala governor and representatives from government agencies, and even the representatives of the CNC. The twelve delegates of local peasant organizations highlighted at the moment (which included UNORCA representatives) all received a round of applause as the sessions opened.[49] The Mexican presence, and the impact on Mexico, was substantial. The conference led several organizations to formally affiliate with the Vía Campesina.[50] UNORCA, though, became the international confederation's official representative voice of Mexico.

Though the vision at the center of the conference was radical and global, it also reflected the moderation of UNORCA's grassroots globalism. The organization maintained a position of changing NAFTA rather than ending it. The CNC and local politicians were there, but the most radical voices of the movement against neoliberalism in Mexico—not only the Zapatistas but the Indigenous/peasant organizations that supported them—were not. As later chapters in this book will show, radical Indigenous organizations in Mexico took up the struggle for land and self-determination in related but distinct ways.

The conference put UNORCA and food sovereignty in the international spotlight in a new way, and UNORCA had invested much effort to ensure its success.[51] To be clear, the event itself mapped onto the same gendered and racialized power dynamics that operated through UNORCA and many organizations in the 1990s. Those who got to communicate internationally with leaders prior to the meeting were the leading men, including Meneses. Women, as one former leader recalled, had a different role.

Although they had influence over what the (limited) women's participation in the conference would look like, most of the women of its Women's Network were stuck with working on logistics.[52] "[The leaders] pretty much would tell the women, 'Now you're going to receive and greet X person,'" she said, or they would instruct the women to "'go greet him at the door. Look, tell him where his room is.'"

During the conference, she said, everyone wanted to hear more about the situation in Chiapas, where the EZLN had launched its insurgency. Indigenous women who were UNORCA members were present at the conference. One (mestizo) leader of UNORCA told Nancy Roman to "'[tell] them to go to the stage in their traditional clothing.' In the moment I wasn't sure I heard correctly, and I said, 'What, you're telling them to get dressed in their traditional clothing?' And he said, 'Yes, just have the ones who are dressed in traditional clothing go up to the stage.'" They just wanted the women as "decoration," Roman said.

These gender dynamics were present not only in UNORCA but in the Vía Campesina and the conference itself. As one Canadian farmer leader noted, only around 20 percent of the participants in the meeting were women, and its prior conference had had a similarly low percentage. Clearly, the confederation hadn't taken the appropriate steps to increase the number. When the confederation split into its seven different regional delegations to elect representatives to the Vía Campesina's International Coordinating Committee, each person nominated was a man.[53] Of the six thematic work groups of the conference, only one dealt with gender, and it was rolled into a much broader panel: "Rural Development, Life Conditions, and Women." Only a quarter of the resolutions of the work group had to do with women or gender specifically.[54]

Yet women created organizational power there. While the women-centered resolutions of the panel weren't numerous, they were blunt and powerful, and included "that the women attending this meeting make a pronouncement to propel our more just and democratic participation, since it is fundamental that we continue the struggle for equality."[55] They proposed (and ultimately won) the creation of an International Women's Commission within the Vía Campesina, which would orient or coordinate additional ways for the confederation to be less male dominated.[56] After it was pointed out that all the international representatives would be men, another debate ensued, and the representatives of the North America region of the organization, which included Mexico and UNORCA, opted to name a woman to the International Coordination Committee.[57] For the first time, women in the Vía Campesina arranged to hold women's assemblies before each international gathering.[58]

FOOD SOVEREIGNTY AND AMBIVALENT NATIONALISM

UNORCA's entrance into the Vía Campesina was paved by its longstanding work on the idea of food sovereignty. UNORCA helped organize a preconference one month prior to the Tlaxcala meeting to create a Mexico-centered vision of food sovereignty. That conference, attended by nearly one hundred representatives of social organizations and NGOs, helped establish the importance of food sovereignty in a country where its impact would soon crescendo. Within a few years, Meneses, as a federal representative, would help pass the Rural Sustainable Development Law (2001), which included a clause about food sovereignty. The clause defined basic grains as strategically important to the nation and identified ways to encourage peasant-based national production, though succeeding presidential administrations have shown little interest in implementing it.[59]

While some versions of sovereignty, and even food sovereignty, have led to forms of "defensive localism," that wasn't the case with food sovereignty in Mexico. *Sovereignty* connotes nationalism, but food sovereignty actually facilitated groups' international collaborations. It created a path for UNORCA into the Vía Campesina, the most extensive peasant confederation in the world. Through Vía Campesina, UNORCA could support other peasants fighting for food sovereignty in their own distinct contexts.

For UNORCA, food sovereignty was never about cultural nationalism or isolating the nation from the world. It wasn't about the nation competing to dominate other nations. It wasn't the kind of nationalism, that, as one agricultural leader recently told me, was about "killing the foreigners." It was an ambivalent kind of economic nationalism that asserted the importance of self-defense, not domination. It centered the importance of

Mexican self-determination in a context of empire, but not as an end in itself.[60] It was about the betterment of the peasants.

Its focus on the transnational corporation is one of the key ways we can see the ambivalence of its nationalism. As targeting the institutions of the world's rich would imply, food sovereignty, for UNORCA, was a question of class as well as nation. UNORCA's clear identification of the problem—the transnational corporation and world agribusiness—indicates the ways its leaders rejected any simplistic idea that US farmers (or any other national group) were the enemy. The binational exchanges that UNORCA helped facilitate were meant to show how small farmers on both sides of the border faced similar threats from global corporate agribusiness. While UNORCA was not an organization of the landless, it was composed of many mestizo and Indigenous small farmers facing immediate financial ruin. As highlighted by its explicit discussion of the Mexican Revolution in the 1980s, defending Mexico implicitly or explicitly meant defending the gains of the Mexican Revolution—and especially social forms of land ownership like the ejido. Like so many anticolonial nationalisms, the goal of national self-determination was part of a project of class equality.

For some in UNORCA, food sovereignty didn't connote a fetishized idea of a timeless, heroic Mexican nation but was really based in the community. UNORCA regional organizations had regularly noted that just increasing national agricultural productivity (as Salinas focused on) was no guarantee that small producers or poor consumers would benefit. Productivity had to be tied to peasant needs and broader issues of wellbeing.[61] As Martha Romero and others recall, UNORCA's membership associated food sovereignty less with national trade balances than with community food production for community benefit. It was about community self-sufficiency, particularly in basic grains.[62]

That said, food sovereignty for UNORCA was based on an anti-imperial nationalism that sought to defend the nation from a new colonial incursion, this one based not on arms but on economics. "We didn't define ourselves as nationalists, but we *were* defending the country," Meneses told me. Salinas de Gotarí and others who supported policies like NAFTA were deemed *entreguistas* (literally, those who handed over something to others). They had betrayed the nation by handing over its resources to the powerful countries.[63]

National sovereignty, as noted in the previous chapter, had been a major focus of recent Mexican political debate. The "revolutionary nationalism" of the authoritarian PRI, which had ruled Mexico for decades, had shaped Mexico for much of the twentieth century. It claimed that the PRI was the heir and true defender of the Mexican Revolution and the national sovereignty it enabled. Yet by the 1980s many Mexicans no longer bought the idea that the repressive PRI had much to do with the revolution. The Salinas camp, in fact, tried to recharacterize the PRI as the modernizing party, one open to new, global realities. It tried to brand its major opponent—Cuauhtémoc Cárdenas, a PRI member who was a vocal critic of NAFTA—as a vestige of an outdated revolutionary nationalism. Meneses supported Cárdenas but recoiled at the labels foisted on them by the opposition. "I wasn't a revolutionary nationalist," he said, repudiating a label that connoted a relationship to the PRI's hypocritical orthodoxy. "I was from the left."[64]

· · · · ·

The above discussion isn't intended to defend nationalistic discourses, which are always dangerous, including those that emerge in anti-imperial contexts in the Global South. The concepts of ambivalent nationalism and grassroots globalism do, however, allow us to better understand not only the history of UNORCA and food sovereignty but also the origins of the global justice movements of later years. While literature about these movements tends to argue that their earliest proponents were either radicals or narrow nationalists, UNORCA was neither. It engaged with global concerns, but from a distinctly national, regional, and local perspective. Its form of grassroots globalism featured the creation of a "networked" union of regional peasant organizations with a goal of organizing particular sectors: producers and the rural poor. It opposed the work of the official, government-supported peasant organizations, even though it strategically engaged with them and government officials in order to secure incremental gains. That said, its vision of a new kind of Mexican agriculture based in the peasantry was a radical, globally infused vision—a vision that the Mexican state of the 1990s strenuously attempted to suppress.

The ambivalent nationalism that UNORCA mobilized was an element of its grassroots globalism, just as it was for another organization that, at least superficially, appears to be completely different: the US alliance of unions and community organizations called Jobs with Justice. The next chapter will help us understand another history of the origins of global justice through the work of that alliance. Together, these two very different organizations show us the ways nation, empire, and grassroots globalism helped shape some of the earliest manifestations of global justice work in North America.

3 The Specter of US Decline

AMBIVALENT AMERICANISM AND THE JOBS
WITH JUSTICE COALITION IN THE 1980S

"Family, Country, Union and Job." The picket sign, hoisted by rallying US workers in the mid-1980s, spoke volumes about the state of the US union movement. Being in a union, and having union rights, was not just about work. It was, as workers and union leaders in a new coalition, Jobs with Justice, argued, part of an "American way of life." And that way of life, they asserted, was disintegrating under a barrage of attacks and new animosities.

Jobs with Justice would soon become a working-class leader of the US global justice movement, particularly after the Seattle protests outside the ministerial of the World Trade Organization in 1999. Yet the origins of its later internationalism emerged in an era known for the emergence of a fiery New Right, whose populism helped lead segments of the working classes into an increasingly nationalist realm of racial resentment and conservative family politics.[1] The logic for building the coalition emerged from founder Larry Cohen, the organizing director of the Communication Workers of America (CWA), who argued that unions and community organizations couldn't stop factory closings, defend strikes, or address antiunion attitudes with temporary alliances. They needed a permanent coalition of progressives. Unions led the way, and the CWA and the Industrial Union Department of the AFL-CIO played key coordinating roles. Citizen Action, the Southern Christian Leadership Conference (SCLC), the National Organization for Women (NOW), and the National Family Farm Coalition (NFFC) served as some of the most important non-union groups in the coalition's founding era.[2]

Some scholars and activists suggest that the US-based popular resistance that emerged in the Seattle era originated in struggles against trade agreements, and particularly against the North American Free Trade Agreement, in the early 1990s.[3] But Jobs with Justice's work before that, in the 1980s, also set the stage for its activities a decade later. It forged innovative worker-farmer coalitions. It developed critiques of the globe-trotting super-rich. It bolstered unions' international trade battles. It explored early "network" organizational forms, distinct from rigid bureaucracies. The organization also began experimenting with direct-action protest and with ways of countering the rise of xenophobic reactions to international trade politics. As this book later shows, in April 2000 the network helped lead the massive protests outside the offices of the International Monetary Fund and World Bank. It played a key role in helping defuse nationalistic reactions that scapegoated China instead of focusing on the role of multinational corporations.

As in Mexico, the popular organizations who crafted early critiques of globalization partly understood it through the categories of the era's popular nationalism. The Mexican peasant farmers of the era sought to defend the Mexican nation from the perceived ascendency of US influence. Jobs with Justice organizers operated in a moment when many unionists hoped to revitalize a US nation that they perceived as being in decline. The "family" and "country" focus of the group's picket sign points to the influence of Reagan-era Americanism on the historical moment. Yet Jobs with Justice, like UNORCA, would articulate nationalistic sentiments ambivalently. Far from being characteristic of an exceptional moment, the tensions around nationalism proved to be an enduring—if contested—component of the US global justice movement.

NATIONALISM AND THE POLITICS OF POPULISM

The US left has frequently framed class in the populist language of the nation, often to fend off right-wing efforts to establish conservatives as the true representatives of the patriotic "plain folk." They have used nationalistic terms of origins and territory to broaden and energize, as well as to narrow and racialize, their struggles.[4] Indeed, extolling community-based values could strengthen undercurrents of the defensive provincialism often used to fend off claims for equal rights, particularly in terms of race, gender, and sexuality.[5] Regardless, by the late twentieth century the right was winning the fight for the folk. By increasingly selling themselves as the community-based custodians of the "breadwinner family,"[6] they portrayed themselves as guardians of the nation's ideals as well as family and community values. Their "plain-folk" evangelicalism and "housewife populism" allowed the "little guy" to stand up to racial, sexual, and neighborhood change, and the protagonists of the ascendant New Right gradually weakened the left's tenuous hold on the "grassroots Americanism" of the plain folk, particularly after the 1960s.[7] By the 1980s, conservatives cited declining economic growth and the loss of the Vietnam War as proof that the country, and its God-fearing families, were "under siege." These Reagan Republicans championed everyday heroes who dared to defend the nation's moral foundation implicitly associated with white producer-citizens and their breadwinner families.[8] They sought to protect that wholesome national community from the state itself, with its hordes of Black welfare recipients, unions and other "special interests," permissive urbanites, dark-skinned foreign immigrants, and all who demanded "special rights"—including abortion—instead of taking "personal responsibility."[9]

As the picket sign mentioned earlier suggests, Jobs with Justice often envisioned unions as extensions of the vulnerable local community and the aggrieved nation. It responded to growing popular distrust of Beltway-based bigness—whether the generalized hostility to "Big Government" or fading faith in "Big Labor"—by reworking the populist appeal of faith, family, and the Founding Fathers that had carried Ronald Reagan to the White House. To counter the right-wing version of this victimized nationalism, however, the coalition tried to redefine the causes of the country's supposed slouch toward the twenty-first century. For Jobs with Justice, the un-American force that threatened the nation's moral core was a "new generation of corporate robber barons" who, like the John D. Rockefellers and Cornelius Vanderbilts of the previous century, weakened the social fabric of the national community with treasonous greed, reckless financial speculation, and deceitful legal and political maneuvering. The efforts of Jobs with Justice to blame national and community decline on ruling financial elites, and not on a dangerous underclass of nonwhite "welfare queens" and criminals, displaced one of the key discursive foundations of 1980s-era US politics.

This cultural history of union organizing in the Reagan era shows that Jobs with Justice hoped to recover momentum by casting unions as representatives of something broader. Though ordaining them as extensions of local and national community helped the coalition challenge claims that unions were mere D.C. special interests, it sometimes reinforced the American exceptionalism at the heart of the New Right's populist patriotism, which celebrated the social harmony and work ethic of a mythically "Main Street" society. In doing so, it largely accepted the interlocking narratives of decline and victimhood that permeated national politics after the 1970s.[10] Imbuing the working class with the credibility of morally exceptional communities and their industrious past could reaffirm a national history of triumph, struggle, and tradition often portrayed and understood in terms of the experiences of white breadwinners. The coalition's Americanism, however, was ambivalent. It sought to use the moral weight of "Middle American" values to extend the economic rights that had been historically proffered to breadwinner communities to social groups long denied them. It pulled away from the most conservative idealizations of the patriarchal family, and it remained wary of the racism and xenophobia that unions' Americanism could ignite. Ultimately, Jobs with Justice animated the story of workers exploited by robber barons by suggesting that morally exceptional local and national communities were at stake. But in doing so it also blurred the contours of class that the coalition so earnestly sought to emphasize.

THE POPULIST POLITICS OF MIDDLE AMERICA

Soon after the coalition's first public rally in 1987, several men and women of the Tennessee Lesbian and Gay Coalition fastened a gay rights banner to a fence at a major Jobs with Justice rally in Nashville. They had displayed the banner at several Tennessee events, including marches against the Ku Klux Klan. But according to the Coalition, the marshals of the rally soon approached and demanded the banner be taken down. They controlled the event, they said. When the activists refused, the marshals physically assaulted one of them—himself a union member. "We had sent in our endorsing form to 'be there' for others in need," one Coalition member wrote later, referencing Jobs with Justice's own emphasis of "being there" in solidarity with others. "Instead," they wrote, "we found ourselves in need of the simplest form of decency," since few other participants had risen to their defense.[11]

One of Jobs with Justice's main goals in its early years was to "highlite [sic] workplace struggles as community concerns" in order to build broad-based coalitions.[12] In some cases, doing so by invoking the populist terms of family or Christian community allowed supporters to articulate deeply held beliefs about the spiritual righteousness of opposing economic inequality.[13] In other cases, it helped the labor left to loosen the right's increasingly tight grip over the era's popular characterization of the nation's moral center, "Middle America." As historian Michael Kazin has shown, Middle America represented the "unstylish, traditionalist expanse between the two coasts" where family folk and unassuming producers felt "squeezed between the penthouse and the ghetto."[14] As Kazin asserts, the term was evidence of the "populist persuasion" in US politics, a long-standing, flexible political language that valorized plainspoken producer-citizens and demonized distant, uncaring elites. The Republicans' "Southern Strategy" counterposed a "Middle America" of down-to-earth whites against "liberal elites," protesters and criminals, and pathological Black and Puerto Rican families, and the Republicans maintained the concept's cozy relationship with morally exceptional white communities as they reenergized it in the 1980s. Nowhere was it more successful than during Reagan's campaign for reelection in 1983–84, when depicting the nation's moral essence as that of a homogenous, white, midwestern hamlet helped lead to his overwhelming victory. In small towns like his own midwestern birthplace, he argued, "a quiet, unselfish devotion to our families, our neighbors, and our nation" made government and unions redundant, and unions unnecessary meddlers.[15]

In its first major rally, Jobs with Justice harnessed the language and anger of 1890s-era Populism to single out the elites in the coalition's crosshairs: the "corporate robber barons." CWA president Morton Bahr repeatedly denounced a "new generation of corporate robber barons" in front of the ten thousand attendees at the rally, which coincided with the annual CWA convention. Another leader lambasted them as "stylish robber barons and their million-dollar consultants."[16] During the proceedings, the three unions confronting Eastern Airlines helped Jobs with Justice to set its sights on its first "robber baron" target: Frank Lorenzo, one of the many '80s-era corporate raiders and owner of Texas Air, which had acquired Eastern in February 1986. The acquisition gave Lorenzo the reins of a company that was one of the few large, unionized employers in the South. He immediately implemented a 20 percent slash in wages for pilots and flight attendants, and managers introduced military rigidity into the everyday routines of Eastern workers. Between December 1986 and September 1988, Lorenzo reduced the Eastern workforce from 43,000 to 29,500.[17] By personalizing the struggle against Eastern as one against Lorenzo, yet by associating individual employers with a dangerous new class, Jobs with Justice rode the anti–Wall Street momentum of late 1987, when many Americans who had made their first, humble bets on Wall Street lost big in the steepest one-day fall in Wall Street history in October. It was at Miami International Airport that Jobs with Justice unveiled its creative direct action, carrying out a "drive-in." It slowed traffic into the airport for hours—including, of course, to the Eastern Airlines counter.

Despite its sophisticated national coordination, the coalition's efforts to cast "workplace struggles as community concerns" meant distancing itself from D.C. politicking and enlisting local allies. Its emphasis on direct action, for instance, stressed "undignified" confrontation, rather than the suit-and-tie negotiating so prized in the AFL-CIO. While Reagan celebrated the private voluntarism of churches and Middle American communities, Jobs with Justice created its "I'll be There" pledge card, through which organizational and individual signers pledged to "be there" for someone else's struggle at least five times in the coming year. The organization's lack of paid staff, early leaders thought, would ensure that organizers from member organizations would become accustomed to initiating activities themselves, instead of waiting for paid D.C. staff to do it.[18] Jobs with Justice affiliates called the group a "campaign" or "network" rather than an "organization." It was meant to prioritize flexibility and local participation.

By late 1987, the coalition had gained most of its attention for the large rallies and marches it organized, and it was relatively active in eight locations nationally. By late 1988, Jobs with Justice coalitions had helped produce concrete union victories in Buffalo and in Nacogdoches, Texas, and the organization claimed to have small local coalitions in around twenty cities.[19] Though national union leaders supplied and ultimately controlled the coalition's funding and made its major decisions, Cohen and others stipulated that local steering committees, elected locally, must feature equal representation of union and "community" organizations. The Jobs with Justice movement wouldn't be led by pencil-pushers, they seemed to argue. As spokesperson Steve Rosenthal of CWA confirmed, "We wouldn't want to make it seem like this came straight out of Washington."[20]

FARMER-LABOR COALITIONS AND THE "NEW POPULISM"

Coalitions of workers, farmers, and peasants would soon be integral components of global justice movements, and collaborations of US progressive farm and labor organizations around trade issues were initiated by Jobs with Justice and others in the late 1980s. Just as UNORCA in Mexico fought economic elites like the World Bank by repostulating the nation's moral center as its (vulnerable) agricultural heartland, Jobs with Justice animated its efforts to situate unions as authentic representatives of the nation's moral values by relating the crisis of workers to the crisis of farmers. Like Mexican peasants, US workers and small farmers were increasingly represented as out-of-step and unproductive. They were dependent victims or clients of the state, and ultimately bound for obsolescence in the modernized and hypercompetitive 1980s-era economy.[21]

Nothing spoke to Jobs with Justice's hopes to claim Middle America more than its efforts in the Midwest and mid-South, where the coalition latched onto a broader development of left-wing "new populism" in the mid-1980s.[22] Savvy activists helped recenter the plight of small producers in the 1980s, and few were as influential in doing so as Jim Hightower, the Texas state agricultural commissioner. Along with US Representative

Lane Evans (D-IL) and Iowa senator Tom Harkin (D), Hightower helped create the New Populist Forum in 1985 to convince Democrats that a rough-and-ready economic populism was the answer to the free market-and-faith version of the Right. Hightower spoke regularly at Jobs with Justice events, like the three-thousand-strong march for workers' rights in Nacogdoches in late 1987, the Jobs with Justice rally at the end of the nearly month-long pilgrimage of the SCLC's "Martin Luther King Memorial March for Jobs with Justice" in April 1988, and dinner meetings at the Industrial Union Department in D.C.[23] Following the lead of his mentor, Fred Harris, who helped spur the liberal response to right-wing populism in the 1970s as a congressman and as a 1976 presidential candidate from Oklahoma, Hightower believed in the necessity of forging a coalition of African Americans, rural whites, unions, and liberals through economic populism. As a member of the "Class of 1982" midterm election sweep by Texas Democrats, he and others helped spur the mid-1980s national populist movement, and his colorful Texas colloquialisms helped some conservative southerners forget that he had gone to Columbia University and worked for Ralph Nader in Washington.

Building Jobs with Justice campaigns through farm-labor coalitions, often with strong church influence, emerged as a significant thread of activity in the alliance's first two years. Hightower and a range of rural groups helped build an organized response to the wave of farm foreclosures that followed Nixon- and Reagan-era policy changes, steep declines in commodity prices, and sharp spikes in interest rates. Two of the main community affiliates of Jobs with Justice in the early days, Citizen Action and the NFFC, celebrated the alliances of farmers and workers who realized that foreclosed farms meant closed-down factories.[24] The NFFC was the primary agricultural group involved in the mid-South and Midwest, and it and Jobs with Justice worked to build farm-union alliances from Jobs with Justice's 1987 rallies through its Labor Day mobilizations the following year. In the Midwest and south through Tennessee, unions, for Jobs with Justice, weren't just about an hourly wage—they were about community economic development.[25]

Though Hightower and Jobs with Justice leaders who conceptualized elites as "robber barons" drew self-consciously from the Populist movement, much of the coalition's early populism was the "small p" variety that celebrated plainspoken producers and the "plain-folk Americanism" of local communities. In Hightower's Texas and elsewhere, the folksy populism was a rhetorical thread between and within the coalition's organizations as it entered its second year, particularly in the nationally coordinated Labor Day events. In Austin, organizers opened the Labor Day program with the Pledge of Allegiance and a prayer and finished the day with "Democratic Caviar"—the coalition's name for beef chili. American flags adorned the Denver route. Though some sites simply used "Jobs with Justice" as a theme for their parade or county fair, those who organized local residents to sign Jobs with Justice pledge cards and take action hailed from Middle America's homeland. Groups in places like Duluth (Minnesota), Iowa, Wisconsin, Kansas City, Nashville, Indiana, and Texas all convinced more than one thousand local residents to sign the cards.[26] All told, seventeen of the $22,000 the coalition spent on local coalitions in 1988 went to those in the South or Midwest.[27] By referring to community roots and no-nonsense Americana, Jobs with Justice's populist initiatives suggested that unions embodied not Beltway bigness but the wage-earning common folk.

If populism was an opportunity for Jobs with Justice to build allies nationally and imbue the working class with Middle American moral credibility, it mostly took shape regionally, and was strongest in white communities in the Midwest and mid-South. There, it relied on a set of long-cultivated tropes of rural white families as worthy victims or sources of democratic renewal. Buttressed by 1980s popular culture that reinforced rural whites' moral exceptionalism and sacralized their connection to the land, the farm organizing tied to Jobs with Justice focused almost entirely on justice for independent white farmers, not immigrant farmworkers or Native Americans.[28]

Whiteness also shaped access to farm-labor populism on the union side. Though the term *working class* in popular discourse had long referred to white workers, by the 1980s the term came to signify a "hardened form of white, male identity politics" and was often counterposed to a pathological "underclass" of Blacks and nonwhite immigrants. Given the historical tenacity of white efforts to deny Black claims to productivity and morality, it's little surprise that Jobs with Justice campaigns with Black majorities campaigned under the broad appeal for "Jobs with Justice" rather than populist producerism.[29] The demand for jobs in general has a long history in Black America, and one of its most ardent proponents, Gus

Hawkins (D-CA), suggested to Jobs with Justice founder Larry Cohen that he make the name of the coalition about jobs, not unions. Finally, populist discourses ascribed an innocence and virtue to white Middle America that few Blacks would have accepted. As scholar Cornel West wrote in a 1986 critique of the left-leaning populism of the 1980s, populism "invest[ed] great confidence in the goodwill of the American people," yet "public acts associated with Black progress" had been ushered in by federal authorities, not "the people." Even the Emancipation Proclamation, he wrote, "would have lost in a national referendum."[30]

West's concerns were likely shared by some of the white farm organizers. As much as blending unionism with invocations of local community and family and with a left-leaning neopopulism promised opportunities, it also portended peril for coalition builders. Unlike the broad-based appeals for "jobs with justice," appeals to community or family could inspire defensive, inward-looking articulations of "tradition" to justify inequalities. Beginning in the late 1960s, conservative Christians increasingly saw individual and national decay in terms of the breakdown of the breadwinner family, and the growing presence of right-wing extremism forced farm and union organizers to challenge its influence. The progressive leadership of the Nacogdoches Texas State Employees Union (TSEU)/ CWA 6186 local hired an organizer who, unbeknownst to them, followed Lyndon LaRouche's "blood conspiracy" theory of the AIDS virus. His white supremacist views helped him mobilize union prison guards to demand that state officials permanently tattoo HIV-positive inmates. The union's refusal to back the plan led the members to leave the local and join a more conservative AFSCME one.[31]

Elsewhere, building farm-labor coalitions meant contending with "Christian Identity" militia and white supremacist groups hoping to take advantage of rural white discontent. Women's rights advocates in the farm organizations responded to Christian fundamentalism with a "Heartland feminism," and one group of rural organizers who often collaborated with the United Auto Workers and the Iowa Farm Unity coalition led workshops with union members to defuse the extremists' growing influence.[32] Kathy Ozer, the farm organizer most closely connected to Jobs with Justice, remembers contending with right-wing extremists in public meetings in the South.[33]

The coalition's main strategy to unite groups around a common economic enemy sometimes deflected, rather than directly confronted, inequalities within and between organizations and communities. As a response to the assault on the gay rights activists in Nashville, for instance, local Jobs with Justice organizers penned a letter that apologized for the behavior but suggested the aggression was merely an isolated action. In its letter, the Tennessee Lesbian and Gay Coalition had demanded wide-ranging gay rights initiatives in the coalition, but the Jobs with Justice apology letter failed to mention them.[34] Part of the national influence Jobs with Justice generated was due to its support from national and local union leaders, and Jobs with Justice campaigns tended to be *for* unions, not *in* unions, where some members faced their own struggles. That men deserved a wage to be the family breadwinner continued to be a common sentiment among unionists, and men in Jobs with Justice–linked unions often expressed hostility or ambivalence about women entering their industries and unions.[35]

Nevertheless, women workers also used the coalition to find allies and frame their causes as community, not simply workplace, matters. In the Eastern Airlines campaign, the Association of Flight Attendants–Transport Workers Union (AFA-TWU) was one of the few women-led and women-dominated unions in the world. The way the AFA's workers sacrificed their well-being by holding off their strike until the contract expiration of the pilots' union was key to the early momentum of Jobs with Justice and the Eastern struggle. Acknowledging the lack of respect they received from both bosses and the Eastern unions, both of whom continued to call them "girls," one flight attendant leader tried to keep morale high by joking about the women's "drone power," doing the dirty work while men enjoyed the benefits.[36] In Miami and elsewhere, female workers used the coalition to show how workers' well-being was about community economic sustainability as well as women's rights, not just a paycheck.[37]

ODE TO THE AMERICAN CENTURY: FOREIGN THREATS AND INTERNATIONAL TRADE

Campaigns against the North American Free Trade Agreement in the early 1990s may have helped shape the era's growing resistance to liberalized trade and investment, but they were hardly its foundation. The main priority for Jobs with Justice's national leadership during the NAFTA negotiations, in fact, was health care reform. The basis for the coalition's later work on international trade lies in its 1980s efforts around domestic trade legislation, when popular ire was rising about the nation's growing trade deficit with other countries. Here, another form of its ambivalent Americanism comes into view. Whereas some populists of the era celebrated the economic vision of "founders like Benjamin Franklin, Mercy Warren, and Thomas Jefferson," or an America "born of hope" and possessing a "unique democratic system," Jobs with Justice's working-class Americanism often situated itself less in a virtuous American essence and more in the shared prosperity of the American Century.[38]

Jobs with Justice increasingly yoked unions to the fate of the nation in 1988 by suggesting that unions' grand victories were entwined with the prosperity and democracy of the American Century. In an early statement, leaders emphasized how in Reagan's America, workers faced "the greatest resistance to unionization in 50 years." That wave of resistance signified how the "collective bargaining rights" so crucial to "the living standards and security of [workers'] families" over the last half century "continue[d] to evaporate." Such sentiments pervaded Jobs with Justice literature, in everything from the campaign's national literature, such as the press material for Labor Day activities in 1988, to that of the spring 1988 activities of the short-lived Alabama Jobs with Justice.[39] The future of unions equaled that of American democracy, since unions' 1930s-era strike wave had led to the nation's shared prosperity and stability. "America," one leader argued, "cannot afford a future" without union and workers' rights. Another leader warned before a rally that "if the interests of organized labor" got smashed, so would "American democracy."[40]

If Jobs with Justice envisioned the attacks of the Reagan era as a break with decades of a broad social compact that had respected unions' role in national prosperity, coalition members animated their critiques by suggesting that the era's robber baron greed was eroding the community-minded ethics that had nurtured the nation and its workers as they built the shared wealth of the midcentury period. The very slogan "Jobs with Justice," one founding member said, invoked "the way we used to be—caring and compassionate.... We lived the true meaning of brotherhood and sisterhood. We were more concerned with people without style than with our own lifestyles."[41] A UAW leader, in a Jobs with Justice – allied action to support the striking Colt Firearms workers of UAW Local 376, defended the union march by explaining that when she "was growing up in Connecticut, that blue-and-gold dome [at Colt's Hartford building] was a source of pride and a symbol of Yankee ingenuity and spirit." But now, she asserted, it had become "the hated symbol of... ruthlessness and a bloody cross upon which 800 people have been suffering for two years."[42] Another Jobs with Justice activist, referring to rampant corporate greed, concluded in 1987 that the disappearance of unions meant the disappearance of "our way of life."[43]

Despite their emphasis on the shameless betrayal of industrious America by the robber barons, identifying unions as extensions of the national community sometimes led Jobs with Justice to conflate perceived threats to the nation with threats to unions, especially manufacturing unions. One of those threats was foreign competition. One early "Call for Jobs with Justice," sent in early 1987 by the coalition's union leaders to convene the original rallies, blamed corporations and politicians who "[used] the cloak of competition to destroy the lives of workers." Accordingly, at rallies during the two-year campaign and strike at Eastern Airlines, Jobs with Justice leaders regularly stressed how foreign governments and companies threatened America. They enjoyed "unfair" advantages, as the "Call for Jobs with Justice" detailed. "The time is now to stop destructive competition: to end unfair foreign competition and mindless deregulation which destroy jobs and devastate the lives of workers," it pronounced.[44] Whether leaders included the term *foreign* or not in their screeds about competition, protecting unions from it was vital for the working class and the nation.[45] Saving unions, early leaders argued, was about "our values," as United Mine Workers of America (UMWA) leader Richard Trumka declared, and those shared values were threatened by foreign competition. At a commemoration of the US Constitution bicentennial that Jobs with Justice helped organize and that associated unionism with Americanism, one Amalgamated Clothing and Textile Workers Union (ACTWU) member punctuated the appeal by referencing the foreign threats he faced: "I'm out of work on account of imports," he said, "[and] walking the streets still looking for a job."[46]

For Jobs with Justice, competition, even the foreign kind, wasn't the only problem for the working class. But shifting the debate to the terrain of national competition deflected blame from the robber barons. Part of the reason the threat of foreign competition gained a presence at all was due to the very real challenges unionized industries faced in the 1980s, a time when falling US productivity, Reagan administration fiscal and labor policy, deregulation and the growth of corporate conglomerates, and increased domestic and international competition defined a world economy considerably different from that of only twenty years earlier. The US trade merchandise balance, which had never ended a year in the red in the twentieth century, descended into deficit after 1970, and by 1987 it hovered at $160 billion, more than four times the size of the deficit even in the early 1980s. Reagan's inaction in the early 1980s regarding the Federal Reserve's policy to cut inflation led to catastrophic drops in earnings for steel and other heavy industries in the 1980s.[47] While in previous years representatives from isolated industries had negotiated with policy makers to establish trade rules, in the 1980s new sectors became increasingly vocal about problems navigating the international markets. Everyone from farmers to producers of high-technology, high-valued-added goods and services like telecommunications (CWA's industry) built coalitions and hired lobbyists to push legislators for favorable policies, including in the congressional trade debates that led to major trade legislation in 1988.[48] Indeed, convincing the International Trade Commission and the Reagan administration that other countries' trade practices were "unfair" could lead to compensation under Section 301 of the 1974 Trade Act.[49]

Confronting union decline by focusing on international competition was an increasingly common strategy for unions in the 1980s. Historian Dana Frank, for instance, has shown how unions collaborated with their employers in "Buy America" consumer campaigns to blame domestic economic malaise on foreign imports, and these collaborations sometimes targeted not simply products and politicians but everyday people. Some blamed Asians, their imports, and even Asian Americans, rather than corporate mismanagement, profiteering, or Reagan administration trade policies. The murder of Chinese American Vincent Chin in 1982 by a laid-off auto plant superintendent foreshadowed a decade of autoworkers bashing Japanese cars in ceremonies of symbolic, sledgehammer-driven violence that urged consumers to buy patriotically.[50]

Despite the presence of the manufacturing unions that helped create the nationalist, anti-Asian sentiments of the 1980s, Jobs with Justice's ambivalent Americanism partly deflected the anti-Asian xenophobia of the day. The coalition complained about Asian competition but often targeted treasonous domestic politicians, not foreign populations, as the root of the problem. Still, its continued appeals to an exceptional America maintained one of xenophobia's constituent elements: ennobling a nation that needed defending. The three-thousand-person crowd at Jobs with Justice's first rally "roared" when CWA president Morton Bahr opened his speech by condemning the erosion of workers' rights, but he brought the crowd "to its feet" when he finished his thought. "What's at stake is not only our rights but our national place in the world," he exclaimed. "Corporate America's solution to the problem of competing in an international economy is lowering American workers' wages to the levels of workers in South Korea and South Africa. That is not the answer. We are angry." Bahr's sentiments were echoed by others in early Jobs with Justice networks, including the populist Hightower, who added Taiwan to the list.[51]

Some members spurred the worker–robber baron antagonism by invoking racialized national rivalries. One local labor leader tried to rile up the Labor Day Jobs with Justice crowd in Odessa, Texas, in 1988 by claiming that the Reagan-Bush administration was "the best President and Vice President of the US that the Japanese have ever had." In August of the same year, the Denver Jobs with Justice coalition, the second-largest local, staged an event on Pearl Harbor Day to decry "AT&T's 'sneak attack' in announcing job reductions a few weeks before Christmas."[52] Disparaging countries like Japan and South Korea was more than mere rhetoric. Both locals were pushing for trade legislation that would protect factory workers and better enable the US to penalize other countries' export practices. Unions overwhelmingly supported the legislation, and union-friendly Democrats were especially zealous about adopting aggressive policies against foreign trade competitors. At the same time, Global South observers and future leaders of global justice movements were highly critical of what they saw as unilateral trade measures by an economic powerhouse.[53]

If defending unions meant militantly defending the economic nation, for some affiliates it also meant militarily defending the American Century's dominant nation-state. Those unions and activists saw foreign competition threatening the guarantor of America's exceptional power—the "security" provided by its armed forces. The Reagan administration had recently introduced monetary policies that made the country an especially attractive target for foreign investors, and some early Jobs with Justice actions targeted arms manufacturers, like a Colt weapons plant in Connecticut, for daring to outsource part of "America's security" and its "national defense" to foreigners.[54] At the October 1987 rally at the Colt weapons plant, as Jobs with Justice union leader William Winpisinger denounced the foreign manufacturing of US armaments, communications workers posed next to a Dutch-made howitzer cannon with their "Buy American" signs seemingly positioned for the newspaper cameras. The Industrial Union Department was actively involved in legislative efforts to limit foreign ownership of certain industries.[55] Jobs with Justice materials, especially those produced by unions like the International Association of Machinists and Aerospace Workers (IAM) and the United Paperworkers' International Union (UPIU), regularly noted that Jobs with Justice's objectives were of and for the "American worker" and that immigrant workers' rights campaigns had little place in early Jobs with Justice.[56] In the Eastern campaign, Jobs with Justice decided that its public discourse would target Lorenzo, not Eastern Airlines, because it could gain a foothold with the public by portraying him as an anti-American tyrant.[57]

Ultimately, targeting competition blurred the fundamental opposition between robber barons and workers that the coalition so earnestly sought to emphasize. Some union leaders, for instance, directly collaborated with employers to pressure government officials to protect their industries, and the president of the Industrial Union Department, Howard Samuel, had a close relationship with industry executives and the "Made in the USA Foundation."[58] One of the organization's first paid staffers, Johnny Carson, had previously worked leading Buy American campaigns in the South. At a Nashville rally, even as Jobs with Justice tried to center attention on class solidarity between the paper workers and other local unions, one local union president and his members stood beneath a sign that suggested US workers had foreigners to blame, not bosses: "Stop Unemployment," it read. "BUY AMERICAN." In Iowa, the State Federation of Labor had endorsed a Buy American clause at the same time it endorsed participation in Jobs with Justice.[59] Though Buy American was more prominent in Jobs with Justice's manufacturing unions, even those supporters with less of a direct economic stake in economic nationalism bought in. In a newsletter to members, Richard Cordtz, the secretary-treasurer of the Service Employees International Union (SEIU), ended his column by turning to purse-string patriotism. "[W]e union members," he wrote, "must practice what we preach. We, too, must buy into America ourselves."[60]

If unions invoked Americanism in part to build coalitions by framing union struggles as being about the local and national community, union leaders ensured that they would continue to powerfully shape the message. Union leaders in CWA and the Industrial Union Department, for instance, became the coordinators of the National Steering Committee and the Executive Council.[61] In initial plans choosing Jobs with Justice local sites, national leaders stipulated that those sites had to have "current labor-management fights" and that "two or more lead unions" would direct local organizing.[62] In its internal documents and publicly, the founders often recruited unions by appealing as much to their self-interest as to their sense of justice. Unions should collaborate with community groups, not to support the community's worthy causes, but because unions could win their own fights only if they had community allies.[63] Though many Jobs with Justice founders hoped to distinguish the coalition from local labor councils by enabling community participation, the long-term reciprocity and shared responsibility they spoke of only sometimes took shape in its founding years.[64]

Though the appeals to uphold an exceptional America overlapped with the New Right's populist Americanism, several factors combined to buffer it from conservative extremes. Jobs with Justice's relationships with liberal civil rights leaders in places like Atlanta, for instance, led the local coalition to present itself as following in the footsteps not of Depression-era union men but of Martin Luther King Jr. In April 1988, the SCLC and the Industrial Union Department jointly coordinated the "Martin Luther

Figure 1. Jobs with Justice march in Montgomery, Alabama (circa late 1980s/early 1990s). Jobs With Justice Photographs #6369, P. Kheel Center for Labor-Management Documentation and Archives, Cornell University Library.

King, Jr., March for Economic Justice," a month-long march from Memphis to Atlanta that organizers saw as part of the growing Jobs with Justice campaign. Beginning on April 4, the day when King was assassinated in Memphis while supporting a janitors' strike, one SCLC leader suggested that "the issues are basically the same as in 1968."[65] The pilgrimage ended with a major rally that featured the Eastern Airlines campaign and the SCLC in Atlanta April 30. While some Jobs with Justice unions had pledged to protect the country's military production, and therefore national security, from foreigners, the president of the SCLC took advantage of one local stop during the pilgrimage to decry how Reagan was both "exporting jobs" and "exporting war" to Third World countries. His organization regularly argued that ending racism and war, in addition to poverty, was the key "to redeem the soul of America." Likewise, the struggle to unionize the largely Black workforce at Stephen F. Austin University in Nacogdoches, Texas, took place alongside a local NAACP campaign against job segregation.[66]

In Atlanta and other Sunbelt sites, some Jobs with Justice campaigns stressed not nostalgia for the stability and social order of an imagined past but the shared hope of overcoming that past—a history marked by racial hierarchy and forced migration. Jobs with Justice organizers in San Antonio and Denver constructed alliances with a new generation of Black and Latinx political leaders, leaders who considered their efforts to be tied to the legacies of César Chávez and King. The SEIU in Atlanta, a key organizer of the 1988 pilgrimage, held Atlanta elites accountable to their claim that the metropolis was a southern economic hub and "a city too busy to hate." When a new manager at a downtown building suddenly forced African American janitors who had been working there for decades to enter the site through the back door, the union rejected the measure by declaring, "This is 1987 not 1950. We want to move forward, not backward!!"[67] Finally, some Jobs with Justice affiliates directly addressed the contradictions of blaming foreign countries for their industries' problems. The UMWA on various occasions invited leaders from the main miners' union in South Africa to speak at Jobs with Justice events. The SCLC as well as the mineworkers campaigned for an end to apartheid and the low-wage labor regime it supported, whose low-cost coal industry threatened UMWA members' jobs. Union leaders like the UPIU's Wayne Glenn, at the November 1987 Nashville rally, argued that US corporations in places like Korea—and not the Koreans themselves—were those underselling domestic US manufacturers.[68]

THE ORIGINS OF GLOBAL JUSTICE

The sweeping rise of neoliberal economic thought spurred breathless visions of the benefits of a hypermodern international economy, powered by unbridled competition and privatization. Planners and economic elites saw small farmers and unions as inconvenient obstacles—or even dangerous roadblocks—to the seamless market efficiency they dreamed of. Like UNORCA in Mexico, Jobs with Justice argued that "plain-folk" producers weren't obsolete or unproductive—they were the moral backbone of the nation. In its vision of a distinctly working-class America, Jobs with Justice saw social class through the framework of a national history of triumph and betrayal portrayed mainly in terms of the experiences of white breadwinners, yet many coalition members used that narrative to demand economic rights for groups long excluded from its benefits. By invoking a vision of Middle America as symbolic of moral values, the coalition's ambivalent Americanism both animated and blurred the antagonism between workers and robber barons that the coalition so energetically developed. Its anticorporate ideologies participated unevenly in the color-blind politics of the post–civil rights era. They contested New Right representations of "plain folk" by highlighting the importance of their labor rights but sometimes reinforced the New Right's notion that national decline and vulnerability threatened America's alleged greatness.

Jobs with Justice wasn't the only group in the 1980s to build the ideological and organizational infrastructure that later shaped the US-based global justice movements of the 1990s. Nor was it the most visible one. The consumer advocates at Public Citizen helped make the international negotiations over the General Agreement on Trade and Tariffs an increasingly prominent cause. So did the Institute for Agriculture and Trade Policy and the NFFC.[69] While nongovernmental organizations offered policy briefs and held press conferences in D.C., Jobs with Justice mainly organized workers in localities throughout the country to defend labor rights.

By the early 1990s, the rapid intensification of neoliberal trade and investment reforms pushed some Jobs with Justice local coalitions further into crossborder organizing or internationalist efforts. Some actively participated in opposing NAFTA. The Washington State coalition organized a demonstration outside of the 1993 Seattle meeting of the Asian Pacific Economic Cooperation group, demanding that any trade deal include workers' rights, human rights, and environmental rights. Larry Cohen and the Communications Workers of America soon developed important coordinating efforts with the major Mexican telecommunications union.[70] The coalition's midwestern farmer-labor work in the 1980s helped generate contacts for its solidarity campaigns in the Illinois "war zone" of the mid-1990s, when a global conglomerate bought out a local corn-processing facility and locked out workers resisting concessions. The national solidarity networks that emerged in response to the Staley lockout drew attention to the power of multinational corporations. They helped lead to the creation of the "Students Against Sweatshops," an important student-based global justice group in the late 1990s. As chapter 7 details, the protests outside the 1999 World Trade Organization ministerial enabled Jobs with Justice to take a more direct and aggressive role in fighting for workers' rights in an international context.[71]

Ultimately, the founding years of the Jobs with Justice coalition in the 1980s serve as a critical moment to think through tensions around questions of labor, trade, and nationalism. Long before the decentralized social movements and "networks" that characterized later global justice movements, Jobs with Justice created its own network form in the late 1980s.[72] Unlike NGOs, it constructed grassroots, working-class resistance to matters of international trade and investment. The ideological contradictions around populism, race, and national identity in Jobs with Justice weren't exceptional for emerging global justice movements; rather, they were in fact enduring components for many working-class and popular organizations.

PART II Racism and Global Justice in a Multicultural Age

4 Against Coca-Colonization

NEOLIBERAL MULTICULTURALISM AND
INDIGENOUS INSURGENCY IN SOUTHERN MEXICO

Few regions in the world were as significant to the rise of global justice networks as southern Mexico. The insurrection of the Zapatista Army of National Liberation (Ejército Zapatista de Liberación Nacional, EZLN) in 1994 inspired Indigenous peoples and non-Indigenous radicals on a global level. Demanding liberation on the first day of the implementation of the North American Free Trade Agreement, the Zapatistas identified neoliberalism as the world-structuring force endangering the lives of the country's Indigenous and working classes. Social movements in Mexico developed a rich and complicated analysis of neoliberalism, a term that was rarely used in the circles of Jobs with Justice, Public Citizen, and other US organizations who would soon play prominent roles in global justice movements. If these US groups often narrowed the issue of neoliberal restructuring to economic "globalization" or "commercial opening" in the 1990s, Indigenous Mexican movements recognized how neoliberalism affected not only production and supply but investment, budgeting, and even policing in local contexts.

Prominent understandings of globalization among Global North activists in the 1990s, in fact, allowed for global capitalism to be understood as a cultural homogenizing force, a view that only partially reflected the experiences of Mexican Indigenous peoples. Globalization-as-homogenization was partially captured by a word often uttered in this era: *coca-colonization*. *Coca-colonization* intended to capture the ways multinational corporations were imposing their values and products on the world's local cultures, in both the North and the South.[1] As I document in chapter 6, this brand of anticorporate ideology could be oriented to defending "cultural diversity" by fighting the standardizing forces of corporate power.[2] These kinds of understandings both visibilized and denounced US empire, even as they could reinforce a liberal benevolence oriented to rescuing the victimized Other whose culture was disappearing.[3] Notable intellectuals emphasized the dangers of homogenization. Naomi Klein fretted about national governments converting themselves into forms of "McGovernment" that were "biased at every level towards centralization, consolidation, homogenization."[4] International Forum on Globalization cofounder Jerry Mander worried about how First World technology was robbing the "Indian Nations" of the sacred.[5] Some Global North activists used a selective reading of the EZLN's writings to articulate a position that centered problems of corporations, money, and trade, rather than bringing out its emphasis on state power and the metaphor of a "war" of extermination that neoliberalism was waging against on "minorities" who were "actually the majority."[6]

This chapter introduces readers to the Popular Indigenous Council of Oaxaca—Ricardo Flores Magón (CIPO-RFM), an alliance of Indigenous organizations founded in the southern Mexican state of Oaxaca in 1997. The groups that forged the alliance were perhaps the state's most important EZLN allies, yet their history is distinctly Oaxacan. CIPO-RFM, in advancing its critique of neoliberalism, created in the 1990s the foundations of its work in the 2000s, even if the organization changed dramatically in later years. By 2003, CIPO-RFM would coordinate the transportation of busloads of Oaxacans to major international globalization protests and would develop its own form of grassroots globalism.

This chapter, in focusing mainly on the state response to CIPO-RFM's original campaigns, argues that the coca-colonization theories of globalization didn't capture the ways in which neoliberal structural reform in Mexico was a profoundly racialized set of transformations. The Mexican state didn't control and repress through standardization and homogeneity—it did so by defining and patrolling difference.

THE 1990S: THE ADVENT OF NEOLIBERAL—BUT ALSO MULTICULTURAL—REFORMS

In both the US and Latin America, racial justice movements in the late twentieth century challenged distinct forms of white supremacy and ethnic assimilation. Elites responded partly by instituting multicultural policies that claimed to inaugurate new forms of ethnic and racial equality, often through the formal governmental recognition of racially subordinated groups. As a range of scholars have noted, while seeming to reproach racism, multiculturalism often reproduced it, reformatting race and ethnicity in ways that served the needs of capitalist expansion and state control.[7] Globalization wasn't simply a threat to multiculturalism—it used it.[8]

In the Latin American context, Charles Hale and others have discussed the growth of "neoliberal multiculturalism," a set of political ideas and practices through which elites allotted a "minimal package of cultural rights" to Indigenous groups but with them introduced "an equally vigorous rejection" of broader demands for collective economic and political justice.[9] This brand of multicultural reform created a distinction between the reasonable multicultural reforms supported by "recognized" Indigenous cultural groups and the threatening demands of "recalcitrant" Indians.[10] As CIPO-RFM's campaigns escalated, the state government and media elites could use newly formed multicultural categories to define and distinguish "good" protesters from "bad" ones, and consequently target the bad for the most aggressive forms of state repression. Tolerating good protesters could be evidence of the state's democratic essence and empathic benevolence. The presence of bad ones constituted evidence that dangerous insurrectionists could be not only roaming the streets but living next door.

More specifically, by celebrating Indigenous participation in state-endorsed forms of tradition and democratic transition, Oaxacan elites isolated what I call a "participating Indigenous subject" from a "protesting" one, stigmatizing CIPO-RFM as "recalcitrant democrats," and justifying the group's repression in early 1998. The state government's politics of tradition and transition helped realign the balance of power enough to contain the further consolidation of radical, antineoliberal Indigenous movements in a moment of insurgency. It did so through a deft construction of a "permitted Indian" and its unauthorized Other.[11] Multiculturalism could indeed be a "menace"—which is precisely what the rise and repression of CIPO-RFM in the late 1990s makes visible.

THE PRI IN PERIL: INDIGENOUS MOVEMENTS AND THE "PERVERSE CONFLUENCE" OF DEMOCRACY AND MULTICULTURAL REFORM

It was not often that public officials in Oaxaca referred to members of the state's sixteen different Indigenous groups as "hordes of savages," as Governor Diódoro Carrasco Altamirano reportedly did in a public statement denouncing CIPO-RFM and its protests in 1998. Though reference to Indians as primitive was certainly common in Mexico leading up to the nationalist revolution in the early twentieth century, officials from the Institutional Revolutionary Party (Partido Revolucionario Institucional, PRI) rarely publicly invoked this kind of racialized terminology in the 1990s. This was particularly the case for Carrasco, who was widely acknowledged as a progressive reformer. While the report of Carrasco's comment on a radio program likely surprised some Oaxacans and provided CIPO-RFM a momentary opportunity to expose what it called Carrasco's "neoliberal disguise" of multiculturalism, Carrasco's public image as a supporter of multicultural democracy was already firmly established after several years of reforms.

Oaxaca's multicultural reforms, as well as an updated version of a politically useful *indio permitido*, emerged in a "perverse confluence" in which seemingly distinct political projects shared—yet struggled over—key notions of multicultural belonging and democracy.[12] They were created at a confluence, which the state government successfully exploited, where elites' "new economy of self-sufficiency and individual choice nicely complemented the indigenous movement's own emphasis on self-determination and autonomy."[13] As elsewhere in Latin America, the corporatist

Mexican state of the mid-twentieth century ruled through incorporating and managing distinct sectors of society, funneling patronage through state-created organizations and leveling violence at those who resisted. Mexican nationalism stressed political integration through an ethnically homogenous mestizo citizenry, bound together by the harmonious mixture of Spanish whiteness and modernity and an imagined "Indigenous soul" forged from the legacies of glorious ancient cultures. By the 1990s, the PRI increasingly replaced its mestizo national-popular imaginary with a multicultural one and extended cultural recognition and rights to Indigenous groups, even as its economic policies, and particularly the North American Free Trade Agreement of 1992, dispossessed them.[14]

Yet opposition parties and movements increasingly challenged one-party rule, and the fall of the long-dominant PRI was particularly threatened in Oaxaca, where the potential spread of the Zapatista insurgency—which Carrasco called a "contamination"—was palpable.[15] The three neighboring states of Chiapas, Guerrero, and Oaxaca had long counted as the country's poorest, with some of the highest percentages of Indigenous residents, and Oaxaca in particular had a long history of social mobilization and struggles for Indigenous autonomy and collective rights. Its statewide, dissident teachers' union local had become a national referent of grassroots pressure for democracy. The union and the state's Indigenous organizations quickly mobilized after 1994 to denounce the repression of the EZLN and advance preexisting struggles for justice and Indigenous rights. In 1996, a new Marxist guerrilla organization named the Popular Revolutionary Army (Ejército Popular Revolucionario, EPR) launched several attacks in Oaxaca (including outside the capital city), and the Carrasco government opened the way for the federal police and army to retaliate in the state's southern mountains.[16]

The 1990s was a decade of mobilization, opportunity, and collaboration for Indigenous movements. Indigenous people formed the EZLN-allied National Indigenous Congress (Congreso Nacional Indígena, CNI) and the National Coordinating Committee of Indigenous Women (Coordinadora Nacional de Mujeres Indígenas, CNMI) in the mid-1990s. In Oaxaca, some of the strongest anti-PRI, pro-EZLN Indigenous and popular organizations created the CIPO-RFM alliance. Yet by the time of its emergence in 1997, the Carrasco government had already constructed its own image of change, based on state-endorsed multiculturalism and a complex blend of transition and tradition.

TRADITION AND TRANSITION: CRAFTING THE PERMITTED, PARTICIPATING INDIAN

In Oaxaca as in other areas of Mexico, recognizing multicultural rights was pivotal both for government responses to Indigenous insurgency and for reform of the Mexican economic and political structure. Elite unease about Indigenous empowerment in Guatemala took shape in distinctly racial terms, as mixed-race Ladinos created neoliberal multicultural rule in response to fear and ambivalence toward social gains by Indigenous Maya. However, the racial coordinates in Oaxaca in the 1990s must be considered in relation to the decline of the PRI, the Indigenous rights momentum generated by the EZLN and Oaxacan Indigenous movements, and the state's distinctive ethnic and class power structure. More than just legitimizing the government and neutralizing a broader Indigenous insurgency, the multicultural reforms in Oaxaca helped shape the popular imagination of what Indigenous politics could look like. They established a permitted Indian whose legitimacy and basic citizenship rights were intimately tied to participation in the state's multicultural and democratic reform.[17] They projected a version of Indigenous tradition that could coexist with goals of preventing rebellion, avoiding postelectoral conflicts, and furthering neoliberal administrative and economic reforms. The administration's savvy cultural politics of transition and tradition presented it as the responsible shepherd of multicultural reform, recalibrating long-deployed representations of Indigenous "folkloric poverty" that was "by tradition, poor, isolated, and community bound" to authorize a certain kind of Indigenous subject for multicultural and democratic reform.[18]

Carrasco's self-presentation as a reformer, and particularly as a responsible steward of multicultural reform who could simultaneously preserve "governability," was crucial to his political legitimacy. He had served in the planning agency of his predecessor, who implemented multicultural reforms partly to control popular protest. Likewise, the Carrasco administration's initial reforms accommodated Indigenous demands, yet with an emphasis on preserving state control.[19] Less than sixty days after the EZLN's uprising on January 1, 1994, the Carrasco administration announced the "New Deal for Indigenous Peoples," which pledged to share decision-making with Indigenous peoples and to reform governmental approaches to Indigenous politics and culture.[20] Carrasco publicized the "vanguard" reforms locally, nationally, and internationally and later noted that they were among the most important accomplishments of his term.[21] Yet in a time of national PRI crisis and local insurgency, Carrasco also identified social stability as a main gubernatorial accomplishment, citing his ability to simply finish his term as evidence. He was only the second Oaxacan governor in twenty-five years to do so.[22]

Indigenous demands for autonomy gained strength throughout the hemisphere in the late twentieth century,[23] and state recognition of Indigenous political systems in Oaxacan municipalities was the hallmark feature of the reforms. The changes allowed Indigenous municipalities to elect their authorities according to their internal rules, without having to register representatives with official political parties. Those municipalities' electoral forms varied, but they relied on rotating positions of authority and administration, communal assemblies for making decisions, and collective work. If the electoral reform helped solidify Carrasco's place as a PRI reformer whose governance facilitated "social peace," it was also a politically opportune tactic. The government feared the spread of the Zapatista rebellion into Oaxaca's rural areas but also noted the ascension of competitor parties in Indigenous Oaxaca since 1988, and its recognition of Indigenous communities' autonomy to choose their representatives without parties sidelined the PRI's electoral competitors in Indigenous areas.

While recognition of the Indigenous political norms in Oaxacan municipalities resonated with the Zapatistas' demands as well as those of Indigenous autonomy movements throughout the hemisphere, it also overlapped with the state's distinctive ethnic and geopolitical landscape.[24] Unlike in Guatemala or in neighboring Chiapas, where the chasm between Indigenous groups and the whiter "Ladino" group helped spur the mobilizations of the 1990s, in Oaxaca a great deal of political conflict occurred among Indigenous groups—and not only between them and racially dominant ones. Oaxaca's geopolitical fragmentation makes it distinct from other Mexican states. It is home to 580 of the nation's total

2,447 *municipios,* many of them significantly Indigenous. This fragmentation has its origins in Spanish colonial attempts to segregate Indigenous populations into their own *Repúblicas de Indios.* Consequently, Oaxaca's Indigenous peoples have developed what Miguel Alberto Bartolomé calls "residential identities" that are closely tied to their localities, and they energetically defend local autonomy. Unlike in Chiapas and other states, land tenure is overwhelmingly defined as "communal land" managed by municipalities and the *agencias* that surround them, instead of demarcated as private property.[25]

If the reforms portrayed Carrasco's administration as introducing a much-needed multicultural transition, they also relied on a savvy politics of tradition that viewed Indigenous politics through a lens of ancient custom. Latin American elites have long deployed representations of Indians as bound to locality and tradition to portray them as unassimilable, deficient, or dangerous. While the demand for government recognition of local political rule in Oaxaca stemmed from the growing movement for Indigenous autonomy, often defended through the language of custom as well, it also partly overlapped with neoliberal multicultural politicians' interests in commodifying local difference and Indigenous tradition.[26] Recognition emerged, in fact, in a "perverse confluence" of contending forces, including the governmental quest for a stable status quo, neoliberal demands for decentralization and foreign investment, and popular pressure for democracy and Indigenous autonomy. This confluence of forces facilitated a recalibrated political formula for distinguishing "good" Indigenous subjects from "bad" ones through adjusting the trope of folkloric poverty for a neoliberal age. The cultural politics of divide-and-conquer not only enhanced the Carrasco's administration's staying power but also served as a new foundation for defining and patrolling legitimate Indigenous subjects of rights.

As Deborah Poole has powerfully argued, diversity has long been a cultural format for rule in Oaxaca. While twentieth-century Mexican nationalism celebrated a singular ancient Indigenous soul as the basis of a unifying Mexican mestizo identity, Poole argues that Oaxaca's elites have articulated a highly curated kind of ethnic diversity as a hallmark of Oaxacan-ness in order to unify the state's antagonistic political forces. These state-endorsed standards of ancient cultural tradition, just like the imagined cultures of "dead Indians" inherent in mestizo nationalism, ultimately functioned to police living Indigenous people. Perhaps the most prominent example is the state's internationally acclaimed Guelagetza festival, which celebrates and stages Oaxacan ethnicities for thousands of spectators every July in the capital city. Initially created in the 1930s as the state's "Homenaje Racial," it has long served as one of the principal means by which state elites christened themselves as official evaluators of ethnic authenticity. Poole shows how the festival helped create the dominant mestizo imagination of Indigenous Oaxaca as fundamentally other, but also "sentimentally 'ours.'"[27]

Declaring the Indigenous to be both "other" and "ours" operates in several ways. Just as PRI reformers supported the limited recognition of Indigenous political autonomy in terms of respecting tradition, the festival and its organizers evaluated participants almost solely in terms of the ancestral authenticity of the Indigenous region and community they attempted to represent.[28] Indigenous women have historically been the symbolic bearers of local tradition in Latin America, and women's bodies garbed in dresses "typical" to their region were the principal way the Guelagetza created "a visual map of the state's diversity." They became increasingly part of an international marketing campaign to sell the state as a "cradle of multicultural diversity," as Carrasco called it, available for easy consumption and investment.[29] While Mexican president Ernesto Zedillo (1994–2000) claimed that recognition of Indigenous autonomy would Balkanize the nation, the Guelagetza imagined Indigenous cultural difference as folkloric packages of customs that safely belonged to the state as cultural patrimony.

Ultimately, the Guelagetza overlapped with the focus on Indigenous tradition, custom, and locality in discussions of municipal autonomy, yet also neatly separated ethnic tradition from broader struggles for economic rights, or from economic pressures that compelled Indigenous people to migrate and adopt increasingly translocal and transborder community identities.[30] As Hale has suggested, the separation of culture and cultural rights from neoliberal economic reform is a crucial component for distinguishing some Indians as authorized subjects of recognition and stigmatizing others.[31] Carrasco's idealized Indian could reconcile perceived contradictions between Indigenous autonomy and neoliberal economic reform. Like the folkloric Indian, long a worthy object of paternalistic modernizers' pity, Carrasco's depiction of Indigenous Oaxacans was that of victims. Rather than being victims of neoliberal reforms, they suffered from the nebulous forces of "ancestral backwardness," "old problems," "centuries-old inertias," or "discrimination" (*marginación*).[32]

Despite the local dynamics at play, the state government's blending of tradition and the 1990s-era ethos of transition overlapped with transnational discourses of efficiency, "ethnic entrepreneurship," and "self-development" circulating among international financial institutions and planners in Latin America.[33] In place of acknowledging neoliberal threats to Indigenous life, Carrasco suggested that extreme precarity and efficiency made Indigenous subjects model economic participants. "Here for each peso you give to the [Indigenous] pueblos, they make one peso 25, one peso 30, one peso 50.... This is the richest experience we have because the communitarian organization is as effective and efficient as any private organization," he said.[34] The decentralized, responsibilized Indigenous community and its collective, unpaid forms of work (like *tequio*) made them important objects of investment in human capital.[35] Carrasco's slogan of "equidad y eficiencia," campaign buzzwords that were also a key slogan of his Plan Estatal de Desarrollo, coupled recognition of Indigenous culture with recognition of the Indigenous as unique participants in the neoliberal economic changes that Carrasco advanced.[36]

The reforms also overlapped with prominent discourses of citizen participation and the PRI's efforts to remake itself as the party of the (neoliberal) democratic transition. While PRIistas rarely invoked the term *transition*, which connoted electoral alternation, embracing the ethos of transition allowed them to imply that they, too, recognized the sins of the past. Carrasco and national leaders obliquely referred to the party's (past) authoritarian excesses and cast their policies in the rhetoric of transition and democratization, thereby suggesting that governmental practice was oriented toward a future good—even if it appeared imperfect or demanded sacrifice. President Zedillo, for instance, emphasized the country's ongoing "democratic development" and the PRI's credentials to continue to direct it. Carrasco asserted that Oaxaca needed "more democracy," and he pledged to "advance" and "perfect" it. Both Carrasco and national-level PRIistas stressed that liberal, cosmopolitan dispositions were compatible with the basic tenets of Mexican nationalism, and celebrated democratic political cultures of "tolerance" and "dialogue."[37] Adhering to a broader neoliberal trend in Mexican governance, Carrasco argued that decentralization challenged the undemocratic centralism of the PRI-state. It could turn recipients (of state assistance) into participants.[38] Decentralizing state investment was one of the four principal themes of the Nuevo Acuerdo, and PRI reformers defended the recognition of indigenous political systems because these involved communities' democratic election of their authorities. The Carrasco government's reforms "decentralized... so that the very pueblos and communities could intervene in the decisions that affect their lives," and the reforms, Carrasco claimed, reflected his "commitment to justice, social peace, and democracy with the Indigenous pueblos."[39] The reforms highlighted the PRI's dedication to democracy and presented them as compatible with neoliberal decentralization and Indigenous autonomy.

Finally, the reforms also featured the participation of Indigenous groups, which further legitimized the changes as part of a democratic and multicultural transition guided by a responsible steward. His government, Carrasco said, "opened its doors" so that all could participate and invited consultations and "an intensely participatory and democratic process" to establish the terms of the Nuevo Acuerdo.[40] Popular pressure made a purely top-down reform politically impossible, and tactically managing citizen participation was already part of Carrasco's multicultural repertoire. While leaders of participating social movements and Indigenous organizations positively considered Carrasco as a dialogue-oriented governor, many were considerably more ambivalent about the reforms, and especially Carrasco's PRI party.[41]

Oaxacan Indigenous peoples' intensifying struggle for autonomy after the 1970s constituted another key element in the contradictory confluence of factors that shaped the recognition reforms of the 1990s. Though the 1994 Zapatista uprising put the spotlight on southern Mexico and Indigenous autonomy, Oaxacan Indigenous people and organizations had increasingly demanded recognition of Indigenous community electoral systems over the decade prior. For instance, political recognition was asserted during an important Indigenous gathering in October 1993, as Sofia Robles of the Mixe organization SERvicios del Pueblo Mixe (Services of the Mixe People, or SER-Mixe) affirmed.[42] The demand, particularly among Indigenous intellectuals and communities in the Sierra Juárez, Sierra Mixe, and Sierra Mazateca, emanated from efforts to defend what some called *comunalidad*—a Oaxacan Indigenous way of being, characterized by shared work, communal celebration, communal service, territory, and consensus-based decision making in collective assemblies.[43] At the same time, Indigenous women increasingly argued that autonomy must include women's rights to fully participate in communal activities, and particularly the communal assemblies. As the 1990s advanced, Indigenous women collectively challenged arguments that characterized patriarchy in Indigenous communities as part of tradition—either to defend it as a valuable heritage or to denigrate it as evidence of Indigenous backwardness.[44]

For some of the organizations that participated in the reform process, agreement to collaborate was accompanied by distrust of the PRI and a dedication to ensuring that the process was led by Indigenous Oaxacans. Indigenous organizations that had long battled for autonomy, yet refrained from actively opposing the PRI, increasingly declared their open opposition to the party in the 1990s. Influential leaders, such as Adelfo Regino, asserted that political parties themselves were the problem: they were "subverting the organizational structures of the Indigenous peoples." For Adelfo Regino, the reforms were an unprecedented historical feat but also only a "first step" toward full autonomy.[45] Regino, a leader of the SER-Mixe organization, and other key indigenous leaders who collaborated in crafting the reform also worked closely with the EZLN and the CNI and were profoundly critical of all political parties.[46]

While participants used the opportunity to push the reforms to be as extensive as possible, their participation did not mean a full endorsement of Carrasco either. The governor's first move to secure support for the reforms revolved around his selection of a group of Indigenous and non-Indigenous advisers, many of them with a background in the Sierra Norte and Sierra Mixe.[47] According to informal adviser Gustavo Esteva, Carrasco suggested early on that his reforms should be "a 'New Deal' in the tradition of the [US] New Deal." However, Esteva said, "We proposed that he make a New Agreement [Nuevo Acuerdo] between the government and the Indian pueblos. It was about governing with the Indian pueblos, not governing at or to them."[48] Zapotec educator and union leader (and EZLN adviser) Aristarco Aquino Solis said at the time that "Governor Carrasco says he defends Indigenous rights" and that Carrasco "proposed a new agreement [*trato*] with the Indigenous. A little beforehand he showed annoyance when community authorities proposed the same thing to him. On March 21 he proposed it as if were his proposal."[49] Nevertheless, Carrasco noted that his years directing infrastructure projects in the prior administration had enabled him to develop personal relationships with influential organizations like SER-Mixe and the Union of Organizations of the Sierra Juárez of Oaxaca (Unión de Organizaciones de la Sierra Juárez de Oaxaca, UNOSJO), and that those groups had spurred the independent forum process and crafted legal language for the reforms.[50] The "perverse confluence" of Indigenous reform in Oaxaca, then, involved the key contributions of pro-EZLN activists, even though the Carrasco administration sought to use the reform precisely to impede Zapatismo in Oaxaca.[51] It relied on the decentralizing logics that accompanied efforts to privatize land tenure and threaten Indigenous territory, yet also featured Indigenous and non-Indigenous claims for the democratic potentials of local autonomy. That overlap was the confluence the state government's politics of tradition and transition exploited.

THE PROTESTING INDIAN: "RECALCITRANT DEMOCRATS" IN AN AGE OF MULTICULTURAL TRANSITION

If the reforms authorized a particular kind of Indigenous subject for the state-endorsed transition to multicultural recognition and formal democracy, Indigenous organizations that failed to comply with—or rejected—the terms of the transition became the recalcitrant Indigenous subjects of the reform era. The recalcitrant subject illuminated here resembles that outlined in other studies,[52] yet it is also distinct. Its construction is highly influenced, not by the terms of terrorism or even insurrection, but by discourses of transition out of authoritarian party rule and into multicultural democracy. As other studies of neoliberal multiculturalism have shown, the distinction between an authorized (*permitido*) Indian and an "insurrectionary" Indian made it difficult for organizations to opt for features of both.[53]

Figure 2. CIPO-RFM member at the organization's first street protest in November 1997 in Oaxaca City, Oaxaca. Photo: NOTICIAS Voz e Imagen de Oaxaca.

CIPO-RFM attempted to do so by strategically combining Indigenous self-determination with petitioning for state resources and advocating an anti-imperialist nationalism. By linking Indigenous autonomy to neoliberal economic reforms, criticizing governmental multicultural recognition, organizing unruly public protests, and blending local demands for rights and services with support for the EZLN, the CIPO-RFM alliance largely worked outside the standards of transition and tradition that were increasingly becoming hegemonic, and in doing so it exposed itself to incarceration or physical repression. At this time, the state and federal government also criminalized the Loxicha (Zapotec) region in Oaxaca as a support base for the guerrilla EPR.[54] Ultimately, the government and media elites successfully typecast CIPO-RFM as "recalcitrant democrats," neither properly traditional nor ready for the limited democratic, multicultural transition.

While many of the CIPO-RFM affiliates had participated in the regional Indigenous forums that helped shape the reforms, not all participating groups or Indigenous intellectuals supported the final product of the reforms. Several later CIPO organizations had pressed for a way to elect congressional representatives outside of political parties, and not just municipal authorities. In 1998, CIPO-RFM leaders criticized the 1998 proposed law in Oaxaca as a top-down maneuver meant to dissolve antigovernment, pro-Zapatista unity. It imposed numerous restraints (*candados*) on Indigenous autonomy, CIPO-RFM leaders claimed, through its use of governmental bodies like regional *delegaciones del gobierno* and an ineffective Procuraduria de Defensa Indígena.[55] The reform, they wrote, reflected the "antidemocratic" and "demagogical" paternalism of the Carrasco administration. At the same time that he celebrated consultation, Carrasco was pushing an energy extraction "megaproject" in the Isthmus region without consulting the affected Indigenous communities. While UNOSJO and SER-Mixe became moral-intellectual forces behind the reform, CIPO-RFM was isolated as its opponent. One exasperated columnist complained that no initiative seemed to be satisfactory for the Indigenous groups, and he directly singled out CIPO-RFM as exemplifying this.[56]

While the Carrasco government imagined an Indigenous subject who could reconcile neoliberal reform and Indigenous rights, CIPO-RFM immediately positioned neoliberal reform as contradictory to Indigenous autonomy. By regularly denouncing the "treason" of state officials throughout 1997, CIPO-RFM argued that the "neoliberal project ... from the [land] reforms to Constitutional Article 27, to the Free Trade Treaty with the countries of the North ... [offers the] total freedom of foreign capital to invest in projects and 'megaprojects.'" For early CIPO-RFM, such "governmental policies ... destroy[ed] the foundations of our national sovereignty." While the Zedillo government had charged the national Indigenous movement with threatening to "Balkanize" the country, CIPO-RFM's founding organizations declared, "We realize that what really destroys our national sovereignty are neoliberal policies imposed by the federal government in collusion with its North American allies."[57] If CIPO-RFM identified the PRI and the rich investors who controlled it as the target of resistance, it formulated what I call the "popular-Indigenous nation" as its subject of resistance. In the first CIPO-RFM statement, leaders conceptualized this aggrieved, multiethnic nation by hailing workers and Indigenous pueblos and situating them in a context of national vulnerability. Though the statement regularly cited the singular nation or

Mexican *pueblo* (people) as victim and agent, it just as regularly asserted the victimhood and collective subjectivity of "los pueblos" or "the majority" of Mexicans.

If the popular-Indigenous nation was the collective subject the organization brandished to expose how elites lacked the ethno-national credentials to speak for the very pluricultural society they claimed to create, women in CIPO-RFM suggested that Indigenous women's autonomy depended on deepening the collective rights at the center of the popular-Indigenous nation. This meant ensuring that women could fully participate in communal affairs.[58] It also meant challenging the state and economic violence that Indigenous women endured. Almost 60 percent of Oaxacan women fifteen years or older had not completed primary school, and 34.6 percent of them could not read—when only 19.7 percent of men were illiterate.[59] To make their own claims, women from the Committee of Defense of the Rights of the People (Comité de Defensa de los Derechos del Pueblo, CODEP), the Indian Organizations for Human Rights in Oaxaca (Organizaciones Indias por los Derechos Humanos en Oaxaca, OIDHO), and the Union of Indigenous Communities in the Northern Zone of the Isthmus (Unión de Comunidades Indigenas de la Zona Norte del Istmo, UCIZONI) founded a Women's Commission inside the CIPO-RFM coalition.[60] Some of the women in CIPO-RFM, like Zoila José Juan, an Indigenous Ayuuk woman from the northern Isthmus region, directly worked with national and international organizations, like the CNMI, which had been recently born at the first National Meeting of Indigenous Women in Oaxaca.

INVALIDATING INDIGENOUS VOICES: THE PRI AND MULTICULTURAL DEMOCRACY

Regardless of its diverse base, PRI politicians and high-profile newspaper commentators branded CIPO-RFM as fundamentally undemocratic. They portrayed its rejection of governmental policy and its penchant for direct action as a remnant of the age of strong-arm brokering, political violence, and Indigenous unruliness.[61] In contrast to SER-Mixe and other Indigenous groups active in the reform efforts in Oaxaca, CIPO-RFM combined its demands for Indigenous autonomy with mass-based pressure politics. The alliance featured some of the most vocal critics of the PRI, with histories of challenging PRI local bosses, or caciques. Unlike UNOSJO and SER-Mixe, they relied on public protests, land takeovers, and road blockades. Yet the PRI itself had long channeled popular discontent into party-based worker and peasant organizations that could be controlled through rituals of protest, negotiation, and patronage. Though the PRI (and Carrasco) frequently denounced corruption, it often compelled organizations or communities to participate in rallies or other mass propaganda activities by threatening the withdrawal of financial support.[62] By establishing a distinction between civil, tolerant, dialogue-based democracy, on the one hand, and the blackmailing self-interest of popular leaders and their passive, corruptible Indigenous subjects, on the other, the PRI and its supporters disqualified for democratic participation the very populations their multicultural democracy claimed to embrace. Those populations were not ready for (multicultural) recognition.

In the first months of CIPO-RFM's founding in 1997, PRI officials continually stressed their dedication to a new, democratic, and multicultural Oaxaca—one based on the oft-repeated principles of dialogue, tolerance, and the transition to a modern multicultural democracy. Former governor and newly elected federal senator Heladio Ramírez López affirmed that the "new political culture" of "opening" prized democracy and "consensus," unlike the "obsolete . . . walled off strongholds of power" and "autocratic decisions" of the party's past.[63] José Murat, the PRI candidate for the gubernatorial elections to be held in August 1998, stressed how his roots in the Isthmus region of the state made him a true candidate for a state whose diversity matched its modern democracy.[64] After CIPO-RFM had decided to end one of its occupations of the central public plaza, Carrasco's secretary of the Interior took credit for the withdrawal, arguing that if the administration "had been intolerant and authoritarian, it would have evicted the protesters." Instead, he said, it had agreed to speak with them and negotiate.[65]

It was CIPO-RFM and other protesters, said the government in the next months, who had intolerantly imposed their will and abused the privileges of a budding democracy. Newspapers, and especially the progovernment *El Imparcial*, continually described Indigenous and popular organizations as disinclined to civil dialogue and prone to blackmail and violence. *El Imparcial* regularly crafted sensationalistic headlines about violence at (CIPO-RFM) protests and *plantones* throughout 1997 and 1998, even though the stories themselves often contradicted the sense of threat and disorder the headlines conveyed.[66] Carrasco himself later noted that while social organizations' demands might have been legitimate, the direct-action methods of some of them were unacceptable.[67] The site of the protests—the capital city's downtown historic district—accentuated the threat they presented. Carrasco's neoliberal economic plan emphasized drawing tourists to the city as a way of attracting foreign investment. The United Nations Educational, Scientific, and Cultural Organization (UNESCO) named Oaxaca City's historic center a World Historic Site in 1987, and one of Carrasco's featured projects was to convert its Santo Domingo plaza into a world-class ethno-historical tourist site. The government had a color scheme for downtown buildings, and it pressured property owners to remove weeds that grew out of the crevices of aging buildings.[68] In December 1997, when CIPO-RFM threatened another mass mobilization, the government expected full hotel occupancy. In April, immediately after CIPO-RFM's *plantón*, one commentator expressed disgust at how "the Government Palace, in the heart of the capital city," had been "usurped by the people" and "converted into a true pigsty."[69]

Critics of CIPO-RFM also tapped into a popular vein of resentment against caciques, politicians, and other supposed leaders who riled up the poor, Indigenous, and popular classes and, according to the PRI, abused the democratic rights the party generously offered. The day before CIPO-RFM's first mobilization, two PRI state officials argued that "he who promotes disorder, intolerance, incivility . . . [and] he who contributes to mobbish protests . . . is not to be trusted." According to these leaders, the state had "advanced and ha[d] had a harmonious development" during the Carrasco term.[70] The prominent *El Imparcial* columnist Humberto Torres, mentioning Cruz and Gatica by name in his essay months later, asserted, "It's already well known that the ways to avoid confrontations, violence, instability, and anarchy are dialogue and legality, for the search for consensus." "Leaders," he said, or "supposed social activists" who threatened "order and tranquility," needed to go forth "with responsibility, with decorum and with civility."[71]

More dangerously, the emergence of the EPR guerrillas granted the government a pretext to further criminalize dissent. The political climate became especially charged after paramilitaries' massacre of forty-five Indigenous Zapatista supporters in Acteal, Chiapas, in December 1997. CIPO-RFM and the Mexican League for the Defense of Human Rights (Liga Mexicana por la Defensa de los Derechos Humanos, LIMEDDH) advanced detailed charges that the PRI supported paramilitaries in rural Oaxaca, which were countered by PRI charges—leveled with no evidence—that political figures like Gatica had ties to the EPR.[72] One report released around the time of CIPO-RFM's founding suggested that the secretary of national defense's "informants" were watching for bandanna-wearing protesters distributing pamphlets or painting graffiti messages. Oaxacan social organizations regularly wore bandannas to express solidarity with the EZLN, and pamphlets and political graffiti were common elements of *plantones*. *Las Noticias,* in fact, displayed a front-page photo of a CIPO-RFM militant with a bandanna on during the organization's first week of mobilizations.[73]

As with the neoliberal emphasis on citizen "participation" elsewhere in Latin America during the democratic transition years, participation in Oaxaca was defined as pure democracy. But recalcitrants like CIPO-RFM, and particularly its leaders, engaged in the corrupt world of *politics*.[74] One PRI paper argued that CIPO-RFM leaders were "disguising [their intentions] as popular demands through which they can try to get personal resources and political benefits."[75] One PRI state deputy claimed that the CODEP organizer Raul Gatica, who was also an important teachers' union leader, did not really care about Indigenous poverty. Instead, he was a mere "tele-leader, a guy who basically lives in Local 22 of the union of education workers, who gets a salary for doing nothing." As a member of CIPO-RFM, he was "part of a ghost organization without support or apology"; he "play[ed] with the needs of the poor" by demanding "resources from the government in name of the Indigenous villages and using them for personal benefit."[76]

Public discourse about leaders often scrutinized the political subjectivities of presumed followers as well. Referencing centuries-old ideas that questioned the readiness for self-rule of the poor and Indigenous, but at the same time avoiding the racialized terminology that defined them as primitive, PRI supporters invoked a political figure the PRI itself had helped produce: the *acarreado*. Referring to herds of livestock guided into trucks for transport (*acarreos*), the term *acarraeados* signified the lowly peasants who were bribed, tricked, or otherwise cajoled by party or organizational officials to travel, often in party cargo trucks or busses, to political events to create the appearance of PRI support.[77]

Without always labeling them as *acarreados*, the government, PRI supporters, and civil society organizations nonetheless implicitly invoked the image in their critiques of Indigenous organizations by suggesting that political and social leaders manipulated peasants. In doing so, they degraded the validity of their participation. The derisive portrayals of leaders mentioned above took for granted that Indigenous peasants were passive victims of canny political operators, and CIPO-RFM critics and social organizations themselves formulated this notion of peasant passivity in a number of ways. For example, LIMEDDH, which supported CIPO-RFM after its repression in April 1998, complained during a multiorganizational *plantón* that some groups occupying the Zócalo "protest under one heading to get to something else" and pleaded with "the leaders" of groups occupying the central plaza (including CIPO-RFM) to "tell [their members] what these mobilizations are really for" and not "use" them.[78] In a state where most rural peasants were Indigenous, questioning peasants' ability to be free, sovereign political subjects—and consequently equipped for democracy—played into long-held beliefs about the incapacity of Indigenous peoples to govern themselves. One newspaper article, referring to CIPO-RFM "peasants," said that they arrived in the capital city like masses herded into an *acarreo* and were typical rural victims of corrupt leaders' "intimidation and trickery."[79]

Racist assumptions about a lack of Indigenous agency were doubly potent for Indigenous women. As the Women's Commission took shape in early 1998, its struggle gathered its greatest public force in its blockade of the city's major highways in March of that same year. In the days leading up to the highway blockades, the Women's Commission led a march and a *plantón* to pressure the governor to attend to their demands for health care, schooling, and other government services. Referencing the mobilizations, members of the commission repeatedly emphasized how their political voice was their own—that they were not, as one Zapotec woman recalled, "*acarreadas*." "What came out in the newspapers," one recalled, "was the government rhetoric, which said that they weren't our decisions, decisions of the women, you know? Instead, it said the [male] leaders were behind us . . . as if invalidating that women were capable of structuring a demand, a proposal, a protest."[80]

In their March 9 public statement, the women stressed how they were independent from the political leaders who tried to manipulate Indigenous women and their ideas with "little gifts," or other "pressure or blackmail."[81] According to a *Noticias* reporter, the Women's Commission emphasized how these mobilizations were "headed and directed by women," and were "without any political overtones." "We don't represent the PRI, and we're not part of the CNC or COCEI," it said, referring to two organizations, the National Peasant Federation (Confederación Nacional Campesina) and the Coalition of Workers, Peasants, and Students of the Isthmus (Coalición Obrera, Campesina, Estudiantil del Istmo), that had ties to political parties. "We're Indigenous women" in "an independent organization." These and other public statements in March repeatedly emphasized how Indigenous women's political subjectivities were not manipulated by politicians, leaders, or other male interlopers.[82]

AUTHENTICITY POLITICS IN A MULTICULTURAL NATION

On April 13, 1998, police arrested two leaders of the Committee for Citizen Defense and Assistance to Rural Communities (Comité de Defensa Ciudadana y Asistencia a Comunidades Rurales, CODECI), setting off a wave of solidarity protests across the state's regions and demonstrating the broad reach of the CIPO-RFM alliance. On the coast, police beat Chatino protesters. In Tuxtepec, the Chinanteco region of CODECI, CIPO-RFM members occupied the regional attorney general's office. CODEP members in the Mixteca blockaded the Putla courthouse with Judge Luis Salvador Cordero Colmenares inside and pledged to remain until CODECI leaders were freed.[83] On April 18, in a national meeting in the teachers' union auditorium in Oaxaca, CIPO-RFM members urged their partners in the Zapatista-linked CNI to continue their support.[84] But the government now paired months of delegitimizing the organization with mass repression. Police charged the courthouse in Putla, arresting eighteen, including a Party of the Democratic Revolution (Partido de la Revolución Democrática, PRD) candidate for state congress.[85] Hundreds of preventative police and state judicial police evicted the Tuxtepec protesters early on the 18th and arrested seventy-six. Most of the detainees were beaten, rumors of two deaths circulated, and a lawyer representing CIPO-RFM was detained without a warrant, according to UCIZONI leader Carlos Beas.[86]

As elsewhere in Latin America, neoliberal multicultural politics in Oaxaca used notions of ethnic authenticity to further distinguish authorized from unauthorized Indigenous groups. Progovernment media sources used then recent controversies over the presence of foreign supporters of the EZLN in Chiapas, including the recent deportation of a French priest, to repeatedly question CIPO-RFM's ethnic authenticity. They suggested that the organization represented more the ideologies of outside agitators than the values of *el pueblo*. In late April, *El Imparcial* published front-page stories about Ana Bayer, a light-skinned German national, and it printed a photo of her, allegedly taken at a CIPO-RFM march, that made her immediately recognizable to multitudes of PRI militants as well as state police. The nationalist constitution of 1917 outlaws foreign participation in domestic politics, so the idea that Bayer joined marches helped to criminalize the organization. It also called into question CIPO-RFM's claims to represent popular-Indigenous Mexico in the face of traitorous neoliberal politicians.[87]

PRI supporters circulated the erroneous rumor that UCIZONI leader Beas was a Chilean as well. Despite a wide-ranging interview that touched on many elements of the prior week's conflicts, the headline directed its partisan venom at CIPO-RFM's ethnonational legitimacy: "THE CHILEAN CARLOS BEAS CHALLENGES THE GOVERNMENT," it read. Below it, "The leader of UCIZONI defends the foreigner Ana Bayer."[88] Beas, for his part, defended himself from what he called a rumor generated by a "pseudojournalist" and denounced the xenophobia that this most recent rhetoric reflected.[89] Though the secretary of the Interior admitted that foreigners had long been part of Oaxacan social life, it pledged to formally investigate Bayer and Beas, because now "more than three hundred foreigners engage in political religions and experimental activities with ethnic groups of the state." According to a Department of the Interior official, "It seems that [foreigners] want to resolve the problems of [the state] themselves."[90]

. . . . .

During a May 1998 radio interview, Carrasco reportedly referred to CIPO-RFM as a "horde of savages." The organization's "irrationality," Carrasco continued, contributed little "to peaceful, organized, and civilized development." While the statement clashed with the progressive public face of his administration, it resonated for groups like CIPO-RFM that had long questioned the meaning of his administration's multicultural reforms. CIPO-RFM spokesperson Alejandro Cruz, in his response to the media, said, "We always thought our ruler was racist but not to the point that he would call Indigenous people savages." "He has governed us," Cruz maintained, "as did the viceroys in past centuries."[91]

The repression of CIPO-RFM did not mean the end of the organization, the end of the Indigenous movement in Oaxaca, or the end of the resistance to neoliberalism. But it did strike a critical blow in a critical moment, in the years immediately following the EZLN uprising. Neoliberal multicultural politics highlighted and reinforced existing divisions in Oaxaca's Indigenous movements—between those who stressed mass protest, for instance, and those who did not, like SER-Mixe and UNOSJO. For CIPO-RFM, the events of the year also created tensions with the CNI, the national Indigenous organization. Carlos Beas, in fact, publicly criticized the lack of CNI support for CIPO-RFM in its time of crisis. By sidelining Oaxaca's most radical Indigenous organization in a state long known for its social mobilization, the repression ultimately weakened national pressure for the implementation of the San Andrés Accords at a time when President Zedillo was implementing new strategies to fragment his Indigenous opposition.[92] In fact, it was soon after the passage of Oaxaca's last major Indigenous rights legal reform in 1998 that President Zedillo paired his stalling on the San Andrés Accords with a suggestion that *all* state governments adopt limited Indigenous autonomy reforms on their own. The Oaxaca experience, Carrasco claimed, convinced the president to do so, and Carrasco would ultimately go on to serve as Zedillo's minister of the Interior from 1999 to 2000.[93]

Sometimes social movements enjoy a steady rise to power and influence. But social movement histories are often stories of sudden peaks and rapid tumbles, unforeseen tragedies and unexpected victories. They are often the stories of repression and violence, particularly in the Global South. The history of a "movement of movements" like that of global justice movements must come to terms with the diversity of experiences that ultimately have helped shape it. It should include the locally driven work that only sometimes results in inspiring triumph or Internet fame. It should discuss how and why some organizations occupy a movement's "edges" rather than its center.[94] The suppression of CIPO-RFM in 1998 was by no means permanent, and its brand of grassroots globalism would become more pronounced in the international protests in the coming years. But the jailing of the council's leaders helped slow the consolidation of antineoliberal resistance in Mexico, particularly the kind driven by Indigenous peoples. The momentum that Indigenous movements enjoyed in the wake of 1994 had been fundamentally disrupted.[95] Far from an isolated case, the state response to the rise of CIPO-RFM illuminates the kind of divide-and-conquer strategies that would penetrate the global justice networks of the coming years, including those of the famed "Battle of Seattle" in 1999.

5 Obscuring Empire

COLOR-BLIND ANTICORPORATISM AND
THE 1999 WORLD TRADE ORGANIZATION
PROTESTS IN SEATTLE

"Teamsters and Turtles, together at last!" The massive protests outside the 1999 World Trade Organization meetings in Seattle exposed the wide-ranging resistance to the trade liberalization of the post–Cold War era. The spectacular events of the week led to hundreds of arrests. They successfully—if temporarily—shut the meetings down. They helped inspire organizations around the world to join massive protests outside economic summits in the coming years—including the three organizations featured in this book. As significant as the protests were for them, these organizations mostly watched Seattle from afar. The funds needed, not to mention the US visas for the Mexican organizations, were insurmountable barriers. Yet the sheer size, scope, and influence of the Seattle protests make them a necessary part of this story. In fact, the fact that these three popular organizations did not play significant roles there illustrates a central point of these two consecutive chapters on Seattle: the far-reaching alliances and undeniable impact of the protests were accompanied by broad exclusions.[1]

The Seattle protests and the global justice movement undoubtedly visibilized international economic inequality in new and important ways. US unions, progressive organizations, and radicals helped build new alliances, including alliances with those in the Global South, to create a more equal global trade system, and their efforts have received significant attention from scholars. With good reason, much of the scholarship on Seattle focuses on the daring direct action that temporarily shut down the meetings.[2] In the wake of the protests, the power of the unlikely coalition between labor unions (the "Teamsters") and environmentalists (the Sea Turtles, as represented by the campaigns of the Sierra Club, Earth Island Institute, and other groups) became perhaps the most enduring narrative of the protests. It was reinforced not only in the news media but in the 2007 film *Battle in Seattle*, starring Charlize Theron and Woody Harrelson.[3] In the aftermath of the protests, one observer marveled about the eclectic "cacophony" of "Teamsters and turtle-lovers, grandparents and Gap clerks, the homeless and computer geeks, high school students and Alaskans, nuns and Jimmy Hoffa, Jr., airplane mechanics and caffeinated slaves from Microsoft," all marching together in the streets.[4]

Yet organizers of color immediately recognized how the narrative that celebrated the power of the Teamsters and Turtles alliance foregrounded some kinds of difference while ultimately obscuring others.[5] As one recounted, there were "all these public education materials talking about sea turtles and labor rights" in 1999, but not about how globalization was "affecting environmental racism in local communities."[6] Organizers of color in Seattle argued that lauding the impact of the Teamsters-Turtles coalition centered the issues, interests, and experiences of middle-class environmentalists and predominantly white organizations. As longtime organizer and intellectual Elizabeth "Betita" Martínez provocatively asked in the wake of the protests, "Where was the color in Seattle?"[7] Martínez's critique mostly focuses on the cultural norms of white countercultures and anarchists in Seattle. This chapter looks at predominantly white progressive organizations and situates the Seattle protests in the political and cultural history of the 1990s.[8]

Analyzing the whiteness of the protest entails thinking about not only who was there but also about how racism and whiteness shaped the very concepts—like globalization—at play.[9] This chapter suggests that the whiteness of the protests, and the ways the "Teamsters and Turtles" narrative reinforced it, were partly due to the ways progressives had framed the problem of globalization in the first place. It discusses the uneasy affinities that white progressives developed with right-wing antiglobalizers in the decade, and it examines the populism and the ambivalent form of Americanism that progressives expressed. Ultimately, it argues that some interpretations of globalization in the 1990s reflected a color-blind anticorporatism, an approach that treated racism and US empire as secondary considerations. In a moment of great interest in international trade, color-blind anticorporate political orientations helped to subtly conceal US empire. And as the next chapter will show, they ultimately invisibilized immigration as well.[10]

TRADE AGREEMENTS AND THE RISE OF THE RIGHT

With some five hundred people languishing in a local jail, outrage filled the air. More than fifty thousand people had marched, protested, blocked streets, and destroyed corporate property. They had forced the WTO to cancel or postpone meetings. The city government had created a "no-protest" zone to manage protesters and secure the meeting perimeter. In a solidarity rally outside the jail, one protester, masked like many of the radical direct actionists of the week, took out a US flag and set it afire. Protesters like him denounced trade liberalization as a new kind of US imperialism. Others there looked at the matter with a different perspective. Soon, a protester nearby—a steelworker from Alabama—approached the flames. Denouncing the flag burner as a national traitor, the steelworker swiftly grabbed the flag and carried it to safety.[11]

The WTO protests were essentially events that said "no." As activist lawyer Patti Goldman recounted, building the protest coalition was relatively easy, since organizations were simply rejecting a model.[12] It's much harder, she said, to agree on an alternative system—to say "yes" to something. The 1990s marked a decade when politicians, consumers, and workers began saying "no" to certain kinds of trade. Consumers fretted about "blood diamonds" extracted from mines in Angola or the Ivory Coast. As imports from East Asia continued to show up on US store shelves, both liberals and conservatives sought sanctions on China for its factories using child laborers or imprisoned workers. Environmentalists, for their part, wanted "dolphin-safe" labels on tuna cans. And Kathie Lee Gifford, one of the best-known television personalities in the country for her work on the morning show *Live! With Regis and Kathie Lee,* came clean on national television about the Honduran child laborers who had sewed the apparel for her booming clothing brand, initiating a new round of debate and activism about international trade.[13]

Forced labor and child labor had been long targeted by union officials and human rights activists in the US and Europe. They received unreserved condemnation on moral grounds. But unions also had an economic stake in the matter. The products that emerged from such abominable conditions—seemingly without safeguards for worker safety or environmental protection—entered global markets at artificially cheap rates. US producers couldn't compete, they said. In response, some unions united with factory owners—the same owners they usually fought with—to create lobbying and advertising campaigns designed to keep out low-priced imports.[14] These campaigns tugged at consumers' heartstrings, as well as their pocketbooks. "Buying American," these unions argued, was the only way to save dying industries. For companies, patriotic purchasing was also about protecting their profits—which they rarely passed on to workers anyway.

Vastly different production conditions in different countries that were all producing for the same global market could easily turn workers and activists in different countries against each other. As the Cold War ended and trade liberalization made it easier for companies to shift factories abroad, US union progressives worried about the creation of a global "race to the bottom," in which companies played countries off each other as they roamed the globe, seeking out production sites with the lowest wages and the least environmental regulation. The creation of the World Trade Organization, they feared, would follow the model of its predecessor, the General Agreement on Tariffs and Trade (GATT), or the recently created regional trade accord between the US, Canada, and Mexico (the North American Free Trade Agreement, or NAFTA). It would accelerate the race to the bottom, applying downward pressure on wages and standards in the US, all with the justification of supporting "free trade" and "open markets" for the benefits of everyone. As debates about creating NAFTA commenced in the early 1990s, some US and Canadian auto workers blamed Mexicans for "stealing our jobs." Mexican farmers looked northward, blaming US farmers for flooding their markets with cheap corn.[15]

To avoid these all-against-all scenarios and the xenophobia they would likely inspire, in the early 1990s Mexican intellectual and activist Jorge Castañeda called for progressives in all countries to work together by enacting a "grand bargain." Progressive groups in each country should oppose multinational trade liberalization agreements by agreeing on a common platform and agreeing to promote the issues that each country cared about—not just their own. US groups, for their part, should mobilize for Mexican demands that the US take the financial boot off the country's neck. Mexico's massive debt made it desperate to maintain low wage levels to attract overseas investment to build up its export industries—all so it could sell goods abroad and acquire foreign currency to pay off its debt. The US government should offer technology transfers, funds for green economic development, and access to the US market so that Mexico could generate sustainable development options, allowing it to foster competitive industries to compete on their own terms. Mexican groups, for their part, should take US concerns seriously, Castañeda argued. US groups were worried about how jobs and investment would flow to Mexico for no valid business reason other than to take advantage of the country's limited labor and environmental protections, and they wanted to see stricter standards implemented domestically.[16] The efforts of Castañeda and others ultimately failed to stop NAFTA, but the moment fostered cross-border collaborations that ultimately helped shape the Seattle protests in 1999.[17]

But not everyone resisting the WTO in the 1990s was so interested in bringing people together across borders. As the Cold War ended and possibilities for new global political arrangements emerged, a growing white supremacist right opposed the WTO in the name of preserving white sovereignty in the face of globalist policies. Globalism endangered what some called a "New World Order"; others simply named the threat "One World."[18] For these conservatives, nonwhites inside the US threatened the sovereignty and freedom of white civilization with criminality, disease, and indolence. Outside the US, Japan, China, and even Mexico posed profound dangers to US dominance, and an international politico-economic cabal—a cabal often implicitly associated with Jews—endangered it from above.[19] White supremacist groups renamed themselves "white nationalists" and argued that most Democrats and Republicans were simply apologists for globalism gone wrong. Long-standing right-wing forces like Lyndon Larouche and the John Birch Society helped lead the right's resistance to globalization, but the decade also featured the quick rise of newcomers like the Christian patriot/militia movement, whose affiliates bombed the Oklahoma City federal building in 1995. The decade also featured the emergence of Trumpian "America First" ideologies, including the message of Donald Trump himself during his first presidential run in 2000.

Perhaps the most prominent representative of this paleoconservative version of antiglobalization was Pat Buchanan, who denounced NAFTA for its endangerment of Euro-American civilization in his 1992 presidential run. Buchanan mainly reviled immigrants and international bureaucracies, and not multinational corporations, but as the decade wore on he increasingly targeted corporations as part of a populist strategy to translate white working-class economic discontent into political capital for himself. After years as a Beltway-based Republican, Buchanan became a rebel. He deserted the party. He ran for the US presidency with the newly formed Reform Party, declaring in the months before the 1999 protests that "we will reclaim every lost ounce of American sovereignty" since "both Beltway parties today conspire to kill our beloved republic. Both colluded to create the WTO. Both voted $18 billion more for the IMF to make the world safe for Goldman Sachs."[20]

Buchanan's masculinist populism relied on raucously encouraging "Middle America" to unite against the elites, who were allowing the world's nonwhite nations to get the better of the US. After he observed tense trade negotiations with Japan in the mid-1990s, Buchanan reminded followers that "since 1970, Japan has purchased 400,000 U.S. cars, while selling us 40 million," and argued that Democratic president Bill Clinton's efforts to punish the Japanese didn't "even qualify as a spanking." Now "that Japan has given Mr. Clinton's trade envoy the wet mitten across the face," Buchanan added, we can see the corporate parties for what they are. They favor middle-class consumers and abstract notions of "free trade" instead of the needs of "Americans who work with their hands, tools and machines."[21] Forgiving Third World debt? That's "just a euphemism for debt transfer onto the backs of the American taxpayers," he complained.[22]

PROGRESSIVE POPULISM: UNEASY AFFINITIES WITH THE RIGHT

Some on the left decided to confront the right by attempting to steal its thunder. Jim Hightower, a featured speaker in Seattle and former Texas state agricultural commissioner, had built a significant following in the 1990s as he hoped to maneuver working-class disgruntlement into left-wing energy and pry the rural working class away from the militia movement. Hightower helped found the *Progressive Populist* web magazine and hosted the folksy *Chat n' Chew* radio show to compete with right-wing talk radio. With his ten-gallon hat and Texas wit, he derided the obsession with the Dow Jones Average and argued that his "Doug Jones Average"— how much daily necessities the proverbial "man on the street" could get from his paycheck—was the true measuring stick for the economy. Unapologetically from the left—but hoping to build a working-class alliance of the "Doug" and "Dottie" Joneses of the world around economic conditions—he titled his 1998 book *There's Nothing in the Middle of the Road Except Yellow Stripes and Dead Armadillos*. To redirect grassroots frustration with international trade and inequality in general, Hightower and his affiliates celebrated a citizenry of rugged, working-class, strong-willed (often masculine) producers. They were the heart of a national project to renew an aggrieved nation and, importantly, the people who built it. He and others worked to reclaim Heartland heritage, community control, and antielite skepticism for the left.[23]

Some progressives, following consumer advocate Ralph Nader, opted to build power by forging new populist blocs with right-wing, working-class whites. Farmer-writer Wendell Berry (discussed in the following chapter) advanced a white populist vision by advocating for the creation of a "Community Party" to unite against corporate Republicans and Democrats. Following the historical populist framework in the US, it would unite the "middling" classes of rural communities, small shopkeepers, and "religious people," and it would also have a new focus on ecological conservation.[24] Global Exchange's Kevin Danaher and Mike Dolan of the national Citizens' Trade Campaign also adopted such a view. Dolan suggested that "it's not about right or left . . . It's about the top and the bottom [of the economic system]."[25] In a 2010 interview, Dolan recounted,

> I was doing populist barnstorming. Sure, it was almost scary. I remember in Phoenix, not too long after the Oklahoma City bombing, I'm driving a big Ryder truck that could have had fertilizer [for a bomb]. I'm doing my events at federal buildings, and that's where this is, so I show them the inside of the truck, and I bring out the podium, and I've called everyone, including the United We Stand America people. To my left was the Sierra Club, Citizen Action, some on labor; on my right, the Teamsters for Buchanan, the "Perotistas," the Schiller Institute, the [Lyndon] LaRouche thing, and this guy said the John Birch Society, and I thought, "Are you kidding, you guys still exist?" Then I had an out-of-body experience, I introduced all these critics, and introducing a guy from the John Birch Society.... That's what populism's about, the ideological continuum on globalization, if we have the bravery... to organize around it.... So I sit down with these people later that night over pancakes, and I said it's not big government, it's the big corporations.... If it comes through to push to shove, what [the left and the right] are all trying to get is some grassroots ownership to vote and be empowered.[26]

Others on the left adopted uneasy affinities with the right wing as they searched for ways to oppose globalization. Beginning in the early 1990s, the Sierra Club, Public Citizen, and the Institute for Agriculture and Trade Policy attended meetings to coordinate their opposition with the right-wing nationalist resistance, including figures tied to Buchanan and the millionaire textile magnate Roger Milliken. Millken, an antiunion archconservative, distributed news clippings about globalization to progressive organizations like the National Family Farm Coalition and Public Citizen throughout the decade.[27] Labor leaders praised the email updates from his deputy, Jock Nash. He sometimes sent as many as fifteen emails per day. In select occasions Nader held joint press interviews with Buchanan, and in later years spoke favorably of his work with him.[28] Right-leaning populist and repeat Reform Party candidate for US president Ross Perot, with his organization United We Stand, occasionally collaborated with Nader and his Public Citizen organization. Reform Party Seattle leader Stan Emert was on one of the first steering committees for protest organization in Seattle.[29] As the next chapter discusses, activist intellectuals tied to the International Forum on Globalization argued that the topic of globalization was beyond right and left. Affiliate and International Forum on Globalization funder Edward Goldsmith spoke at several right-wing events.

For the US progressives, these were new affinities, but uneasy ones. Progressives I interviewed said they were determined to keep the meetings with the right wing secret. They called it the "No-Name Group." Even thirty years later, they only spoke about it to me off the record.[30]

AMBIVALENT AMERICANISM: FRAMING THE WORLD TRADE ORGANIZATION IN THE 1990S

Arch-conservative Pat Buchanan in a sea turtle costume at a street demonstration? The thought of it made him chuckle in an interview shortly after the 1999 protests. "I have my costume in my closet," he joked. Turning more serious, Buchanan affirmed that "where I agree with the sea turtles and the porpoises and [consumer activist] Ralph Nader and [conservative] Howard Phillips and the union guys is, when you make a law in the United States of America, no international organization should have the right to tell us that we've got to alter or change our laws."[31] For Buchanan, the struggle against the WTO was the "decisive battle in a second war of American independence, to recapture sovereignty from global bureaucrats." America, as he titled his 1999 book, was a "republic, not an empire."[32] The WTO's imperial inclinations were threatening *it*.

In the 1990s, Nader, much like Buchanan, adopted a focus on the injured and eroding state of US sovereignty in the face of globalization. He and his consumer safety organization, Public Citizen, created the Citizen Trade Campaign, which became a leading voice on antiglobalization in the 1990s. Operating from the left but flirting with the right and its anger about these "international organizations," Nader's early campaigns for US president were efforts to unite constituents from the right and the left against trade agreements and other corporate-friendly policies that both Democrats and Republicans sponsored.[33] Nader first won fame in the 1960s by pressuring automobile companies to install seatbelts, framing it as a question of "consumer safety," and in the process deftly divorcing corporate malfeasance from global corporate greed and US empire. To the chagrin of much of the US left, he never took a public stand on the Vietnam War.

Nader and the Citizen Trade Campaign's Americanism, unlike Buchanan's, was ambivalent, rather than full-throttled and explicit. Nader rarely took stands on gender and racial equality. He implied that ending *Roe v. Wade* wouldn't be a disaster and reportedly referred to identity politics as "gonadal" politics.[34] He refrained from overt criticism of Milliken. The same is true of Buchanan and his positions on women's rights and multiculturalism. He implied that regardless of things to disagree on, both he and Buchanan cared about "improving democracy."[35] In a 1998 political stunt, Nader asked the country's one hundred largest corporations to recite the Pledge of Allegiance before their shareholder meetings. When most proved noncommittal, Nader distributed the results to prominent commentators, and Buchanan himself used the results to pen a column decrying their lack of patriotism.[36] Nader's ambivalent Americanism came into focus during the months in 1995 when the US Congress debated whether the US should join the newly created WTO. Nader framed the problem of globalization in terms of a vulnerable American nation witnessing the erosion of its sovereignty at the hands of faceless international bureaucrats and foreign competitors, particularly from Asia and Latin America.

Nader helped popularize the problem of the WTO in terms of protecting American national sovereignty. While the pro-whiteness populism of Buchanan's conservatism lashed out at poor countries in explicit terms, Nader's ambivalent brand blamed both corporations and competitor countries.[37] It invested in the legitimacy of US nationalism, even if it fretted about reinforcing the racism and xenophobia such a vision could entail. In short, explicit pro-whiteness was problematic, but the basic populist script was important. In Nader's reading, America was innocent, if imperfect.

The WTO's proposed one-country, one-vote policy was especially problematic to the right-wing and left-wing populists. Republican Speaker of the House Newt Gingrich denounced it for creating a "Third-world dominated" structure and a new "world government."[38] Buchanan incredulously asked how a country like Bangladesh could have the same vote as the mighty US. Nader adhered to the general nationalist format, denouncing the WTO as an "autocratic world government," and warned that in the WTO, "Any two little dictatorships can outvote the U.S."[39] Pat Choate, operating more from the political center but supportive of the progressive populist push, steered away from the racialized fear-mongering about the Global South; he criticized the WTO plan for subjecting the US to equal treatment to Slovakia—which he cited for its small population—rather than contrasting US power with generic symbols of Third World poverty and corruption, as Buchanan and Gingrich did (and Nader implied).[40]

Nader, for his part, lamented how the WTO structure denied the US a form of veto power, akin to what it had on the United Nations Security Council. He suggested that the World Bank model—where countries simply bought influence—was fairer.[41] Nader's organization, Public Citizen, lamented how the WTO would no longer permit the US to employ unilateral trade sanctions, an important component of US imperial overreach. In contrast to Public Citizen, the National Rainbow Coalition played down the sovereignty threat and emphasized how US insurance and banking interests were using the WTO model to take over the domestic markets of Global South nations.[42]

Sovereignty was at the center of the WTO debate, which followed several years in which Nader and Public Citizen had drawn attention to this issue in campaigns against the GATT (the WTO predecessor) and NAFTA.[43] The sovereignty theme had already created tensions in emerging anti-WTO coalitions internationally, including between organizations interested in a multicountry alliance, or "grand bargain" kind of strategy, as Castañeda had called it. In struggles against NAFTA, Mexican organizations had chafed at how easily some US organizations could adopt the rhetoric of threats to US sovereignty, given the way US unilateral action had for so long violated their nation's sovereignty.[44] Australian and European activists criticized the national sovereignty framing that had emerged.[45] The sovereignty theme also created tensions with the more internationalist organizations within the US. They tended to favor long-term, transnational coalition building, rather than Public Citizen's realpolitik strategy of garnering anti-NAFTA and anti-WTO support from both the left and the right within the US.[46] For their part, Global South progressives had much to criticize about the GATT and early WTO discussions, but they rarely singled out the voting structures and dispute settlement procedures that Nader so maligned for their diminishment of national sovereignty.[47] Upon arrival in Washington, D.C., for an event in the mid-1990s, a Canadian global justice leader was (unpleasantly) surprised to be picked up none other than Jock Nash, who had been sent by Nader's Citizen Trade Campaign on the errand.

SOVEREIGNTY AND THE TUNA-DOLPHIN DEBATES

Protecting US sovereignty had been a central theme of Nader and Public Citizen's signature case against the WTO predecessor in the early 1990s: the "tuna-dolphin" controversy. Protecting sea creatures like turtles and dolphins from commercial fishing businesses had been a central plank for Nader and his middle-class consumer and environmental allies in the 1980s and 1990s. The tuna-dolphin case could capture the point that Nader (and Buchanan) were making about US victimhood. Sovereignty, for them, was a zero-sum game. If organizations at the global level had more, the US had less.[48] The US Congress, after all, agreed in the early 1990s to ban from US markets any tuna caught in nets that also ensnared dolphins. The organizations that led fight for the ban—the Earth Island Institute and allies like Greenpeace, Public Citizen, and the Sierra Club—celebrated the historic win, but not for long.[49] The Mexican government took the legislation to the GATT (and later the WTO), which promptly ruled that the ban constituted an unfair barrier to international trade. It would need to be lifted, or the US would need to pay countries like Mexico and Peru for the damages.

Public Citizen and US environmentalists framed the battle as epic and unambiguous: scrappy and altruistic environmental organizations passionately protecting sea mammals, only to have outsiders strip away all the protection they had won. Their enemies? GATT bureaucrats whose only real interest was private enterprise, not to mention the callous foreign fishermen who hunted "dirty tuna," stained from the "slaughter" of innocent dolphins."[50] It was the monster-like "GATTzilla," they said, "versus Flipper," the cuddly dolphin from the so-named 1960s-era television show.[51] But then something unexpected happened. Greenpeace Mexico, and other environmentalists in Latin America, decided to oppose Nader, the Earth Island Institute, and even Greenpeace International. The Union of Environmental Groups in Mexico (Unión de Grupos Ambientalistas de México, UGAM) criticized the US groups publicly. The tuna-dolphin controversy wasn't just about dispute settlement for them. It was about empire.

While tuna harvesting was a rather small industry in the behemoth US economy, it was a critical one for a Global South nation struggling under a mountain of debt to the World Bank, the IMF, and First World banks. Tuna harvesting had created a double benefit for Mexico, and the government began promoting it, if unevenly, in the 1970s. First, the debt crisis of the 1980s had created new poverty and hunger throughout the country, and tuna was a cheap protein source.[52] Second, Mexicans could also sell tuna outside their borders. Mexico was compelled to support export industries like tuna because of their desperate need for US dollars to pay off long-standing debts to major banks and international financial institutions.[53]

Global South activists had long argued that negotiations with the US, the world's biggest market and most powerful country, were highly unequal. They needed access to the US market for economic survival, but the mighty US didn't need any single market to survive—and certainly not a small Global South country's. The US shouldn't be able to unilaterally impose a solution, particularly an embargo on other nations. Greenpeace Mexico, in fact, argued that the US bill, and the ban it imposed, was really about protecting US financial interests, and particularly the US tuna fishing industry—which was being required to use dolphin-safe fishing methods. The Earth Island Institute, for instance, collaborated with and directly promoted some US tuna brands.[54] The Latin American environmentalists argued for a multilateral solution, a kind of "grand bargain" approach. Multinational negotiations, akin to the process for creating the international convention against ivory, would allow stakeholders to discuss protecting dolphins, but to do so in a way that wouldn't further exacerbate global inequality between North and South. The US should reduce the debt, as Global South countries were demanding, and allow for transfers of netting technology and resources so that the industries could strive to compete.[55]

Yet that context was mostly absent in the work of US environmentalists. The Earth Island Institute's coverage of the tuna-dolphin issue in the 1990s vilified Mexican fishing vessels, in one case connecting them to ocean-bound "narco-traffickers." Early in the decade, an environmental organization's ship encountered a Mexican tuna boat in the open seas and intentionally "rammed into" it, forcing it to flee.[56] While the dolphin issue was only one issue among many in Seattle, the organizations involved actively publicized the matter among activists. Public Citizen's fliers and reports were so prolific, in fact, that rumors emerged about it possibly receiving funding from Milliken.[57] In the weeks leading up to the Seattle protests, the sovereignty framing continued to circulate. The radical Direct Action Network, in the organizing packet it sent out to activists to draw them to the 1999 protests, featured the dolphin case and failed to mention the highly unequal economic contest between the countries, or the compromise efforts by Mexico, Greenpeace Mexico, and Latin American countries to reduce dolphin deaths. Instead, according to the Direct Action Network, a powerful and immoral Mexico was maintaining its "dolphin-killing" methods and wielded lawsuits and threats to force the US to back down. The US had no choice and so "eliminated the law" protecting dolphins.[58]

· · · · ·

The United Steel Workers' protest and rally in Seattle captures some of the contradictory elements of the moment—and helps contextualize the confrontation between the steelworker and the flag burner recounted at the beginning of the chapter. The day after the major rally, protests, and arrests, the union staged a ceremonial Boston Tea Party on the Seattle docks.[59] Clamoring around the slogan "No globalization without representation" and with more than two thousand people in attendance, steelworkers dumped pounds of "steel" (it was actually Styrofoam) into the water. Recalling the fervor of the spirit of 1776, and expressing a similar nationalism, the action denounced the "dumping" of steel onto world markets by China—which had led to dramatic declines in steelworkers' "American" jobs. As one observer noted, "Speaking from Seattle's drizzly docks, Steelworkers President George Becker point[ed] to an American flag sewn into the lining of his jacket and attempt[ed] to lead the crowd in chanting

'U-S-A! U-S-A!'"⁶⁰ For Becker and his allies, protesting the WTO was perhaps about social justice, but it was certainly about imports and industrial survival.⁶¹ We might contrast Becker's approach with that of Glen Mpufane, a Black mineworker from South Africa. A day before the steelworkers' events, Mpufane took the stage at the major labor rally. Corporate globalization, he said, was far from simply an economic process. It was also a geopolitical one designed to keep the colonizing countries powerful. For Mpufane, neoliberal globalization wasn't just economics, it was empire.

To be clear, Becker's politics weren't reflective of the protests as a whole. Then again, neither were Mpufane's. Instead of thinking about nationalists as entirely distinct from internationalists in the global justice movements, we can see in Seattle an ambivalent and contradictory spectrum. The ambivalent Americanism of the age allowed progressives to simultaneously single out how the WTO hurt US sovereignty *and* how it hurt the Global South, all the while occasionally indulging in rhetoric of American exceptionalism. The Direct Action Network may have repeated the sovereignty framing, but—like Nader and Public Citizen—it also highlighted many cases about the inequality the Global South faced. Nader, on the campaign trail, could rail against the evils of global inequality, while also helping finance a billboard in Seattle that featured an image of the US Bill of Rights with a large "X" through it. The WTO, it warned, meant an end to US democracy.⁶² The King County Labor Council, led by progressive unionist Ron Judd, could publish a column in its monthly newsletter about how the WTO would particularly harm Global South workers, yet overlay the article's text on the same image of the US Bill of Rights with an "X" through it.⁶³

While the organizing for the Seattle protests began in earnest in early 1999, it reflected more than a decade of advocacy and organizing, as countless groups and activists developed strategies against trade and financial liberalization. The problems of the protests that Betita Martínez and others pointed out—namely, their whiteness—stemmed from those roots as well.⁶⁴ For the progressives discussed here, the US wasn't the *only* victim of the WTO regime, but it was the one they usually made most visible. As with Buchanan and the right wing, progressives often portrayed the US as vulnerable and injured. Yet unlike Buchanan, their attempts to defend the country were ambivalent, recognizing that Global South countries also suffered.⁶⁵ Whether through ambivalent Americanism or through uneasy affinities with the racist right during the decade, white progressives' interpretations of globalization sometimes reflected a color-blind anticorporatism, an orientation that treated racism as a secondary consideration. It visibilized global inequalities but could simultaneously conceal and obscure the idea of US empire. As the following chapter shows, color-blind anticorporatism could invisibilize immigration as well.

6 Invisibilizing Immigration

COLOR-BLIND ANTICORPORATISM AND
THE 1999 WORLD TRADE ORGANIZATION
PROTESTS IN SEATTLE

"The true environmentalist doesn't believe in immigration," said Brian Derdowski, a former King County councilor who was the only Seattle-area councilor to oppose the WTO and its arrival in the city in 1999.[1] Derdowski, a Republican, met with me in 2019 in the Seattle suburb that he represented. A deep spirt of conservation had long shaped his thinking, he said. To be clear, Derdowski didn't advocate stopping immigration to the US. He was speaking hypothetically. But he had long campaigned against "growth" in his affluent district. "Immigrants," he told me, "would consume ten times more or create ten times more contamination migrating than if they stayed at home."

At first glance, Derdowski may appear an unlikely ally of the antiglobalization protesters in the 1990s. Yet as the previous chapter demonstrated, the left didn't own the issue of opposing globalization. White supremacists like Pat Buchanan argued that US Americans needed another "war of independence" to reestablish national self-determination in the face of the sovereignty-stifling World Trade Organization, which mostly represented the interests of Global South nations and (Jewish) international financiers. The US left, for its part, offered a different interpretation, tending to criticize the WTO for representing multinational corporations and spurring global inequality.

For Derdowski, the fight against the WTO was partly about the power of transnational corporations and global inequality. But it was simultaneously about conserving a way of life, including in the largely white localities like his own. Derdowski had long argued that "development pressures" like new roads, buildings, and populations, were "ruining our northwest quality of life."[2] One observer christened him the "John the Baptist of the slow-growth movement."[3] His localism propelled him, along with progressive allies, to lead a fight in Seattle in the late 1990s against the Multilateral Agreement on Investment (MAI), a draft agreement among rich countries to create a universal set of guidelines for foreign investment. He and other antiglobalization activists called it "NAFTA on Steroids" for the way it loosened rules on capital mobility. In arguing for Seattle to constitute an "MAI-free zone," Derdowski and his left-wing allies argued that the MAI constituted a dire threat to sovereignty and democracy. It would allow foreign investors to sue local governments if their laws were found to be detrimental to foreign investors.

Let's contrast Derdowski's ideas—or the color-blind anticorporatism from the last chapter—with those of the Seattle-based organization Legacy of Equality, Leadership, and Organizing (LELO). In the months after the Battle in Seattle, LELO members, in addition to activist intellectual Elizabeth Martínez, criticized the whiteness of the protests, which were already being celebrated as cacophonous and diverse. LELO, as an organization with decades of experience organizing for racial and economic justice in Seattle's working-class communities of color, fought for global justice partly by building campaigns with local migrant workers displaced by trade agreements. When it sought allies and support to focus on mobilizing local immigrants for the WTO activities, it mostly got silence from local and national progressives.

This silence, this chapter suggests, was partly due to how these organizations—as well as iconoclastic figures like Derdowski—had defined globalization in the first place. The color-blind anticorporate ideologies that took shape in the 1990s, whether the populist and nationalist variants of the last chapter or the "global village multiculturalism" discussed here, ultimately helped invisibilize immigration at the protests. Few people knew more about globalization than the displaced Global South migrants in Seattle, many of whom had experienced firsthand the economic consequences of global trade agreements. Yet color-blind anticorporate understandings of globalization generated a deep unease about immigration, particularly in middle-class and largely white environmental organizations. By situating the emergence of the US global justice movement in the political and cultural history of the 1990s, this chapter shows how some tendencies within the movements made immigrants' rights seem unrelated—or inconvenient—to questions of border-crossing trade and investment.

IMMIGRATION AND TRADE: FROM NAFTA TO THE WTO

How could Randy Hayes, a leading environmental activist and founder of the Rainforest Action Network, oppose the immigration of Latin Americans to the US but simultaneously help lead high-profile campaigns in support of poor Latin Americans against US oil companies? The following sections argue that such a seemingly contradictory position reflects a particular brand of color-blind anticorporatism that I call global village multiculturalism.

Immigration issues have long been agenda items in trade and investment negotiations. The construction of the European Union, for instance, included broad, if contradictory, efforts to harmonize income inequalities on the continent and prevent massive migration to richer countries. Predicting how NAFTA would affect Mexican migration to the US was a major topic of discussion for trade officials and observers and experts in the early 1990s, and most agreed that many rural Mexicans would be displaced. In initial NAFTA negotiations, Mexicans had tried to broach the issue.[4] Mexican unions supported them, but the US union leadership, which maintained an official policy of opposition to immigration, resisted, as did others. Leaving immigration outside of NAFTA framed trade politics as the movement of goods across borders, but not the movement of peoples. The latter was consigned to the realm of security and policing. This made immigration—and the increasing anti-immigrant sentiment of the era—seem naturally outside the purview of the anti-WTO advocacy networks that developed in the decade.[5]

Ironically, the union whose participation in the Battle of Seattle came to most characterize the protest's diversity—by way of the Teamsters and Turtles duo—was one of the most explicitly anti-immigrant and anti-Mexico. The Teamsters' general president, James Hoffa, had long blamed both global corporations *and* poor countries when it came to trade, sometimes aligning himself with racist stereotypes and those who voiced them. Shortly after the Seattle protests, he told a crowded press conference on international labor rights that "there's always someone who will work cheaper. There's always some guy in a loincloth." Hoffa's response to the WTO protests in Seattle (where he spoke at the major labor rally) was to attend the next major global justice protest a few months later at the IMF/World Bank meetings in Washington, D.C. He personally invited Pat Buchanan, who saw Global South immigration as intimately connected to trade issues. For Buchanan, it was a threat to the cultural fabric of white Western civilization. Rumors swirled about Buchanan asking Hoffa to serve as his running mate for his Reform Party campaign for US president in 2000.[6]

Hoffa and the Teamsters' nationwide press blitz in the 1990s to oppose allowing Mexican truckers to operate in the US generated particular consternation. Playing on long-standing stereotypes about Mexico as crime-ridden, corrupt, and contaminated, the campaign sought to provoke fear in the American public about the dirtiness and disrepute of Mexican truckers, who, according to the campaign, were often secretly shuttling illicit drugs in their stashes.[7] Future Green Party presidential candidate Ralph Nader sometimes followed Hoffa in tone, working up fear about NAFTA by saying the trade agreement was like a "giant Mexican truck in your rear view mirror."[8] The machinists' union ran a story about a Mexican trucker using marijuana and cocaine on the job.[9] One observer, noting that many of the early anti-NAFTA coalition members in the US were nongovernmental organizations without extensive grassroots memberships, registered an illuminating irony. In a moment with great potential for creating cross-border alliances, "the only case of a bottom-up U.S. protest that blocked part of the NAFTA implementation" was the Teamsters trucking campaign, he wrote. That was the very campaign that "many Mexican free trade critics considered to be anti-Mexican in tone."[10]

Among the progressives who, along with the Teamsters and other unions, hoped to build lasting coalitions to challenge NAFTA and the

WTO, immigrant rights was a vexed and controversial topic. For its part, the AFL-CIO maintained a position that favored restricting the entry of immigrants in the 1990s.[11] Nader, whose electoral base was largely white and who attempted to attract disaffected Republicans to his presidential campaigns, refrained from taking a stance on controversial anti-immigrant policies in 1996. In 2000, he spoke out against bilingual education indicating that children must learn English first.[12] Nader's Public Citizen organization attended meetings with right-wing anti-globalists in the early 1990s (as discussed in chapter 5), some of which included representatives from the Federation for American Immigration Reform, the leading anti-immigrant organization at the time. The *Wall Street Journal* reported that "anti-Mexican banter was not unusual" at those meetings. Public Citizen also received money from the anti-immigration Foundation for Deep Ecology. Progressive populists who wanted to fight corporate globalization by creating left-right populist coalitions against corporate Republicans and Democrats tried to avoid the issue.[13] The *Progressive Populist* magazine, which frequently featured Nader and Jim Hightower, published relatively few stories about the struggles of immigrants or farmworkers in the 1990s.[14] In some of the widely circulated progressive political writing about globalization by these organizations in the 1990s, the term *immigration* almost never appears. Nor does *race* or *racism*.[15]

IMMIGRATION AND ENVIRONMENTALISM

Nowhere in these early global justice coalitions was the controversy about immigration as heated and public as in the Sierra Club—and Randy Hayes was in the middle of it. Middle-class environmentalism has a long history of equating the "clean" natural environment with white lifestyles and differentiating them from the threatening dirtiness of nonwhite others. By the 1970s, many in these white-led environmental networks began to support global population reduction measures because of Paul Erlich's best-selling book *The Population Bomb*, which popularized the idea that population growth, not Global North industrial overreach, was the key factor in environmental destruction. Critics argued that the eugenicist tactics of targeting Third World fertility replayed older white supremacist scripts. Ehrlich once argued that US aid should be withheld to any nation that refused to sterilize men after the birth of their second child, though he later walked back such comments.[16] As immigration from Latin America and the Caribbean increased in the 1980s, racists and eugenicists gained power by pressing for "English-only" legislation in their state legislatures, and prominent anti-immigrant organizations like FAIR began to argue that conserving the US environment was a critical reason to oppose further immigration.

The immigration debate came to a head in the Sierra Club only a year before the organization would help lead the Seattle WTO protests. Some of its anti-immigrant energy emerged from the Club's official "Population Committee," with many arguing that immigration restriction was necessary for deterring US population growth and its deleterious effects on natural environments. The Club's vote for limiting immigration in 1988 accompanied the era's growing racial backlash against "dirty" Latin American immigrants, and after divisive debate in 1996, the organization compromised and expressed "neutrality" about immigration. In 1998, neutrality was reaffirmed by membership vote, but it was relatively close: 60 percent voted in favor, and 40 percent were opposed (though only 13 percent of the membership voted).[17] Anti-immigration forces were well organized.[18] Hayes, who was a Club board member, voted for restriction in the 1998 population reduction vote. He was an acquaintance of Ehrlich's. His other acquaintances, like militant Earth First! founders Dave Foreman and Paul Watson, voted for restriction as well. Sierra Club board member Watson and others led an anti-immigrant campaign inside the organization in the early 2000s and nearly won majorities of the board.[19]

Hayes is best known for founding the Rainforest Action Network in 1986, an organization that helped lead campaigns against multinational corporations and other economic interests encroaching on South American and Asian rainforests, which were often the home of Indigenous groups. Hayes's work there occupied an ideological and strategic position distinct from the white, middle-class moderation of the Sierra Club but also distinct from another extreme of the era's environmental politics: the conservationist Deep Ecology of figures like Foreman, who created the radical direct-action network Earth First! in 1980. Foreman helped coin the

Earth First! slogan "No Compromise for the Wilderness"—and he meant it. Earth First! sabotaged bulldozers and powerlines near mines and dams, sometimes installing metal spikes in tree trunks that would shatter loggers' saws if they made contact. Sometimes called a misanthrope for his lack of concern for humans (like the loggers mentioned above), in the 1980s he argued, with a dose of grandiosity, that he stood proudly "with the bears" in the "genocidal [human] warfare against nature."[20]

Immigration became a flash point for Foreman. Foreman saw himself as a "conservationist," not an "environmentalist." The former, he said, defended nature regardless of its effects on humans.[21] Foreman and his close associate Edward Abbey, the famous conservationist writer who inspired much of Earth First!'s work, staked out a number of racist positions in the 1980s. Foreman suggested AIDS and Ethiopian famine should be allowed to continue (to winnow the population), and both called for militarizing the US/Mexico border. Abbey argued throughout the 1980s that Latin American and Caribbean immigrants were "culturally-morally-genetically impoverished people" and constituted a threat to "Latinize" the "Northern European culture" of the US.[22] Foreman offered apologetic "second thoughts" about his comments in 1991, yet even the apology reflected the masculinist stridency of the man who once proudly identified as a "Redneck for wilderness." Foreman stated that "while Ed Abbey's proposal to send every illegal refugee that is caught home with a rifle and a thousand rounds of ammunition may be considered flippant and impractical," the left wing too often ignored the "merit" of the statement's "underlying spirit."[23]

Unlike Foreman's more strident racism, much of the Sierra Club anti-immigrant bloc advanced a color-blind version that downplayed the racial coordinates of immigration restriction. Hayes told me, in a 2022 interview, that "he got a lot of flak" for his vote on immigration. He said that the Sierra Club director, Carl Pope, told him that he just wanted the issue to go away. Hayes's position, unlike Abbey's, was tied not to inferiority of Latin Americans but to concerns about population growth and contamination. As for the Sierra Club resolution itself, "I would have to take a look at the wording of it to see what I would do now," he said. "But I guess my general sentiment was that, you know, population numbers and carrying capacity are important issues and can be scary." Hayes suggested that most people don't want to migrate and that organizations should fight the global processes that displace them.[24] Ultimately, the hesitancy of the Sierra Club in general—as reflected in merely claiming "neutrality" on the issue—shows the difference between Hayes, the Sierra Club, and another, growing tendency within US environmentalism. Environmental justice movements emerged in the decade and argued that protecting wilderness areas primarily benefited middle-class whites and recreationists. The structural racism of capitalism created have-nots and compelled them to live and work amid the most toxic contaminants. These have-nots—often working-class immigrants of color—should be the focus of the environmental movement, not its enemy.

Hayes and other Sierra Club activists adopted color-blind positions about the Global South immigrants in their midst. They rejected the explicit racism and xenophobia of Edward Abbey, yet downplayed and deflected the impacts of racist xenophobia, viewing them as secondary to goals of environmental carrying capacity. At the same time, figures like Hayes expressed a deep respect for Global South peoples in faraway lands, and he wasn't alone. Hayes and other progressives' unease with immigration can be seen as tied to the broader political orientation of global village multiculturalism.[25]

GLOBAL VILLAGE MULTICULTURALISM

Why weren't the Zapatistas from Mexico on the list of speakers for the major international "teach-in" on globalization a few days before the November 30 protests in Seattle? It was a signature event of a packed week of activities, held in the packed, 2,500-seat Benaroya Hall, with overflow crowds waiting outside. The Zapatistas, for their part, had led an uprising on the first day of NAFTA's implementation and had emerged as icons of the antiglobalization left. They had convened the People's Global Action network, one of the main sources of direct-action energy behind the civil disobedience of the week. They had a savvy and active internet presence, a charismatic and entertaining spokesperson, and a multitude of manifestoes about the stated topic for the evening: "global economic inequality."

But they also drank Coca-Cola.

As thousands of Europeans and US Americans visited Chiapas in the years after 1994, the fact that the indigenous Zapatistas bought, sold, and drank the beverage became an occasional tension within global solidarity circles.[26] Some were incredulous. After all, Coke symbolized the global corporate power they opposed. Other activists were understanding. But the fact that it became a source of conversation reflects how the topic engaged with deeper cultural assumptions about the peoples of the Global South, and especially about the Indigenous.

The organization that convened the teach-in was an international network of scholars and activists named the International Forum on Globalization (IFG), and Hayes was one of them. Mobilizing a brand of Deep Ecology and bioregionalism closely attuned to questions of international development, prominent voices in the IFG had long advocated confronting the problem of globalization with "relocalization." They envisioned challenging the homogenous "One World" of globalization by creating a "globe of villages," small communities closely in tune with their distinct local ecosystems.[27] Some conceptualized the villages of a relocalized world as something like their vision of Indigenous peoples' communities. And drinking Coke wasn't part of the vision.

Hayes was one of many voices in the IFG; its affiliate intellectuals included writer-critic Vandana Shiva (from India) and others from Asia and Latin America, though most were from the US or England. The organization was sponsored and led by two US business executives who had come to see their industries as part of an economic and technological system destroying the environment and local communities. One was former advertising executive Jerry Mander, and the other was his personal friend Douglas Tompkins, the (antiunion) owner of Esprit fashion corporation. Tompkins funded the IFG, particularly in the beginning.[28] It specialized in crafting reports and leading workshops about globalization. The IFG led or participated in dozens of teach-ins about globalization in the 1990s, particularly on college campuses. They gained a large following, which helps explain why the *New York Times* once referred to Mander as "a patriarch of the anti-globalization movement."[29] Mander, along with IFG cofounder and personal friend Edward Goldsmith, compiled and edited a key text—perhaps *the* key text—for the emerging global justice movements in the 1990s: *The Case against the Global Economy* (1996).

Mander, in his best-selling books, advanced a vision of the global economy that identified "megatechnology" as a dire threat to cultural and biological diversity, but particularly to nature and to those beings and practices he understood as "sacred." As author of a book decrying television (and celebrating authors who wrote their books in longhand), he united a critique of computing and genetic technologies with an anticorporate analysis of what he called the "*megatechnological* age."[30] Many might find Mander's perspective extreme, but no one defended the sacred as zealously as Goldsmith. Goldsmith, who spoke at the IFG's major Seattle event on November 26, argued in his texts that the bonds of religion and the (patriarchal) family were the key things that held "traditional" societies together in balance with nature. This allowed them to resist the dulling consumerism of globalizing corporate culture. His associates in Green politics in the UK and elsewhere acknowledged that his positions on multiculturalism and "women in the home" were controversial.[31] As his longtime coeditor at *The Ecologist* magazine wrote in a tribute, Goldsmith "was no racist: on the contrary, he reveled in the extraordinary diversity of cultures and peoples. But he saw danger . . . through mass immigration or through the imposition of colonial rule."[32] Goldsmith yearned for a world of traditional villages that could preserve the "ancient" that still existed. In the 1990s, Mander and Goldsmith argued that now "only the bows and arrows of ancient tribal people stand in the way of Western development assault."[33]

ENVISIONING THE INDIGENOUS

Yankton Dakota scholar-activist Vine Deloria once noted that "it was the strangeness of Indians that made them visible, not their humanity."[34] White radicals and counterculturalists have been frequent cultivators of stereotypical, ill-informed visions of "eco-Indians"; such figures serve as "satisfying legends," archetypes who embody the promise of "stone-age economics" and validate movements for ecological change.[35] Mander, for his part, criticized intellectuals who reduced the Indigenous to a "vanishing race" or to the "Noble Savage"—the tragic, passive, and disappearing Native American.³⁶ But Mander and IFG associates also faced criticism for their sometimes one-dimensional portrayals.

Let's take as an example Mander's best-selling *In the Absence of the Sacred: The Failure of Technology and the Survival of the Indian Nations* (1991). The decades before the publication of the book were marked by the urbanization of Native America, and radicals in organizations like the American Indian Movement organized Native youth in cities as well as on rural reservations. Yet those aren't the images of Indigeneity that appear in Mander's work. *In the Absence of the Sacred* mostly tells the tale of television and consumer technology despoiling formerly isolated Indigenous cultures.³⁷ The Zapatistas and others used the internet to build important solidarities and protect themselves from government repression. Yet Mander's message for Native Americans is to discard their computers. Mander and the IFG scarcely mention the Zapatistas in their work in the 1990s.

In *The Case against the Global Economy* (1996), Mander and Goldsmith include the work of IFG colleague Helena Norberg-Hodge, whose research focused on the Ladakh people of India. According to her essay, Ladakh society was irrevocably transformed—and its traditional family structures and social institutions were destroyed—by the global economic forces after the 1970s. Yet other anthropologists have disputed Norberg-Hodge's representation of the Ladakh in 1974 as a "traditional society," given the processes of colonization, modernization, and state building over the prior century.³⁸

The Indigenous people represented in Mander's and Norberg-Hodge's work in the 1990s have little hope leading hybrid lives that are both modern and traditional. It's the unmodernness of the Indigenous that makes them "visible" in the IFG's environmental ideology. Unlike immigrants—and unlike the Indigenous peoples who drank Coca-Cola—these far-away Indigenous subjects are Native peoples in their "expected" places—as authentic bearers of ancestral tradition against a corrupt modernity. They are different, but in entirely expected ways.³⁹

Like Norberg-Hodge and Mander, Hayes was attracted to a world of "ancient futures" that Indigenous peoples could represent. For the Rainforest Action Network (RAN), saving rainforests meant supporting the people who lived there. Hayes founded RAN in 1985, and its early campaigns to save rainforest in the Amazon region of South America contributed to the rapid internationalization of the struggles of Amazonian Indigenous groups in the 1980s and 1990s. As Indigenous groups translated long-standing languages of self-determination into environmental discourses for consumption in US and European environmental circles, they became quick media sensations. The weekly magazine *Parade* and others penned cover stories about the ancient headdresses and exotic body jewelry of the last traditional inhabitants of the Amazon. The rock singer Sting flew in for a visit. So did reporters from *Vogue* and *People* magazines. The owner of the Body Shop cosmetic brand, who was an acquaintance of Hayes and Mander and spoke at the Benaroya Hall event, stated that the Amazonians Indians "symbolized purity." That's why she featured them in an advertising campaign for the Body Shop's latest hair conditioner.[40]

RAN's materials from this period represent Indigenous peoples as more complicated than the proud—but ultimately passive—stereotypes. They're fighters. They build organizations. They launch lawsuits. Hayes, for his part, was critical of mainstream Global North environmental organizations that opened up offices in the Global South rather than operating through partnerships with local organizations. He was also critical of Global North environmentalists buying land in the South in the name of conservation.[41] Yet what links RAN's representations of the Indigenous with those of other critics in IFG circles is the appeal of authenticity. As RAN's newsletters from the 1990s show, their appeal was their presumed distance from Western ways. They were often one-dimensionally pure, authentically inhabiting their place and—until now—untainted by capitalistic greed and consumerism. Articles in RAN's Action Alert in the late 1990s were coupled with photos of shoeless "tribesmen" with spears and prominent jewelry. The Yanomami people were "still living in relative isolation" from outsiders, yet recent incursions by miners had led these "proud hunters" to a life of "begging."[42] The Kyopo and others were naturally noble—inhabiting Edenic forests and conserving their "ancient" cultures.[43] One regional director said that the U'wa people (of Colombia, who were contesting new oil extraction by the Occidental Oil Company) were the perfect "poster child" for the organization's goals, and supporting the U'wa was one of the group's most successful campaigns.[44] In 1997, its popular website showcasing information about its campaigns, along with images of Indigenous life, was garnering twenty-three thousand hits per day.[45] RAN advertised Goldsmith's *Imperiled Planet* (1994) book in its newsletters in the 1990s as "essential reading."

FROM ECO-INDIANS TO ETHNO-HOMELANDS

In 1987 Kentucky writer and small farmer Wendell Berry published an essay entitled "Why I Am Not Going to Buy a Computer." His decision, he wrote on the essay's opening page, was made possible because "my wife types my work on a Royal standard typewriter bought new in 1956 and as good now as it was then."[46]

Berry's valorization of his 1956 typewriter, not to mention the conservatism reflected in who uses it, signals his nostalgic lionization of tradition and local rural place—key elements of his contribution to the IFG's determined pursuit of relocalization in the face of homogenizing globalization.[47] Berry's essay in Mander and Goldsmith's *The Case against the Global Economy*, a volume subsequently revised, updated, and reprinted several times, was titled "Conserving Communities." Like Mander, Berry argues that the new wave of bigness threatens (rural) smallness. The global economy will mean that "supranational corporations and the governments and educational systems that serve them" will "disallow" the local "cultures that preserve nature and rural life."[48]

The turn toward the typewriter, for Berry, is not a whimsical writing habit but a component of his quest to embody a traditionalist and "conservationist" response to what he calls the "military-industrial state" and its fantasies of mass consumption and extraction. Berry saturates his essays with accounts of the trust, interdependence, and "neighborly acts" of small-town Kentucky before the Big Institutions came, whether the universities and their "experts" or the corporations and their staff. Because strip-mined coal is so destructive of local land, he refuses to buy a computer for the electricity it would consume. "How could I write conscientiously about the rape of nature," he asks, "if I were, in the act of writing, implicated in the rape?" Berry proceeds to explain that he does all his writing before dinnertime. "For that same reason," he continues, "it matters to me that my writing is done in the daytime, without electric light."[49]

In the essay, Berry presents himself as one of the few remaining men of principle in a corrupt world. Elsewhere in this multiessay volume, he defends another such figure: none other than Edward Abbey.

In "A Few Words in Favor of Ed Abbey" (1985), Berry acknowledges the criticism Abbey has faced for his statements about immigrants but casts Abbey much as he represents himself: as a principled, determined, and masculine martyr figure, one of the few with the courage to "go it alone" to resist the consumerism, group-think, and superficial political correctness of US society. For Berry, the problem with the reaction to Abbey's anti-immigrant statements is that many readers and critics see him as an "environmentalist." Because of that label, Berry notes, they expect a certain kind of "sober, informed, and logical" voice. But Abby is not an environmentalist, Berry asserts. He is an "autobiographer," a "conservationist," and a "traditionalist," hoping to save nature and "human nature" with it.[50] Berry never directly condemns Abbey's statements about immigrants. Certainly, Berry writes, Abbey is "a poor excuse" for "a political activist." But it's the reader's fault for holding him to that standard.[51]

In an age when "diversity" became an increasingly productive category for economic and racial elites, Berry's essays in the 1990s advocate a distinctly deracialized kind of diversity as a way to counter the forces of globalization. Berry's insistence on the sovereignty of small places is partly driven by his view of the fundamental power inequality in society: not between women and men, or Black and white, but between rural and urban, the small and the big. It's the global economic system and its "one-world economy" against a world with local diversities.[52] Berry compares the plight of his mid-South plain folk with those brutalized by overseas imperialism, arguing that the rural has been made into a "colony," conquered by an urban world dedicated to resource extraction. It has also been victimized by contemporary multiculturalism, a logic that demands you "quit talking bad about women, homosexuals, and preferred social minorities" but at the same time utter anything you please about "people who haven't been to college, manual workers, country people, peasants, religious people, [and] unmodern people."[53] Today's multiculturalism, Berry suggests, is inadequate since it fails to recognize the true, landed diversity of small-town America. Forming "adequate local cultures" in rural areas, he argues, would constitute "authentic multiculturalism."⁵⁴

Berry's quest for an authentic multiculturalism of global villages led him to send a blunt message to the emerging audience of antiglobalization sympathizers in 1996: abandon the Republicans and Democrats and build a "community party" of local hard workers and churchgoers. The distinctions between conservatives and liberals, and between communists and capitalists, are now "useless," he argues, since they all have turned against rural communities. However, a new political schism is "beginning to take form" around local community. One political bloc "holds that community has no value; the other holds that it does. One is the party of the global economy; the other I would call simply the party of local community," which is "only now coming aware of itself." The "natural members of the community party consist of small farmers, ranchers, and market gardeners; worried consumers; owners and employees of small businesses; self-employed people; religious people; and conservationists."⁵⁵

Berry, like his IFG associates, downplayed the divisions between the left and right. From different angles, they valorized place and tradition in a way that legitimized assumptions by right-wing antiglobalizers. While Berry held positions shared with the political right, Goldsmith moved to establish links with the New Right in the 1990s. Goldsmith visited and conversed with French New Right organizations, speaking twice at a notable New Right conference in the 1990s. Arguing for a kind of ethno-cultural isolation and "right to difference," the French-origin European New Right movement (ENR), like IFG environmentalists, argued that populations should (re)discover their organic connections to their "homelands," including their natural environments. The ENR mobilized a romanticized notion of the ethno-homelands of European communities before the growth of states, nationalism, industrial economies, and even massifying Christianity.⁵⁶ The ENR fervently opposed the entry of immigrants from the Global South and advocated breaking up European nation-states into ethno-cultural regions. Goldsmith supported an anti-immigrant Green party in the late 1990s as well, and his conservative collaborations with the right and conservative positions on gender and race led to a schism in the editorial board of *The Ecologist* in the 1990s.⁵⁷

There are many reasons the Zapatistas weren't included in the IFG's teach-in days before the Battle of Seattle.[58] The Seattle protests featured tens of thousands of activists, including Indigenous activists and speakers. Yet the inattention to both the Zapatistas and immigrants in the work of IFG affiliates in the 1990s reflects a pattern. Neither quite fit into the worldview of one of the main US voices on globalization in the 1990s. Activist intellectuals connected to the IFG, whether Randy Hayes defending immigration restrictions, Wendell Berry defending Edward Abbey, or Norberg-Hodges focusing on the "ancient futures" of eco-Indians, privileged the purity of place, not the traversal of space.[59] Ultimately, the many contours of global village multiculturalism—from the eco-Indians to the European ethno-homelands—helped whiten the ways some progressives understood globalization in the 1990s. In an essay about how liberal multiculturalism celebrates diversity and difference but simultaneously stifles substantive social change, scholar-activist Angela Davis discussed how some deployments of difference don't really "make a difference."[60] Global village multiculturalism favored the different, but only if it was distant, ultimately helping marginalize many of those who best knew the impacts of globalization.

NOVEMBER 30, 1999

Seattle was ready for a global event. The city possessed a major port and a growing and international tech sector. Washington, for its part, was a trade-dependent state. In the week leading up to the protests, one Seattle restaurant owner "[anticipated] watching the world pass" by his windows, he told a local magazine, as the city welcomed officials and staffers from all over the world. That week, the reporter informed us, "His bartenders would serve up a new drink du jour called—what else?—the WTO. It contains French cognac, Indonesian cinnamon stick, American orange slice and sugar."[61]

If local businesses anticipated the arrival of delegates—and dollars, other observers were excited about the diversity of the protests, and particularly the unlikely pairing of the Turtles and the Teamsters. Yet in the weeks following the protests, activists from LELO and Elizabeth Martínez offered alternative perspectives on the protests' diversity. Earlier in 1999, LELO was one of groups who criticized national organizers for their failure to connect with local organizations, despite their deep experience organizing for global justice locally. The main protest alliance, People for Fair Trade/No WTO, which was coordinated by Public Citizen's Mike Dolan, made only limited efforts to do outreach to Seattle's own working-class communities of color.[62] The Direct Action Network, an expansive civil-disobedience network, mostly stuck to its crowd of young white radicals and progressives.[63] The Sierra Club lead organizer admitted that its Seattle mobilizing and media strategy was mainly oriented to "soccer moms."[64] In a letter to African American community leaders in Seattle, LELO cofounder and influential Black unionist Tyree Scott noted that "probably no one [has] reached out to you about this."[65] When the iconoclastic Republican Brian Derdowski brainstormed promoting the protests to his white, wealthy East Seattle communities, his staffer suggested the IFG's David Korten, who was buttoned-up and legitimate enough for the job. But when LELO organizers offered to organize working-class communities of color for the Seattle protests, they were denied support or funding by People for Fair Trade/No WTO. In the weeks before the protests, LELO ultimately created a separate protest coalition of Seattle-based working-class (community) organizations called the "Workers' Voices Coalition."[66]

The last two chapters have examined color-blind anticorporate approaches to globalization, and two of the big events of the week illuminate these. First, the IFG organized one of the largest teach-ins in Seattle—the Benaroya Hall event. Reflecting the global village multiculturalism discussed in this chapter, the teach-in featured a multinational collection of speakers—but left out the locals. Mander, Goldsmith, and numerous white Europeans spoke at the proceedings. The teach-in featured Filipino intellectual-activist Walden Bello (about globalization's effects on the Philippines) as well, but not representatives from Seattle's own substantial population of Filipinos, including its radical activists. The latter, in fact, organized their own march on November 30, distinct from those of the main labor and environmental marches.[67]

For all the anticorporate focus on protecting local place and saving the small-scale, the local residents of Seattle became an afterthought. "I just think they brought in some pretty heavy hitters," LELO cofounder Cindy Domingo said. "[The International Forum on Globalization] was traveling around the world. It included Walden Bello. They had this big forum at the Benaroya Hall, the symphony hall, in which I think there were six or eight really nationally and internationally known people who came to speak on the issues. . . . I think the difference is they didn't really care. The national organizers that came here didn't really care about what the organizing around the WTO would mean for the local population, what they would leave here locally with."[68] And LELO, in noting the lack of immigrant workers in the Seattle proceedings, opted to create their own event with immigrant and international women workers on December 4. Despite efforts by local Seattle organizations, immigrant workers and activists, many of whom were displaced by the very free trade deals the IFG criticized, were largely absent from the major events sponsored by progressives.[69]

The other event was the major labor rally at the Seattle Coliseum on November 30. Union leaders rejected LELO's proposal for Tyree Scott to speak at the rally, despite his union pedigree and years of experience. Yet a short time later and only shortly before November 30, AFL-CIO leaders realized they lacked international labor representatives for the labor rally. They called LELO. After they asked if they could use the workers that LELO, with its limited funds, had recruited on its own, LELO obliged.[70] Despite these last-minute efforts, one of the main AFL-CIO organizers of the rally later admitted that the rally stage turned into a string of white male union leaders like Jimmy Hoffa. They spoke so long, he said, they cut off the Black musical act, Sweet Honey in the Rock. The workers attending the rally, he added, started streaming out of the stadium to go to the marches even before the leaders finished speaking.[71]

The color-blind anticorporate ideologies discussed here were only part of the story of Seattle, where organizers and activists put global inequality on the map in profound ways. In building on Martínez and LELO's critiques of whiteness of the protests, this chapter, as well as the one before it, has endeavored to think about who was at the protests, but also about the ways white experiences, assumptions, and political needs shaped understandings of globalization in the 1990s. Unlike the populist and nationalist variants of color-blind anticorporatism that stressed the homogeneity of the (American) nation and people, the global village multicultural variant stressed heterogeneity. Yet both made it possible for activists to treat racism and xenophobia directed at immigrants as unfortunate, but of secondary importance. The way global village multiculturalism curated difference ultimately led to whitened perspectives on globalization that marginalized the political and economic needs of some of those affected by neoliberal trade and investment reform. The tensions evident in 1999 in Seattle, and particularly the questions of nationalism, whiteness, and US American exceptionalism there, created a space for Jobs with Justice to intervene in the following months. That's the story of the next chapter.

PART III Two Protests

GROUNDING GLOBAL JUSTICE IN
THE TWENTY-FIRST CENTURY

7 "Localizing" Global Justice

CLASS, NATION, AND THE JOBS WITH
JUSTICE COALITION AFTER SEATTLE

Cliff and I embodied the "Teamsters and the Turtles," that grand and unlikely coalition that, according to some perspectives, reflected how the "Battle of Seattle" had been a struggle for the future of everyone, even those as different as labor unionists and environmental conservationists.

My great-uncle was a card-carrying member of the white rural poor. He was a small farmer, lived in the small North Dakota farmhouse he grew up in, and advanced a kind of "America First" narrative long before Donald Trump would carry it into the presidency. I had just graduated from the University of Minnesota as an upper-middle-class idealist. I heard the World Bank and WTO were bad from a part-time Spanish instructor during our morning course in Folwell Hall.

Despite this book's focus on the *limitations* of the Teamsters-Turtles frame, the pairing undoubtedly captured something about one segment of the burgeoning global justice movement in the US. Without reducing either of us to caricature, I would say Cliff saw trade in a context of American greatness and the threat it faced from imports and international bureaucrats, whereas I saw trade in a context of American empire—just more of the same from an abusive superpower. He saw it in relation to economic need—maintaining the viability of small farming in the age of agribusiness. I saw it in relation to abstract ideals of justice and equality.

Despite our differences, my great-uncle and I were part of Seattle's after-party. These were months of breathless celebrations of the protest's power.[1] One leader of a manufacturing union exclaimed that he and others felt as if they were "walking on air" after returning from Seattle to their home in postindustrial Massachusetts.[2]

In the aftermath of Seattle, one organization tried to harmonize aspects of the two distinct kinds of globalization politics my great-uncle and I represented.[3] The Jobs with Justice coalition sought to "localize the movement for global justice." In doing so it advanced another kind of grassroots globalism. This chapter considers the unacknowledged role of Jobs with Justice in forging a brand of global justice that brought working-class realities to the center but simultaneously built on the creative militancy emerging more from the young radicals and street protesters. This chapter helps show how the nature of the Seattle protests, including the tensions around race, nationalism, and "color-blind anticorporate" ideas, continued to shape how working-class organizations would respond to what became one of the most powerful social movements of the early twenty-first century.

COLOR-BLIND ANTICORPORATISM: "NO TO THE WTO" OR "NO TO CHINA"?

"My last job was working at Arvin Industries," stated Sherry Benton, a longtime resident of tiny Providence, Kentucky, halfway between the Ozarks and Appalachia on the edge of the US South. Arvin Industries, she said, had fled to set up shop in Taiwan nearly twenty years ago.

Benton had been working at the Moen plastics factory since then, and making more than $10 an hour. But now *that* factory was moving, she said. Its new home would be in Mexico. "After 19 years working at Moen and at age 50, I'm starting over again," she lamented.[4] In Providence, words like "Mexico" and "Taiwan" were often uttered with disdain. Moen's new workers in Nogales would be earning a full $3.50 per day.

Nationalist scapegoating had long influenced how workers and unions responded to plant relocations; the new homes of their factories were racialized as different and dangerous. These were "our" jobs—and now "they" had taken them, the narrative went. But Seattle, according to many left-wing observers, had started to change that. Now, they wrote, workers and unions were starting to see the problem wasn't the foreigners—it was the multinational corporations moving the jobs in the first place.[5]

Organizers for the next global protest, in April 2000 outside the meetings of the International Monetary Fund and World Bank in Washington, D.C., would quickly realize that any such paradigm shift stood on fragile foundations. In the wake of Seattle, was the Teamsters-Turtles coalition as internationalist as it seemed? Would labor unions working with people like Sherry Benton continue to target the corporation, or would they blame the foreign nations? The answer is both, as we see a different and more egregious brand of color-blind anticorporatism, one that criticized corporate excess but participated in the code language and "dog whistles" of xenophobic racism in the post-civil rights era.[6]

In D.C., the objective of many of the direct-action protesters was the same as in Seattle—to blockade and shut down the meetings. But the IMF and World Bank were different targets than the World Trade Organization. They were created after World War II with the stated premise of reducing economic conflict between nations, in hopes of avoiding more economic depressions and world wars. Yet they were also component parts of the US-led effort to contain Soviet communism, and by the late twentieth century they were propelled by neoliberal ideologies that promoted unbounded forms of trade and investment liberalization.

Mexico is a great example. As previous chapters have shown, the IMF forced Mexico to embrace austerity measures to pay off loans to rich international banks and governments. It pushed them to embrace agribusiness and to export food for cash (to make debt payments), rather than feed the population. The World Bank's "Structural Adjustment Programs" forced nations into similar arrangements, and by the 1980s many Global South countries were carrying impossible debt burdens. As the Seattle protests "shook the world," Mexican university students continued a strike against educational privatization that they saw as inspired by pressure from the World Bank. For activists heading to D.C. for the April 16 (or "A16") protests, the goal was to "Defund the Fund, Break the Bank, and Dump the [Third World] Debt."[7]

Yet only weeks after Seattle, it became clear that the Teamsters and the Turtles might not even be there. They had a different target: China.

For the Sierra Club and the AFL-CIO, a pending legislative proposal for China to receive "permanent normal trade relations" (PNTR) with the US was the main priority in the world of trade. As they saw it, such a proposal would implement a new stage of the "race to the bottom"—of footloose corporations moving production to the nations with the least labor and environmental regulation. For them, thousands of manufacturing jobs would be lost to highly polluting Chinese factories. China's human rights abuses, they said, showed how the Bill Clinton presidential administration (and many Democrats and Republicans) would avert their gaze from the worst kind of authoritarianism—communism, no less—if it meant getting cozier with their corporate funders. This was the newest incarnation of the Teamsters and the Turtles, and they decided they would stage their own D.C. rally. It would be on April 12, four days before the A16 protests, and would solely be dedicated to campaign against permanent normal trade relations with China.

As in the lead-up to Seattle in the 1990s, the Turtles and the Teamsters sometimes flirted with the populist right, embodied best (once again) by former Republican Pat Buchanan. The Reform Party nominee for US president campaigned about the threat PNTR posed to US manufacturing jobs. He focused and reinforced long-standing anti-Chinese racism by raving about Chinese spies. Buchanan and other Republicans criticized the country's atheism and human rights abuses. How would we allow communists so much access to our consumer market? he asked.

China was the major focus of the labor unions who helped rally the crowds on April 12, and there was plenty of anti-China hyperbole.[8] The messaging reflected their mixing with the right. James Hoffa, the nationalist Teamster president, won praise from trade progressives like Lori Wallach, even though he invited none other than Pat Buchanan to speak to the fifteen-thousand-strong crowd.[9] While the Teamsters and major industrial unions almost always endorsed Democratic presidential candidates, they withheld their endorsement in 2000 and flirted with both Buchanan and left-wing populist Ralph Nader.

At the rally, union leaders and Buchanan denounced "godless" China, and union T-shirts depicted the Chinese "as ruthless killers and torturers."[10] Teamsters posters from the rally featured historic photos of executions, firing squads, and arrests in China. A former Teamsters staffer told me that "I was instructed [by Hoffa's office] to never say 'China,' and only say, "*communist* China.'"[11] The AFL-CIO initiated its "No Blank Check for China" campaign, despite the exaggeration built into the name. Hardly a "blank check," the proposal would only mean that China would receive the same trading status as many other countries.[12] In the days surrounding the rally, Teamsters from Pennsylvania pushed through the halls of Congress to lobby against the PNTR bill.[13] The United Steel Workers union dedicated the days to legislative lobbying as well.[14] The Sierra Club dedicated most of its work to the anti-China fight, putting less energy into A16, and major figures in the Seattle organizing, like Ralph Nader's Public Citizen and its affiliate the Global Trade Watch, focused on China but supported the IMF/World Bank demonstrations as well.[15]

Yet critical voices on the left took aim at the China analysis. While IMF/World Bank protesters called for debt relief for the Global South, the anti-China liberals were attacking what some called the only Global South nation that could actually challenge the Euro-American world order.[16] Some of these critical voices raised a series of questions about the corporate "race to the bottom" narrative that the anti-China campaign foregrounded. Creating factories in low-wage countries had actually spurred worker and democracy movements in those countries, movements that had, in some cases, raised standards. The recent period of liberalization in China (since the 1970s) had been characterized not simply by oppressive authoritarianism but by worker organizing and campaigns for higher standards.[17]

The "race to the bottom" idea implied that US capital was investing all of its resources in the Third World, and at the expense of "American" jobs. Yet most foreign direct investment was actually flowing into the US, not out, and international investors were partly attracted to the US for its own lax labor and environmental standards. The US was an economic powerhouse, but simultaneously the world's biggest debtor.[18] As a Korean activist pointed out in the weeks after Seattle, Global North workers were losing jobs because of other forms of restructuring, not just outsourcing.[19]

For other critics, the newest manifestation of Teamsters-Turtles unity smacked of paternalism and ignorance. The AFL-CIO and others justified their position in the name of "human rights" in China, yet they seemed to have no real relationship with working-class Chinese voices on these matters.[20] The fact that Chinese workers and activists themselves had no clear consensus on PNTR reinforced the idea that US unions were really only interested in protecting their own manufacturing jobs.[21] One influential Global South analyst argued that advancing human rights in other countries required more than merely punishing other countries' workplace abuses through punitive trade sanctions: labor standards and wage levels had to be tied to national levels of development.[22] Besides, concern about the race to the bottom should make labor progressives *want* capital to shift to China instead of countries with weaker governments. The Communist Party–controlled government could at least resist the most abusive corporate models.[23] China's past workers' movements (e.g., the Chinese Revolution) had never relied on charitable outsiders for help. Why would they need it now?

What's more, the race-to-the-bottom view invisibilized US empire. Citing Amnesty International's recent report about the US use of mass incarceration as a form of social control, Filipino critic Walden Bello noted that China's violence toward workers could hardly compare to the violence of US capitalism and war-mongering abroad. The US had all kinds of prison labor, yet US unions denounced it in China, not in their own backyard.[24] The Sierra Club focused on China's pollution, but the Global North nations were the world's main polluters. For some Global South representatives, the idea that the US could unilaterally decide which countries could be part of the liberalizing order or the WTO was itself an imperial imposition.[25] To characterize Global South nations as simply "the bottom" was objectively inaccurate and reinforced dangerous forms of nationalist racism.

Ultimately, some on the left argued that the focus of the unions should really be the IMF and World Bank. Their austerity programs, which cut wage and social supports for workers abroad, had arguably led to US job loss and wage reduction as much as China had.[26] Echoing UNORCA's idea of rural development in the Global South, Bello and Mittal argued for the abolition of the IMF, the World Bank, and the WTO. They argued that poor countries should promote development by catalyzing dynamic domestic markets driven through high wages, instead of focusing on exports to the rich countries. Instead of promoting "indiscriminate globalization," Global South nations should create regional trade blocs with other developing nations. Foreign direct investment should be met with requirements that multinational corporations create local jobs, spur domestic markets, and transfer technology.[27]

Finally, critics noted how the focus on China played up racist anti-Asian sentiment, the kind that had caused the killing of a Chinese American by white auto workers at the height of anti-Asian hysteria (about imports) in the 1980s. As one union educator recalled, the "dislike of Japanese and Mexicans was often palpable" among the United Auto Workers in the late 1990s. But even "progressive unionists," he said, looked the other way on union xenophobia. They had agreed that, in theory, they "should be careful not to encourage union members to think of the WTO protests in a potentially chauvinistic way." They had also agreed that "there were plenty of sweatshops and prison-made goods right here in the United States." Yet, the educator stated, "I was told that we had to meet the unions 'where they were at'" on China rather than rock the boat.[28]

Finally, U.S Marxists offered some of the most critical interpretations of the AFL-CIO's flip from "No to the WTO" to "No to China." For some, the "No Blank Check" campaign showed a blatant "national-chauvinism." It showed how US workers, as a "privileged" sector of the world working class, could be turned against Global South workers. The federation's larger argument, that the WTO was acceptable as long as it included social clauses about labor standards, showed how Global North trade unions would side with capitalist imperialism instead of the global proletariat.[29]

Yet the AFL-CIO didn't simply leave behind its Seattle anticorporate critique and exchange it for an anti-China one.[30] It integrated the two. The AFL-CIO, for its part, had been run by progressives since the mid-1990s. As one local Jobs with Justice leader recounted, its leadership "had been developing a critique of neoliberalism that became quite explicit" by Seattle. As previous chapters have shown, anticorporate discourses in the US could be captured by the political right. Anticorporate ideologies weren't necessarily free from "chauvinism"; they sometimes reframed it for a "color-blind" era.

The AFL-CIO president's comments in the days before the protest perhaps capture it best: "We cannot relinquish our only economic leverage against a country that offers up its people as sacrifices to multinational corporations, then persecutes them, puts them in prison and even puts them to death when they protest," he said.[31] According to the federation's color-blind anticorporatism, both multinational corporations *and* oppressive China were to blame for the erosion of workers' rights and "global fairness."[32]

JOBS WITH JUSTICE: CHALLENGING UNIONS

As much as my uncle and I agreed about the WTO, he wouldn't have known I had hopped into a van of strangers on a chilly April midnight to head to D.C. I don't think I even told my parents (whom I lived with at the time). Like so many of the protesters inspired by Seattle, I wanted to help blockade the IMF and World Bank. And like so many others, I had scoured the email listservs tied to the A16.org website to find a ride.[33] A group of Winnipeg anarchists with a few boxes of vegan snacks greeted me as I stepped into their rented minivan for the twenty-two-hour ride to the activist Convergence Center on Florida Street in Washington, D.C.

Jobs with Justice would have respected my efforts, but they also wanted to redirect all that energy into specific campaigns for justice for workers. While debates swirled about the issue of China among activist intellectuals and within union legislative offices, Jobs with Justice continued its dedication to grassroots mobilization and coalition building, rather than policy or proposal briefs. Its mobilizing around the power of "corporate greed" helped it leave its particular stamp on the global justice organizing of the era, and the A16 protests specifically.

Jobs with Justice, as a nationwide union-community coalition dedicated to workers' rights, had changed radically since the 1980s. It was no longer fighting the conservative, anticommunist AFL-CIO. Progressives came to power in the federation in a stunning election in 1995 and essentially recognized Jobs with Justice as an ally, not an enemy.[34] It also grew dramatically, even in the years immediately before A16. The number of local coalitions had multiplied from twelve in 1992 to nearly forty throughout the country in 2001. Its database featured thousands of names and jumped from thirty-three thousand to thirty-eight thousand in a single eight-month period in 2000-2001.[35] Jobs with Justice's work influenced the campaigns of hundreds of thousands of workers. The number of national staff in recent years had risen from one to three.

Like other grassroots globalisms, Jobs with Justice's was based in a network model of organization. Local coalitions were formed as joint ventures between local area unions, community organizations, progressive churches, and labor activists. They were dedicated to forging a vision of solidarity that compelled each of its distinct affiliates to stand up for the others if they came under attack. These local coalitions named their own steering committees and leaderships and mostly raised their own funds. The groups in Boston, Washington State, or Portland (Oregon), not the national staff, took the lead on questions of global justice in the 1990s. They had participated in struggles against NAFTA in the early 1990s, even when NAFTA wasn't the main focus of the national leadership.

Even though the organization's national staff were growing and enhancing their role, much of their work was dedicated to strengthening the local coalitions.[36] They initiated efforts to fortify them in the 1990s and launched their own fundraising efforts to offer grants to local coalitions. Few local groups had paid staff members, and the national office helped fund them. The organization moved from having a board of only national union leaders to allowing local coalitions and community members to serve on the board.[37] The locals helped control the national office.[38] Yet this kind of grassroots networked model wasn't based on the cyber-activist global justice networks that had also begun to emerge in those years. In fact, the internet and email remained minor components the organization's work. Jobs with Justice's list of thirty-eight thousand names included only two thousand email addresses. One goal in 1999 was simply to be able to reach each local coalition electronically. Some coalitions still had no email in 2001.[39]

Like the grassroots globalisms of UNORCA or CIPO-RFM, the coalition existed in a dynamic and contradictory relationship with the sectoral organizations that had historically represented the working class.

Nationally, powerful labor leaders (including Communications Workers of America president and Jobs with Justice founder Larry Cohen) were still on the executive board. Unions and union goals, rather than community or "social justice" struggles, were often its biggest objectives. Its "Right to Organize" campaigns geared toward union organizing rights were perhaps its single biggest efforts in the late 1990s. In many cases local coalitions were not simply phone-banking for union causes; they were closely advising and developing strategies in union campaigns.[40]

Yet Jobs with Justice also pushed beyond the limitations of both unions and traditional NGOs. Working there was different from working for unions, one staffer said, because unions could never see beyond their current campaign. Instead of short-term fixes, Jobs with Justice was oriented toward building social movements. It "was known to be in it for the long haul," she said.

Some of these factors made Jobs with Justice a slightly less hostile place for people who looked different from the union organizer archetype: a heterosexual white male. By the late 1990s the "vast majority" of its local directors or staff were "women or people of color." As some of these leaders attested, they wanted to work for the working classes but had found Jobs with Justice's movement-oriented approach better than that of either unions or NGOs.

One organizer who worked in unions said that many union campaigns involved Black and Latinx workers. However, she said, "I think the hardest situation . . . [is that] it's very clear you [as an organizer] are there because you're Black or Latino." For her, "There was no thought about bringing you into the larger union culture, that you were going to be a leader. You weren't going to have input. 'We need some Latino and some Black people,' and then when the campaigns are over, we'll be cut. The joke was that if you were Black or Latino or Spanish there's always work for us, but there's never a permanent job. . . . It felt very much like you were temporary or being used."[41]

Even as Jobs with Justice's national office presence grew—and it was the national office that took the lead on the A16 protests—it resisted becoming an office-based professional NGO with no relationship to working-class communities. You could see the difference in the meetings, one staff member recalled. In Jobs with Justice, people worked through ideas on large sheets of butcher paper. At a D.C. advocacy group she had previously worked at, staffers handed out strategy sheets. "It felt like it had all been figured out beforehand," she said. "We "weren't even looking to the voices of the people being profoundly affected" by oppressive social forces.

GRASSROOTS GLOBALISM: *AGAINST* GLOBALIZATION, OR *FOR* WORKERS' RIGHTS?

Before we get to the A16 story, let's turn back to Sherry Benton. She lost her job—twice. If she could ever retire, it wouldn't be at sixty-five. Instead of simply blaming the Mexicans, though, she broke bread with them as part of a workers' delegation to the site where the Moen plant was relocated. The organization that led the delegation—Kentucky Jobs with Justice—wanted to show people that the problem wasn't Mexicans, it was the multinationals.

For Jobs with Justice, targeting corporations made it possible to push beyond local unions' nationalist response to factory closings: that since China (or Mexico) was taking our jobs, we needed to blame them and get everyone in the US to be a true patriot and Buy American.[42] Jobs with Justice's anticorporate approach would also counter the *other* common framing of the issue, the one you would see in the newspaper: that offshoring and overseas speculation were really "free trade," an exciting brand of globalization that promised consumer choice to all.

Writing after Seattle, one Jobs with Justice local leader wrote that in those years, anytime workers opposed trade liberalization they would be called defensive nationalists, self-interested protectionists, or hapless hicks. If Seattle had merely been a labor rally outside without the disruptive direct action and protest creativity, its only legacy, he wrote, would have been "a 2-minute clip on the nightly news, with something like, 'A bunch of inefficient union workers from the rustbelt marched for a return of the bad old days. Fortunately, the WTO delegates largely ignored these bits of roadkill on the way to the new economy. Although they are hopeless Luddites, it is true that something must be done for the losers in the new world economy who are too old and hidebound to run a computer.'"[43]

The Kentucky coalition sought a workers' rights vision of the situation that moved beyond nationalist scapegoating but could counter charges that dissenting unionists were irrationally "against globalization," stuck in a factory era that no one really liked anyway. As chapter 3 has shown, Jobs with Justice's early years were characterized by leaders' efforts to expand unionists' sense of their self-interest by showing how "community" problems like water contamination or farm foreclosures were advanced by the same corporations attacking unions. Likewise, a variety of local Jobs with Justice coalitions had embraced the power of worker-to-worker delegations in the 1990s to humanize the fraught relationship between US industrial workers and the "foreign" workers they imagined. These efforts sought to contextualize US factory workers' suffering and steer them toward campaigns against the trade agreements and wage competition that pitted workers against each other.

This focus on root causes, and particularly what Jobs with Justice consistently denounced as "corporate greed," allowed the scrappy Kentucky coalition to pull together a range of interests for its Mexico delegation. Benton, for her part, had been a member of the United Steelworkers union, which faced dire threats both from the relocation of factories like Moen and from imported steel. The USW had recently been collaborating with United Students Against Sweatshops (USAS), a new organization launched in the wake of the high-profile sweatshop scandal of celebrity Kathie Lee Gifford.

News of the inhumane working conditions in the Honduran production units of Gifford's clothing brand had helped turn national attention to the question of outsourcing. University students launched a wave of campaigns to make local universities buy university apparel from factories inspected by an independent labor monitor. In the same year that Moen announced its relocation, USAS at the University of Kentucky and at small Transylvania University spearheaded campaigns against their own universities, with support from some local unions.[44]

As with the USAS campaigns, Benton's delegation was meant to show that the off-shoring regime created few winners. It allowed delegates the chance to witness the distressing social conditions of Nogales life. Mexican workers weren't stealing jobs; NAFTA and the liberalized economy were displacing them from the countryside and compelling them to take dangerous and low-paying jobs. Sherry Benton and her companions, who stayed in the homes of the struggling Mexican Moen workers, saw that the newest Moen employees themselves were losing. "'I came here with the attitude that the Mexicans are taking our jobs,' one laid-off worker said. 'But I learned that it is not like that. They are victims of the situation, too.'"[45]

The grassroots globalism this book discusses wasn't based simply on utopian global dreaming or high-minded ideals, but rather developed in organizations that fought for massive structural changes even as they engaged with messy, contradictory, and often conservative local institutions—including unions.[46] In the Kentucky coalition, as in most local Jobs with Justice coalitions, local union dues had historically constituted the biggest part of the funding stream, yet the Kentucky coalition was barraged with requests for support from community organizations and student groups advancing causes that local unions were ambivalent about. In Kentucky, organizers acknowledged, it was "hard to get middle-class student activists to respect union culture" and understand that their members were "struggling to put food on the table." For union organizers in Kentucky, the students were too unwilling to engage in militant actions, like picketing or confronting local employers.[47]

Developing trust between stakeholders could be one of a local coalition's most difficult tasks, and money and resources were often scarce. The Kentucky coalition patched together a budget, usually of less than $50,000, but most of its work was completed through volunteer efforts. At one point, the local director, after ruefully listing some of her tasks in 2000, acknowledged that "I wish this were *all* I had to work on."[48] Things like organizational infrastructure, she said, were being neglected.

The work of the Kentucky organizers shows how in the face of the rapid circulation of capital, Jobs with Justice affiliates—both in Kentucky and elsewhere—didn't have any easy answers for the global problems at hand but knew they had to move beyond simply blaming foreigners and globalization. Jobs with Justice wanted to embrace the high-minded justice ideals of churches or students who opposed sweatshop conditions overseas, but they also wanted to ensure that affected workers themselves would have a voice.

While the leadership of the United Food and Commercial Workers International Union (UFCW) denounced how a taxpayer-funded institution like the University of Kentucky did not invest in Kentucky jobs by supplying its apparel locally, the union's ultimate demand wasn't to take jobs back but rather to get the university to buy from providers who had met code of conduct standards. For a United Steelworkers representative who went to Nogales with the delegation, "'It is difficult to know what the solution is. We do know that we want to inform the community and members of tour organizations about the living and working conditions which we saw. We are committed to holding our elected officials accountable for allowing American companies to move to countries for low-wages, non-existent and non-enforced labor and environmental laws. We want to work with workers in other countries to bring all workers to a fair standard.'"[49] They supported using tax dollars to "Buy American," but they also agreed that standards elsewhere had to be raised.

As these forms of capital flight continued to affect US workers, labor progressives argued about how best to respond but criticized corporate messaging that implied that standing up for your US job made you a union dinosaur, a mere "hard-hat" defending "labor protectionism" and outdated ways of life.[50] For one labor leader and Jobs with Justice activist, painting a "stark contrast between self-interest and altruistic arguments" was misleading in portrayals of unions and others fighting plant closings. "They can go hand in hand," said Jeff Crosby, president of IUE/CWA Local 201 at General Electric in Massachusetts. "People want to defend their jobs, and when I meet with people in other countries, I never find they have a big problem with that. They're trade unionists. They get that." The progressive presidential candidate Jesse Jackson, he said, captured these sentiments well in the 1990s. Jackson, according to Crosby, would say that "'it wasn't the Chinese that took your jobs.'" It was the major corporations. But, Crosby recounted, "[Jackson] didn't say, 'Don't fight for your jobs.'"[51] Even Walden Bello, the Filipino critic of the US left's approach to China, respected how the AFL-CIO stood up for US jobs. Just don't do it in the name of standing up for Chinese citizens you have little knowledge of, he said.

Ultimately, the wave of plant closings from Kentucky to Massachusetts and beyond meant that unions couldn't afford to lock themselves into a local, or even national, framework. According to Azcarate, "For people working on a contract campaign at [General Electric] or in an appliance factory in Louisville ... you can't just beat [a global corporation] in Louisville or Lynn, Massachusetts. You need to fight that one company but [also] the whole neoliberal system that is causing those job shifts, that are causing this globalization."[52]

PLANNING FOR A16: LOCALIZING THE MOVEMENT FOR GLOBAL JUSTICE

We arrived at the Florida Street Convergence Center for the next day's A16 protests at about 4 a.m.—a few hours before the police raided the building, yelling and intimidating the sleepy travelers like us. The reason for the raid? The site's arts and crafts materials weren't to make puppets, they said, but to make weapons.

Thousands of protesters blocked intersections around the IMF and World Bank buildings the next day, but the delegates entered their meetings before dawn, including through underground security tunnels. That evening, the Mobilization for Global Justice, the NGO-driven alliance that had organized much of the week's activity, met to take stock of the plans for the next day. In addition to the failure of the blockades, nearly one thousand had been arrested. For our part, the Winnipeg group and I attended the "spokescouncil" meeting of the hundreds of direct-action affinity groups. In the basement of Calvary Baptist Church in Northwest D.C., this decentralized "Anti-Capitalist Convergence" was dedicated to direct democracy. Agreeing that disruption was the only way to make change, we started to chart our own strategy for the following day.

China-bashing unions, progressive NGOs, Christian groups, and direct-action anarchists. It was a difficult task, but one organization—the national office of Jobs with Justice—tried to convene them all to redirect global justice for the working class. While activists like me had been planning last-minute strategy on April 15, Jobs with Justice was leading its own global justice march to a parking ramp owned by the Interparking company. The large regional parking business was cutting the benefits to its largely Ethiopian American workforce, much as the World Bank and IMF loan structures forced companies into austerity management in Global South countries. With efforts like its Interparking campaign during A16, Jobs with Justice was, in its words, "localizing the movement for global justice."

In the months before the protest, the scenario was radically different than even a year earlier. One Portland staffer told me that when she had called the Jobs with Justice national office about plans for Seattle in mid-1999, "They were like, huh?"[53] One of its national field organizers, Simon Greer, noted that the national office really didn't understand what its role could be in 1999. For people like Fred Azcarate, the shift to global justice represented a major opportunity. Azcarate, the son of Filipino immigrants whose college years were marked by fighting against tuition increases and hate crime in the State University of New York system, had led the national office since 1992. He spent lots of time working on NAFTA in the years immediately after he stepped into Jobs with Justice. "There were local mobilizations, he said, "but not a focal point" as there was now.[54]

Still, there wasn't much time, though some of the local coalitions were doing their best to capture the Seattle energy. As staff member Cassie Waters recalled in Boston, several local unions had sent people to Seattle, "but [Massachusetts] Jobs with Justice was mostly focused on its rally outside the Federal Reserve [in Boston]" on November 30. For the coalition, their local Boston event was more than a single rally. "It activated a good number of folks," she said, "and we were pretty diligent about signing up everyone on the clipboard, and there would be a follow-up kickoff of a local network, and that became the Boston Global Action Network [BOGAN]. Jobs with Justice was pretty instrumental."[55] BOGAN and Jobs with Justice would help lead Boston's global justice activities in 2000 and after.

Even in early 2000, though, the national staff in D.C. was unsure about the best role its members could play. As Azcarate remembers it, things really began when "we got approached by the broader global justice community, like "50 Years Is Enough!" and some other organizations. And we made the decision, and went to our leadership, that we could play a bridge role and bring parts of the labor movement into these specific sets of action."

Indeed, progressives had been asking unions to join them for A16 but had struggled to get them on board. Unlike some of the D.C. progressive groups, though, Jobs with Justice had developed long-standing relationships with union leaderships.[56] For A16, the steelworkers were the first to sign on after Jobs with Justice asked. They were followed by CWA and others, and finally by the AFL-CIO.

Despite the trust Jobs with Justice enjoyed, these weren't easy requests for them to make.[57] For the AFL-CIO, April 12 was a date safely before the images of tear gas and masked protesters that would undoubtedly circulate after A16. Associating unions with anarchists would jeopardize the AFL-CIO's China legislative efforts and damage the reputation of the Democrat running for president, whom they had endorsed despite his pro-"free trade" stances. Besides, the AFL-CIO's move to focus on China in the first place made it clear that any high-minded ideas about global justice for developing nations was much less of a priority for the national labor federation. In addition, the AFL-CIO was an important funder of Jobs with Justice.[58] Ultimately, Azcarate and Greer couldn't rely only on trust; they also had to make convincing political arguments for unions to join them. They told the unions leaders that unions' absence at A16 would make it impossible to leverage this social discontent for their big-picture plans about US trade and globalization.[59]

THE A16 PROTESTS AND BEYOND

After union leaders began to sign on, things moved very quickly. As Massachusetts Jobs with Justice staff member Cassie Waters recalls, "[A16] was totally a fly-by-night situation, I don't even know all the adjectives [to use], it was just thrown together. It was a really, really amazing experience, and my job ... was to pretty much fax this flyer about the labor action pretty much to every union local east of the Mississippi. I faxed, and I called, and I faxed, and I called."

The organization also wanted to manage its relationship with the direct-action protesters in a new way. Greer had stated that Jobs with Justice's approach to the direct action and arrests had to be based on forging a relationship with protesters, not simply trying to stay as far away as possible. That, he added, had been the Seattle strategy for union leaders. That said, Greer's position was to keep union members safe and out of jail. As Waters recalled, protest trainer Lisa Fithian had trained hundreds of activists in direct-action methods in the weeks leading up to A16. But "she had [also] worked with SEIU, and we ran into her at this rally, ... and Simon [Greer] was just talking about our concerns, [and she said,] 'Why don't you come to the meeting and talk about that?'" Following the conversation, Azcarate and union leader Stewart Acuff went to a meeting with the protesters, and "They talked about their concerns, but also gave a real message of solidarity from the labor movement. All of that went really far so people understood what the different perspectives were."[60]

On the day before the actions, Jobs with Justice was helping both the protesters *and* the labor unions. As Waters explained, "Simon had brought this guy from Philly to make these banners, [and] the folks making the puppets got raided, they got kicked out, so I was sent down to get the key for the SEIU local." This, she said, was the night before A16. She said she told the protesters to just "clean up the stuff on the floor when you're done, but some guy needed some help painting, so I was running, plus they wanted help to step up the stage" for the labor rally. "I didn't have the right crew," she said, chuckling. "So random people were helping set up, which was probably a huge safety hazard."[61]

Once A16 arrived, Jobs with Justice's new idea of "localizing the movement for global justice" took shape in two ways. First, local coalitions who were unable to go to D.C. themselves led their own events, not about China, but about trade and development. Locals like Massachusetts and Tennessee organized rallies. Reflecting the more conservative and Christian mid-South, the Kentucky coalition had a community-religious event about sweatshops.[62] In September, the Jobs with Justice national office organized a wave of solidarity rallies in US cities for protesters confronting the ministerial in Prague, Czech Republic.

Second, the national office organized side marches of A16 protesters to targets of ongoing workers' struggles in D.C. itself. In April and later in September they directed protesters to a facility of Interparking. In September, three hundred marched and thirty-two were arrested in a nonviolent civil disobedience action blockading a street.[63]

According to Greer, a high point was when we "got global justice protesters in D.C. going to support parking lot attendants and janitors, when they were coming out and supporting hotel workers who were looking for the right to unionize." Greer said that these struggles showed protesters

Figure 3. Jobs with Justice activists and staff members during the week of protests against the International Monetary Fund and World Bank in Washington, D.C. From left (seated): Bonji Beard, Sarita Gupta (seated in front), Fred Azcarate, Cassie Waters, Simon Greer, and M. B. Maxwell (standing behind Greer). Walking behind them (without backpack) is Russ Davis, executive director of Massachusetts Jobs with Justice. Jobs with Justice Photographs #6369, P. Kheel Center for Labor-Management Documentation and Archives, Cornell University Library.

how global justice could be localized. "Some of the workers had been through war in Ethiopia and Eritrea," he said. "Global organizing was big, and they said they had to get a job as a parking attendant because of the global economy." For Greer, "You can't say we just do local, [or] we just do global. It's more connected than that."

· · · · ·

In the wake of it all, the AFL-CIO's push against China failed. Their election drive to vote in a loyal Democrat—despite his being a "pro-China free trader"—also failed. It wasn't the best year for the federation, but it was a crucial year for Jobs with Justice. It succeeded in making sure the legacy of Seattle would not be *only* middle-class Global North activists or China-bashing workers and unions.

That's not to say Jobs with Justice's work on global justice was narrowly self-interested. The organization pulled groups together with a version of anticorporatism it had been developing for more than a decade, including an anticorporatism it had used to contest US trade policy in the 1980s.[64] Its "Stop Corporate Greed" poster—seen around the country in countless protests since the 1990s—dovetailed well with what activists were clamoring for: "People before Profits." Its annual meeting in summer 2000 featured an "International Plenary on Global Justice," where workers from Kentucky and several countries agreed to keep fighting "to hold corporations accountable!"[65] In short, and in part because of its highly malleable anticorporate frame, Jobs with Justice was well positioned to be the kind of "bridge" organization that D.C. NGOs had asked for.

As the Jobs with Justice leaders took stock of the year's events, they realized that "global justice" frameworks could galvanize local labor struggles, just as labor struggles needed to be a part of global justice. Fighting "corporate-led globalization," Azcarate said, "gave some unity to the network" at a time of rapid growth. "It was dramatic," he said. For Jobs with Justice, this work had "brought tangible organizational benefits for many local coalitions." Even a year later, they recognized that "the energy and vibrancy" of global justice movements could "help us meet our [labor movement] goals . . . if we can tap into this energy."[66] What's more, linking workers' rights campaigns to global justice fights made it possible to "protect ourselves from attacks on 'labor protectionism.'"

While the grassroots globalisms of organizations like Jobs with Justice emerged to confront new forms of economic restructuring in the 1980s and 1990s, the grassroots globalism of the twenty-first century differed in a key way. After the mid-1990s, but especially after Seattle, a growing movement challenging global injustice was forming around organizations like Jobs with Justice, UNORCA, and CIPO-RFM. Now one of the goals of their grassroots globalism was to make sure the working classes had a voice in them.

For the US movement, the 9/11 attacks altered the context of protests. They justified the unleashing of new techniques of repression, now unveiled with greater political legitimacy.[67] The USA Patriot Act created new surveillance repertoires, and cities cracked down on mask wearing as a way to target direct actionists.[68] Protests shrank. The IMF/World Bank protests scheduled for Washington, D.C., in September 2001 were anticipated to be enormous as summer 2001 ended, yet they fundamentally changed after 9/11. The IMF/World Bank ultimately called off their meetings late in the month because of concerns about security.[69] The protests were reduced to a much smaller antiwar event. The 2003 protest in Miami for the "Free Trade Area of the Americas" summit was met with harsh policing, now closely integrated with antiterrorism security measures. The AFL-CIO backed away from partnerships with groups that opposed wars in Afghanistan or in Iraq.[70]

That said, the movement didn't end. Some of it "spilled out" into the antiwar movement, whose highlight was the February 15, 2003, wave of global protests against the proposed US invasion of Iraq. Other segments of the global justice movement changed, basing themselves more in community work or the World Social Forum (or regional social fora). As the following chapters indicate, the strategy of mass protest remained, despite new repressive techniques. The momentum changed, but the tides didn't turn. Global justice movements continued to successfully push back against the neoliberal current—and win.[71]

8 The WTO Is Back

UNORCA, THE VÍA CAMPESINA, AND THE STRUGGLE OVER AGRICULTURE IN CANCÚN

A security fence separated the South Korean farmers from the Mexican federal police on the other side. The convention center holding the 2003 World Trade Organization ministerial in Cancún, Mexico, was far in the background, behind the shields and helmets of the specially trained forces, many of them in short sleeves. The breeze from the Caribbean, only a few hundred meters away but out of sight, was blocked by the massive hotels lining the shore. Cancún's streets and boulevards were steamy even in normal times, but especially with around ten thousand people confronting police and demanding, among other things, the end to WTO regulation of agriculture.

After several attempts by the farmers to pull down the fence, Lee Kyung-hae grabbed its rungs and hoisted himself up, slightly above the crowd. The trade ministers a few blocks away held the future of Global South agriculture in their hands. Would South Korean rice and apple farmers face a new wave of cheap imports from China or the US? Would plants and organic materials from Mesoamerica be patented by Northern corporations? Would farmers have to compete with genetically modified food products coming from factory farms?

Reportedly saying, "Don't worry about me, just struggle your hardest," Kyung-hae slipped a blade out of his pocket. Moving swiftly, he nestled its tip four centimeters into his chest, puncturing his heart's left atrium.[1] For his South Korean comrades as well as those from UNORCA and the Vía Campesina, their movement now had a martyr. Kyung-hae, his comrades argued, had been driven to suicide by the state of peasant agriculture.

Fifteen years later, I walked the avenue where Kyung-hae took his life. Later in the week, I left the city and meandered down the small roads in the rural parts of the state of Quintana Roo. There I spoke to people who had also been at the protests—peasants, peasant leaders, and others whose voices haven't been captured in the literature on these movements. Their first memory? Kyung-hae's dramatic, sorrowful death.

This chapter begins by looking at how UNORCA, through a form of grassroots globalism that challenged both global institutions and national leaders, generated an alternative vision of Global South development. Its critical vision, which continued to make visible the structures of imperialism and colonialism within contemporary globalization, led it to make the Cancún protests a major organizational priority. Once it was there, its local planning and organizing *grounded* the work of the global justice movement in new and powerful ways.

FROM EMPIRE TO BIO-COLONIALISM

We were all worried about the Sargasso.

The creeping red algae had recently appeared up and down the Gulf of Mexico coastline in southeastern Mexico. The pristine Caribbean coast, an attraction that lured millions of travelers to the nearby city of Cancún, was the fundamental source of income for the states of Yucatán and Quintana Roo.[2] Rumor had it the algae was first spawned from agro-chemical runoff in Brazil. Circulating in the Atlantic southerly currents, it choked out native sea plants and organisms and made it impossible to swim or sunbathe, since the sticky, shiny weeds pasted the beaches after the sea currents deposited them, only to bring back more the next day. I had just returned from the home of Pedro Dzib Puc in the regional town of José María Morelos, a four-hour drive from Cancún. I was staying in a lodge with oceanfront access in the touristy coastal town of Tulum, and I was hoping the beach was open—and that the noisy tractors used to dredge out the Sargasso had finished their work for the day.

Known for its cattle and forestry, but mostly for its tourism and Mayan archaeological sites, Mexico's Southeast is a study in contrasts. Dzib Puc, an Indigenous (Mayan) farmer, knew that Sargasso threatened the broader economy of the state. Since the 1960s, the Mexican state had assiduously tried to make the Cancún area a destination for foreign investment via tourism. Yet at the same time, Dzib Puc and his crops seemed worlds away from the consumer and service economy of the state's coastline. Still, Dzib Puc knew Cancún well. He was one of the thousands of UNORCA members who had camped, walked, listened, and marched during the week of intense activity outside the WTO meetings in Cancún in 2003—the first WTO meeting in the Americas since the Battle of Seattle.

The Sargasso crisis of 2018 resembled, in some ways, the threat of trade and investment liberalization fifteen years earlier. Sargasso, like the WTO, arrived from outside the country and was spawned partly by the work of major transnational corporations. Its origins and operations were opaque and difficult to comprehend. It was created by technological and economic forces but would have profound effects on the everyday life and ecology of seemingly isolated regions like central Quintana Roo.

Nothing better represented these dynamics than UNORCA's latest and newest target: genetically modified crops.

For the UNORCA of the 1980s and 1990s, protecting (food) sovereignty meant defending against the importation of US corn. It meant an end to those countries "dumping" their excess supply on poor countries, thereby ruining the market for domestic producers. While those issues were still prominent, sovereignty was also threatened by invasive forces penetrating the body public in new, cellular ways. In one of the latest developments in the agribusiness arsenal, and one of the newest issues in the WTO, companies like Monsanto or Cargill could alter genes in crops and seeds with the premise that such modified or "enhanced" plants would produce more food. Genetically modified corn was already grown throughout the US.[3]

Yet these plants took the shape, in the eyes of UNORCA, of an "invisible enemy" not so different from the spread of Sargasso: silently seeding itself until it fundamentally reshaped society. Indeed, in 1999 scientists confirmed what the Vía Campesina had long warned: that Mexican corn crops had already been cross-pollinated with GMO corn. Corn, like most plants, pollinated through the wind's transfer of seeds. It was a Mexican staple crop with an important place in Indigenous cosmovision, and peasant families had been selecting and saving harvested corn kernels for generations: those kernels would be next year's seeds. Many ecoregions and mountain valleys in Mexico, then, had their own kind of corn bred for that specific microclimate. Now that corn was contaminated with seeds from the North.[4]

While these seed varieties likely spread through some combination of wind, travel, migration, and accident, they foreshadowed a much more concerted attempt by Northern corporations to confine and control seeds. These issues were not limited to Mexico; indeed, WTO officials and Northern trade ministers hoped they would play center stage at the Cancún meeting. An early agreement on agriculture, they hoped, would allow for a discussion of several other agenda items, including how commercial interests could patent living material like seeds.

Such an agreement could threaten the legality of Mexican peasants saving and sharing seeds. Intellectual property rules in some nations were already allowing corporations to patent organisms in ways that made it illegal to share and use saved seed. Since saved seeds hadn't been certified and registered, there was no way for the state to know if a business interest elsewhere had technically patented them. If the seeds had been cross-pollinated with patented seed, saving or breeding them was technically forging counterfeit, "pirated" products.[5]

Northern corporations, for their part, argued that without the ability to certify and patent life forms as intellectual property, businesses would never invest in research, development, and innovation, depriving the world of the improved products needed to face global problems, like hunger. Yet farmers worried that they would be forced into accepting high-priced corporate seeds, and having to purchase them each year, rather than saving seeds from last year's harvest. Farmers in Europe had been fined for sharing seeds they had saved. Monsanto's Round-up Ready Gene Agreement permitted the company to visit farmers' fields without permission, to check if they had illegally reproduced the company's seeds. Its

"Terminator" gene was engineered for seeds so that a plant's fruits (e.g., a corn kernel) would be useless as future seed.[6]

UNORCA'S ALTERNATIVE VISION OF DEVELOPMENT

For one Vía Campesina activist, "One thus finds powerful institutions (World Bank, USAID, Rockefeller Foundation) compelling peasant farmers to abandon native subsistence crops (millet, taro, quinoa) in favor of export driven monocultures (coffee, cotton, cocoa) while at the same time forcing communities in the South to privatize their common property resources (land, biodiversity, water) and convincing consumers everywhere to 'enjoy' dangerous value-added imports (biotech corn, antibiotic beef, processed junk food)—all in the name of competitive advantage and economic efficiency."[7] For UNORCA and its ally, Vía Campesina, the dominant model of agriculture revolved around capital and chemicals. Matters like GMOs had to be understood as part of this broader food system and as threats to sustainability, local and regional food needs, traditional or Indigenous knowledges, and well-paying rural employment. Food systems were not simply about food but about environmental and social stability.[8]

As in the 1980s, UNORCA saw these matters through a lens that recognized the older forms of imperialism within the system now called "globalization."[9] In its campaign to prohibit the Ministry of Agriculture, Livestock, and Rural Development (Secretaría de Agricultura, Ganadería y Desarrollo Rural, SAGAR) from subsidizing the purchase of transgenic seeds for Mexico, UNORCA argued that by adopting NAFTA, the government had put Mexicans' health at risk because "we imported millions of tons of [GMO] corn and other products, which go into our food." Western scientific technologies are good for some things, UNORCA wrote, but not for the people's food. The country was so subservient to US corporate interests that it had been reduced to taking corporate leftovers. Since crops using these seeds actually had decreased 25 percent in the US in recent years (probably because of the EU ban on importing GMO food), Mexico was just getting the leftovers. Monsanto needed to unload its unsold seeds, so SAGAR was "just solving Monsanto's problem."[10]

A WTO agreement on biotechnology could also create incentives for Northern corporate entrepreneurs to descend on the South in search of life forms to patent and sell. The term that emerged to describe this kind of transnational research and development—*bioprospecting*—itself recalled the mineral prospecting of older forms of colonialism. Indian social critic Vandana Shiva, who had denounced the practices in a speech at the Seattle WTO protests, dubbed it "biopiracy."[11] Basing its statement on a range of scientific studies, UNORCA argued that Mexico had the kind of diversity of plants and animals, not to mention "productive cultures" in the countryside, that could be "destroyed" by the sicknesses or problems transgenics could introduce.[12] UNORCA's emerging position on these issues helped push the Mexican government to sign a multinational agreement slowing the spread of transgenics in 2000.[13]

MEXICO: GLOBAL SOUTH OR GLOBAL NORTH?

In the months leading up to the Cancún protests, it became clear that the Mexican government's negotiating team mostly sided with the US government's negotiating positions (with the idea of buttressing their trading bloc against competition from the EU). UNORCA, however, believed that Mexico shouldn't be the US's junior partner. The organization could have followed the US and focused its qualms on Europe's trade practices as well. Getting the EU to undo its ban on GMO beef would indeed allow medium-size Mexican producers to have a shot at exporting beef (fed with GMO corn or not), and Mexican producers needed any help they could get. Instead of adopting such a short-term brand of thinking, though, UNORCA sided with the positions emerging from the Global South—and against the production of GMO beef in general, even though major Mexican agribusiness outfits were already trying to produce it. Months before the Cancún protest, UNORCA's general coordinator heralded the symbolic importance of the US-Mexico border, not because it was the gateway to the North, but because that line marked the place "where Latin America starts."[14]

UNORCA established its position on trade in a way that resonated with other Global South experiences: as tied to a longer history of austerity imposed by the IMF and World Bank (see chapter 1). Technically, the initial 1995 WTO agreement on agriculture allowed countries to bypass trade liberalization if it significantly affected "noncommercial interests" like water and rural stability.[15] But although the Cancún negotiations were part of what was called the "development" round of negotiations, the reduced profit margins and austerity linked to liberalization made it difficult for Global South societies to adequately protect these interests.[16] UNORCA, like other Global South nations, asserted agriculture's "multifunctionality," the technical term that refers to how agriculture is intrinsically embedded in environmental, social, and cultural matters.[17]

Histories of austerity had also limited how Global South countries could respond to liberalization. Like other Global South nations, UNORCA and the Vía Campesina argued that developing countries should receive "special and differential treatment": that is, that they should be treated differently than the rich countries by the WTO rules. While extended negotiation had granted the Global South longer time periods to liberalize and reduce its subsidies, many countries had already dismantled subsidies because of IMF and World Bank loan conditionalities. For many Global North negotiators, the answer to most of these problems was getting access to Global North markets. But limited access to these markets for products like coffee and bananas had not made much of a difference.[18]

Yet, as with many grassroots globalists, much of the organization's work against neoliberal reform in general, including around WTO questions of domestic subsidies and corn imports, was at the national level. UNORCA was particularly interested in pressuring the national state, so much so that it disagreed with other developing countries' positions to put a "development box" into the WTO framework. Through such a mechanism, Global South governments would be given more options (for instance, to maintain higher tariffs). Yet, as UNORCA showed, countries like Mexico were so controlled by neoliberal politicians that they hadn't imposed higher tariffs, even when the rules allowed them to do so. In addition, Mexico needed an expansive set of agricultural extension services to best serve farmers and to lead them away from biotech crops. But the national government wouldn't invest more in domestic, small-scale agriculture.[19]

UNORCA's focus on the national government, not just global institutions, was never more clear than in the year leading up to the Cancún protests. The Zapatistas had long lamented how major producer organizations like UNORCA had never really taken a stand against NAFTA. But now they did, because, as they began to argue in late 2002, "The countryside can't take it anymore." [20]

UNORCA AND NATIONAL-LEVEL PROTEST

The international bridge between Juárez and El Paso was a long-standing connection between Mexico and the US, but that's not why the new coalition—called El Campo No Aguanta Más (The Countryside Can't Take It Anymore)—launched its campaign there. The bridge also symbolized the fraught situation in which NAFTA had positioned farmers. Alberto Gomez, UNORCA's new leader, was one of the first speakers to address the crowd during its first rally on January 1, 2003. The coalition's constituent organizations released a statement from Juárez that same day. "Here," the coalition declared, "food that is frozen for ten years, that is scrap, that is transgenic, that's junk food—comes to steamroll our national production."[21]

Since NAFTA's implementation in 1994, food imports from factory farms in the US had skyrocketed. Peasant and farmer leaders from the coalition chose the site because it represented a fundamental inequality: US food products could cross the bridge en masse, even though US producers were so highly subsidized they could easily undersell Mexican farmers in their own country. The Mexicans didn't have a chance. The date the coalition chose—New Year's Day 2003—also meant something. That day, NAFTA's third round of mandatory tariff reductions went into effect. Wheat, rice, and some meat and poultry had remained protected since 1994—but no longer.[22]

The campaign brought UNORCA together with eleven other major peasant and farmer organizations, many of them from different political perspectives. At Juárez, a group of peasant leaders went on an eight-day hunger strike. Three weeks later, peasants, unionists, and activists from a variety of organizations protested. In one state, they occupied offices of the Agricultural Ministry and threatened to occupy more.[23] Meanwhile, the country's major business interests demanded that Mexico's president,

Vicente Fox, "apply the rule of law in full" to control the growing wave of protests. Fox himself met with the new World Bank liaison to the country the same week as these later protests.[24]

That the new peasant coalition made demands on Vicente Fox, a national leader, and not only global institutions is indicative of how UNORCA believed change had to be made at both the global and the national level. Many had hopes that Fox *would* constitute a real change. Unlike the last two presidents, he had gone to college in Mexico, not at Harvard or Yale. He was the first non-PRI president in seventy-one years. For many, this represented Mexico's long-awaited "transition to democracy." Yet the Mexican left had less hope about significant reform. Fox was a former Coca-Cola executive, he came from the right-wing, free-trade party the PAN (Partido Acción Nacional / National Action Party), and he had continued to allow national agricultural investment to decline.

Even though this was a national movement pressuring for national changes, UNORCA and its allies here shaped their demands around the concepts at the center of the WTO agriculture debates. One of their six main demands was for a long-term agricultural plan for the year 2020 "based in the central objectives of food sovereignty, multifunctionality of agriculture," and a sustainable national agricultural model. In the days before the Cancún protest, they renewed their calls for Fox to stand up to the pressures of the Global North and to "raise his voice" about agricultural dumping. They campaigned for him to demand "special and differential treatment" for Mexico.[25] The Countryside Can't Take it Anymore movement dedicated its work to changing national politics—for instance, increasing the percentage of GDP spent on agriculture—yet in doing so it denounced global plans, like the Free Trade Area of the Americas.[26]

The campaign's biggest moment came thirty days after the International Bridge action on January 1. The organizations coordinated one of the biggest marches in Mexican history. One hundred thousand people departed by foot from the historic "Independence Angel" statue in Mexico City and walked to the city's central plaza a few kilometers away. In Cancún, they would voice the demand "Agriculture out of the WTO!" Here they insisted on a moratorium on NAFTA, and the entire exemption of corn and beans from the deal.[27] They denounced the "complicity of Vicente Fox" with the imperial designs of US president George W. Bush. The US refusal to suspend the NAFTA tariff reduction, they claimed, was "just one more piece of a belligerent strategy, as the same thing happens with controlling gas in Central Asia to the oil of Iraq and Venezuela and the food supply of Mexico."[28]

The show of unity and power on January 31 forced the federal government to agree to eight roundtables for intensive discussions about the country's agricultural future.[29] This movement constituted the first time that food sovereignty, a concept that UNORCA had been developing since the 1980s (see chapter 1), served as the dominant guiding principle of a broad-based opposition force to neoliberal agriculture in Mexico.[30] Yet the government's responses over the coming months also fragmented the opposition. UNORCA, then an organization of four thousand members, refused to sign the government's proposal. It was too weak on biotechnology and GMOs.[31] UNORCA's next step: make many of these same demands, but with many other allies, at the next major international protest for global justice.

THE ROAD TO CANCÚN

"There aren't any radicals here."

That's what Irish anarchist Ramor Ryan thought after he and a multinational group of anarchists had spent a few weeks in Cancún, with hopes of preparing for the WTO protests in September. Ryan and his comrades had arrived in July 2003 after leaving the state of Chiapas, where they had been supporting the Zapatistas.[32]

By the time the massive forums, rallies, and protest marches got underway in early September, around four thousand peasants from the countryside around Cancún converged on the city. Cancún may have lacked the particular kind of radical Ryan looked for, but these members of local UNORCA chapters—including Pedro Dzib Puc—showed up en masse to the city, some of them for the first time in their lives. Cancún's residents, sometimes friends or relatives of the marchers, hosted some of the UNORCA protesters in their own homes. They might not have been "activists" in a way legible to certain kinds of Western anarchism, but they nonetheless demonstrated their own kind of solidarity.

The area's UNORCA affiliates in the states of Quintana Roo and Yucatán had their own histories of militancy. Regional activists in UNORCA Quintana Roo, like Marcelo Carreón, had long been pushing for Mayan peasants to get a fair price for their lumber and agricultural goods.[33] After the EZLN uprising in 1994, they paid a penalty. As regional leader Victoria Santos recalled, "The Zapatista movement came out on January 1 of 1994, and a week later they were saying that we were an arm of the Zapatistas, and we had a hidden arsenal. That was all false."

It was a dangerous situation. National papers descended on central Quintana Roo. Some people heard *Washington Post* reporters were in the area. Soon, authorities started asking around about the whereabouts of the leaders of their local organization, the "Union of Forestry Ejidos of the Mayan Zone," which was affiliated with UNORCA. "Fortunately," Santos said, "people hid them. People were taking them in and moving them. Each night they slept in a different community." Several of the leaders and activists, including Carreón and Santos, fled for Mexico City. "But even there," she said, "the media kept saying, 'They're going to go after the leaders regardless of the consequences.'"[34] That, she said, was when UNORCA's national leadership intervened.

Its leaders set up a meeting with the federal Ministry of the Interior, and nearly ten local members from Quintana Roo went. The minister said that the commotion was all over nothing. Looking at the members, he said, "You all don't look like what they are saying you are. You all are hardworking people; go back to Quintana Roo, and continue with your work." When the official later met with the Quintana Roo governor, along with UNORCA's Luis Meneses, Meneses reportedly said to the governor, "Stop with this silliness. Say that you're sorry publicly because you have a tourist state, and you can't be going around saying that there are guerrillas. You're going to scare away all your tourism."[35]

Nine years later, Zapatismo remained an important presence in the minds of many protesters. UNORCA's leadership had sent the EZLN a letter a month before the protest in search of its endorsement of the Cancún protests. UNORCA, like Jobs with Justice and CIPO-RFM, partly oriented its grassroots globalism in the early 2000s to ensuring that the global justice movement featured, or was led by, the voices of the working class and the peasantry. In Cancún, that meant turning out those who knew Cancún best—the peasants and farmers from the region.

PLANNING FOR THE PROTESTS

By 2003, UNORCA's Alberto Gomez had directed the Vía Campesina presence in Mexico for several years. The first time I met Gomez, in 2017, we talked in a small apartment in Mexico City studded with Vía Campesina goods. As an informal Mexico headquarters for the Vía Campesina, it was swathed in green—the bandannas and flags that accented the room's windows all exhibited the Vía Campesina's signature color. The UNORCA members who marched in Cancún had created a sea of green with their bandannas and flags.

Part of Gomez's role was to help plan the protests and the countersummit, a complicated endeavor given the range of groups looking to attend. The National Union of Workers (Unión Nacional de Trabajadores, UNT), a progressive labor federation, was hoping to create a Latin American network of unions against privatization. Mexican women tied to the Gender and Economy Network (Red de Género y Economía, or REDGE) built a committee called "Women toward Cancún." They aimed to fortify feminist perspectives on globalization's impact on women.[36] The National Indigenous Congress (Congreso Nacional Indígena, CNI), loosely affiliated with the Zapatistas, held frequent meetings and planned a two-day Indigenous Forum.[37] Fair Trade Mexico was helping coordinate a Fair Trade concourse, where people could sell locally made, fair-trade Mexican products as an alternative to corporate goods.[38] Radical youth had issued a call of their own.[39]

Perhaps the most widely known convening group, however, was a nongovernmental organization named the Mexican Network in the Face of Free Trade (Red Mexicana ante Libre Comercio, RMALC). Tied to the Hemispheric Social Alliance, it had worked with UNORCA and US and Canadian organizations in the years leading up to NAFTA (see chapter 2).[40] RMALC's effort to create what it called the Mexican Space against the WTO (Espacio Mexicano Contra la OMC) aimed to pull together global justice organizations and plan a "Forum of the Peoples" as a countersummit to the WTO meetings. During this time it led meetings in the poor, Indigenous part of the country, though RMALC itself primarily consisted of academics and intellectuals.[41]

RMALC had been one of the first organizations in Mexico to speak out about the dangers of liberalized trade in the early 1990s. Yet by the early 2000s, peasants and Indigenous organizations wanted action, and they wanted to speak for themselves. At several convenings, direct actionists and UNORCA attested that RMALC intellectuals "monopolized discussion." RMALC had published a variety of books and had sponsored the publication of widely circulated articles. One UNORCA activist argued that RMALC wanted "to speak for the movements" since, as an NGO, "they have no social base."[42] Some activists in Cancún were frustrated by the "armchair communism" of some of the NGOs. "One time I was joking," a Fair Trade Mexico leader said, "that it seems like the most important point on the agenda of [NGO] forums is where the next one's going to be." When RMALC and others hosted a "Road to Cancún: The Southeast Resists" preparatory forum in early August, none of the local peasant organizations attended.[43] UNORCA and the Vía Campesina had their own meeting on August 4.[44]

Part of both UNORCA's and the Vía Campesina's work was to generate spaces for working-class and peasant voices in the world of NGOs and private foundations. One Mayan leader who led UNORCA's local efforts in Cancún had grown frustrated with German foundations and their unwillingness to fund activities that questioned the Mexican government.[45] Though the Mexican government was more restrictive than other countries about allowing "civil society" representatives into the WTO ministerial as sponsored guests, the WTO did offer an avenue to do so in Cancún. Its new "Participation and Consultation" component was oriented directly to NGOs. Those who would enter, of course, would be vetted by governments and WTO officials, and groups like RMALC took the opportunity.[46] The Vía Campesina saw these offers as efforts to co-opt and divide global justice movements; the opposition should be outside the summit, united, it said. That said, some interpreted the political positions of Vía Campesina as problematic, unilateral, and largely based on the decisions of its central committee, rather than its members.[47]

Meanwhile, much of UNORCA and Vía Campesina's work was out in the small towns, including with Victoria Santos and Marcelo Carreón, the alleged gun-toting Zapatistas who nine years earlier were forced to flee persecution. UNORCA's national office first reached out to ask them for help in getting people excited to come to Cancún. Vía Campesina delegates, though, also took on important roles.[48] UNORCA's national office had dedicated weeks of time to arrange for travel, lodging, and visas for Vía Campesina's international peasant affiliates and its leadership council. Here in towns like Felipe Carrillo Puerto or José María Morelos, hours away from Cancún, the delegates and representatives arrived and addressed the residents.[49] The major demand of the Vía Campesina and UNORCA, they said, would be the demand they first articulated in Seattle: "Agriculture out of the WTO."

For the residents of rural Quintana Roo, standing up to the WTO was about standing up for their corn and beans, and for peasants worldwide. Local community leaders, some of whom have since died, took it upon themselves to get their own communities to go.[50] These regional affiliates didn't go to Cancún "for a local demand," but rather to stand up for poor countries against the rich. One thing that organizer Rosa Hernández would say to the local members was that "we need to be there because they're making agreements that affect all the peasants and poor countries, but the peasants from other places are very far away. It is our turn here because we are close. If [the summit] was in Africa, those from there would be going." She went on to say that "it is a question of capitalism, of how it affects poor people," and that members should "go to represent the peasants of the world."

For the members of UNORCA Yucatán, three hours up the road, hundreds of Mayan peasants planned to make the trip, knowing that "we are fighting against the World Trade Organization, we are fighting to protect our seeds, [we are fighting] to protect ourselves from transgenics, and to protect the environment." Pablo Duarte, a Maya-speaking UNORCA leader with an office in the regional city of Mérida, said that he had been bringing information to communities about issues related to trade deals and the dangers of agribusiness. He would get the information in Mexico City at political events, since local UNORCA members would chip in for his transportation costs. Some of it came from documents carried by

Figure 4. Farmers affiliated with Vía Campesina at the 2003 protests outside the World Trade Organization meetings in Cancún, Mexico. Photo courtesy of Alamy.

friends or comrades in meetings of the UN's Food and Agriculture Organization (in Europe) or elsewhere. Duarte said that the members of UNORCA Yucatán who planned to attend the Cancún protests had reasoned that "we've never been to Cancún [and] it's a tourist site, but we're going to go and see what's going on."[51]

For those in Quintana Roo, the organizers had worked everything out to the last detail. UNORCA Quintana Roo would take charge of all logistics, and the Vía Campesina would pay for the transportation and arrange for food. The Vía Campesina ultimately arranged for seventy buses to pick people up early on September 8. Marcelo Carreón, who at that time was the state's forestry director, spent time in Cancún getting logistics and permits ready there. However, and much as had happened nine years earlier in the wake of the Zapatista uprising, just as the group was exercising its influence, rumor mills and fear-mongering emerged to imperil their work.

According to Santos, people hired by state government showed up in the small communities "to tell people not to go." They used fear. They told the locals that "they would be beaten, they would be stripped, that they would get water sprayed at them, and things like that." The tactics worked, to a degree. "Many," she said, "got scared, but someone [also] said something like, 'If I'm going to die in my hammock, I die. If it's my turn, it's my turn. Yes, *I* will go." According to Duarte, a PAN-affiliated local newspaper slandered the Yucatán group, saying publicly that they were forcing people to go to the protests. The media sent the message that "hey, that guy went [to the communities] to heat things up [*calentar*]. He's an enemy of the government—this has got to be ended." For many of these organizations, the repression of the local government was precisely how the national UNORCA leadership had first gained its trust and presence there—sticking up for them in the face of hostile local officials.[52]

Still, the main language about violence at the protests was used to describe the protesters themselves. Panic overcame the local Cancún media in the month leading up to the protests, which reporters and commentators preordained to be the "Battle of Cancún."[53] In the city, the Association of Shopping Malls asked for police backup.[54] The airport was covered with new police units. The ministerial conference, happening on Cancún's hotel strip, a miles-long coastal peninsula separated from the main city by a canal, was heavily fortified. Two sets of fences (and an inner and an outer one) were erected to keep out the protesters, nearly a kilometer in front of the conference's actual entrance.

That said, the history of the Cancún protests shouldn't be told simply as a melodrama pitting the impoverished masses against greedy governments and omnipotent police. Like other forms of grassroots globalism, UNORCA's work involved campaigning for radical demands (such as "food sovereignty" and "agriculture out of the WTO"), but at the same time patiently working with local institutions, including the government.

Cancún's mayor collaborated relatively closely with UNORCA's Marcelo Carreón and others. He agreed to allow some of the city's park spaces to be used for camping, and some city buildings to be used for teach-ins. The city, by early September, said that it had invested 5 million pesos in arranging for the services. It asked the federal government for additional loans, since the alternative countersummit was important: its events would reflect "the convergence of an infinity of organizations looking for a space for expression."[55] (The thousands of protesters, of course, would also bring business to Cancún's central city.) Carreón had pressured the secretary of agriculture and the governor to allow him to be in Cancún in the first place and played an important role in mobilizing the communities.[56]

While the city's major newspaper indeed played up the potential for violence, it did also offer more nuanced views of the proceedings. In one issue alone, it featured two political cartoons lampooning the overblown security efforts, such as the massive walls to keep the protesters out, and the poverty faced by many of the peasants protesting. It offered a detailed story about activist claims that a young Mexican "activist journalist" was actually a police infiltrator. It also offered stories about peasants arriving from different parts of the country and the world. It even published an editorial denouncing agricultural dumping by the US and Europe—a topic central to UNORCA and Vía Campesina's claims.[57]

Negotiating teams themselves were uncertain how the ministerial would go. The US trade representative said that it was unlikely that the next step of integration—the Free Trade Area of the Americas—could happen without an agreement on agriculture in Cancún.[58] Earlier in the summer, Franz Fisher, the commissioner of agriculture for the European Union, said that if the bloc of twenty developing countries "wanted to keep pursuing their [unrealistic demands] . . . they will end up with empty hands."[59] Later, in June, European Union governments agreed to modestly roll back subsidies to large agribusiness. Would the Global South countries see this and other reforms as enough to warrant opening up new areas for foreign investment? No one knew the answer, but the stakes were high.

THE WEEK OF THE PROTESTS

Nothing went quite as planned for the protest organizers once September 8 arrived. According to Santos, municipal officials in several county seats shipped in beer the day before the protests. Offering it free to residents, the functionaries hoped they wouldn't be in condition to board the Vía Campesina buses the next morning. Santos observed that the scare tactics—about getting stripped or sprayed with water—may have scared some, but mostly the PRI-leaning residents in the ejidos. Santos and others quickly realized the seventy buses weren't enough. Moving rapidly and using UNORCA Quintana Roo funds, they arranged for nearly thirty vans to supplement them. But then they hit another roadblock, literally. Key roads were mysteriously blocked on the way to Cancún. They had to take the long way.[60]

The Cancún they encountered was unlike the Cancún of any moment in the city's brief history. At least twelve buses of people from Chiapas, Oaxaca, Guerrero, and Mexico City had already arrived, coordinated by UNORCA. Peasants from more than a dozen countries were arriving as well.[61] Teach-ins dotted the landscape of the city. Because of frustrations with organizers from RMALC, UNORCA, and the Vía Campesina created their own forum, with collaboration later secured from the National Indigenous Congress. They held this International Peasant and Indigenous Forum at the municipal House of Culture and the Kuchil Baxal Gymnasium, which would be the first stop for the regional peasants.

The park surrounding the gymnasium was where many of the UNORCA members slept during the night. Massive tents covered the grounds of the large outdoor complex, perhaps a mile from the hotel zone. "We didn't bring anything," Santos said. "The people just went with their bandannas or little flags from the Via Campesina, their caps, [and] that was what they brought."[62] Duarte said they endured the hot, muggy conditions. "They slept in trucks, or below tarps or sunshades," he said.[63] It wasn't just the regional peasants who stayed at the park. It was a wide range of people, including Korean farmers and peasants, and different varieties of street protesters. The Quintana Roo group even saw protesters on stilts there.[64]

The protest marches, of course, were central to the events. While shutting down the ministerials was no longer a realistic goal for most organizers, the waves of nearly daily marches were meant to disrupt activities. Some NGOs had rallies in parks, others on beaches. The major march on September 9 set the stage for the week, but it also featured Kyung-hae's suicide. Later that evening, as UNORCA members recalled, the South Korean ambassador scolded the Korean farmers for letting it happen.[65] Kyung-hae quickly became a martyr in the eyes of the peasant movements there. In a later march, his comrades offered flowers to the security police on the other side of the fence.

· · · · ·

On the night before September 14, the Mexican government, which was overseeing the ministerial, said that an agreement among the nations was imminent. After encountering the "Battle of Seattle" in 1999, and then holding its next meetings in Doha, Qatar, to get away from protesters, the WTO needed some good news. If the ministerial coordinators were right, the Doha round goal of reaching consensus on agriculture by 2005 would be fulfilled, and two years early, at that.

But it wasn't to be. A "Group of 20" nations, led by Argentina and Brazil (as major food exporters), hesitated at what they saw as the lack of clarity from the US and Europe about the old issues of market access and about reducing subsidies. With that, negotiations, and the ministerial, ended. Before September, WTO officials said the meeting was of utmost importance. After its failure, they began to claim it hadn't been important at all.[66]

For UNORCA, as with other kinds of grassroots globalism, the importance of its activities extended beyond what happened in boardrooms to effects on its organizing capacity. Santos recalled telling Carreón that "we can't allow ourselves to not do this well, because if it doesn't go well, there are going to be many repercussions, for the Vía Campesina [and] national UNORCA and obviously for the state UNORCA branch." The UNORCA national leadership was happy to receive a letter from the EZLN right before the peasant forum. The statements, which Gomez read aloud to the attendees, confirmed the EZLN's support for the event and the work of UNORCA and the Vía Campesina.[67]

For Duarte, the protest was an overwhelming success. It "gave us credibility," he said. Now the people "recognized that what we were saying was true, [and] that we weren't lying." And before Cancún, he said, "the people were scared." "It scared them to go out into the street. To do a *plantón* [occupation] was a sin." But "after Cancún, [they'd say,] 'We're going to take Zariapa—let's go.'" After Cancún, we occupied the government palace [in the town of Zariapa] four times; we'd fill it with four hundred, five hundred people." Some days they had even more in the plaza outside, and "the people [from the organization], using the microphone, [would] let it all out about what bothered them."

For one regional leader, the protests solidified UNORCA's ability to bring different groups together, partly through its mobilizations in the coalition The Countryside Can't Take It Anymore. "We could still interact in Cancún with the [telephone workers' union], with the youngsters they gave the name of 'Black Bloc' to, [and] the youth that came from international movements." Its work in that capacity was particularly important given that the masses of young people from the rest of Mexico failed to appear in numbers that many expected. The direct-action segment of the protests, likewise, was more tame than that of other Mexican global justice protests. Following the suicide of Kyung-hae, the Vía Campesina helped steer an agreement with the Black Bloc about respecting the Koreans' wishes to have a peaceful vigil at the security fence. Ultimately, the relatively small size of the protests—perhaps around ten thousand people—brings into relief the critical impact of UNORCA's and the Vía Campesina's work, given that they alone brought thousands of people.

These dynamics, of radical direct actionists alongside peasants and unionists, are part of the story for this book's final chapter on grassroots globalism: how the anarchistic influences of one of the era's most radical Indigenous alliances led it as well to the historic WTO protests in Cancún.

9 The Radical Road to Cancún

ANARCHISM AND AUTONOMY FOR THE
POPULAR INDIGENOUS COUNCIL OF
OAXACA—RICARDO FLORES MAGÓN

A resident of Plan de Zaragoza, a small, rural hamlet in southern Mexico about four hours from the capital of Oaxaca, once told me about the day a politician came to visit. The regional party official had come under the pretext of evaluating local farming practices, but certainly also to drum up support for his upcoming electoral bid. He tried to walk up to the mountainside community from the riverbed below, where the gravel road ended. He made it about halfway, and promptly fainted.[1]

The people who live in this Ñuu Savi (Mixtec) town of Plan de Zaragoza walk for hours to get to their small plots of corn, coffee, and beans. Many of their children walk two hours to get to school in the morning. The difficult climbs and steep descents are especially challenging for outsiders. While a complex maze of foot-worn trails in the area allows residents to reach the town square as quickly as possible (and avoid the switchbacks and dust of the road), anyone unfamiliar with the area can easily get lost. And the hike from the riverbed—which can take about an hour—is almost straight uphill in some places.

The lack of roads, lack of schools, and lack of services are precisely why Ñuu Savi residents denounced the Mexican government for its forgetting (*olvido*) of them. And that's largely why they joined the Popular Indigenous

Council of Oaxaca—Ricardo Flores Magón (Consejo Indígena Popular de Oaxaca—Ricardo Flores Magón, CIPO-RFM) in the early 2000s. They could have continued to wait for political representatives to help, even if many Indigenous Oaxacans had lost faith in the Institutional Revolutionary Party (Partido Revolucionario Institucional, PRI), which had governed the state for nearly seventy years. CIPO-RFM's organizing approach, though, placed power and management more within the hands of the community members themselves. Shaped by Oaxacan Indigenous politics, the Oaxaca-born revolutionary Ricardo Flores Magón's unique brand of anarcho-communism, and broader Mexican and Latin American "autonomous" movements, CIPO-RFM's work in the era marked a novel crystallization of grassroots globalism at the turn of the twenty-first century.[2]

It's much easier to get to the center of this small town from the riverbed today. The courage and efforts of Ñuu Savi residents, as part of CIPO-RFM, pushed the state government to release the funds necessary to build a bridge so cars could traverse the river, even during the rainy season that begins in May. Instead of hiring a state contractor for the work, who would likely pocket some of the funds and skimp on materials, the residents decided to do it themselves. CIPO-RFM had established itself as a pan-ethnic Indigenous alliance in 1997, and since then it had built solidarity relationships with local unions. The unionists agreed to help design and plan the bridge, and the residents and CIPO-RFM volunteers helped with the construction.

Today, every time a car or van passes over the compact white bridge near the small fish farm and gentle waterfall, passengers see the message painted in bright red letters on its railings: "Autonomía y Autogestión: CIPO-RFM" (Autonomy and Self-Management: CIPO-RFM).

Bricklayers and small farmers. Civil engineers and Indigenous communities. Government unionists and teachers. These aren't the pairings we typically associate with the global justice movement—or with anarchism, for that matter. Yet these actors were each vital participants in CIPO-RFM's journey to the 2003 World Trade Organization protests in Cancún. CIPO-RFM resembled some of the anarchist-oriented organizations in Latin America in the early 2000s, and perhaps some of those in the Global North, but the picture of anarchism and autonomous politics in this chapter is also quite different from the kind generally associated with the global justice movements. CIPO-RFM, after all, was a membership organization, not an affinity group. It was run by lifelong Oaxacans, not guided by the virtual connections of radical cyber-networks or media collectives. Unlike a "culture jamming" arts organization, it focused on material realities, even as it made important contributions to the "street theater," "guerrilla art" aesthetic tied to direct-action global justice networks.[3] To be clear, CIPO-RFM identified itself as a Magonista organization, not an anarchist one. Yet it worked with anarchists in a variety of capacities. Given the importance of young people, anarchism, and punk rock in the broader global justice struggles, this chapter focuses on the young people who entered the organization in this era and ends with an examination of the multigenerational group of CIPO-RFM members who traveled to the WTO protests in Cancún in September 2003.[4]

CIPO-RFM AND AUTONOMOUS POLITICS

The growing resistance to neoliberal reforms in the early 2000s was due in part to the rise of "autonomous" movements in the Americas. They no longer relied on traditional organizations or parties to mediate their demands.[5] Argentina after the 2001 financial crisis was one important site for the emergence of anarchistic kinds of autonomous politics. After the crisis forced millions of citizens into bankruptcy or poverty, workers took over their factories. Poor people organized neighborhood assemblies. They coordinated food exchanges in neighborhoods and blocked major highways in the cities to demand change.

Such movements were heralded in North American and European anarchist circles, and among the left more generally, as they sought to build solidarities around global justice politics. Anarchist websites and listservs discussed their work, and local activists helped organize tours and events for Argentine activists and others to speak.[6] They reached such mainstream recognition that global justice figurehead Naomi Klein produced a high-profile film about Argentina's worker-owned factories.[7] The work of the Zapatistas in Mexico and the land takeovers of the Landless Workers' Movement in Brazil continued to represent the hopes of inspiring an analogous kind of resistance in the US and Europe well into the 2000s.[8]

CIPO-RFM was part of this wave of autonomous movements, yet its version of autonomy was quite distinct. The meaning of Indigenous autonomy was at the center of debates over recognizing Indigenous political structures in the 1990s, and Oaxacan Indigenous activists ultimately convinced the Zapatistas to embrace a brand of community level autonomy in the same time period. The meaning of autonomy for CIPO-RFM also came from the writings of Mexican revolutionary Ricardo Flores Magón (1873–1922). Building on a number of Oaxacan, left-wing interpretations of his work, the organization took inspiration in part from Flores Magón's argument that Mexican Indigenous peoples had created their own forms of "communism," where "mutual aid was the rule," where "everybody had a right to land, water for irrigation, and the forest for wood," and where the state was mostly absent.[9] Flores Magón's idealized portrait captured the spirit of many of the demands arising from Indigenous Mexico after the 1960s. Instead of electing politicians or representatives in organizations tied to political parties, Indigenous peoples fought for ways to do things themselves, whether controlling their local decision-making structures or controlling their territory. CIPO-RFM argued that *expanding* these kinds of collective efforts, mutual aid, and skepticism toward the state could allow Indigenous people and workers to collectively run their farms, factories, and communities.[10] Political parties and other authorities, they argued, were paternalistic at best and repressive at worst.

The CIPO-RFM in this chapter—in the years leading up to the 2003 WTO protests in Cancún—was quite different from that of the late 1990s (see chapter 4). In a highly controversial shift, the organization in 2001 moved from being an alliance of organizations to an alliance of communities. Some from one of the major founding organizations, the Indian Organizations for Human Rights in Oaxaca (Organizaciones Indias por los Derechos Humanos en Oaxaca, OIDHO), argued that activists linked to the influential organizer Raúl Gatica had led a takeover of CIPO-RFM. Gatica had been a former leader of the Committee in Defense of the People (Comité de Defensa de los Derechos del Pueblo, CODEP). A CODEP member told me in 2010 that the change in CIPO-RFM was due to "arguments among leaders"—that is, closed-door, personal disputes. Few were privy to the full details.[11] Still others claimed that OIDHO had left CIPO-RFM voluntarily.[12]

Despite this contested history, this period is significant not only because of high-profile activists. It's also the story of a diverse group of Indigenous members and organizers who helped make CIPO-RFM what it was in these years: a council of roughly twenty Indigenous communities around the state of Oaxaca, with eight major committees (on everything from "communications" to "human rights") and a track record for winning concrete victories in local communities as well as maintaining a broader vision of resisting oppression. In these years, CIPO-RFM stood up to the neoliberal reforms and abuses of the PRI. While CIPO-RFM would target the global forces shaping economic and political systems in places like Cancún, much of its everyday work was focused on engaging and confronting local state officials on the front lines of these larger processes.

As chapter 4 discussed, many communities had gained some distance from the PRI when the state government, after Indigenous pressure, agreed to formally recognize a limited version of Indigenous self-rule, or autonomy, in 1995. The Zapotec community of San Isidro Aloapam, in the coffee belt of the state's northern mountains, represented the situation of other CIPO communities at the time. This small town of around seven hundred residents operated largely through its own internal systems of governance (commonly known as "ways and customs," or *usos y costumbres*, but better defined as "normative internal political systems").[13] Each year, it elected community members (usually men) to take up key roles, including that of the mayor (the *autoridad*) and the communal land commissioner (the *comisariado de bienes comunales*). Votes were taken by voice at the monthly town assembly (the *asamblea*), and these positions were unpaid and obligatory. Anyone who refused to serve would no longer have right to use land in the community. These roles were part of a system of duties (*cargos*) that allowed the community to function, and to do so without political parties, particularly without the PRI. They operated through a deeply entrenched system of reciprocity that was common in rural areas.

While these kinds of internal political systems generated space between communities and political parties, the county seats (*cabeceras municipales*) of these small towns were often the sites of continued PRI rule, even if the *muncipio* adhered to its own internal political system. San Isidro Aloapam, for its part, had initiated a decades-old struggle against its *municipio*, which was controlled by the PRI. PRI *municipios* could withhold federal money to the small towns (*agencias*) around them and keep it for themselves.[14] And that's exactly what the county seat of San Miguel Aloapam did. In addition to denying San Isidro funds from important federal budget lines, they denied representation to the *agencia* by claiming that more than four hundred San Isidro residents were not communal land holders.[15] By doing so they were able to extract the timber from the area's mountainside forests more aggressively and to lock out San Isidro residents from receiving benefits. Most of San Isidro Aloapam had resisted the increased logging anyway, worried that it would despoil the territory and its watersheds.

These conditions forced a wave of the town's young men and families to migrate to the US in the 1990s and after, some of them to escape the political pressure. As soon as residents of San Isidro began standing up for themselves, the state police (again, controlled by the PRI) launched arrest orders. Dozens were arrested on dubious charges in the 1990s and early 2000s.[16] In the months after Cancún, CIPO-RFM and San Isidro residents would launch a *plantón* (occupation) of the capital city's Zócalo, only to face an early-morning violent eviction, in which fifteen CIPO-RFM leaders and San Isidro residents were jailed for two months.[17]

YOUTH AND GRASSROOTS GLOBALISM

By 2003, global justice protests were known for creating spectacles—and the Cancún protests promised to be similar. Yet Cancún certainly wouldn't be the first time CIPO-RFM had pushed for change in daring and creative ways. One day, a year before the trip to Cancún, CIPO-RFM released rats into the governor's office in Oaxaca.[18] Sometimes they marched with monster puppets (of political figures) and with faces painted as skulls.[19] In late 2002, two members scaled the governor's palace and theatrically hanged themselves with ropes, with the words "land, liberty, and justice" painted on posterboard strapped to their chests. On Mother's Day 2002, women wrote their demands in their own blood.[20] Later, after they established an occupation outside the government building they situated their grills and cooking equipment near the palace's ground-floor windows. They roasted chili peppers over flames to release a peppery, smoky mix of gases into the palace offices where the governor's functionaries were trying to work.[21]

What did the activists from CIPO-RFM want? They wanted more government funding for community infrastructure and agricultural projects; they wanted an end to PRI corruption and intimidation in rural Indigenous areas; and they wanted justice and freedom for Indigenous people more broadly. When they carried crucifixes to the plaza outside the Oaxacan State Government Palace in late December one year, their banners explained how government policies were generating the slow death of their communities. "The poor don't get a merry Christmas," their flyers read. They declared themselves "against neoliberalism and capitalist globalization."[22] These tactics were partly why a diverse group of Indigenous youth found a space in CIPO-RFM during these years and found ways to make it their own.

A young Indigenous-descendant Ayuuk woman named Concepción was representative of one segment of the young people that helped lead CIPO-RFM in the years after its takeover of the state attorney general's office in 1998 (see chapter 4). Originally from a regional Indigenous town a few hours' drive from the Oaxaca state capital, she, like so many others of her generation, had migrated to live in Oaxaca City when she was a child. Life in Mexico's countryside, for all the economic reasons discussed in the previous chapters, had become increasingly difficult. In Oaxaca, people like Concepción's family lived in settlements on the edge of the city, where they had purchased or squatted on dusty land and built homes, far from urban amenities like running water, paved roads, and electricity.[23]

Concepción's first engagement with the Oaxacan left was through the school system, as some of her relatives worked as teachers or school workers and were therefore members of Local 22 of the National Education Workers Union (Sindicato Nacional de Trabajadores de la Educación, SNTE), one of the most radical union locals in the country.

She participated in local Oaxacan support brigades for the Zapatistas after their 1994 uprising, and there she was recruited by the Marxist organizers of CODEP. CODEP grew out of the land struggles in the 1970s and by the late 1990s had an important base of young people like Concepción. Some, like Concepción, took a few classes at the local public university. Some of these youth, like Concepción, worked as street vendors when they could, selling CDs or candy to cover basic living costs. They attended study groups about Leninism or the left-wing guerrillas in Colombia.[24] Ultimately, when recounting her political experiences with me in 2008, Concepción said that the Marxism of CODEP was a little "square" (*cuadrado*) for her.

By the early 2000s, a growing number of young people turned to CIPO-RFM for their political work. Some had worked with Zapatista support groups and Marxists, and some had also worked with slightly more moderate Indigenous rights organizations, such as SERvicios del Pueblo Mixe (Services of the Mixe People, or SER-Mixe) or the University Workshop on Human Rights (Taller Universitario de Derechos Humanos, TUDH). Still others were active in the anarchist, punk rock scene. On weekends they assembled do-it-yourself concerts (*toquines*), usually in old garages or homes, and featured bands from far beyond Oaxaca City, like Guadalajara or Mexico City. These gatherings served as venues where they could trade or sell their zines, or homemade pamphlets (*fanzines*), about everything from Zapatismo to antiglobalization protests to animal rights. With time, many came to see CIPO-RFM as their ideological home.[25] Often they were hungry and broke. One told me he liked to show up at the CIPO-RFM office with hopes that one of the older members, who were often schoolteachers, would have a few *tamales* or sandwiches to share.[26]

As with other forms of grassroots globalism in the US and Mexico, the organization they entered operated through a network structure, yet one that differed from the global justice networks of anarchist affinity groups. It also differed from the internet-based cyber-activism and media work emerging within global justice circles. One of these young people said that he associated the internet with the United States at that time. Even a young man who attended the local state university told me he had little internet access in the early 2000s.[27] CIPO-RFM's hybrid network structure wove grassroots horizontalism together with the hierarchy and structure often associated with more traditional working-class organizations, such as trade unions.

CIPO-RFM's structure built on the centrality of the Indigenous community assembly. Each affiliate community would elect a rotating "base council" to carry out the decisions made by the town assembly. Each town assembly would also name a delegate to CIPO's "council of councils," which would decide on major strategic directions. It would also name the general coordinator of the organization and the organizing committee. All positions were rotating, one-year positions, with the exception of the general coordinator, which was a three-year term.[28] As with the rule of one-year rotations, the organization agreed that no positions would be paid. This model of rotating, voluntary terms cultivated a deep core of membership. These roles were seen as acts of service (*cargos*), just as leadership positions were in Indigenous Oaxaca communities like San Isidro Aloapam. In a poor, mountainous state with seven major Indigenous regions and with politicians skillful at keeping communities divided through highly vertical patron-client politics, CIPO-RFM's networked power came in part from its ability to convene different Indigenous towns, speaking different languages, into a single association of communities.[29]

One of the young women who joined at this time commented that during CIPO-RFM's introductory workshops for communities, organizers explained that "what is happening to you all is happening to the comrades of the Sierra, it's happening to the comrades on the coast, and it's happening to the comrades in the Mixteca [region]." Recruitment and orientation workshops thus organized people by situating their problems in larger patterns and a larger geographic region. The organization's aspiration toward popular power based in collaboration, not verticality, was captured in the slogan that many of its pamphlets from the era highlighted: "CIPO-RFM: many hands and one heart to struggle."[30]

As with other grassroots globalisms, CIPO-RFM's work in local community struggles was guided by a broad vision of confronting neoliberal economic reform. The young adults of the organization were also central to circulating the organization's systematic vision. One of the committees they most actively participated in was the communications committee. There, many used skills honed in Zapatista or anarchist pamphleteering or doing photography or communications work in organizations like SER-Mixe. Influenced by the anarchist wave of do-it-yourself media in the global justice networks, they created pirate radio stations and circulated a series of pamphlets, booklets, and videos about CIPO-RFM.[31]

These pamphlets discussed how the organization situated its work simultaneously within but against a system of neoliberalism. They were intended either for a local activist readership or for use in guiding conversations with Indigenous communities about these topics. One popular pamphlet discussed the Plan Puebla Panama, a formerly secret plan to create a transportation corridor through southern Mexico to Panama. The PPP, the pamphlet said, was the epitome of neoliberalism in that it functioned like "poisoned candy" (*dulce envenenado*). Such regionalist development enterprises seemed good on the outside, yet would inevitably import a corporate model that "would be imposed on our country."[32]

Another pamphlet was titled "How Neoliberalism Affects All Women." Presented in the style of a comic, it opens with a story scenario that highlights neoliberalism's intensification of work. "If you want to eat fruit," one woman says to the other, "take care of my tree and I will give you an apple each day." But the next year, the tree owner has more fruit and more seed, so plants more trees. While the tree owner acquires more and more fruit and sells it, the other woman continues to only get one apple a day—and has to take care of more and more trees.

Unlike the definitions of neoliberalism outlined by other organizations in this book, the one that emerges here illuminates how the system affects both productive labor and the reproductive labor of the home.[33] The pamphlet continues by noting how women are half the world's population but hold only a fraction of the wealth. It concludes with the prediction that neoliberalism will allow the rich to privatize water and electricity supplies, making them cost more, which will make women's reproductive labor in the home harder: "You're going to have to walk farther to bring water ... [and] when there's no more gas, you'll have to cook with firewood, which damages your health."[34]

ANTIMODERNIST AUTONOMY? RECLAIMING INDIGENOUS OAXACA

What did autonomy and mutual aid even mean in an age of globalization and major economic reforms? As much as CIPO-RFM energized these issues in the Indigenous movement, it didn't have a monopoly on them. The anarchist youth of Oaxaca City themselves introduced important examinations of the work of Flores Magón and elaborated a punk-infused notion of self-management and mutual aid.

Taking inspiration from Flores Magón and many others, they argued that authority could only be parasitical and that people and workers could self-manage their own societies. As one Oaxacan anarcho-punk zine quoted from Magón, "Anarchists [*los libertarios*] aren't accustomed to having leaders. You're not fighting to exalt anyone to power, because that would be making a sacrifice to [simply] have a new persecutor."[35]

For many anarcho-punks in Mexico in the late 1990s and early 2000s, mutual aid was about running do-it-yourself punk rock concerts and donating the proceeds to political prisoners throughout Latin America.[36] They ran skill-shares, where attendees would teach each other how to sew, screen-print and reproduce images, and do photography and basic carpentry. They traded zines or bought and sold them to cover the cost of production. The well-known Oaxaca City zine *Fortaleza Libertaria* (Libertarian Strength) cost two pesos in the late 1990s. Sometimes these anarchists organized free discussions, or events featuring local intellectuals like Humberto Escobedo Cetina or Benjamin Maldonado, both of whom had written about the relationships between the contemporary Indigenous movement and the historical anarchism of Flores Magón.[37]

These anarcho-punks saw an overlap between anarchism, Indigenous autonomy, and antiglobalization. They resided in Oaxaca City but had lived in communities operating under Indigenous, assembly-based political systems. One Oaxacan anarcho-punk zine included calls to support the Zapatistas alongside denunciations of the Free Trade Area of the Americas and the treatment of women maquila workers in Oaxaca. It reclaimed the writing of Flores Magón for contemporary anarchists alongside invocations to oppose McDonald's and to "globalize the resistance," an important slogan of global justice networks worldwide.[38]

For CIPO-RFM, self-management and mutual aid were very much tied to Oaxacan Indigenous forms of collective work. In Oaxaca, the collective work arrangement called *tequio* was commonplace. Just as Indigenous communities required service through *cargos*, they also required participation in unpaid work, perhaps on projects dedicated to refurbishing a road or clearing away fallen branches after a storm. *Tequio* was even common in places like Oaxaca City, where the presence of Indigenous migrants and lack of services meant neighbors often collaborated to get work done. Local school committees and parent-teacher associations all engaged in regular *tequio* projects at local schools.[39]

CIPO-RFM, then, tried to refashion and reclaim Indigenous collective labor as one part of its larger push for Indigenous autonomy and self-management. It created a cooperative to sell Indigenous artisanal goods in the CIPO-RFM office. It temporarily tried to launch a "communitarian tourism" project to attract socially conscious international travelers to CIPO-RFM affiliates.[40] One of the organization's major campaigns in 2001–2 was to defend an Indigenous transportation cooperative in the town of Yaviche from falling under the control of a local PRI regional boss. The productive projects that CIPO-RFM won from the state government (for instance, vegetable seeds and fertilizer) were often worked collectively, rather than granted to individual community members.

CIPO-RFM and anarcho-punks weren't the only groups to reclaim *tequio*. For some, *tequio* was a component of "sustainable development." The Center Centeotl, an NGO based outside Oaxaca City, advocated small-scale artisanal production as "self-management" and called its newsletter *El Tequio*. For the influential Zapotec and Mixe theorists of the *comunalidad* concept, which identified Oaxacan Indigenous life with an essence of communitarian harmony, *tequio* was at the core of Oaxacan collective life and Indigenous self-determination.[41]

CIPO-RFM, for its part, embraced *tequio*, though it resisted what it saw as romanticization of Indigenous customs divorced from contemporary politics. In one declaration that situated its work outside moderate and technocratic forms of development politics, a CIPO-RFM flyer noted that "we have to conserve the naming of our representatives in assemblies, continue with *tequio*, with *guetza*, and not wait for politicians to resolve our problems." The piece continued by saying that "this means that we declare ourselves in rebellion, to disobey imposed laws and walk down the path of illegality, because we can't respect laws that go outside of reason and justice."[42]

Was the embrace of *tequio* in the era an example of the "antimodernism" of anarchism—of a tendency to idealize a communal past as a path for a future? Particularly in the US and Europe, a strain of primitivism or "green anarchy" in anarchist global justice networks at the time emphasized the essentially harmonious and sustainable communal societies before the rise of technology.[43] One activist from the Popular Revolutionary Movement (Movimiento Popular Revolucionario, MPR), a Maoist organization based in Oaxaca City, was less sanguine about *tequio*. He told me that his organization considered Oaxaca to be in the semifeudal stage of production and felt that it still needed to transition to modern capitalism to forge a modern and revolutionary proletariat. Such a form of unwaged productive labor, he said, was more appropriate for the feudal era than for today.[44]

As scholar Maia Ramnath has indicated, distinctions between the modern and antimodern lead to flawed understandings of anarchistic politics.[45] In chapter 4, this book argued that the nature of Oaxacan society challenged the "coca-colonization" perspectives on globalization: that Global North corporations were imposing cultural homogenization and steamrolling all that was different and local, particularly Indigenous cultures. The CIPO-RFM of those years, the earlier chapter showed, wasn't calling for a return to an idealized world of yesterday. It was not confronting a system that merely forced its affiliated communities into consumerist sameness; rather, it was confronting the state government's strategic politics of difference and selective redeployment of Indigenous "traditions" as exotic commodities to be sold to foreign tourists.[46]

Likewise, CIPO-RFM's vision of autonomy wasn't posited as a return to an idyllic communitarian past and a rejection of modernity. It meant defending territory and collective practices that Indigenous communities had developed, along with pressuring the state for schools, funding, and roads. It was oriented to ending the racism and the forgetting of Indigenous communities. These communities wanted better prices for their coffee, which, to be clear, was grown to sell, not for self-subsistence.[47] CIPO-RFM backed public sector unions' battle for better wages and protections—that's partly how they got structural engineers to plan the aforementioned bridge project. The Women's Committee, in particular, rallied against Indigenous communities where men kept women out of the town *asamblea* on the rationale that doing so was "tradition" or "custom." "Those are bad traditions," one CIPO-RFM member said, so they needed to be disposed of.⁴⁸ The organization's support of *tequio* didn't spring from a narrow nostalgia.⁴⁹

If anything, CIPO-RFM's vision of autonomy might be antimodernization, not antimodern. It resisted the development strategies driven by the modernization theories of the Cold War and the agricultural "modernization" of the PRI. Those strategies suggested that development would come only by getting rid of "backward" small towns and moving their residents to work in a growing industrial sector.⁵⁰ What autonomy meant for one resident of Plan de Zaragoza was about choice and control. Speaking of large chain stores, she said, "If the people of the town permit them, then it could happen, but not so they just enter because they want to. It's true that we are poor in this town, we are modest, but we don't allow them to trick us just because they feel like it. That's what I understand as autonomy. We need to take care of our ways and customs, as we say, and take care of our town so that they don't enter just because they want to."

Still, it's true that CIPO-RFM's relationship to the state and its social projects *was* a point of tension for some of its members. On the one hand, Concepción argued that pressuring and protesting the state for productive projects, like a bread-baking project in Plan de Zaragoza, was part of a goal to forge self-managing communities.⁵¹ Others justified state funding because it was, after all, the people's money, since it originated from their taxes.⁵²

Yet other members had mixed feelings. One young person said that while the organization often trumpeted how it was "demanding" (*exigir*) projects from an unwilling government, it was sometimes more like "requesting" (*pedir*).⁵³ The government was happy to fund projects, he implied, likely as a way to steer community residents into PRI circles or force the organization to depend on government support for follow-through or additional supplies. One of the teachers in CIPO-RFM suggested from the beginning that getting and managing these projects should always be just a first step to gain the trust of community members. CIPO-RFM's long-term plan, he said, was to generate excitement about

Magonismo, and they expected that only a few town residents would someday become committed adherents.⁵⁴

CANCÚN: CIPO-RFM ON A WORLD STAGE

Abram felt lost. As a Ñuu Savi member of CIPO-RFM from Plan de Zaragoza, he had never left the state. He had never been on an airplane and had rarely eaten at a restaurant. But CIPO's growing profile and its Indigenous peasant membership had caught the eye of Greenpeace Mexico, a large US-based environmental activist group. Greenpeace organizers had big plans for Cancún. They were going to send their own ship to block export vessels attempting to carry transgenic corn out of Mexico for sale. But they also had plans for the many forums and events. They wanted Abram to talk about what it was like to be a peasant in the "free trade" era.

Because he had Greenpeace's financial support, Abram left Oaxaca alone early in the morning of September 7 to board a flight to Cancún, before CIPO-RFM's two buses departed from Oaxaca. Greenpeace had put him up in a Cancún hotel for the week, but Abram wouldn't be there for long. As soon as CIPO-RFM's companions arrived the next night, he quietly left the hotel. CIPO-RFM leaders picked him up. Abram wanted to be with the group—even though they were sleeping in a crowded park in muggy, rainy, Cancún with no showers and limited bathrooms.⁵⁵

The world tourist destination of Cancún is indeed a long way from Plan de Zaragoza. For the five people from the area who journeyed to Mexico's Caribbean coast for the WTO protest, only one had ever left Oaxaca. But they constituted a core group of the two buses that CIPO-RFM was able to fill for the twenty-two-hour bus ride to the state of Quintana Roo. Some CIPO-RFM members, not unlike those in UNORCA and the Vía Campesina, found it especially important to have a voice at these major protests.

The Women's Area, in particular, had confronted over the years the ways large NGOs, usually represented by non-Indigenous women, captured many of the funds and speaking opportunities. The Area had criticized a recent international event, the 2002 First Indigenous Women's Summit of the Americas, for mostly inviting NGO-based speakers to represent the voices of Indigenous women. They wrote a letter to the directors in protest and were subsequently invited to the panel.⁵⁶ One of the Women's Area's most significant statements about the problems that neoliberalism presented for women criticized "mestiza women from the city" who failed to comprehend rural Indigenous women's workload and who attempted to speak for them in meetings.⁵⁷ In Cancún, the major women's network in Mexico, the REDGE (Red de Genero y Economía / Gender and Economy Network), hosted its women's forums at the Best Western hotel, where its leaders stayed.⁵⁸ The class and race difference between their experiences and those of the Indigenous peasant women were mapped into the landscape of the countersummit. The REDGE members were on Cancún's hotel strip, the CIPO-RFM members in a park in the central city. The CIPO-RFM women ultimately went to the Peasant and Indigenous Forum, not the "women's" sessions on the hotel strip.⁵⁹

For its part, the CIPO-RFM contingent wasn't the only Oaxacan group in Cancún.⁶⁰ The Maoists from the Popular Revolutionary Movement were also there. Its members, mostly university-age youth, intended to build on its protests at former economic summits, and its goal, one member said, was internationalizing the struggle of the proletariat.⁶¹ As he told me, starting in August he and his comrades would go out "bucketing" (*boteábamos*) in Oaxaca City. They would take "a little bucket and get on buses, and explain what the WTO meant, the World Trade Organization, and its repercussions for the countries of Latin America, Asia, and Africa." It created a profound "economic dependence," they would say to the passengers.

People, he said, would help out. "We'd ask for a little money [*una cooperación*], and our goal was to get forty people at a minimum." Their popularity might have been because of the general buzz about the WTO and globalization. "There was a boom—we'll put it that way," he said. "There was a boom because of all those movements in Italy, the US, [and] other countries."⁶²

It was a little different for CIPO-RFM. Like other grassroots globalists, it had developed relationships with unions and other kinds of groups that some of the most radical leftists mistrusted. For example, it had longstanding relationships with Local 22, the education workers' local.⁶³ They supported the demonstrations. The local, in fact, hosted an event right after the 2000 Seattle protests that featured US activists talking about how they had shut down the meetings.⁶⁴ General coordinator Raul Gatica and others had recently built ties with the local public employees' union in

Oaxaca as well. That group faced a wave of state cuts. For some CIPO leaders, the possibility of uniting a radical *Magonista* organization with a union of four thousand workers was an opportunity too important to pass up. CIPO-RFM leaders had a litmus test for working with them, though. Their first question to the union's leader was if he opposed the Puebla-Panama Plan. Instead of using the bucket method, CIPO-RFM was able to get two buses donated because of its solidarity with Ruta 100, the radical Mexico City union organization. These bus drivers donated their time and the buses to drive CIPO-RFM members to Cancun.[65]

While the global justice literature tends to focus on the horizontal, transnational connections of activist networks, CIPO-RFM's prior international work also paralleled older forms of international solidarity. These connections, for CIPO-RFM, were much more North-South than South-South. In 2002 three members traveled to Spain and Catalonia to conduct workshops and participate in fundraising events with everyone from local anarchist info-shops to Catholic social gospel groups.[66] In 2003 two other members went on a similar trip to France. CIPO-RFM members who traveled rotated so different people would get the opportunity, and they took detailed notes so they could report back to the other members upon their return to Oaxaca. In 2002 an anarchist union federation in Spain, the Confederación General de Trabajadores (CGT), began supporting CIPO-RFM, and CIPO-RFM signed on as an affiliate in their International Section.[67]

Like the EZLN in Chiapas, CIPO-RFM had constant visits and collaborative work with European anarchists and activists. One CIPO-RFM member called it a kind of activist "circuit"; first they would see CIPO-RFM, then they would head to Chiapas. The long-term visits of French, Swiss, Swedish, and Spanish activists had a profound impact on some CIPO-RFM members, including three from Plan de Zaragoza. Two Ñuu Savi residents who went to Cancún, Jorge and Esperanza, fondly remembered the months that European women lived with them during extended support trips for CIPO-RFM. Demonstrating the solidarity experienced during these trips, one Spanish activist told me that when the police came to a CIPO-RFM land protest in Huatulco, the local CIPO-RFM members told the two Spaniards to pose as tourists so they wouldn't get arrested.[68]

Once in Cancún, CIPO-RFM members attended a range of activities, and different activist organizations hosted dozens of teach-ins and rallies.

Figure 5. Protester carrying a CIPO-RFM banner at the 2003 protests outside the World Trade Organization meetings in Cancún, Mexico. Photo courtesy of Alamy.

As one said, "We were going around to listen and share ideas with other peoples who are close, where there is poverty.... We shared ideas, like about what you can plant there and what you can't."[69] Abram spoke at the peasant forum, and an emerging women's leader participated in a panel on Indigenous women's rights.

The marches, of course, were memorable. The MPR from Oaxaca, along with many groups from throughout Mexico and elsewhere, arrived with ideas of disrupting the meetings as best they could. Some wore white overalls like Italy's radical direct actionists the Tute Bianche.[70] The CIPO-RFM representatives from the Mixteca were near the front, and ultimately not far from where the Korean farmer Lee Kyung-hae (see chapter 8) killed himself. As Jorge recalled, part of the march had the chaotic, carnivalesque character of other global justice protests, as well as the fear and anger in facing police repression. "We were sitting with Koreans, talking with them, and I started to talk to them about what kinds of things they plant, and there it started. Some groups entered, with some kind of music, but they were dressed in black and were playing [music] with their sticks. I saw that they had entered peacefully, dancing, but I'm not sure what kind of meaning it all really had."

Then, he said, some of the confrontations with the police at the fence happened. "I saw lots [of activists] start to enter with sticks and with some big jackets, and below them they had machines to cut fences, and that's when I saw the confrontation start, and some of the Koreans said, 'Let's get up, we'd better look for where to run if we have to, and if we have to turn ourselves in I guess there's no other option.'" But, he said, "Thanks to others who said, 'We're not going to run, we have to grab the stones around us [to fight back],'" he concluded that many were committed to holding their ground.

In Cancun protesters faced both police repression and a range of additional difficulties. One Ñuu Savi woman's bags were searched by police, who said they thought she might have rifles hidden with the hand-crafted textiles she hoped to sell. At least two of the CIPO members hoped to sell artisanal goods on the side, but they found it difficult to spare the time. Police repression was a big fear for many of them.[71] Some panicked when a long-term leader was separated from the group, although they later determined he was safe.

While right-wing Mexican critics hoped to delegitimize UNORCA's efforts by saying they were forcing or bribing their peasant members to attend the protests, the CIPO-RFM members who attended hoped to advocate for the political positions CIPO-RFM had developed on questions of globalization.[72] Jorge and Marcelino told me that they had gone to Cancún to confront the "big stores" and the government, as both had plans to privatize corn seeds and water. They faced police intimidation there because, as Marcelino said, "The government didn't want [CIPO-RFM] to participate, since CIPO is struggling against the government to make it support us poor *pueblos*." Jorge wanted to protest because "they want to send us the transgenic corn, which has seeds that we can't use to plant [for next year]." Plus, he said, their own products, like bananas and beans, didn't have a decent selling price.[73]

For Josefina, the corn question was similar to that of water—it posed new threats to their autonomy. "That's why we don't let other people come and try to trick us. Instead, we have to take care of the land. The land—because it's *here* we were born, *here* we eat, and *here* where we have our water," she said. "If we don't have it, we're not going to live."

· · · ·

For CIPO-RFM members who traveled to Cancún, hearing about how other peoples faced conditions of poverty had a strong impact. Josefina recalled that some of the speakers she heard discussed "how their people were [also] suffering." They showed that "not just in Oaxaca, but in other countries, people suffer from poverty." Esperanza fondly remembered dancing with the Koreans one evening at the camp. Jorge stated that "for me the struggle was hard, to be there, but thanks to God that it was like that and that the government realizes that the peoples [*pueblos*] have the courage to fight for the needs that we have."

Unlike UNORCA and Jobs with Justice, CIPO-RFM had little access to mainstream progressive foundations. They had little access to powerful international confederations, like the Vía Campesina. Yet despite their differences from the other organizations in this book, CIPO-RFM's presence at the Cancún protests reflected a brand of grassroots globalism. Like UNORCA or Jobs with Justice, they combined networked forms of organization with traditional vertical structures. They endeavored to fight frontline battles even as they were guided by a global vision of the threat of neoliberalism.

CIPO-RFM contributed to the global justice movement's momentum by supplementing its efforts at Cancún, where the crowds ultimately helped push Global South negotiators to hold strong against Global North attempts to insert agriculture into WTO regulation (see chapter 8). Like UNORCA and Jobs with Justice, it helped ensure that poor people had a voice in the growing, multifaceted global justice networks that ultimately helped tarnish the image of some of the era's most important international financial organizations.

Epilogue

"Ground pork or beef?" I asked yesterday at my neighborhood grocery store. "Good luck," the store manager told me. "Pork might be here tomorrow. Try to show up before noon." As I left the market frustrated with the prospect of another meatless dinner, I was tempted to try another store—the third of the day—but I had to get home. A landscaping company was delivering the topsoil and seeds I needed for planting. I had reached my limit: I would be trying to grow my *own* food for the summer of 2020.[1]

Food lines, rationing, and empty shelves. The Covid-19 pandemic brought these specters of scarcity into the living rooms and refrigerators of even middle-class US Americans. Capitalism, after all, was supposed to be about consumer plenty. Even if our wallets were empty, the shelves were always stocked. The dusty display cases in US grocery stores in early 2020 illuminated the frailties and limits of our own economic system. This was US capitalism, Covid-19 style. It was globalization—subjected to global pandemic.

Covid-19 quickly led to a new wave of skepticism about globalization. Global sourcing and supply chains? In early 2020, "buy local" shifted from an ethical appeal to a life-and-death consideration. I quickly realized that I wasn't the only one with vegetable seed and fertilizer on my mind.

Despite the social distancing and "shelter-in-place" mandates of the year, business boomed for garden stores and seed companies as people rushed to plant gardens.[2]

More broadly, most governments and many corporations grew wary of global trade. They hustled to guard their supplies and limit international commerce in the midst of the pandemic, and officials from China to Canada to Mexico began reassessing their capacity for national self-sufficiency. Fox News commentators suggested that sending face masks or ventilators outside the country, as some US companies did, should constitute a kind of treason. *The Economist* fretted about an era of globalization "in trouble" and "unwound." A headline from an Italian newspaper tersely declared that globalization was "dead."[3] Such pronouncements represent a dramatic shift from the tone of most journalists and observers only a few decades earlier, when globalization was often assumed to be irreversible.

This book has endeavored to think through those early years, when the organizations at the center of this book dared to begin criticizing neoliberal trade reforms. Part I, "(In)visibilizing Empire: Ambivalent Nationalism and the Origins of Global Justice," begins in rural Mexico in the 1980s. In a moment when Global South countries found themselves submerged in oceans of debt, peasant/farmer organizations like UNORCA refused to let the rural working class take the blame. The bankers and experts wanted to replace farmers with factory farms and push the farmers to work in urban factories and create exportable goods. For UNORCA, maintaining fair prices for crops was both a way to save the farmers *and* a way to feed the people. The first two chapters help us understand how UNORCA was articulating an idea of food sovereignty as early as 1985, even though most observers associate that concept's origins with the mid-1990s. While notions of national sovereignty can lead to isolationist attitudes and ethno-national scapegoating, the language of food sovereignty in Mexico visibilized the imperial contours of the international food system. It created a pathway for UNORCA to become part of an emerging international peasant federation—Vía Campesina. With veteran farm leaders as well as a new group of women leaders, UNORCA went on to host the 1996 Vía Campesina meeting in the Mexican city of Tlaxcala.

That said, left-wing UNORCA leaders were wary of taking an uncritical stance on national sovereignty. The same could be said for a new union-community coalition in the United States—the Jobs with Justice coalition. In an era of rising conservatism and industrial competition from Asia, union progressives sometimes embraced a working-class Americanism and populism, but did so uneasily. Imbuing the working class with the credibility of morally exceptional communities and their industrious past could invisibilize US empire and reaffirmed a national history of triumph, struggle, and tradition that centered the experiences of white breadwinners. The coalition's Americanism, however, was ambivalent. It sought to use the moral weight of "Middle American" values to extend the economic rights historically proffered to breadwinner communities to social groups long denied them. Americanism proved to be an enduring—if contested—component of the US global justice movement in the 1990s.

Part II, "Racism and Global Justice in a Multicultural Age," further analyzes the workings of race, nation, and empire in grassroots global justice organizations but does so in the context of increasingly prominent notions of global multiculturalism. Chapter 4 introduces the third major organization of the book: the Popular Indigenous Council of Oaxaca—Ricardo Flores Magon. As a radical Indigenous alliance dedicated, like the nearby Zapatistas, to undoing neoliberal reforms like NAFTA, CIPO-RFM squared off with not only the harsh repression of the state government but also a kind of neoliberal multiculturalism. Critiquing the metaphor of the "coca-colonization" of globalization, the chapter suggests that the organization was confronted not so much with homogenization as with the Mexican state's brand of neoliberal multiculturalism, which sought control not by eliminating difference but by creating, defining, and patrolling it.

Chapters 5 and 6 take up activist-intellectual Elizabeth "Betita" Martínez's question, "Where was the color in Seattle?" The chapters argue that the whiteness of the 1999 Seattle World Trade Organization protests is partly evident in the framing of the problem of globalization in the first place. US progressives in predominantly white organizations in the 1990s developed an approach to neoliberal trade and investment reform that I call "color-blind anticorporatism." Color-blind anticorporate perspectives and strategies led them in conservative directions: they developed occasional affinities with racist and right-wing antiglobalization advocates and elaborating interpretations of globalization shaped by new languages of ambivalent Americanism. While the protests, including the progressives, undoubtedly helped to spotlight global inequality in new ways, they could also obscure questions of US empire in the process. Chapter 6 focuses on one variant of color-blind anticorporatism that I call global village multiculturalism. This political orientation, which arose among a number of influential progressive and radical antiglobalization activist-intellectuals, celebrated global and multinational difference and the relocalizing of economic systems, yet simultaneously demonstrated a deep concern about immigration from the Global South. The broad circulation of global village multiculturalism in the 1990s is partly why the events and activities of the 1999 Battle of Seattle largely invisibilized questions of immigration and immigrant workers' rights. It made questions of immigration seem unrelated to matters of trade and investment, despite the ways local immigrant workers in Seattle had experienced firsthand the displacements and abuse of globalization.

While Parts I and II examine the origins of three popular organizations and their role in developing global justice activity, Part III examines how they also helped build major international protests after 1999. Titled "Two Protests: Grounding Global Justice in the Twenty-First Century," Part III considers the development of grassroots globalism in mass demonstrations outside economic summits after 1999. Chapter 7 shows how the tensions around racism and nationalism in Seattle created a space for Jobs with Justice to "localize global justice" in the next major protests: those outside the International Monetary Fund and World Bank just months after the Battle of Seattle. Chapter 8 examines how UNORCA, with the Vía Campesina, mobilized thousands of its members to go to Cancún in September 2003 to protest the first meeting of the WTO in the Americas since Seattle. Chapter 9 discusses the grassroots globalism of CIPO-RFM as it prepared for the 2003 Cancún WTO protests and focuses on how their *Magonista* brand of autonomy and anarchism differed from the anarchism in the wider global justice movement. Both chapters show how these organizations envisioned alternative ways of being, even as they protested and said "no" to neoliberal capitalist reforms.

So did globalization really die in 2020? While the answer is "no," it was changing dramatically, and not in the ways that radicals from the 1990s would have wanted. The pandemic revealed how rich governments rushed to hunker down and hoard necessary items—like vaccines. That fortress mentality unveiled itself in the Global North after several years of increasingly frequent calls to halt globalization's growth.[4] The United Kingdom left the European Union. The Mexican president elected in 2016 had long been the face of the national opposition to neoliberalism, trade agreements, and NAFTA. Donald Trump was elected on an "America First" platform and vowed to undo NAFTA and other trade policies. In short, a combination of patriotic product hoarding and geopolitics changed the calculus of further liberalizing international trade and investment. Thomas Friedman gained a reputation in the 1990s by celebrating how the World Trade Organization would solidify peace and prosperity through a rule-based international trading system. Many readers were convinced by his "Golden Arches theory," which held that no two countries with McDonald's franchises would ever go to war.[5] Twenty-five years later, such a theory seems completely untenable. Russia had 842 McDonalds franchises but still invaded Ukraine in 2022, and the saber-rattling between China and the US continues to escalate despite the brisk sales of Big Macs in both countries.[6]

One of the goals of this book was to think through the ways both nationalism and multiculturalism shaped, and limited, the power of the movement in the late twentieth century. And the growing invocations to rein in globalization in recent years were articulated largely in terms of narrow nationalisms. Resisting globalization had increasingly become a right-wing issue in the US, driven by the xenophobia and racism of the Trumpian right. Their focus on a white republic victimized by China, by Global South immigrants, and by international financial bureaucrats and liberals draws from elements of right-wing antiglobalization sentiment developing at least since the 1980s.

As in previous years, the case for protecting US national sovereignty drew supporters from both the left and the right, even if the most prominent critics came from the right. A Republican senator, Josh Hawley, published a prominent op-ed in the *New York Times* in May 2020, arguing, as the headline stated, that "the WTO should be abolished."[7] Far from advancing new arguments, these conservatives rehashed the themes of the 1990s with a China-bashing so energized it recalled the 1890s. Branding "Chinese imperialism" as "the single greatest threat to American security in the twenty-first century," Hawley argued that "there is no going back to the world before Covid-19." And since that era's liberalized trade regime had so imperiled US sovereignty, "We shouldn't want to." The *Patriot Post* conservative news digest heralded Donald Trump's foresight in steering production out of China even "way back in August 2019 BC (Before Coronavirus)."[8] Senator Tom Cotton demanded that the US government limit visas to Chinese students. Not to be outdone, presumptive Democratic presidential nominee Joe Biden leveled his own brand of anti-China ire as polls showed the majority of US Americans favored a more aggressive policy against the country.[9]

Nationalist responses to trade and investment liberalization also surfaced during the recent negotiations over NAFTA, in both the US and Mexico. Claiming that the original deal symbolized the weak-kneed internationalism of past governments, Trump officials argued that the US could only be "made great again" by standing up to Mexico and Canada. In Mexico in late 2019, federal senators raised a last-minute cry of alarm: US "inspectors" would be allowed to ensure that Mexican work sites were meeting labor standards. For NAFTA opponents—who in this case were center/right opponents of the left-leaning president Andres Manuel López Obrador—the presence of US inspectors was a clear violation of national sovereignty. Late that evening, the presidential negotiating team cleared the air, at least enough for the revision to pass congressional muster: we would call them consultants, rather than "inspectors," and their teams would have the power only to offer guidelines, not to enforce policies, they said. The political leadership in Mexico continued to advocate a kind of left-leaning and populist brand of protecting Mexican sovereignty. Obrador could use it both to defend Mexico's oil supplies from international investors and to criticize a growing feminist movement as anti-Mexican and inauthentic, overly influenced by US and European women's movements.

If nothing else, the increasingly negative views of globalization that have developed in the last decade show that the organizations that helped create the global justice movements of the late twentieth century were on to something. Their efforts, and those of many others, threw into relief the profound limitations of the arguments against globalization today. They help us see the parochialism and presidentialism of presidentialism of López Obrador's nationalism, and the empty expediency of simply blaming China in the US. They illuminate today's approaches because these organizations struggled with many of the same questions, tensions, and assumptions that people today do: the opacity of complicated trade regulations, the ease of blaming interlopers and outsiders, and the dominance of conventional explanations, with their often white, middle-class, and US-centric assumptions.[10]

Yet if there are continuities between now and then, the ground has also dramatically shifted. Grassroots globalism emerged in the 1980s, but it transformed after 2003.[11] The Miami and Cancún protests were the last major protests of the era in the Americas. Much of the grassroots globalism in the US was redirected into opposing post-9/11 US militarism, and also into environmental justice activism and the Occupy Wall Street movement. In addition, organizers of color, including key leaders in Jobs with Justice, created an organization titled Grassroots Global Justice (GGJ) in 2005 to confront the exclusionary nature of global justice movements, particularly in relation to the World Social Forum. That process led in part to the US Social Fora, which were led by influential organizers, many of them tied to GGJ or its affiliates. In short, organizers of color in local organizations built on their own (often unrecognized) work during the 1990s to create their own kind of grassroots global justice movement, one more radical and more deeply antiracist and anti-imperialist than Jobs with Justice.[12]

In Mexico, things went downhill. The government's militaristic War on Drugs claimed nearly fifty thousand lives in a single presidential term, that of Felipe Calderón (2006–12). In the following administration, Enrique Peña Nieto (2012–18) pushed through the neoliberal structural reforms that the Mexican left had so successfully opposed, including a partial privatization of the country's petroleum and massive educational and fiscal reforms. CIPO-RFM and UNORCA struggled with internal factionalism, repression and threats against key leaders, and the mass migration of Mexican Indigenous peasants to the US. Most of the anarchist youth tied to CIPO-RFM left it; key organizers left both organizations, often moving to the US in search of work. The women's network formally split from UNORCA, and new leadership steered one faction into the right-wing National Action Party (Partido Acción Nacional, PAN).

When we think about the history of these movements, their local-level work created forms of social movement activity that would later become key parts of their global justice activism: the way they created networks, the alliances they forged, and the traditions of street protest and direct action that they practiced. While they often were guided by visions of global futures, their articulations of demands like jobs, food, and autonomy were often targeted to local, regional, and national authorities. They engaged with government entities and incrementalist politics in ways that differed from some radical activist groups, yet their base-building work could open doors to stronger alliances with global justice movements later. Despite the profound differences between the organizations discussed here, they all forged variations of what I have called grassroots globalism. That approach challenged both neoliberal reforms *and* global justice movements to take working-class and poor people's concerns into account.

So, in a world of global pandemic, Trumpian white power movements, and a struggling global justice movement, where do we go from here? Any advance in today's world must explore what happened the last time these issues came to the fore. And this study offers a few key lessons.

First, any global justice organizing with working-class communities in the US must make confronting racism and xenophobia a central component of its work. What would have happened in Seattle in 1999 (or in Washington, D.C., in 2000) if the global justice movement had included masses of immigrant workers? Or collaborations between Chinese and US workers to conceptualize a powerful and inclusive "globalization from below"? We will never know the answers to these kinds of questions, but the rise of the Trumpian right shows the danger of any brand of US nationalism, including those deemed progressive (chapters 3 and 5–7). The "Make America Great Again" narrative overlaps in dangerous ways with historical narratives evoked by some US progressives in the 1980s and 1990s. In Mexico, AMLO's selective celebration of the country's anti-imperial past (e.g., the 1938 oil expropriation) shows how antiglobalization discourses can be articulated for exclusionary ends.

Another concrete lesson we can draw from this involves disruptive tactics. All three organizations were at the height of their powers when they could lead many people into the street. CIPO-RFM's Women's Commission blockaded Oaxaca City toll booths in 1998. UNORCA organized three thousand peasants to arrive for the 2003 Cancún WTO protest. In addition, as indicated in chapter 7 with UNORCA, massive global justice protests inspired them to engage in more protests locally. Jobs with Justice galvanized more than fifty solidarity protests for a global rally in Prague in

2000, and thirty-two activists tied to the organization were arrested in protest of Interparking's treatment of its immigrant workforce. As other commentators have asserted, the massive, disruptive protests outside the summits of world financial institutions twenty years ago stained the reputation and diminished the influence of institutions that had withstood decades of criticism from development NGOs and Global South communities.[13]

A final lesson revolves around the importance of grassroots internationalist exchanges. The Kentucky-Sonora worker exchanges that Jobs with Justice organized in the 1990s and early 2000s changed US workers' approach of blaming Mexican workers for their communities' problems. Both UNORCA and CIPO-RFM members were strongly influenced by their opportunities to work, talk, and share food with South Korean farmers during the Cancún 2003 ministerial. UNORCA's work with US farmers in the early 1990s allowed Mexicans to see that US farmers themselves weren't the problem, the agribusiness model was. Juan Garcia, a longtime Jobs with Justice activist and community organizer in Rhode Island, stated in a recent meeting that Jobs with Justice's efforts to bring him to the World Social Forum in Brazil created one of the most important moments in his activist life.

If anything, the last several years have shown the world what happens when we don't have multiracial and influential working-class organizations proposing their own visions of globalization. Right-wing antiglobalizers have always been there, but have recently emerged with force, despite the efforts of today's global justice activists, who have taken aggressive stands on issues like climate injustice.[14] Perhaps the Covid-19 pandemic will usher in the most just and sustainable forms of self-sufficiency and self-determination. But that future remains clouded. Regardless, new and continuing work on the histories of globalization and global justice must be at the center to ensure that, as global justice activists have long proclaimed, "another world" is indeed "possible."[15]

Notes

INTRODUCTION

1. Jeffrey St. Clair and Alexander Cockburn, *Five Days That Shook the World* (London: New Left Review, 1999).
2. Thomas L. Friedman, *The Lexus and the Olive Tree* (New York: Farrar, Straus, Giroux, 1999). For analysis, see "Movements at the Millennium: Seattle+20," special issue of *Socialism and Democracy* 34, 1 (2020): 1–268.
3. All translations from Spanish in this book are by the author.
4. Jeremy Brecher, John Brown Childs, and Jill Cutler, eds., *Global Visions: Beyond the New World Order* (Boston: South End Press, 1993).
5. Jerry Mander and Edward Goldsmith, eds., *The Case against the Global Economy: And for a Turn toward the Local* (San Francisco: Sierra Club Books, 1996).
6. Richard Falk, "Resisting 'Globalisation-from-Above' through 'Globalisation-from-Below,'" *New Political Economy* 2, no. 1 (March 1, 1997): 17–24, https://doi.org/10.1080/13563469708406281; Jeremy Brecher, Tim Costello, and Brendan Smith, *Globalization from Below: The Power of Solidarity* (Cambridge, MA: South End Press, 2000).
7. John Keane, *Global Civil Society?* (Cambridge: Cambridge University Press, 2003).
8. Direct Action Network Against Corporate Globalization, information packet, ca. late 1999, Accession no. 5177-003, Box 1, Folder 1, WTO Seattle Collection, Special Collections, University of Washington Libraries.

9. Elizabeth "Betita" Martínez, "Where Was the Color in Seattle? Looking for Reasons Why the Great Battle Was So White," *Colorlines*, March 10, 2000.

10. Janet M. Conway, *Edges of Global Justice: The World Social Forum and Its "Others"* (New York: Routledge, 2013); David Featherstone, *Solidarity: Hidden Histories and Geographies of Internationalism* (London: Zed Books, 2012); and Arturo Escobar, *Territories of Difference: Place, Movements, Life, Redes* (Durham, NC: Duke University Press, 2008); See also Anti-Fascist Forum, ed., *My Enemy's Enemy: Essays on Globalization, Fascism and the Struggle against Capitalism* (Montreal: Kersplebedeb, 2003); and Kristine Wong, "The Showdown before Seattle: Race, Class, and the Framing of a Movement," in *The Battle of Seattle: The New Challenge to Capitalist Globalization* (New York: Soft Skull Press, 2002), 215–24.

11. Amory Starr, "How Can Anti-imperialism Not Be Anti-racist? The North American Anti-globalization Movement," *Journal of World-Systems Research* 10, no. 1 (2004): 119–51, https://doi.org/10.5195/jwsr.2004.308; Marc Edelman, "Peasant-Farmer Movements, Third World Peoples, and the Seattle Protests against the World Trade Organization, 1999," *Dialectical Anthropology* 33, no. 2 (2009): 109–28.

12. Brecher, Costello, and Smith, *Globalization from Below*, 104. While the authors seem to be arguing that whites should respect Blacks' own responses to globalization, their position also minimizes white racism and the overall power dynamics that Martínez's essay points to. Brecher et al. assert that the predominantly white movement hasn't become "closed off" to Blacks or people of color (104), which is partly what Martínez and others claimed. Blacks and other "groups will inevitably develop their own responses and follow their own itineraries" about global justice issues, they say (104). Another argument used to counter Martínez is that the global economy might have more violent effects on Blacks than racism itself (104). Readers could turn to Cedric Robinson or many others on how racism is an intrinsic part of global capitalism, not separate from it. See Cedric J. Robinson, *Black Marxism: The Making of the Black Radical Tradition* (London: Penguin UK, 2021). Finally, Brecher et al.'s book also obscures the place of immigrant rights or immigrant worker rights movements in "globalization from below." This book discusses that matter directly in chapter 6. On a similar note, while Jeffrey Juris notes the importance of how organizers of the 2007 US Social Forum worked to undo a legacy of whiteness in US global justice movements, he ultimately suggests that the increased presence of working-class organizations of color led to the "exclusion" of predominantly white groups. These efforts to shape the demographics of such events could threaten the tradition of "open space" at such events. Instead of adopting a zero-sum approach to the *amount* of participation (e.g., more of one group means less by the other), the author may have asked how the new diversity and new voices may have offered

new channels for historically overrepresented groups to change their *kind* of participation (e.g., to adopt roles as allies, partners, or listeners instead of protagonists.). The author fails to explain why the new racial and ethnic diversity didn't constitute a valuable source of exchange and translation (a "contact zone"), while an "open space" model with less diversity did. See Jeffrey Juris, "Spaces of Intentionality: Race, Class, and Horizontality at the United States Social Forum," *Mobilization: An International Quarterly* 13, no. 4 (December 1, 2008): 354, https://doi.org/10.17813/maiq.13.4.232j1557h7658813.

13. See the essays in Donatella Della Porta, ed., *Global Justice Movement: Cross-national and Transnational Perspectives* (London: Routledge, 2015). See also Marianne Maeckelbergh, *The Will of the Many: How the Alterglobalisation Movement Is Changing the Face of Democracy* (London: Pluto Press, 2009). Others elide the Global South origins of the movements. For examples, see Kevin Michael DeLuca and Jennifer Peeples, "From Public Sphere to Public Screen: Democracy, Activism, and the 'Violence' of Seattle," *Critical Studies in Media Communication* 19, no. 2 (June 2002): 125–51, https://doi.org/10.1080/07393180216559, and Andy Opel and Donnalyn Pompper, "Introduction: An Emerging Paradigm?," in *Representing Resistance: Media, Civil Disobedience, and the Global Justice Movement* (Westport, CT: Praeger, 2003), ix–xvii.

14. André C. Drainville and Saskia Sassen, *Contesting Globalization: Space and Place in the World Economy* (London: Taylor and Francis, 2004). Drainville, for example, discusses how global justice protests created place-based diversity, as did the 1894 London Dockworker strikes and (proslavery) Tammany Hall political machine of New York City in the nineteenth century. A better example might have been Marcus Garvey's Harlem in the 1920s, which became a springboard for the United Negro Improvement Association to build a worldwide network in forty countries. For more on Marcus Garvey and globalization, see Robbie Shilliam, "What about Marcus Garvey? Race and the Transformation of Sovereignty Debate," *Review of International Studies* 32, no. 3 (2006): 379–400.

15. Andy Opel, "Punishment before Prosecution: Pepper Spray as Postmodern Repression," in Opel and Pompper, *Representing Resistance*, 44–60. Opel asks why "there was so much support" for Rodney King, the victim of police brutality in L.A. in 1991, and not for "nonviolent environmental protesters" to whom police applied pepper spray at a 1996 protest.

16. Daniel Faber, "Building a Transnational Environmental Justice Movement: Obstacles and Opportunities in the Age of Globalization," in *Coalitions across Borders*, ed. Joe Bandy and Jackie Smith, People, Passions, and Power (Lanham, MD: Rowman and Littlefield, 2005), 43–70. Maecklenberg argued that the global justice movements were able to be so "diverse" because they "overcame ... identity politics." See Maeckelbergh, *Will of the Many*, 19–21.

17. Many of the numerous collections of essays about the movements make admirable efforts to cover the Global South. Yet that format limits the analysis of

any particular place or movement to a short chapter. See "The Revolt of the Globalized" in Eddie Yuen, Daniel Burton-Rose, and George N. Katsiaficas, eds., *The Battle of Seattle: The New Challenge to Capitalist Globalization* (New York: Soft Skull Press, 2001). Single-authored works do as well. See Amory Starr, *Global Revolt: A Guide to the Movements against Globalization* (London: Zed Books, 2005).

18. Anthony Bogues, *Black Heretics, Black Prophets: Radical Political Intellectuals* (New York: Routledge, 2003), 227n84. Bogues argues that the lack of attention in contemporary antiglobalization movements to the 1970s demands of neocolonial African nations reflects the long-standing neglect of African history and political thought. Prashad is one of the few to consider this history in relationship to global justice movements. See Vijay Prashad, *The Poorer Nations: A Possible History of the Global South* (London: Verso Books, 2013).

19. Adom Getachew, *Worldmaking after Empire: The Rise and Fall of Self-Determination* (Princeton, NJ: Princeton University Press, 2019). For more on Mexico's role, see Christy Thornton, *Revolution in Development: Mexico and the Governance of the Global Economy* (Oakland: University of California Press, 2021).

20. Laura Briggs, *Reproducing Empire: Race, Sex, Science, and U.S. Imperialism in Puerto Rico*, American Crossroads 11 (Berkeley: University of California Press, 2002); Amy Kaplan, *The Anarchy of Empire in the Making of U.S. Culture*, Convergences (Cambridge, MA: Harvard University Press, 2002); Fernando Ortiz, *Cuban Counterpoint: Tobacco and Sugar* (Durham, NC: Duke University Press, 1995); Nick Estes, *Our History Is the Future: Standing Rock versus the Dakota Access Pipeline, and the Long Tradition of Indigenous Resistance* (London: Verso Books, 2019); Edward W. Said, *Culture and Imperialism* (New York: Knopf Doubleday, 2012); Robin D. G. Kelley, *Freedom Dreams: The Black Radical Imagination* (Boston: Beacon Press, 2002); Greg Grandin, *Fordlandia: The Rise and Fall of Henry Ford's Forgotten Jungle City* (London: Picador, 2010). María Josefina Saldaña-Portillo, *The Revolutionary Imagination in the Americas and the Age of Development*, Latin America Otherwise (Durham, NC: Duke University Press, 2003); and Christina Heatherton, *Arise! Global Radicalism in the Era of the Mexican Revolution* (Oakland: University of California Press, 2022).

21. The discussion of how human rights discourses were "grounded" in Chiapas helped inspire my understanding of grounding in this work. See Shannon Speed, *Rights in Rebellion: Indigenous Struggle and Human Rights in Chiapas* (Stanford, CA: Stanford University Press, 2008). See also Manisha Desai, *Subaltern Movements in India: Gendered Geographies of Struggle against Neoliberal Development* (Abingdon, Oxon, New York, NY: Routledge, 2016).

22. Donatella Della Porta and Sidney G. Tarrow, eds., *Transnational Protest and Global Activism*, People, Passions, and Power (Lanham, MD: Rowman and Littlefield, 2005); Jackie Smith, *Social Movements for Global Democracy*, Themes in Global Social Change (Baltimore: Johns Hopkins University Press,

2008); David Graeber, *Direct Action: An Ethnography* (Edinburgh: AK Press, 2009); Heather Gautney, *Democracy, States, and the Struggle for Social Justice* (New York: Routledge, 2009); Jeffrey S. Juris, *Networking Futures: The Movements against Corporate Globalization* (Durham, NC: Duke University Press, 2008); Geoffrey Pleyers, *Alter-Globalization: Becoming Actors in a Global Age* (Cambridge: Polity, 2010); Catherine Eschle and Bice Maiguashca, *Making Feminist Sense of the Global Justice Movement* (Lanham, MD: Rowman and Littlefield, 2010); Lesley J. Wood, *Direct Action, Deliberation, and Diffusion: Collective Action after the WTO Protests in Seattle*, Cambridge Studies in Contentious Politics (Cambridge: University Press, 2012); Tamara Kay, *NAFTA and the Politics of Labor Transnationalism* (New York: Cambridge University Press, 2011); Susan A. Aaronson, *Taking Trade to the Streets: The Lost History of Public Efforts to Shape Globalization* (Ann Arbor: University of Michigan Press, 2001).

23. In doing so it joins an adjacent literature that analyzes some of the significant popular organizations that participated in the movement, although those works sometimes make their efforts with global justice movements a relatively small part of the story. Gwyn Williams, *Struggles for an Alternative Globalization: An Ethnography of Counterpower in Southern France* (Farnham: Ashgate, 2008); Escobar, *Territories of Difference*; Angus Lindsay Wright and Wendy Wolford, *To Inherit the Earth: The Landless Movement and the Struggle for a New Brazil* (Oakland, CA: Food First Books, 2003); Alex Khasnabish, *Zapatistas: Rebellion from the Grassroots to the Global* (London: Zed Books, 2013). See also Boaventura de Sousa Santos, *The Rise of the Global Left: The World Social Forum and Beyond* (London: Zed Books, 2006); Boaventura de Sousa Santos, *Another Production Is Possible: Beyond the Capitalist Canon*, Reinventing Social Emancipation 2 (London: Verso, 2006); Guiomar Rovira, *Zapatistas sin fronteras: Las redes de solidaridad con Chiapas y el altermundismo* (Mexico City: Ediciones Era, 2009); Timothy A. Wise, Hilda Salazar, and Laura Carlsen, eds., *Confronting Globalization: Economic Integration and Popular Resistance in Mexico* (Bloomfield, CT: Kumarian Press, 2003); and Kara Zugman Dellacioppa, *This Bridge Called Zapatismo: Building Alternative Political Cultures in Mexico City, Los Angeles, and Beyond* (Lanham, MD: Lexington Books, 2009).

24. Paul Adler, *No Globalization without Representation: U.S. Activists and World Inequality* (Philadelphia: University of Pennsylvania Press, 2021); Michael Denning, *Culture in the Age of Three Worlds* (London: Verso, 2004). See also Steve Striffler, *Solidarity: Latin America and the US Left in the Era of Human Rights*, Wildcat Series (London: Pluto Press, 2019). Historian Christy Thornton is working on a history of institutional responses to the movements.

25. In doing so I am drawing on the work of Featherstone, *Solidarity*; Conway, *Edges of Global Justice*; Escobar, *Territories of Difference*; Prashad, *Poorer Nations*; Anne Garland Mahler, *From the Tricontinental to the Global South: Race, Radicalism, and Transnational Solidarity* (Durham, NC: Duke

University Press, 2018); and Nancy A. Naples and Manisha Desai, *Women's Activism and Globalization: Linking Local Struggles and Global Politics* (New York, NY: Routledge, 2002). See also contributions in Yuen, Burton-Rose, and Katsiaficas, *Battle of Seattle;* Santos, *Rise of the Global Left.* My interpretations of whiteness and racism in working-class movements have been highly influenced by Robin D. G. Kelley, *Race Rebels: Culture, Politics, and the Black Working Class* (New York: Free Press, 1994); David R. Roediger, *Towards the Abolition of Whiteness: Essays on Race, Politics, and Working Class History* (London: Verso, 1994).

26. The US-based organization Jobs with Justice frequently used this slogan in the early 2000s. See Part III of this book for more.

27. In this regard and others I distinguish grassroots globalism from "grassroots globalization," a concept mainly about nongovernmental organizations that "speak for the poor," rather than popular organizations based in working-class and disenfranchised communities. See Arjun Appadurai, "Grassroots Globalization and the Research Imagination," *Public Culture* 12, no. 1 (January 1, 2000): 18, https://doi.org/10.1215/08992363-12-1-1.

28. My analysis of nationalism here draws from many sources, but in particular from J. Kehaulani Kauanui, *Paradoxes of Hawaiian Sovereignty: Land, Sex, and the Colonial Politics of State Nationalism* (Durham, NC: Duke University Press, 2018); Natividad Gutiérrez Chong, *Women, Ethnicity and Nationalisms in Latin America* (New York: Routledge, 2016); M. Jacqui Alexander and Chandra Talpade Mohanty, *Feminist Genealogies, Colonial Legacies, Democratic Futures* (New York: Routledge, 2013); Claudio Lomnitz-Adler, *Deep Mexico, Silent Mexico: An Anthropology of Nationalism,* Public Worlds 9 (Minneapolis: University of Minnesota Press, 2001). I have been influenced as well by debates about nationhood in national liberation struggles, particularly in Puerto Rico. See Frantz Fanon, *The Wretched of the Earth* (New York: Grove Press, 1968); Andrés Torres and José Emiliano Velázquez, *The Puerto Rican Movement: Voices from the Diaspora* (Philadelphia: Temple University Press, 1998); Jose Soler, "Jose Soler: A Life Working at the Intersections of Nationalism, Internationalism, and Working-Class Radicalism. An Interview with Eric Larson," *Radical History Review,* no. 128 (May 2017): 62–76.

29. Scholars and activists generally cite that meeting as the origin point of the concept of food sovereignty.

30. Martínez, "Where Was the Color." My analysis of color-blind anticorporatism draws on the work of several theorists of race and racism: David R. Roediger, *Colored White: Transcending the Racial Past* (Berkeley: University of California Press, 2003); Roediger, *Towards the Abolition of Whiteness;* Kelley, *Race Rebels;* Eduardo Bonilla-Silva, *Racism without Racists: Color-Blind Racism and the Persistence of Racial Inequality in America,* 4th ed. (Lanham, MD: Rowman and Littlefield, 2014).

31. Luis Fernandez has analyzed the policing of these protests. See Luis Fernandez, *Policing Dissent: Social Control and the Anti-globalization Movement,*

Critical Issues in Crime and Society (New Brunswick, NJ: Rutgers University Press, 2008).

1. FOOD SOVEREIGNTY

1. Edelman et al, for instance, states that the "canonical account" pinpoints the term's origins in the efforts of Vía Campesina in 1996. See Marc Edelman, "Food Sovereignty: Forgotten Genealogies and Future Regulatory Challenges," *Journal of Peasant Studies* 41, no. 6 (November 2, 2014): 961, https://doi.org/10.1080/03066150.2013.876998.

2. This chapter builds on the work of Marc Edelman, who first traced the origins of the term *food sovereignty* (*soberanía alimentaria*) to Mexican government circles in the 1980s. See Edelman, "Food Sovereignty." Contemporary observers of Mexican food policy also noted the government's change in language. See James E. Austin and Gustavo Esteva, "SAM Is Dead—Long Live SAM: Birth, Death and Reincarnation in Mexican Food Policy," *Food Policy* 10, no. 2 (May 1, 1985): 123–36, https://doi.org/10.1016/0306-9192(85)90005-3, and John Richard Heath, "El Programa Nacional de Alimentación y la crisis de alimentos," *Revista Mexicana de Sociología* 47, no. 3 (1985): 115–35, https://doi.org/10.2307/3540495. See also Cassio Luiselli Fernández, *Agricultura y alimentación en México: Evolución desempeño y perspectivas* (Mexico City: Siglo XXI Editores, 2019). The chapter also builds on the work of Lucas Henrique Pinto, who has discussed how UNORCA articulated food sovereignty in the 1980s. See Lucas Henrique Pinto, "El surgimiento de la UNORCA y el debate sobre la autonomía campesina: Breve análisis de la trayectoria de construcción del concepto de soberanía alimentaria en México," *Estudios Rurales* 8, no. 14 (2018): 120–52. Edelman also notes that peasant organizations in Costa Rica in the 1980s used the term. See Marc Edelman, *Peasants against Globalization: Rural Social Movements in Costa Rica* (Stanford, CA: Stanford University Press, 1999).

3. C. Clare Hinrichs, "The Practice and Politics of Food System Localization," in "International Perspectives on Alternative Agro-Food Networks: Quality, Embeddedness, Bio-Politics," ed. David Goodman, special issue, *Journal of Rural Studies* 19, no. 1 (January 1, 2003): 33–45, https://doi.org/10.1016/S0743-0167(02)00040-2; P. Allen, "Realizing Justice in Local Food Systems," *Cambridge Journal of Regions, Economy and Society* 3, no. 2 (July 1, 2010): 295–308, https://doi.org/10.1093/cjres/rsq015. The *defensive localism* term is from Allen. See also Amy Trauger, "Toward a Political Geography of Food Sovereignty: Transforming Territory, Exchange and Power in the Liberal Sovereign State," *Journal of Peasant Studies* 41, no. 6 (November 2, 2014): 1131–52, https://doi.org/10.1080/03066150.2014.937339.

4. For a critique, see Joanne Barker, *Sovereignty Matters: Locations of Contestation and Possibility in Indigenous Struggles for Self-Determination* (Lincoln: University of Nebraska Press, 2005).

5. In contrast, proponents of "Indigenous food sovereignty" have attempted to shift sovereignty away from Western notions of dominant control to ideas of sovereignty that emphasize restoration, ecology, and Indigenous self-determination. See Kyle Powys Whyte, "Indigenous Food Sovereignty, Renewal, and US Settler Colonialism," in *The Routledge Handbook of Food Ethics*, ed. Mary Rawlinson and Caleb Ward (London: Routledge, 2016), 354–65. For critical perspectives on exclusionary forms of food sovereignty, see T. L. Pendergrast et al., "Introduction to the Symposium: Rethinking Food System Transformation—Food Sovereignty, Agroecology, Food Justice, Community Action and Scholarship," *Agriculture and Human Values* 36, no. 4 (December 1, 2019): 819–23, https://doi.org/10.1007/s10460-019-09952-z; Alison Hope Alkon and Teresa Marie Mares, "Food Sovereignty in US Food Movements: Radical Visions and Neoliberal Constraints," *Agriculture and Human Values* 29, no. 3 (September 1, 2012): 347–59, https://doi.org/10.1007/s10460-012-9356-z; Alison Hope Alkon and Christie Grace McCullen, "Whiteness and Farmers Markets: Performances, Perpetuations . . . Contestations?," *Antipode* 43, no. 4 (September 2011): 937–59, https://doi.org/10.1111/j.1467-8330.2010.00818.x; Julie Guthman, "'If They Only Knew': Color Blindness and Universalism in California Alternative Food Institutions," *Professional Geographer* 60, no. 3 (August 2008): 387–97, https://doi.org/10.1080/00330120802013679; Allen, "Realizing Justice"; Kenneth MacDonald, "The Morality of Cheese: A Paradox of Defensive Localism in a Transnational Cultural Economy," *Geoforum* 44 (January 31, 2013), https://doi.org/10.1016/j.geoforum.2012.03.011.

6. Susan M. Gauss, "The Politics of Economic Nationalism in Postrevolutionary Mexico," *History Compass* 4, no. 3 (2006): 567–77, https://doi.org/10.1111/j.1478-0542.2006.00326.x. Gauss shows how mid-twentieth-century protectionists and liberalizing industrialists *both* promoted their plans in the language of protecting the economic sovereignty of the nation.

7. Leopoldo Solís M., *La realidad económica mexicana: Retrovisión y perspectivas*, El Mundo del hombre. Economía y demografía (Mexico City: Siglo Veintiuno Editores, 1970), 114–16. Yet the Mexican government routinely expressed a popular anti-Americanism even as it catered to US business and foreign investment. Julio Moreno, *Yankee Don't Go Home! Mexican Nationalism, American Business Culture, and the Shaping of Modern Mexico, 1920-1950*, The Luther Hartwell Hodges Series on Business, Society, and the State (Chapel Hill: University of North Carolina Press, 2003).

8. One of the outliers in this was Mexican president Gustavo Díaz Ordaz (1964-70), who argued that the country should save "millions of pesos" and import basic grains rather than paying for their production in Mexico. See

Gustavo Díaz Ordaz, "Primer informe de gobierno del Presidente Gustavo Díaz Ordaz," *El Día*, September 2, 1965.

9. The Spanish term was *autosuficiencia alimentaria*. The term for "food sovereignty" is *soberanía alimentaria*.

10. Jonathan Fox, *The Politics of Food in Mexico: State Power and Social Mobilization*, Food Systems and Agrarian Change (Ithaca, NY: Cornell University Press, 1993). Various scholars have noted how keeping urban food prices low was also a strategy of keeping urban working-class wages low. See David Barkin, Rosemary L. Batt, and Billie R. DeWalt, *Alimentos vs. forrajes: La sustitución entre granos a escala mundial* (Mexico City: Siglo XXI, 1991). For a history of government intervention in food and agriculture, as well as of official uses of the idea of food self-sufficiency, see Enrique Ochoa, *Feeding Mexico: The Political Uses of Food since 1910* (Wilmington, DE: Rowman and Littlefield, 2000). Thanks to Luis Hernández Navarro for assistance on this topic.

11. The president felt confidence in asserting Mexico's political independence given its economic strength, which was driven by high oil prices. See Fox, *Politics of Food*, 66–68.

12. Fox, *Politics of Food*, 66–68, 73. The decision was likely made for a variety of reasons, including to seek stability for the nation and avoid discontent in the countryside, all the while restoring Mexico's self-conception as revolutionary and powerful. See Fox, *Politics of Food*, 63n46, for more.

13. Fox, *Politics of Food*, 66–67, also 72n61.

14. As Solís and others have argued, a focus on supporting the peasantry in the 1930s quickly changed to a focus on industrialization, with low agricultural wages and prices designed to subsidize urban industrial growth. Leopoldo Solís M., *Alternativas para el desarrollo*, Cuadernos de Joaquín Mortiz (Mexico City: Editorial J. Mortiz, 1980).

15. As de la Madrid identified, it was one of two main goals of his food policy. See Alejandra Lajous, *Las razones y las obras: Gobierno de Miguel de La Madrid; Crónica del Sexenio, 1982–1988, Sexto año* (Mexico City: Fondo Cultura Económica, 1988), 360.

16. For more, see B. Suárez and F. Pérez-Gil, eds., "La modernización del campo y la alimentación: Un recuento de los últimos años," in *Sector agropecuario y alternativas comunitarias de seguridad alimentaria y nutrición en México*, ed. L. M. Espinoza (Mexico City: UAM/CECIPROC/INNSZ/Plaza y Valdés, 1999).

17. For de la Madrid, "Under the concept of food sovereignty, the nation retrieves and retains exclusive control of decisions regarding the satisfaction of the population's basic food needs." Miguel de la Madrid Hurtado, introduction to "Summary Description of PRONAL" (October 17, 1983), in chap. 15 of *Food Policy in Mexico: The Search for Self-Sufficiency*, ed. James E. Austin and Gustavo Esteva (Ithaca, NY: Cornell University Press, 1987), 316. John Heath has argued

that the lofty rhetoric of sovereignty of PRONAL never matched the Mexican government's implementation of the program and that the "principal restrictions" on fully developing the program were the terms established with the International Monetary Fund. See Heath, "Programa Nacional de Alimentación," 115. For more, see Austin and Esteva, *Food Policy in Mexico*. De la Madrid, as minister of planning in the López Portillo administration, had seen the growth of the SAM as a potential bureaucratic threat to his own agency. See Fox, *Politics of Food*, 60–70.

18. *Food independence*, as noted by the agricultural commissioner of the General Accounting Office of the Federation, was a term being used to replace *food self-sufficiency*. It meant finding ways to produce tortillas, even if the country was not self-sufficient in corn (e.g., by replacing corn with sorghum or amaranth). Ramón Fernández González, "Posibilidades para la producción de alimentos en México," in *Por la soberanía alimentaria: Enfoques y perspectivas*, ed. Julian Rodríguez Adame (Mexico City: Centro de Estudios Históricos del Agrarismo en México, 1984), 25–37, 31. This book stemmed from a symposium "For Food Sovereignty" and generally explored food in the context of hunger in both Mexico and the world, and the needs of the population projected to the year 2000.

19. Antonio Tenorio Adame, opening address, February 27, 1984, Mexico City, in Rodríguez Adame, *Por la soberanía alimentaria*, 4.

20. This 1988 collection of essays on subsidized food and food storage in Mexico was another key site of the administration's articulation of food sovereignty. Raúl Salinas de Gotarí, *Diconsa en la modernización comercial y la regulación del abasto popular* (Mexico City: Instituto Nacional de Administración Pública, 1988).

21. Luis Meneses, telephone interview with the author, December 19, 2017.

22. Barry Carr and Martha Tappan, "El Partido Comunista y la movilización agraria en La Laguna, 1920–1940: ¿Una alianza obrero-campesina?," *Revista Mexicana de Sociología* 51, no. 2 (June 1989): 115–49; Alan Knight, "Cardenismo: Juggernaut or Jalopy?," *Journal of Latin American Studies* 26, no. 1 (February 1994): 73–107. For more on the troubled, state-led efforts to collectivize ejidos in the 1970s, see Ricardo Gamboa Ramírez et al., *Historia de la cuestión agraria mexicana* (Mexico City: Siglo Veintiuno Editores; Centro de Estudios Históricos del Agrarismo en México, 1988), 332–40.

23. Gerardo Otero, "The New Agrarian Movement: Self-Managed, Democratic Production," *Latin American Perspectives* 16, no. 4 (1989): 28–59.

24. See Jonathan Fox and Gustavo Gordillo, "Between State and Market: The Campesinos' Quest for Autonomy," in *Mexico's Alternative Political Futures*, ed. Wayne A. Cornelius, Judith Gentleman, and Peter H. Smith, Monograph Series 30 (La Jolla: Center for U.S.-Mexican Studies, University of California, San Diego, 1989), 131–72; and Otero, "New Agrarian Movement."

25. To be clear, many peasant organizations continued to fight for land in the 1980s and after, including the groups that would ultimately coalesce to create the Zapatista Army of National Liberation (EZLN). See Marco Estrada Saavedra, *La comunidad armada rebelde y el EZLN: Un estudio histórico y sociológico sobre las bases de apoyo zapatistas en las cañadas tojolabales de la selva lacandona (1930-2005)* (Mexico City: El Colegio de México, 2016); Neil Harvey, *The Chiapas Rebellion: The Struggle for Land and Democracy* (Durham, NC: Duke University Press, 1998). For more on appropriating the productive process, see Armando Bartra, "Pros, contras y asegunes de la apropiación del proceso productivo: Notas sobre las organizaciones rurales de productores," in *Los nuevos sujetos del desarrollo rural*, ed. Armando Bartra, Cuadernos Desarrollo de Base 2 (Mexico City: ADN Editores, 1991), 3-22, cited in Jonathan Fox, "Political Change in Mexico's New Peasant Economy," in *The Politics of Economic Restructuring in Mexico: State-Society Relations and Regime Change in Mexico*, ed. Maria Lorena Cook, Kevin J. Middlebrook, and Juan Molinar Horcasitas (San Diego: Center for U.S.-Mexican Studies, University of California, San Diego, 1994), 243-76. Note that improving the productivity of ejidos has often been a politically safer claim for Mexican politicians than creating new ejidos, which requires redistributing privately held land. For an example, see Tore C. Olsson, *Agrarian Crossings: Reformers and the Remaking of the US and Mexican Countryside* (Princeton, NJ: Princeton University Press, 2020), 133-35.

26. Meneses, telephone interview, December 19, 2017.

27. Nidia Hidalgo Celarié, Verónica Vázquez García, and Emma Zapata Martelo, "Experiencias de crédito y ahorro entre mujeres: El caso de la Sociedad de Solidaridad Social (SSS) Susana Sawyer de Álamos, Sonora," in *Antropología de la deuda: Crédito, ahorro, fiado y prestado en las finanzas cotidianas*, ed. Magdalena Villareal (Mexico City: Editorial Miguel Ángel Porrúa, 2004), 233-56.

28. Various organizations, "Acuerdos sobre el Encuentro sobre Crédito y Aseguramento y Precios de Garantía Celebrado en el Ejido de Estanzuela de Romero, Municipio de Jerécuaro, Guanajuato, 10 y 11 de Abril de 1983," in *UNORCA: Documentos para la historia*, comp. Nuria Costa (Mexico City: Costa-Amic Editores, 1989), 82. For more on UNORCA history, see Fox, "Political Change."

29. Neil Harvey, *The New Agrarian Movement in Mexico, 1979-1990*, University of London, Institute of Latin American Studies, Research Paper 23 (London: Institute of Latin American Studies, 1990), 26.

30. Costa, *UNORCA*; UNORCA, "Convenio de concertación propuesto por UNORCA al gobierno federal," in Costa, *UNORCA*, 102. As Hernández shows, this demand was one of the six fundamental tenets of its 1985 proposal for an agreement with the government, which was discussed at the organization's first full meeting, September 27-29, 1985. The meeting was partly about the emergency response to the catastrophic earthquake. UNORCA also argued that the

ejido and the Indigenous community were central to food sovereignty at the "Defense of the Ejido Forum" in 1985. Meneses quote about food sovereignty from Meneses, telephone interview, December 19, 2017.

31. Luis Meneses, interview with the author, May 14, 2018, Mexico City.

32. Meneses, telephone interview, December 19, 2017. Similarly, in a 1990 commentary, journalist Iván Restrepo urged for food sovereignty to be understood not only as "reaching the sufficient volume of foodstuffs to satisfy national needs" but as "rais[ing] the well-being" of rural people, particularly those who found themselves in extreme poverty and nutritionally deficient—a population whose numbers had increased in the 1980s. Iván Restrepo, "La alimentación de los mexicanos," *La Jornada*, September 24, 1990, sec. El País, 4.

33. Harvey, *New Agrarian Movement*. See also Gustavo Esteva, "El desastre agrícola: Adiós al México imaginario," *Comercio Exterior* 38, no. 8 (August 1988): 663. Yet agriculture did better than much of the crisis economy until 1986. The administration established wage ceilings, limiting people's ability to buy food. It limited CONASUPO (Compañía Nacional de Subsistencias Populares / National Company for Subsidies for the Population) substantially. It dramatically cut social spending—which could be used for agricultural technical instruction, insurance programs, etc.—and sought out foreign direct investment to make up for the gap. See Marilyn Gates, *In Default: Peasants, the Debt Crisis, and the Agricultural Challenge in Mexico* (London: Routledge, 1993), 46–49. Many of the promises of food sovereignty in PRONAL and government rhetoric were contradicted or simply unfulfilled in practice, as federal money across the board was slashed. Fox, *Politics of Food*.

34. Cuauhtemoc Cárdenas, "1988 Plataforma Común del Frente Democrático Nacional," Jalapa, Veracruz, January 12, 1988, www.memoriapoliticademexico.org/Textos/7CRumbo/1988-FDN.html. As Jonathan Fox suggested, hunger and malnourishment "undermine[d] the legitimacy of what [was] officially called the "institutionalized revolution" of the PRI. Dependence on food imports was seen to "compromise national sovereignty." For Fox, "The class issue of hunger intersects with the nationalist question of sovereignty," so food "reflects and refracts the most basic tensions" of Mexico. Fox, *Politics of Food*, 4.

35. Miguel Armando López Leyva, *La encrucijada: Entre la protesta social y la participación electoral (1988)* (Mexico City: Plaza y Valdés, 2007), 75–76 and 88–95.

36. López Leyva, *Encrucijada*, 95. One Trotskyist group labeled Cárdenas's vision of sovereignty as part of a "bourgeois-populist nationalism" that was about cross-class collaboration, rather than class warfare. "México: Erupción sobre elecciones," *Spartacist*, October 1988, Español edition, 2.

37. Indeed, most scholars and activists writing from the left about Mexico in the 1980s use *food self-sufficiency* or *food autonomy* (*autonomía alimentaria*) rather than *food sovereignty* (*soberanía alimentaria*). To my knowledge the

same is true of Pablo Gonzalez Casanova and Héctor Aguilar Camín. A 1989 case study of Mexico (assisted by Fernando Rello, a Marxist scholar from the Universidad Nacional Autónoma de México, who had written about transnationals) noted the key importance of food sovereignty and the use of self-sufficiency in basic grains as a basis for food sovereignty. See Inter-American Institute for Cooperation on Agriculture, *Plan de acción conjunta para la reactivación agropecuaria en América Latina: El caso de México* (Coronado, Costa Rica: Inter-American Institute for Cooperation on Agriculture, 1989).

38. UNORCA, "Manifiesto a la nación" [ca. 1988], in Costa, *UNORCA*, 340–45.

39. UNORCA, "Manifiesto a la nación," 342.

40. UNORCA, "Manifiesto a la nación," 345.

41. UNORCA, "A los campesinos del mundo. A la opinión pública" [ca. 1988], in Costa, *UNORCA*, 350. This public letter indicated that, as new statistics emerged about how currency devaluation was leading to declining nutritional standards for Mexicans, food sovereignty wasn't just about the peasants' interests—it was also in the national interest. The progressive wings of UNORCA, and Meneses, were the real home of the food sovereignty discourse. The term doesn't appear at all in the work of another UNORCA leader, Gustavo Gordillo. Gustavo Gordillo, *Campesinos al asalto del cielo: Una reforma agraria con autonomía*, Economía y Demografía (Mexico City: Siglo Veintiuno Editores, 1988).

42. The transnational corporation had recently become an object of study and critique in Latin American Marxism and dependency theory. Chilean academic Osvaldo Sunkel wrote important works, including "Capitalismo transnacional y desintegración nacional en América Latina," *Estudios Internacionales* 4, no. 16 (March 1971): 3–61. Other scholars discussed the "transnational turn"; they sought to distinguish between the (new) transnational capitalism and the (old) "international" capitalism. See Martin Godfrey and Steven Langdon, "¿Socios en el desarrollo? La tesis de la transnacionalización en el contexto Keniano," *Estudios Internacionales* 11, no. 44 (December 1978): 45–70. The question of the Green Revolution had been discussed among the Mexican left by David Barkin and Blanca Suárez San Román, who wrote about Green Revolution technological packets in *El fin de la autosuficiencia alimentaria* (Mexico City: Centro de Ecodesarrollo, 1985). Barkin's Centro de Ecodesarrollo in Mexico and the Instituto Latinamericano de Estudios Transnacionales published important work on these themes in the 1970s. Susan George's work had been translated in some cases to Spanish as well and circulated among the Mexican left. For a more popular work by a famous Latin American writer, see Julio Cortázar, *Fantomas contra los vampiros multinacionales: Una utopia realizable* (Mexico City: Excelsior, 1975). See also the work of Raúl Prebisch on dependency.

43. The debt is a major theme of the 1988 Rural Forum that Meneses participated in.

44. Luis Meneses, "Autonomía organizativa y soberanía alimentaria," in *Primer Foro Nacional sobre Reforma Rural en México*, ed. Herminio Baltazar C. (Mexico City: Universidad Autónoma de Chapingo, 1989), 161. Silver and Arrighi argue that after World War II, the US, in order to secure global hegemony, offered "national self-determination" (e.g., juridical sovereignty) and "development" packages oriented to increase production and growth through First World technological practices. They did this instead of offering a welfare state society built on middle-class mass consumption and full employment. See Beverly J. Silver and Giovanni Arrighi, "Workers North and South," *Socialist Register* 37 (2001): 55, https://socialistregister.com/index.php/srv/article/view/5755.

45. Elena Gallegos and Arturo García, "Posible cumbre en Mexico sobre la integración de AL," *La Jornada*, September 30, 1990, sec. El Pais; Notimex, "Incluir servicios en la Ronda Uruguay, pedirá Mexico," *La Jornada*, September 23, 1990, sec. Economía; Salvador Guerrero Chiprés, "Buscará México avanzar hacia una zona de libre comercio en AL," *La Jornada*, September 28, 1990, sec. Economía.

46. UNORCA, *Una propuesta para el movimiento campesino* (Mexico City: Fundación Friedrich Ebert, Representación en México, 1992). Independent advisers such as Ana de Ita Rubio and Luis Hernández Navarro were also part of the authorship team. The book was one of the few of this foundation's series called "Work Documents" that dealt with agriculture; most concerned challenges to manufacturing and energy sectors.

47. Versions of this view also can be found in a manifesto by a UNORCA affiliate organization in the southern state of Guerrero. See Coalición de Ejidos de la Costa Grande de Guerrero, "La Coalición de Ejidos de la Costa Grande de Guerrero frente a los nuevos retos del siglo XXI," *La Jornada*, August 10, 1991.

48. Unlike the "Manifiesto a la nación" published four years earlier, the proposal does not frame the quest for food sovereignty as explicitly tied to the legacy of the Mexican Revolution, even if defending the ejido is central to the work. Several scholars have shown how Mexican nationalism fundamentally changed during these years. See Lynn Stephen, *Zapata Lives! Histories and Cultural Politics in Southern Mexico* (Berkeley: University of California Press, 2002).

49. UNORCA, *Propuesta*, 10–17.

50. UNORCA, *Propuesta*, 15.

51. Or, UNORCA argued, they hoped to increase production to ensure the steady supply of profit from marketing and distribution, the part of the supply chain that was the most profitable and that they already controlled. See UNORCA, *Propuesta*, 9.

52. UNORCA proposed to protect against "dependence on imports" by imposing tariffs and import controls, particularly on corn, beans, and other crops, for which Mexico should strive for "food self-sufficiency." UNORCA, *Propuesta*, 60–70, esp. 63. For UNORCA, globalization needed to be tied to a vision of "com-

plete and sustainable rural development" (desarrollo rural integral y sustentable), the foundation of its vision of national development.

53. Meneses, interview, May 14, 2018.

2. AMBIVALENT NATIONALISM

1. Vía Campesina and Conferencia Internacional de la Vía Campesina, *La Vía Campesina: Memoria de la II Conferencia Internacional de la Vía Campesina, Tlaxcala, Mexico, 18 al 21 de abril de 1996* (Brussels: Ediciones NCOS, 1996). Peasants from sixty-nine organizations and thirty-seven countries attended.

2. One of the themes "we most . . . defended" there, he said, "was food sovereignty, based in what we called the appropriation of the production process of the small producers." Luis Meneses, telephone interview with the author, December 1, 2017.

3. This passage is a paraphrase of the description of NAFTA's effects by a leading Mexican agricultural critic, Armando Bartra. See Armando Bartra, "Los nuevos campesinos," in *El impacto social de las políticas de ajuste en el campo mexicano* (Mexico City: Instituto Latinoamericano de Estudios Transnacionales, 1995), 206.

4. For more on Mexico's corn policy since NAFTA, see Jonathan Fox and Libby Haight, eds., *Subsidizing Inequality: Mexican Corn Policy since NAFTA* (Washington, DC: Woodrow Wilson International Center for Scholars, 2010), 1–181.

5. Carlos Salinas de Gotarí, *Plan nacional de desarrollo, 1989–1994* (Mexico City: Secretaría de Programación y Presupuesto, 1989), 12.

6. "La inversión extranjera no menoscaba la soberanía," *La Jornada*, September 30, 1990, sec. Economía; "Grave crisis en el sector agropecuario en AL," *La Jornada*, September 26, 1990, sec. Economía.

7. Luis Hernández, "Respuestas campesinas en la época del neoliberalismo," *El Cotidiano*, no. 39 (1991). quoted in Ana de Ita, "PROCEDE: A Failed Programme to Reduce Poverty and Inequalities in Mexico," WIDER Working Paper, July 2022, United Nations University, World Institute for Development Economics Research.

8. Meneses is credited with being one of the early initiators of cross-border (US/Mexico/Canada) dialogues after 1990, and he helped found the Center for Studies for Change in the Countryside (Centro de Estudios para el Cambio en el Campo Mexicano, CECCAM), which helped coordinate some of them. See Karen Lehman, "Farmer Organizations and Regional Integration in North America," in *Cross-border Dialogues: U.S.-Mexico Social Movement Networking*, ed. David Brooks and Jonathan Fox (San Diego: Center for U.S.-Mexican Studies, University of California, San Diego, 2002), 168–69. See also Annette Aurélie Desmarais,

La vía campesina: La globalización y el poder del campesinado (Madrid: Editorial Popular, 2007).

9. David Brooks and Jonathan Fox, "Movements across the Border: An Overview," in Brooks and Fox, *Cross-border Dialogues*, 44–45. The quotation is from Victor Suárez.

10. Salvador Mena Munguía and Mario Ramírez Martínez, eds., *Panorama de la agricultura en México* (Guadalajara: Editorial Universitaria and CUCBA, Universidad de Guadalajara, 2014). See contributions by Esperanza Fujigaki Cruz and Enrique Semo Calev.

11. Luis Hernández Navarro, "Doce tesis sobre el nuevo liderazgo campesino," in *Autonomía y nuevos sujetos sociales en el desarrollo rural*, by Julio Moguel, Carlota Botey, and Luis Hernández Navarro (Mexico City: CEHAM; Siglo Veintiuno Editores, 1992), 49–81. For more on UNORCA's approach, see Fox and Gordillo, "Between State and Market."

12. In addition, for the influential *Linea Proletaria* current in Mexican Marxism, the crisis represented the need for a change of tactic, toward negotiation and away from confrontation. Harvey, *New Agrarian Movement*, 24–27. UNORCA leader Javier Gil remarked in 1989 that they had little choice. "Maybe we won't even figure in the picture that is Mexico in the year 2000. Maybe we will be overrun by the multinationals," he said. "But for that reason we have to act now. . . . We cannot wait and expect the State to intervene out of the goodness of its heart and protect us." Harvey, *New Agrarian Movement*, 8.

13. Hernández Navarro, "Doce tesis," 70–71.

14. Hernández Navarro, "Doce tesis," 70–71.

15. Alejandra Safa Barraza and Erna Mergruen Rentería, *Las mujeres campesinas se organizan* (Mexico City: UNORCA, 1993), 4. For a comparative discussion of how a Costa Rican peasant movement tried to transition "from protest to proposal," see Edelman, *Peasants against Globalization*, chap. 5.

16. Meneses, telephone interview, December 19, 2017. See also Guillermo Trejo, *Popular Movements in Autocracies: Religion, Repression, and Indigenous Collective Action in Mexico*, Cambridge Studies in Comparative Politics (New York: Cambridge University Press, 2012).

17. The term *central* signified "headquarters" or "main office" in Mexico. Organizations operated largely by political parties were often called *centrales*.

18. UNORCI, "Reglamento de la UNORCI que propone la Unión de Ejidos Lázaro Cárdenas, de Ahuacatlán, Nayarit," in Costa, *UNORCA*, 130. Some founding organizers proposed the name "UNORCI," the term *independent* replacing *autonomous*. The organization was to be "of masses, not of *cúpulas*" (131). To hold power in UNORCA, the bylaws stated, you had to be a peasant. The debate that was most divisive at the time was whether technicians should or could become leaders or whether they must be held distant from more authentic peasant representative leadership. Hernández Navarro, "Doce tesis," 66.

UNORCA's focus on the "regional" wasn't coincidental. It called for different development plans given the needs of different regions, including the poverty of the South and the wealth of the North, the distinct crops raised, and the differing eco-regions that farmers inhabited. It called for differentiated kinds of credits and subsidies. And its insistence on self-management granted an important role to regional peasant organizations, who would establish agreements with the federal government to tie production quotas (for farmers) to credits and subsidies. See UNORCA, *Propuesta*. For more on UNORCA history, see Jonathan A. Fox, "Democratic Rural Development: Leadership Accountability in Regional Peasant Organizations, Development and Change," *Development and Change* 23, no. 2 (April 1, 1992): 1–36.

19. Whereas the Coordinating Committee of the National Plan of Ayala (Coordinadora Nacional Plan de Ayala, CNPA) is concentrated mainly in the southern and central states in regions of high Indigenous population, UNORCA-affiliated groups tend to be concentrated in relatively more prosperous regions such as Comarca Lagunera in Durango and Coahuila, Sonora, Chihuahua, Nayarit, Guerrero, and the Bajio region of Jalisco and Guanajuato. UNORCA has a smaller presence in Sinaloa, Zacatecas, San Luis Potosí, Hidalgo, the State of Mexico, Puebla, Tlaxcala, Veracruz, Morelos, Michoacan, Oaxaca, Tabasco and Chiapas. See UNORCA, "Open Letter to H. Cámara de Diputados and Gabinete Agropecurario," in Costa, *UNORCA*, 356–57; Harvey, *New Agrarian Movement*, 45n45.

20. Erna Mergruen Rentería, interview with the author, June 5, 2018, Mexico City.

21. For example, some of its membership supported Salinas de Gotarí, though substantial numbers supported the insurgent candidate.

22. Hernández Navarro, "Doce tesis," 59.

23. UNORCA was beginning to see its proposal-based politics as a new form of engaged bargaining (*concertación*) between the government and peasant organizations. Salinas himself frequently trumpeted the importance of *concertación*.

24. Former UNORCA leader Gustavo Gordillo was central to this process. Some UNORCA affiliated leaders, like Hugo Andrés Araujo, were asked to be subsecretaries of agriculture under Salinas.

25. Bartra, "Nuevos campesinos," 23.

26. The CNPA and the National Coordinating Committee of Indigenous Peoples (Coordinadora Nacional de Pueblos Indígenas, CNPI) refused to enter the CAP. As quoted in Bernardino Mata G., "La autogestión campesina en el desarrollo rural," in *El sector agropecuario en el futuro de la economía mexicana*, ed. Juan Pablo Arroyo Ortiz (Mexico City: Fund. Friedrich Naumann, 1991), 170. UNORCA had an important seat on the CAP (Gil was cochair). They were willing to work with the CNC.

27. Hubert Carton Grammont, *Neoliberalismo y organización social en el campo mexicano* (Mexico City: Plaza y Valdes, 1996), 255.

28. The reform ultimately ended the Mexican government's commitment to (re)distribute land to small farmers, a key stipulation of the laws of the Mexican Revolution, and opened up the *ejido* and other lands to private investors, including corporations. See also Michael W. Foley, "Privatizing the Countryside: The Mexican Peasant Movement and Neoliberal Reform," *Latin American Perspectives* 22, no. 1 (1995): 67–68.

29. María Guadalupe Acevedo López, *Reestructuración económica y desarrollo en América Latina* (Mexico City: Siglo XXI, 2004).

30. UNORCA, *Propuesta*. The organization was disappointed in the final wording of the reform. The quotation is from Victor Suárez, interview with the author, January 5, 2018, Mexico City.

31. Grammont, *Neoliberalismo y organización social*, 255, 256.

32. Nancy Roman, interview with the author, June 8, 2018, Mexico City.

33. Hidalgo Celarié, Vázquez García, and Zapata Martelo, "Experiencias de crédito"; Roman, interview, June 8, 2018.

34. Safa Barraza and Mergruen Rentería, *Mujeres campesinas se organizan*, chap. 1.

35. Roman, interview, June 8, 2018. As in UNORCA in general, and most Mexican peasant organizations, leadership and coordination was distributed among experienced political and agricultural organizers (like Meneses), peasant producers, and technical specialists who helped carry out agricultural planning or accounting or assisted with the onerous and complicated management of government forms and agency visits. The work of Nancy Roman and others is one vantage point to better understand UNORCA's early grassroots globalism, including its moderation and incrementalism. Some radical voices in the peasant movement warned of how technical (agricultural or political) specialists could lead to the institutionalization or co-optation of the movement. See Hernández Navarro, "Doce tesis." In contrast, UNORCA's vision of peasant self-management and appropriation of the productive process—in a broader context of demanding food sovereignty—facilitated the recognition that leadership and coordination demanded technical skills that often only experienced organizers or college-educated staffers could provide. Even in UNORCA, though, establishing structures to limit the power of technical staff or the agronomists from government agencies or universities had always been a discussion. Technically, elected leaders of the organization were required to be peasant farmers.

36. Mergruen Rentería, interview, June 5, 2018. The first pamphlet was about commercialization of farm products.

37. Mergruen Rentería, interview, June 5, 2018; Roman, interview, June 8, 2018.

38. Ana de Ita was part of CECCAM.

39. Erna Mergruen Rentería, interview with the author, January 7, 2018, Mexico City.

40. Martha Romero, interview with the author, June 17, 2018. Romero was a member of the Women's Area.

41. Sponsoring women's productive projects connected their work to UNORCA's quest to appropriate the productive process and to galvanize peasant self-management (Romero, interview, June 17, 2018).

42. Roman, interview, June 8, 2018.

43. Luis Meneses, interview with the author, May 14, 2018, Mexico City.

44. Jesús Andrade, telephone interview with the author, December 21, 2019. See also Meneses, interview, May 14, 2018.

45. Meneses, interview, May 14, 2018. The Vía Campesina was formed in 1993.

46. Matilde Pérez U., "Acto de Vía Campesina: Pugnan productores por la soberanía en materia alimentaria," *La Jornada*, April 18, 1996, sec. El País.

47. Pérez U., "Acto de Vía Campesina."

48. Meneses, telephone interview, December 19, 2017.

49. Vía Campesina, *Proceedings from the II International Conference of the Vía Campesina, Tlaxcala, Mexico, April 18–21, 1996* (Brussels: NCOS Publications, 1996), 5. The Mexican organizations applauded there were UNORCA, CNPA, the Center for Independent Agricultural Workers and Peasants (Central Indepiendente de Obreros Agrícolas y Campesinos, CIOAC), and the Democratic Peasant Union (Unión Campesina Democrática, UCD).

50. Suárez, interview, January 5, 2018. His organization, the National Association of Campesino Marketing Organizations (Asociación Nacional de Empresas Comercializadoras de Productores del Campo, ANEC), also joined the Vía Campesina at that time.

51. Andrade, telephone interview, December 21, 2019; Roman, interview, June 8, 2018; Jaime Castillo, interview with the author, June 15, 2017.

52. Roman, interview, June 8, 2018.

53. Nettie Wiebe, "Women of La Via [sic] Campesina: Creating and Occupying the Spaces Which Are Our Right," in *Report: IV Women's Assembly of La Vía Campesina*, 7–11 (Harare, Zimbabwe: October 2014), https://viacampesina.org/en/wp-content/uploads/sites/2/2015/06/2015-06-06%20LVC%20women%20articulation%20report%20EN-rev1-c.pdf.

54. Vía Campesina, *Proceedings*.

55. Vía Campesina, *Proceedings*, 34–35.

56. Annette Aurélie Desmarais, "The International Women's Commission of La Vía Campesina," in *The Women, Gender, and Development Reader*, 2nd ed. (London: Zed Books, 2011). See also Vía Campesina, *Proceedings*, 35.

57. Wiebe, "Women of La Vía [*sic*] Campesina."

58. Vía Campesina, *Proceedings*; N. Wiebe, "Women of La Vía [*sic*] Campesina."

59. Meneses, interview, May 14, 2018.

60. Alan Knight, "Peasants into Patriots: Thoughts on the Making of the Mexican Nation," *Mexican Studies / Estudios Mexicanos* 10, no. 1 (1994): 135–61, https://doi.org/10.2307/1051969. Knight usefully breaks down some kinds of nationalist expression in Mexico and distinguishes economic nationalism from other types. He builds on other work showing Mexican nationalism to be particularly broad and powerful, at least compared to other countries in Latin America. For a study of Mexican ideas about the US in particular, see Stephen D. Morris, *Gringolandia: Mexican Identity and Perceptions of the United States*, Latin American Silhouettes (Lanham, MD: Rowman and Littlefield, 2005).

61. "Acta de Acuerdos del VII Encuentro Nacional Campesino Celebrado en la Ciudad de Cuetzalan, Puebla, los dias 30 y 31 de Marzo de 1985," in Costa, *UNORCA*, 144–49.

62. Romero, interview, June 17, 2018.

63. Meneses, interview, May 14, 2018; Knight, "Peasants into Patriots," 153. Knight shows how PRI candidates were equated with *gachupines*, or Spanish colonizers.

64. Meneses, telephone interview, December 19, 2017.

3. THE SPECTER OF US DECLINE

1. See Dana Frank, *Buy American: The Untold Story of Economic Nationalism* (Boston: Beacon, 1999); Leon Fink, "When Community Comes Home to Roost: The Southern Milltown as Lost Cause," *Journal of Social History* 40, 1 (Fall 2006): 119–45, https://doi.org/10.1353/jsh.2006.0079; Jefferson Cowie and Lauren Boehm, "Dead Man's Town: 'Born in the U.S.A.,' Social History, and Working-Class Identity," *American Quarterly* 58 (June 2006): 353–78; Jefferson Cowie, *Stayin' Alive: The 1970s and the Last Days of the Working Class* (New York: New Press, 2010); Robert Self, *All in the Family: The Realignment of American Democracy since the 1960s* (New York: Hill and Wang, 2012).

2. Members, staff, and officials from unions like the International Association of Machinists and Aerospace Workers (IAM), the United Mine Workers of America (UMWA), the Service Employees International Union (SEIU), the Association of Flight Attendants (AFA), and the American Federation of State, County, and Municipal Employees (AFSCME) most actively developed the union side of the alliance. The Industrial Union Department was created in the 1955 merger of the AFL and CIO. Its mission was to further the social commitments of the CIO and was funded by its affiliate industrial unions. For other examples

of labor liberals building coalitions after the 1960s, see Andrew Battista, *The Revival of Labor Liberalism* (Urbana: University of Illinois Press, 2008).

3. Rebecca Solnit, *Hope in the Dark: Untold Histories, Wild Possibilities*, 3rd ed. (Chicago: Haymarket Books, 2016); Thomas Davies, *NGOs: A New History of Transnational Civil Society* (Oxford: Oxford University Press, 2014); Aaronson, *Taking Trade to the Streets*; Adler, *No Globalization without Representation*. In contrast, Aaronson suggests that resistance began with struggles against the General Agreement on Tariffs and Trade in the late 1980s, mostly with NGOs. Adler discusses how "public interest" globalization activism began in the 1970s, with consumer-based NGOs leading the way. Tamara Kay notes that US unions responded to trade politics in the 1980s, but not in the collective and coordinated way they did in the 1990s. See Kay, *NAFTA and the Politics*, 358.

4. *Populism* in the Latin American context generally refers to forms of politics driven by charismatic strongmen who forge a mass base through patronage and promises of uplift for the poor. Karen Kampwirth, *Gender and Populism in Latin America: Passionate Politics*, foreword by Kurt Weyland (University Park: Pennsylvania State University Press, 2010); Kenneth M. Roberts, "Neoliberalism and the Transformation of Populism in Latin America: The Peruvian Case," *World Politics* 48, no. 1 (October 1995): 82-116. In the US, though, populism can also be understood as a malleable discourse that pits virtuous producer-citizens against distant elites. It was first forged in settler narratives that suggested that Europeans could make the US an exceptional nation of independent-minded small producers, free from the status hierarchies of European aristocracy, despite the presence of enslaved Africans and dispossessed Native Americans in their midst. See Michael Kazin, *The Populist Persuasion: An American History.*, 2nd ed. (Ithaca, NY: Cornell University Press, 2017). For these dynamics in twentieth-century US history, see Gary Gerstle, *Working Class Americanism: The Politics of Labor in a Textile City, 1914-1960* (Cambridge: Cambridge University Press, 1989); Michael Denning, *The Cultural Front: The Laboring of American Culture in the Twentieth-Century* (London: Verso, 1996); Lizabeth Cohen, *Making a New Deal: Industrial Workers in Chicago, 1919-1939* (Cambridge: Cambridge University Press, 1990); Mary L. Dudziak, *Cold War Civil Rights: Race and the Image of American Democracy* (Princeton, NJ: Princeton University Press, 2000); Gerald Zahavi, "Passionate Commitments: Race, Sex, and Communism at Schenectady General Electric, 1932-1954," *Journal of American History* 83, no. 2 (September 1996): 514-48; and Rebecca Hill, *Men, Mobs, and Law: Anti-lynching and Labor Defense in U.S. Radical History* (Durham, NC: Duke University Press, 2008). See also Frank, *Buy American*.

5. Left-wing populism has sometimes veered rightward over time. See L. Fink, "When Community Comes Home"; James N. Gregory, *American Exodus: The Dust Bowl Migration and Okie Culture in California* (New York: Oxford University Press, 1989); Bethany Moreton, *To Serve God and Wal-Mart: The*

Making of Christian Free Enterprise (Cambridge, MA: Harvard University Press, 2009); Neil Foley, *The White Scourge: Mexicans, Blacks, and Poor Whites in Texas Cotton Culture* (Berkeley: University of California Press, 1997); C. Vann Woodward, *Tom Watson: Agrarian Rebel* (New York: Oxford University Press, 1938); Michael Pierce, "Orval Faubus and the Rise of Anti-labor Populism in Northwestern Arkansas," in *The Right and Labor in America: Politics, Ideology, Imagination*, ed. Nelson Lichtenstein and Elizabeth Tandy Shermer (Philadelphia: University of Pennsylvania Press, 2012), 98–113; and Kazin, *Populist Persuasion*, chaps. 7–11.

6. Self, *All in the Family*. Self defines the breadwinner family as a "white middle-class nuclear family headed by a patriotic and heterosexual male" (4).

7. For "grassroots Americanism," see Kazin, *Populist Persuasion*, 112. For "plain-folk" evangelicals, see Darren Dochuk, *From Bible Belt to Sunbelt: Plain-Folk Religion, Grassroots Politics, and the Rise of Evangelical Conservatism* (New York: W. W. Norton, 2012). For "housewife populism," see Michelle Nickerson, *Mothers of Conservatism: Women and the Postwar Right* (Princeton, NJ: Princeton University Press, 2012). For effects on L.A. union efforts, see Becky M. Nicolaides, *My Blue Heaven: Life and Politics in the Working-Class Suburbs of Los Angeles, 1920–1965* (Chicago: University of Chicago Press, 2002).

8. Natasha Zaretsky, *No Direction Home: The American Family and the Fear of National Decline, 1968–1980* (Chapel Hill: University of North Carolina Press, 2007), 18; Eric Porter, "Affirming and Disaffirming Actions: Re-making Race in the 1970s," in *America in the Seventies*, ed. Beth Bailey and David Farger (Lawrence: University Press of Kansas, 2004), 50–74.

9. As Self, *All in the Family*, convincingly shows, conservatives used the breadwinner family to help them portray feminism and abortion rights as "anti-family." Their tightening hold on the breadwinner family led to a "realignment of American democracy." For the values of "Middle America," see Kazin, *Populist Persuasion*, chap. 10.

10. Zaretsky, *No Direction Home*, 18.

11. Tennessee Gay and Lesbian Rights Coalition, statement to Mid-South Jobs with Justice, November 3, 1987, Industrial Union Department, unprocessed records at George Meany Memorial Archives (hereafter IUD records); and Melba Fiser and Freddie Wright to Gerry Scoppettuolo, November 5, 1987, IUD records.

12. George Kohl to "Participants in the Austin, Friday Morning Dialogue," February 19, 1992, Joe Uehlein personal collection. The document is a retrospective statement on the coalition's first two years.

13. For ideas of unions as outsiders, see Nelson Lichtenstein and Elizabeth Tandy Shermer, eds., *The Right and Labor in America: Politics, Ideology, and Imagination* (Philadelphia: University of Pennsylvania Press, 2012). See especially Pierce, "Orval Faubus." Many of Jobs with Justice's leading figures had

long histories articulating struggles for justice in terms of Christian or Jewish ideas of rights, redemption, and the value of labor. Many of their early political experiences were in support of civil rights or farmworkers' movements. See Randy Shaw, *Beyond the Fields: Cesar Chavez, the UFW, and the Struggle for Justice in the 21st Century* (Berkeley: University of California Press, 2008); and Doug Rossinow, *The Politics of Authenticity: Liberalism, Christianity, and the New Left in America* (New York: Columbia University Press, 1998). For a discussion of the backgrounds of a number of Jewish labor leaders who helped build Jobs with Justice, see Nathaniel Popper, "Working Legacy: Jews and the Labor Movement," *Forward*, April 23, 2009, http://forward.com/articles/105047/new-labor-leaders-take-a-page-from-history/.

14. Kazin, *Populist Persuasion*, 253.

15. Kazin, *Populist Persuasion*, 251, 262. Quote taken from Kazin, *Populist Persuasion*, 262, quoted in Paul D. Erickson, *Reagan Speaks: The Making of an American Myth* (New York: NYU Press, 1985), 109. For more on the working-class politics of the Southern Strategy, see Cowie, *Stayin' Alive*, chaps. 1–4.

16. For "stylish robber barons" quotation, see Erik Gunn, "Unions Unite for Campaign" [clipping], *Milwaukee Journal*, June 25, 1987, Jobs with Justice national office files (hereafter JwJ files).

17. William Stockton, "Tearing Apart Eastern Airlines," *New York Times*, November 6, 1988, 36; and International Association of Machinists and Aerospace Workers, District 100, "What Are the Issues at Eastern Air Lines?," handout for the Jobs with Justice Rally, July 29, 1987, IUD records.

18. George Kohl, telephone interview with the author, June 20, 2008; Jobs with Justice, "Procedures of the Jobs with Justice Campaign," March 24, 1988, IUD records.

19. "Jobs with Justice as a Strategy—Not Just a Rally: A Paper to Stimulate Discussion at the Placid Harbor Meeting," December 1987, Joe Uehlein personal collection.

20. Leaders hoped their coalitions would function like local labor councils, but with an organizing vision. Quotation from Reinaldo Ramos, "Thousands Rally for Union Rights" [clipping], *Miami Herald*, July 30, 1987, JwJ files.

21. Andy Welch, "Hightower Present: Save-the-Family-Farm Act Introduced in Congress," *Texas Gazette* (Newsletter of the Texas Department of Agriculture), February 1987, 1.

22. These populists emphasized reclaiming the presumed voluntary tradition in US communities and combining it with government programs. For more, see Harry Boyte, Heather Booth, and Steve Max, *Citizen Action and the New American Populism* (Philadelphia: Temple University Press, 1986), 30–31.

23. The New Populist Forum was a politically engaged think tank that founded the short-lived *Populist Message* newsletter in 1986. For more on the Forum, see Lane Evans, Tom Harkin, and Jim Hightower, "Renewing, Reclaiming Populism,"

Lodi News-Sentinel, June 6, 1986, 4; and "View from Hightower Is That Texas Is Populist State," *Houston Chronicle*, June 8, 1986, 34. Republicans lost two seats in the Senate and gained only a few in the House in 1984, so Reagan had little congressional support for initiatives. See Joshua B. Freeman, *American Empire: The Rise of a Global Power, the Democratic Revolution at Home, 1945–2000* (New York: Viking, 2012), chap. 15. The Nacogdoches newspaper in the week leading up to the Jobs with Justice rally focused much more on Hightower's scheduled appearance than on Jobs with Justice or the workers.

24. The crisis would mean the imminent elimination of "thousands of UAW farm-equipment workers' jobs," some claimed. See Evans, Harkin, and Hightower, "Renewing, Reclaiming Populism." The UAW was an important Jobs with Justice founder and funder. For more on farm-crisis coalitions in the Midwest, see William C. Pratt, "Using History to Make History? Progressive Farm Organizing during the Farm Revolt of the 1980," *Annals of Iowa* 55, no. 1 (1996): 24–45. Jobs with Justice founder William Winpisinger had collaborated with Citizen Action's Heather Booth and other populists since the 1970s. See Boyte, Booth, and Max, *Citizen Action*, 30–31, 61–62.

25. "Jobs with Justice Organizing Checklist," October 8, 1987, IUD records. The "Harkin Plan," drafted by Iowa senator and populist Tom Harkin, was the populist answer to Reagan-era farm policy and stipulated that a combination of production controls and subsidies were needed to save small farmers. Jackson named Merle Hansen, an Iowa farm activist, his agricultural adviser, and Jim Hightower was a longtime Jackson supporter. Many national union leaders with ties to well-funded Zionist organizations would not openly support Jackson's campaign.

26. Jobs with Justice, "Labor Day Jobs with Justice Status Report," July 21, 1988, JwJ files. By the end of 1987, the coalition claimed to have a total of thirty thousand cards signed, despite the lack of a single paid staff member. "Jobs with Justice as a Strategy."

27. Though by the end of 1987 Jobs with Justice was active in around eight localities, its strongest areas were Iowa, Florida, and Tennessee. Much of that early funding went to the SCLC, which coordinated much of the work in the South. See "Jobs with Justice Organizing Checklist." For more on leadership in different areas, see Howard Samuel to Participating Officers, "Unions Participating in Jobs with Justice Campaign," May 18, 1987, Joe Uehlein personal collection. The miners and paper workers took the lead in Nashville. For funding, see "Jobs with Justice 1988 Statement of Income and Expenses," June 9, 1988, JwJ files.

28. The NFFC board of directors in the late 1980s consisted of forty whites, two Blacks, and zero members of other nonwhite groups. NFFC, unnamed grant application, ca. 1989, p. 3, organizational files of the NFFC, Washington, DC. The wide appeal of the nationally televised "Farm Aid" fundraiser in 1985 and John "Cougar" Mellencamp's *Scarecrow* (1986) album exemplifies this, but a

series of films had already dramatized the struggle of noble white farmers to keep their land. Examples include *The River* (1984), *Country* (1984), and *Places in the Heart* (1984).

29. That was the case in Nacogdoches, for example. For background, see Danny Fetonte and Larry Braden, "Showdown at Nacogdoches: The CWA in Texas," *Labor Research Review* 1, no. 15 (1990): 25–35.

30. Cornel West, "Populism: A Black Socialist Critique," in *The New Populism: The Politics of Empowerment*, ed. Harry Boyte and Frank Riessman (Philadelphia: Temple University Press, 1986), 208.

31. Danny Fetonte, interview with the author, November 16, 2010, Austin, TX.

32. See William P. Browne, "Challenging Industrialization: The Rekindling of Agrarian Protest in Agriculture, 1977–1987," *Studies in American Political Development* 7, no. 1 (Spring 1993): 1–34; and Judith Ezekiel, *Feminism in the Heartland* (Columbus: Ohio State University Press, 2002). For more on the UAW, Iowa Farm Unity, and churches, see Rev. David Ostendorf and Daniel Levitas, "Education for Empowerment and Social Action in Rural America," *Mid-American Review of Sociology* 12, no. 1 (1987): 55–64. For broader context, see Kathleen Belew, *Bring the War Home: The White Power Movement and Paramilitary America* (Cambridge, MA: Harvard University Press, 2019).

33. Kathy Ozer, telephone interview with the author, September 10, 2012.

34. Local organizers, in a statement, expressed regrets for the incident and claimed that "the person who did this does not reflect the view of the Mid-South Jobs with Justice Campaign." Fiser and Wright to Scioppettulo, November 5, 1987, JwJ files.

35. Unions tied to Jobs with Justice or Jobs with Justice organizers in the United Food and Commercial Workers (UFCW), the CWA in Texas and Ohio, the UMWA, and the Eastern unions and Florida building trades unions all exhibited such ambivalence or hostility. For the UFCW case, see Deborah Fink, "Reorganizing Inequity: Gender and Structural Transformation in Iowa Meatpacking," in *Unionizing the Jungles: Labor and Community in the Twentieth-Century Meatpacking Industry*, ed. Shelton Stromquist and Marvin Bergman (Iowa City: University of Iowa Press, 1997), 218–41; Karen Clarke, telephone interview with the author, October 11, 2008; Joe Uehlein, interview with author, August 10, 2008, Washington, DC. Gay male flight attendants struggled against homophobia in and through flight attendants' unions, for example. See Philip James Tiemeyer, *Plane Queer: Labor, Sexuality, and AIDS in the History of Male Flight Attendants* (Berkeley: University of California Press, 2013).

36. Andy Banks, telephone interview with the author, June 30, 2008; Mary Jane Barry, telephone interview with the author, June 11, 2008.

37. Kit Rafferty, interview with the author, August 5, 2011, Washington, DC; Barry, telephone interview, June 11, 2008; Fetonte and Braden, "Showdown at Nacogdoches."

38. Fetonte and Braden, "Showdown at Nacogdoches," 34, 27. Boyte, Booth, and Max, *Citizen Action*, 18, also draw attention to how everyday Americans had legitimate concerns about distant, bureaucratic unions as well as corporations, while Jobs with Justice leaders almost never expressed ambivalence about unions.

39. "Jobs with Justice," ca. January–February 1987, IUD records; Jobs with Justice, "Labor Day Activity to Focus on Jobs with Justice," Joe Uehlein personal collection; Alabama Jobs with Justice, "Rally!!!" June 4, 1988, brochure, Joe Uehlein personal collection.

40. "Nation's Largest Unions Launch Campaign for Workers' Rights," *John Herling's Labor Letter,* July 4, 1987, 1–2, IUD records; W. Morgan Mallard, "Unions Planning Series of Pro-labor Political Rallies" [clipping], *Atlanta Constitution,* June 24, 1987, JwJ files. See also "A Call for Jobs with Justice," ca. April-May 1987, IUD records.

41. The words of CWA District One vice president Jan Pierce come from Betty Brickson, "Labor Calls for New Solidarity" [clipping], *Wisconsin State Journal,* September 6, 1988, JwJ files.

42. Bob Vacon, "Thousands Attend Rally to Support Colt Strikers," *Hartford Courant,* September 28, 1987, 1, 9.

43. "Jobs with Justice"; "CWA, Union Leaders Kick Off Jobs with Justice Campaign," *CWA News,* June 11, 1987, 6; "Nation's Largest Unions."

44. "Call for Jobs with Justice."

45. Owen Bieber testimony, September 16, 1987, *Congressional Record,* 105th Cong., 2nd. sess., 1987, 55.

46. Edward Power, "Labor Chiefs Rally to Urge Rights Bill," *Philadelphia Inquirer,* September 17, 1987, 9b.

47. See I. M. Destler, *American Trade Politics,* 4th ed. (Washington, DC: Institute for International Economics, 2005), 46; Freeman, *American Empire,* Part III.

48. Those debates led to the creation of the Omnibus Foreign Trade and Competitiveness Act of 1988. The stock market crash of October 1987 spurred anxieties about the country's economic decline as well, but the administration had aided export industries that Jobs with Justice unions had a stake in. It protected them by imposing Voluntary Export Restraints on products like semiconductors (CWA), autos (UAW), steel (USW), and textiles (ACTWU). See Stephen Grubaugh and Scott Sumner, "Monetary Policy and the U.S. Trade Deficit," in *The Reagan Years: The Record in Presidential Leadership,* ed. Joseph Hogan (Manchester: Manchester University Press, 1990), 237–58.

49. Targeting some of those practices, like dumping and export subsidies, was common for unions and sometimes included calling for changes in the 1974 trade legislation.

50. Photo caption in "Buy American: Should We Follow That Flag?" *Labor Notes* Special Section, May 2009, 2. For unions and Yellow Peril ideas, see Frank, *Buy American.*

51. Jobs with Justice made the same comment in its media kit. "Jobs with Justice Media Information Kit," November 1987, IUD records; Morton Bahr, speech transcript, Miami Jobs with Justice rally, July 1987, IUD records. For Hightower comment, see his speech to United Food and Commercial Workers, April 28, 1987, San Antonio, Jim Hightower Papers, Box 4Ja50, AFL-CIO Folder, p. 9, Briscoe Center for American History, University of Texas.

52. Bryan Abas, "Look for the Union Label: Jobs with Justice Has a Label for One Local AFL-CIO Official: Spy," *Westword*, April 12–18, 1999, 18.

53. For criticism, see Martin Khor, "Free Trade and the Third World," in *The Case against "Free Trade": GATT, NAFTA, and the Globalization of Corporate Power*, ed. Ralph Nader and Lori Wallach (San Francisco: Earth Island Press; Berkeley, CA: North Atlantic Books, 1993), 97–107. For more on the fight over trade, see Associated Press, "Reagan Vows to Veto Omnibus Trade Bill," *Idahonian/Daily News*, April 28, 1988, 2a. For more on the bill, see David E. Birenbaum, "The Omnibus Trade Act of 1988: Trade Law Dialectics," *University of Pennsylvania Journal of International Business Law* 10, no. 4 (1988): 653–61. Invoking the threat of foreign competition sometimes obscured the realities of corporate conglomerates. Though producers in Japan and South Korea did indeed compete with domestic US industries, so did those in the European Economic Community, and especially West Germany. See Oswald Johnson, "Omnibus Trade Bill Passed by Congress: Reagan to Measure Stiffening Ability to Retaliate against Unfair Actions Abroad," *Los Angeles Times*, August 4, 1988, http://articles.latimes.com/1988-08-04/news/mn-10208_1_trade-bill; and "Reagan Vows to Veto." The coal companies that the UMWA battled competed not only with foreign companies but with other subsidiaries inside the energy conglomerates who owned them. See Stephen L. Fisher, *Fighting Back in Appalachia: Traditions of Resistance and Change* (Philadelphia: Temple University Press, 1993), 176. During the Cold War, US unions notoriously embraced the government's anticommunism, which turned them away from supporting workers' rights in poor countries, and Jobs with Justice affiliates could have considered how the growth of Japanese and West German productive capacity stemmed in part from the same Cold War "security" industries they sometimes valorized. The US strategically targeted prospective Cold War allies with funding through the Marshall Plan and other aid. See Paul Buhle, *Taking Care of Business: Samuel Gompers, George Meany, Lane Kirkland, and the Tragedy of American Labor* (New York: Monthly Review Press, 1999); see also Grubaugh and Sumner, "Monetary Policy," 254.

54. His agreement to lower the dollar's value in the mid-1980s helped manufacturing unions hoping to export goods but also made US industry

the target of foreign investors from Asia and Europe. Freeman, *American Empire,* chap. 15.

55. "Jobs with Justice" [clipping], *IUD News,* November 1987, 16, Joe Uehlein personal collection; IUD officers, "1988 IUD Officers' Report / Report to AFL-CIO Council," July 17, 1988, IUD records.

56. Though SEIU and its organizing director Andy Stern were tied to Jobs with Justice, a permanent L.A. coalition never formed, and Property Services organizers within SEIU built their own ties to community groups in Los Angeles for its well-known Justice for Janitors campaign. Jono Schaffer, telephone interview with the author, October 14, 2008. While some Jobs with Justice–affiliated unions had immigrant members (though few leaders), campaigns about immigrant worker rights in Jobs with Justice would not occur until the 1990s. Jaime Martínez recounted resistance to organizing immigrants in some Jobs with Justice unions in the South in the 1980s. Jaime Martínez, interview with the author, July 11, 2012, San Antonio, TX.

57. Larry Cohen and Steve Early, "Jobs with Justice: Community in Action," 1994, 2–3, JwJ files.

58. Their collaborations, with IUD and CWA leaders and others, helped lead to the passage of the 1988 Omnibus Trade Act; see "1988 IUD Officers' Report / Report to AFL-CIO Council." The Labor-Industry Coalition on International Trade (LICIT), for instance, included Bahr and IUD president Howard Samuel, who was a LICIT co-chair. In 1986, Samuel and Corning Glass (now Corning, Inc.) vice president Allan Cors exchanged notes and guidebooks about their family vacations to France. Howard Samuel to Allan Cors, March 26, 1986, IUD records. On Made in the USA Foundation, see Joel Joseph to Howard Samuel, August 15, 1990, IUD records.

59. Johnny Carson, résumé, 1988, IUD records; "Jobs with Justice" [clipping], *IUD News,* IUD records; Brian Turner to "Files: JOBS [*sic*] with Justice Program," March 13, 1989, IUD records.

60. Richard Cordtz, "Concerned about Trade," *SEIU Update* (Public Division) 1, no. 2 (Fall 1987): 23. The Congressional Black Congress and Black organizations launched their own boycott on Japanese-owned companies because of their discriminating against Black workers. Howard Samuel, "Foreign Investment in the U.S.: A Labor View," *Looking Ahead,* May 1989. Heather Booth and other "progressive populists" supported domestic content legislation given that "thirty-two countries have domestic content laws." Though supporting "full employment" and workers' rights in the Third World was crucial, Booth argued, such domestic content legislation was important since "raising Third World livings is a very long term solution." Other progressives advocated targeting corporate power by creating restrictions in corporate charters. See Boyte, Booth, and Max, *Citizen Action,* 182. In contrast to the tone of some of Jobs with Justice affiliates on trade, one important founding activist in the coalition, Rand Wilson

from Boston, had helped create union-based internationalism and solidarity for Central American workers during the 1980s. Another resource for internationalist activists at the time would have been early work on the global economy. One example would be Walden Bello, *Brave New Third World? Strategies for Survival in the Global Economy* (San Francisco: Institute for Food and Development Policy, 1989). For other forms of labor internationalism, see Henry J. Frundt, *Trade Conditions and Labor Rights: U.S. Initiatives, Dominican and Central American Responses* (Gainesville: University Press of Florida, 1998), 6–10, 84–90.

61. See Jobs with Justice, "Procedures." In addition, organizations paid their own costs for participating. That meant that community-based groups in low-income areas, particularly those without an office in D.C., would have less of a voice in major decisions. MacDowell to Lori et al., March 4, 1991, JwJ files. National leaders were almost entirely white and mostly male.

62. See Jobs with Justice, "Procedures." Union support for a community campaign is not discussed.

63. "Jobs with Justice Organizing Checklist"; "Jobs with Justice as a Strategy"; Abas, "Look for the Union Label."

64. MacDowell to Lori et al.; "Jobs with Justice as a Strategy."

65. The march received more national Jobs with Justice funding than any other single event. Patrick Peterson, "King March Unlike 60s; Issues Remain," *Sun Herald* (Biloxi, MS), April 10, 1988, b1.

66. For "exporting war" quotation, see Ron Colquitt, "SCLC President Leads March against IP Lockout," *Mobile Register*, April 11, 1988, b1; untitled photo in "Southern Pilgrimage for Jobs with Justice," special issue, *People's Daily World*, April 28, 1988, 19a. For more, see Marilyn Bechtel, "June 11 Rally: 'More Important Than Ever,'" *People's Daily World*, April 28, 1988, 3a. For Nacogdoches, see "Mattie Stegall," in *Jobs with Justice: 25 Years, 25 Voices*, ed. Eric D. Larson (Oakland, CA: PM Press, 2013), 1–3.

67. Justice for Janitors Organizing Committee, *Organizer* newsletter, no. 1 (October 1987): 1, Atlanta Justice for Janitors—1987 folder, Organizing Department, Box 1 (of 7), SEIU Collection, Walter P. Reuther Archives. For the "city too busy to hate," the union was responding to the Dust-Away contractor. Justice for Janitors (SEIU), *Dust-Away Refuses to Meet with Justice for Janitors*, brochure, ca. 1987, Atlanta Justice for Janitors—1987 folder, Organizing Department, Box 1 (of 7), SEIU Collection, Walter P. Reuther Archives.

68. Mary Wingreen and George Kohl to Jobs with Justice Labor Event Coordinators, August 17, 1988, JwJ files; Wayne E. Glenn, "President Glenn Addresses Jobs with Justice Rally," speech transcript, *The Paperworker*, November 1987, 21.

69. Adler, *No Globalization without Representation*.

70. For Seattle, see Washington State Jobs with Justice, APEC flier, November 1993, Washington State coalition 1993 folder, JwJ records; for CWA, see Larry

Cohen, telephone interview with the author, January 9, 2023. See also Larry Cohen and Steve Early, "Globalization and De-unionization in Telecommunications: Three Case Studies in Resistance," in *Transnational Cooperation among Labor Unions*, ed. Michael Gordon and Lowell Turner (Ithaca, NY: Cornell University Press, 2000), 202–22; and Larry Cohen and Steve Early, "Defending Workers' Rights in the Global Economy: The CWA Experience," in *Which Direction for Organized Labor?*, ed. Bruce Nissen (Philadelphia: Temple University Press, 1999), 143–64.

71. Steven K. Ashby and C. J. Hawking, *Staley: The Fight for a New American Labor Movement* (Urbana: University of Illinois Press, 2009), 107. The Staley lockout and two major strikes (at Bridgestone/Firestone and at Caterpillar Inc.) in central Illinois led unionists to refer to the region as the "war zone." See also Stephen Franklin, *Three Strikes: Labor's Heartland Losses and What They Mean for Working Americans* (New York: Guilford Press, 2002). As Ashby and Hawking note, Jobs with Justice was an active participant in solidarity work for the Staley lockout. See also "Russ Davis," in *Jobs with Justice: 25 Years, 25 Voices*, ed. Eric Larson (Oakland, CA: PM Press, 2013), 56–61. The moment was an important one for transnational solidarities. Workers in other countries pressured Bridgestone/Firestone and helped save US workers' jobs. See Brecher, Costello, and Smith, *Globalization from Below*, 48. Some Jobs with Justice local coalitions, for instance in Massachusetts, were active in progressive struggles against NAFTA as well.

72. Juris, *Networking Futures*.

4. AGAINST COCA-COLONIZATION

1. First emerging amid anxieties about Americanization in post–World War II Europe, the term became increasingly used in the 1990s in terms of the Americanizing influence of trade, internet, and advertising policies in Europe and Asia. The United Nations took on the issue. See United Nations, "World Must Reap Benefits of Globalization without Eroding Cultural Diversity, Republic of Korea Tells Second Committee," press release, October 22, 1997, https://press.un.org/en/1997/19971022.GAEF2770.html. While the threat of cultural homogenization was present in the era's major books on globalization (e.g., those of Thomas Friedman or Benjamin Barber), it also became part of the contentious trade politics of the decade. See Michele Belluzzi, "Cultural Protection as a Rationale for Legislation: The French Language Law of 1994 and the European Trend toward Integration in the Face of Increasing U.S. Influence," *Penn State International Law Review* 14, no. 1 (1995): 27; see also Randy Kluver, "Globalization, Informatization, and Intercultural Communication," *American Communication Journal* 3, no. 3 (2000), http://ac-journal.org/journal/vol3/Iss3/spec1/kluver.htm; and Steven Flusty, *De-Coca-Colonization: Making the Globe from the Inside Out* (New York: Routledge, 2004).

2. In centering the omnipotence of multinational corporations, some of these interpretations offered simplistic representations of Global South governments as either noble victims or complete authoritarians.

3. See chapter 6 for more on how US settler colonialism and empire employed brands of benevolent "rescue anthropology" in the face of genocide. Jean M. O'Brien, *Firsting and Lasting: Writing Indians out of Existence in New England*, Indigenous Americas (Minneapolis: University of Minnesota Press, 2010).

4. Naomi Klein, "Reclaiming the Commons," *New Left Review*, June 2001, https://newleftreview.org/issues/II9/articles/naomi-klein-reclaiming-the-commons. She refers to the dangers of coca-colonization in her first book, *No Logo: No Space, No Choice, No Jobs* (New York: Picador, 2000).

5. Jerry Mander, *In the Absence of the Sacred: The Failure of Technology and the Survival of the Indian Nations* (San Francisco: Sierra Club Books, 1991).

6. Subcomandante Marcos regularly described a "Fourth World War" of neoliberalism that aimed to "eliminate" the "minorities" of the world. As war, it was about elimination, not homogenization. See discussion of the war metaphor in Jérôme Baschet, "¿Más allá de la lucha por la humanidad y contra el neoliberalismo?," *Revista Chiapas*, no. 16 (2004): 31–50, https://chiapas.iiec.unam.mx/No16-PDF/ch16baschet.pdf.

7. See, for example, Jodi Melamed, Bruce Burgett, and Glenn Hendler, "Diversity," in *Keywords for American Cultural Studies*, 2nd ed. (New York: New York University Press, 2014), 84–88; Roderick A. Ferguson, *The Reorder of Things: The University and Its Pedagogies of Minority Difference* (Minneapolis: University of Minnesota Press, 2012); Avery Gordon and Christopher Newfield, eds., *Mapping Multiculturalism* (Minneapolis: University of Minnesota Press, 1996); Lisa Lowe, *Immigrant Acts: On Asian American Cultural Politics* (Durham, NC: Duke University Press, 1996); Glen Sean Coulthard, *Red Skin, White Masks: Rejecting the Colonial Politics of Recognition*, Indigenous Americas (Minneapolis: University of Minnesota Press, 2014); Sara Ahmed, *On Being Included: Racism and Diversity in Institutional Life* (Durham, NC: Duke University Press, 2012); Paul Gilroy, *There Ain't No Black in the Union Jack: The Cultural Politics of Race and Nation* (London: Routledge, 2006).

8. Néstor García Canclini, Inderpal Grewal, and George Yúdice all examine the ways globalization was characterized not by standardization but by hybridity. See, for example, Néstor García Canclini, *Imagined Globalization*, trans. George Yúdice, Latin America in Translation/En Traducción/Em Tradução (Durham, NC: Duke University Press, 2014); Inderpal Grewal, *Transnational America: Feminisms, Diasporas, Neoliberalisms*, Next Wave (Durham, NC: Duke University Press, 2005).

9. Charles R. Hale, "Does Multiculturalism Menace? Governance, Cultural Rights and the Politics of Identity in Guatemala," *Journal of Latin American Studies* 34, no. 3 (2002): 485.

10. Hale, "Does Multiculturalism Menace?"; V. de la Cruz and R. Laura, "La política de la multiculturalidad en México y sus impactos en la movilización indígena," in *Identidades, etnicidad y racismo en América Latina*, ed. FLACSO-SEDE Ecuador (Quito: Congreso Latinoamericano y Caribeño de Ciencias Sociales, FLACSO, 2008); James D. Bowen, "Multicultural Market Democracy: Elites and Indigenous Movements in Contemporary Ecuador," *Journal of Latin American Studies* 43, no. 3 (2011): 451–83, https://doi.org/10.1017/S0022216X11000769.

11. See Charles R. Hale and Rosamel Millamán, "Cultural Agency and Political Struggle in the Era of the Indio Permitido," in *Cultural Agency in the Americas*, ed. Doris Summer (Durham, NC: Duke University Press, 2006), 281–304. The authors cite Bolivian scholar Silvia Rivera Cusicanqui as coining the term *indio permitido* in a 2001 workshop.

12. Evelina Dagnino, "Citizenship: A Perverse Confluence," *Development in Practice* 17, nos. 4/5 (2007): 549–56.

13. Rebecca Overmyer-Velázquez, *Folkloric Poverty: Neoliberal Multiculturalism in Mexico* (University Park: Pennsylvania State University Press, 2010), 135.

14. Rosalva Aída Hernández Castillo, *Histories and Stories from Chiapas: Border Identities in Southern Mexico* (Austin: University of Texas Press, 2004), 188–89.

15. Diódoro Carrasco Altamirano, interview with the author, August 15, 2015, Mexico City.

16. Jorge Hernández Díaz, *Reclamos de la identidad: La formación de las organizaciones indígenas en Oaxaca* (Oaxaca: Universidad Autónoma Benito Juárez de Oaxaca; Mexico City: Miguel Angel Porrúa, 2001); Lynn Stephen, *We Are the Face of Oaxaca: Testimony and Social Movements* (Durham, NC: Duke University Press, 2013).

17. Although Carrasco was part of the multicultural reforms of the administration of his predecessor, it was only after the EZLN uprising that he seriously discussed broad reforms. See Jorge Hernández Díaz and Victor Leonel Juan Martínez, *Dilemas de la institución municipal: Una incursión en la experiencia oaxaqueña*, Colección Las ciencias sociales (Mexico City: H. Cámara de Diputados, LX Legislatura; Oaxaca: Universidad Autónoma Benito Juárez de Oaxaca; Mexico City: Miguel Angel Porrúa, 2007): 77.

18. Overmyer-Velázquez, *Folkloric Poverty*, 7.

19. The former governor Heladio Ramírez managed left-wing groups and producer organizations through patronage, populist appeals, and largely symbolic multicultural reforms like altering Article 16 of the state constitution to recognize the state's pluri-ethnic character. See David Recondo, *La política del gatopardo: Multiculturalismo y democracia en Oaxaca*, Publicaciones de la Casa Chata (Mexico City: CIESA; CEMCA, 2007); Alejandro Anaya, *Autonomía indígena, gobernabilidad y legitimidad en México: La legalización de los usos y*

costumbres electorales en Oaxaca, Política (Mexico City: Universidad Iberoamericana; Plaza y Valdés, 2006).

20. Recondo, *Política del gatopardo*, 202. Soon after the announcement, the Carrasco administration changed Article 16 of the state constitution to guarantee protection of indigenous languages. Carrasco Altamirano, interview, August 15, 2015; Recondo, *Política del gatopardo*. However, the most significant change to be fully implemented was the recognition of Indigenous internal political systems discussed below.

21. Carrasco Altamirano, interview, August 15, 2015; Recondo, *Política del gatopardo*, 207n75.

22. I. Rendón, "Debe México saldar su deuda con Oaxaca," *Palabra*, November 30, 1998.

23. Kay B. Warren and Jean E. Jackson, *Indigenous Movements, Self-Representation, and the State in Latin America* (Austin: University of Texas Press, 2002).

24. The Mexican government has long used the municipality to control local populations, but Indigenous peoples (including the EZLN) have also tried to reclaim it as theirs. See Miguel González Pérez, Aracely Burguete Cal y Mayor, and Pablo Ortiz-T., *La autonomía a debate: Autogobierno indígena y estado plurinacional en América Latina*, Foro (FLACSO Sede Ecuador) (Quito, Ecuador: FLACSO Ecuador; Cooperación Técnica Alemana, GTZ; Ministerio Federal de Cooperación Económica y Desarrollo; IWGIA; CIESAS; UNICH, 2010). The Zapatistas had first tried to establish regional autonomy frameworks but later concentrated on creating autonomous municipalities. Saúl Velasco Cruz, *El movimiento indígena y la autonomía en México*, Colección Posgrado 23 (Mexico City: Universidad Nacional Autónoma de México, 2003). As Mattiace analyzes, competing visions of autonomy (particularly in terms of its scale) were subject to extensive debate in the 1990s within and around the neo-Zapatista movement. See Shannan L. Mattiace, *To See with Two Eyes: Peasant Activism and Indian Autonomy in Chiapas, Mexico* (Albuquerque: University of New Mexico Press, 2003).

25. R. G. Mendoza Zuany, "Dealing with Diversity in the Construction of Indigenous Autonomy in the Sierra Norte of Oaxaca," *Bulletin of Latin American Research* 27, no. 3 (2008): 351–67. Bartolomé's term is cited on 352. Oaxaca also has a smaller proportion of ejidos, state-owned land titles granted to peasants after the Mexican Revolution. Guillermo de la Peña, "Social Citizenship, Ethnic Minority Demands, Human Rights and Neoliberal Paradoxes: A Case Study in Western Mexico," in *Multiculturalism in Latin America: Indigenous Rights, Diversity and Democracy*, ed. Rachel Sieder, Institute of Latin American Studies Series (London: Palgrave Macmillan UK, 2002), 129–56, https://doi.org/10.1057/9781403937827_6.

26. de la Peña, "Social Citizenship."

27. Deborah Poole, "An Image of 'Our Indian': Type Photographs and Racial Sentiments in Oaxaca, 1920–1940," *Hispanic American Historical Review* 84, no. 1 (February 1, 2004): 37–82, https://doi.org/10.1215/00182168-84-1-37.

28. Indigenous governance systems were termed *usos y costumbres*, a phrase that referred to local customary practices and that many indigenous leaders argued was simplistic and racist. The term often used now is *sistemas normativos internos* (internal normative systems).

29. Carrasco also promoted Oaxaca as a *mundo mágico*, a term borrowed from Heladio Ramírez; see Carrasco's *Plan estatal de desarrollo*. Gobierno Constitucional del Estado Libre y Soberano de Oaxaca, *Oaxaca, Plan estatal de desarrollo, 1992–1998* (Oaxaca: El Gobierno, 1993), 31.

30. As Poole, "Image of 'Our Indian,'" has shown, the Guelagetza distinguished (and celebrated) cultural diversity as Oaxacan but elided notions of biological race and framed racialized Afro-Mexican dancers as foreign, different, and inferior. For more on transborder identities, see Lynn Stephen, *Transborder Lives: Indigenous Oaxacans in Mexico, California, and Oregon* (Durham, NC: Duke University Press, 2007).

31. Hale, "Does Multiculturalism Menace?"; see also Maria Teresa Sierra Camacho, Rosalva Aída Hernández Castillo, and Rachel Sieder, *Justicias indígenas y estado violencias contemporáneas* (Mexico City: FLACSO; CIESAS, 2013).

32. Diódoro Carrasco Altamirano, "Ley de los Derechos de los Pueblos y Comunidades Indígenas del Estado de Oaxaca," Gobierno del Estado de Oaxaca, March 21, 1998, 4–5, www.diputados.gob.mx/comisiones/asunindi/oaxregla.pdf.

33. Monica Christine DeHart, *Ethnic Entrepreneurs: Identity and Development Politics in Latin America* (Palo Alto, CA: Stanford University Press, 2010); Nancy Grey Postero, *Now We Are Citizens: Indigenous Politics in Postmulticultural Bolivia* (Stanford, CA: Stanford University Press, 2007).

34. Rendón, "Debe México saldar su deuda."

35. *Tequio* is a form of collective, communal work common in Indigenous Mexico but especially in Oaxaca. The efficiency of the *pueblos*, Carrasco continued, was why the state must invest in the *pueblos*, why "you have to give them information, training, resources, instruments to move forward." While the term *pueblos* can mean "small towns" or (Indigenous) peoples, those terms often coincide in Oaxaca. Here Carrasco is referring to Indigenous peoples; see Rendón, "Debe México saldar su deuda."

36. Gobierno Constitucional del Estado Libre y Soberano de Oaxaca, *Oaxaca, Plan estatal de desarrollo*.

37. Mexico, Poder Ejecutivo Federal, *Plan nacional de desarrollo, 1995–2000: Programa de desarrollo informático* (Mexico City: INEGI, 1996), 42.

38. In Oaxaca, shifting administrative and executive power to local municipalities coincided with neoliberal efforts to decentralize (Recondo, *Política del*

gatopardo, 288–92). For relationships between decentralization and Indigenous politics, see Nancy Grey Postero and Leon Zamosc, *The Struggle for Indigenous Rights in Latin America* (Brighton: Sussex Academic Press, 2004).

39. Gobierno Constitucional del Estado Libre y Soberano de Oaxaca, *Oaxaca, Plan estatal de desarrollo*, 4.

40. Gobierno Constitucional del Estado Libre y Soberano de Oaxaca, *Oaxaca, Plan estatal de desarrollo*, 6–7. See also Anaya, *Autonomía indígena*, 159.

41. This was confirmed by interviews with different leaders on separate occasions. Gustavo Esteva, interview with the author, January 21, 2015, Oaxaca City; Sofia Robles, interview with the author, June 18, 2015, Tlahuitoltepec (Oaxaca); Adelfo Regino, interview with the author, January 22, 2015, Oaxaca City.

42. The event was the Simposio Indolatinoamericano. Robles, interview, June 18, 2015.

43. Floriberto Díaz, Sofía Robles Hernández, and Rafael Cardoso Jiménez, *Escrito: Comunalidad, energía viva del pensamiento Mixe = Ayuujktsënää'yën— ayuujkwënmää'ny—ayuujk mëk'äjtën* (Mexico City: Universidad Nacional Autónoma de México, 2007), 39–40.

44. Maylei Blackwell, "The Practice of Autonomy in the Age of Neoliberalism: Strategies from Indigenous Women's Organising in Mexico," *Journal of Latin American Studies* 44, no. 4 (2012): 703–32; Aracely Burguete Cal y Mayor and International Work Group for Indigenous Affairs, *Indigenous Autonomy in Mexico* (Copenhagen: IWGIA, 2000); Sara Lovera and Nellys Palomo, *Las Alzadas* (Mexico City: Comunicación e Información de la Mujer; Convergencia Socialista, 1999); Guiomar Rovira, *Mujeres de maíz: La voz de las indígenas de Chiapas y la rebelión zapatista* (Barcelona: Virus, 1996); Shannon Speed, Rosalva Aída Hernández Castillo, and Lynn Stephen, *Dissident Women: Gender and Cultural Politics in Chiapas* (Austin: University of Texas Press, 2006).

45. Regino, interview, January 22, 2015; Anaya, *Autonomía indígena*, 137.

46. Mattiace, *To See with Two Eyes*, chap. 4. Influential anthropologist Salomón Nahmad and Luna, along with Esteva, were advisers for both Carrasco and the EZLN.

47. Indigenous leaders rejected the federal government's efforts to sponsor forums throughout the country and created their own. That process was led by groups like SER-Mixe and UNOSJO; see Anaya, *Autonomía indígena*, 97. Carrasco and Esteva had a friendly relationship that dated back more than a decade. Esteva said he was close friends with Carrasco's adviser Armando Labra, who was the head of advisers in this effort (interview, January 21, 2015). Esteva, Labra, and Nahmad had worked together in the Ramírez government as well; see Jorge Hernández-Díaz and Victor Leonel Juan Martínez, *Dilemas de la institución municipal: Una incursión en la experiencia oaxaqueña*, Colección Las ciencias sociales (Oaxaca: Universidad Autónoma Benito Juárez de Oaxaca: Mexico City: M. A. Porrúa, 2007), 76.

48. Esteva, interview, January 21, 2015.

49. Aristarco Aquino Solis, "Las inquietudes en la Sierra Norte no se deben a la rebelión en Chiapas," in *Usos y costumbres, caciquismo, e intolerancia religiosa (entrevistas a dirigentes indios de Oaxaca)* (Oaxaca City: CAMPO, 1996), 36. The date March 21, 1994, was when Carrasco publicly announced the Nuevo Acuerdo. March 21 is the birthday of Oaxaca-born national hero Benito Juárez, and the announcement was made at the Juárez celebration ("Inquietudes," 34–39).

50. Carrasco Altamirano, interview, August 15, 2015; Recondo, *Política del gatopardo*, 226–30.

51. For an analysis of Zapatismo in Oaxaca in the 1990s, see Stephen, *Zapata Lives!*

52. Bowen, "Multicultural Market Democracy"; Lynn Stephen, "The Construction of Indigenous Suspects: Militarization and the Gendered and Ethnic Dynamics of Human Rights Abuses in Southern Mexico," *American Ethnologist* 26, no. 4 (November 1, 1999): 822–42, https://doi.org/10.1525/ae.1999.26.4.822; Carmen Martínez Novo, *Who Defines Indigenous? Identities, Development, Intellectuals, and the State in Northern Mexico* (New Brunswick, NJ: Rutgers University Press, 2006), 43–44.

53. Patricia Richards, "Of Indians and Terrorists: How the State and Local Elites Construct the Mapuche in Neoliberal Multicultural Chile," *Journal of Latin American Studies* 42, no. 1 (2010): 59–90, https://doi.org/10.1017/S0022216X10000052.

54. Stephen, "Construction of Indigenous Suspects."

55. *Delegaciones de gobierno* were regional offices accountable to the governor's office and widely seen by PRI opponents as modules for vote buying and corruption. The appointed officeholders were often not from the Indigenous communities they served; see Gabriela Kraemer Bayer, *Autonomía indígena: Región Mixe, relaciones de poder y cultura política* (Mexico City: Plaza y Valdés; Consejo Nacional de Ciencia y Tecnología; Universidad Autónoma Chapingo-Dirección de Difusión Cultural, 2003), 59–60.

56. While some advisers for the state reforms were also EZLN advisers, Carlos Beas of UCIZONI was an EZLN adviser but was not asked to be part of the state reform process. See Hernández Díaz and Martínez, *Dilemas*, 82n169; Recondo, *Política del gatopardo*, 226; Carlos Beas, "Testimonio: Los retos del movimiento indígena mexicano," *Cuadernos del Sur* 14 (1999): 141–52. Beas and UCIZONI had, in fact, closer relationships to Carrasco than the other main CIPO organizations.

57. CODECI, OIDHO, and UCIZONI, "Untitled Declaration," April 7, 1997, unprocessed records of the Organizaciónes Indias por los Derechos Humanos de Oaxaca, Oaxaca City.

58. N. G. Sibaja, "Realizarán indígenas más movilizaciones," *El Imparcial* (Oaxaca), March 12, 1998.

59. Instituto Nacional de Estadística, Geografía e Informática, *La mujer en Oaxaca* (Aguascalientes, AGS: INEGI, 1995), 58, 61.

60. Dora Avila, interview with the author, December 15, 2011, Matias Romero (Oaxaca).

61. As in the rest of Mexico, the PRI exerted considerable power over the media through its control of government funds. Newspapers in Oaxaca were especially dependent on government contracts, though, because of the extreme lack of private wealth in the state. According to Carrasco, the administration arranged these contracts with local newspapers (interview, August 15, 2015). Both major newspapers in Oaxaca were progovernment (PRI) in the 1990s. The respected journalist Pedro Matias of *Proceso* magazine recalls how Carrasco tried to damage his reputation after he printed a critical article about Carrasco's status with Indigenous Oaxacans in the 1990s. Pedro Matias, interview with the author, January 17, 2017, Oaxaca City.

62. For background, see Trejo, *Popular Movements in Autocracies*.

63. Heladio Ramírez López, "El partido y el futuro," *El Imparcial* (Oaxaca), December 2, 1997.

64. A. López Morales, "Sí habrá desarrollo en el istmo, promote José Murat en Juchitán," *Las Noticias,* March 11, 1998; A. G. Sumano and J. A. Márquez, "Propone Murat un gobierno que sea incluyente y tolerante," *Las Noticias,* March 10, 1998. Note that Murat was of Iraqi immigrant descent. Thanks to Jonathan Fox for the clarification.

65. G. Ramírez, "Emplaza oposición a canjear la intolerancia por acuerdo político," *El Imparcial* (Oaxaca), November 22, 1997. The secretary was Hector Anuar Mafud.

66. O. R. Avendaño, "Actos violentos en protestas del CIPO," *El Imparcial* (Oaxaca), April 23, 1998.

67. Carrasco Altamirano, interview, August 15, 2015.

68. J. H. Robles, "Promueven imágen visual en calles de la ciudad," *El Imparcial* (Oaxaca), December 6, 1997.

69. L. C. Osorio, "Anarquía," *El Imparcial* (Oaxaca), April 27, 1998. In November, another commentator labeled CIPO-RFM's *plantón* as "a grotesque spectacle" that was "blackmailing the government and the population." Readers should note that *plantones* often lasted weeks or months; to maintain the encampment demonstrators usually cooked, slept, and washed themselves there.

70. D. Ezcárraga and G. Pinto, "Desarrollo y retos," *El Imparcial* (Oaxaca), November 16, 1997.

71. Humberto Torres, "Rechazo a la violencia," *El Imparcial* (Oaxaca), April 28, 1998.

72. M. García, "Movilizaciones, anuncian indígenas," *Marca,* January 9, 1998. The EZLN supporters were members of the pacifist group "Las Abejas." Gatica sought political asylum in Canada in 2005 and later received it.

73. C. Román, untitled photograph, *Las Noticias*, November 19, 1997.
74. Bowen, "Multicultural Market Democracy," 470–73.
75. H. R. Granados, "Nuevas alianzas," *El Extra*, November 20, 1997.
76. S. G. Servin, "CODEP es una organización fantasma: Diputado Priísta," *Las Noticias*, January 13, 1998.
77. One commentator in *El Imparcial* in 1998 deplored how *acarreados* had disrupted "the civility" of a government-sponsored classical music concert in the Zócalo. See H. Beltrán Garcia, "Política partidista sobre las manifestaciones de la cultura," *El Imparcial* (Oaxaca), March 11, 1998.
78. C. Morales, "Generan movilizaciones inestabilidad," *El Imparcial* (Oaxaca), March 14, 1998.
79. Granados, "Nuevas alianzas."
80. Avila, interview, December 15, 2011.
81. Women of the Popular Indigenous Council of Oaxaca—Ricardo Flores Magón, "Declaración Política de Mujeres," March 9, 1998, unprocessed records of the Organizaciónes Indias por los Derechos Humanos de Oaxaca, Oaxaca City.
82. O. V. Ascencio, "Siguen mujeres en plantón pues 'no hay respuestas concretas,'" *Las Noticias*, March 12, 1998; Sibaja, "Realizarán indígenas más movilizaciones."
83. M. A. Vásquez, "Marchan 500 de CODECI, por la detención de sus líderes," *Cantera*, April 17, 1998.
84. O. V. Ascencio, "Ocupa CIPO-RFM juzgados en 6 ciudades; Demandan libertad de dirigentes," *Las Noticias*, April 18, 1998.
85. CIPO-RFM, press release, April 19, 1998, unprocessed records of the Organizaciónes Indias por los Derechos Humanos de Oaxaca, Oaxaca City.
86. V. R. Arrazóla, "Cuestiona Carrasco que líderes quieran exoneración," *La Jornada*, May 20, 1998. This was corroborated by a CIPO-RFM member in a confidential interview, June 19, 2009.
87. Immigration officials denied on April 24 having received a petition from the attorney general to investigate her, which suggests that the PRI and its media supporters had little proof of illegal activities or were most interested in using the issue as a scare tactic; see G. R. Hurtado, "Ninguna petición para expulsar a Ana Bayer," *El Imparcial* (Oaxaca), April 24, 1998.
88. J. Vega, "La detención de dirigentes del CIPO-RFM, 'No se va a quedar así,'" *Cantera*, April 24, 1998. The article in the pro-PRI *El Sur* reported that she was detained during the Tuxtepec demonstrations and was the wife of Cruz.
89. O. V. Ascencio, "Definirán indígenas acciones vs. 'política represiva' de Zedillo," *Las Noticias*, April 18, 1998; Humberto Torres, "No se atiende," *El Imparcial* (Oaxaca), April 28, 1998.
90. C. Morales, "SEGOB investigará a extranjeros," *El Imparcial* (Oaxaca), April 29, 1998.

91. Arrazóla, "Cuestiona Carrasco."

92. Trejo, *Popular Movements in Autocracies*. C. Beas, "Testimonio," argued that the national Indigenous movement had to decide if the state reforms were opportunities or distractions (*esquiroles*).

93. Carrasco Altamirano, interview, August 15, 2015.

94. Eschle and Maiguashca, *Making Feminist Sense*; Conway, *Edges of Global Justice*.

95. Gilberto López y Rivas, *Autonomías: Democracia o contrainsurgencia*, Biblioteca Era (Mexico City: Era, 2004); Stephen, "Construction of Indigenous Suspects"; Overmyer-Velázquez, *Folkloric Poverty*.

5. OBSCURING EMPIRE

1. The expense and distance proved difficult for UNORCA and CIPO-RFM to surmount. CIPO-RFM was still recovering from the repression of 1998. The national office and Washington State Jobs with Justice played relatively minor roles in Seattle. The local chapter was struggling with leadership transitions and budget limitations at the time. Jonathan Rosenblum, interview with the author, June 10, 2019, Seattle, WA; Rosalinda Aguirre, interview with the author, January 15, 2020, Seattle, WA.

2. Graeber, *Direct Action*; Wood, *Direct Action*; Yuen, Burton-Rose, and Katsiaficas, *Battle of Seattle*; Alexander Cockburn and Jeffrey St Clair, *Five Days That Shook the World: The Battle for Seattle and Beyond* (London: Verso, 2000).

3. The focus on the unions and environmental activists, particularly to demonstrate the "cacophonous" diversity of the protesters, is also common in the scholarship. See, for example, DeLuca and Peeples, "From Public Sphere"; Opel and Pompper, "Introduction"; *Battle in Seattle*, directed by Stuart Townsend, 2007.

4. Jerry Crangi, "Report from Seattle: How the IA Shut Down the WTO (with a Little Help from Our Friends)," *IATSE District 1 History* (blog), December 1999, http://iatsedistrict1.org/oldhistory/end1999.htm. Quote from filmmaker Michael Moore, originally published in Michael Moore's Newsletter, December 7, 1999, wvw.michaelmoore.com. (no longer an active web site).

5. Wong, "Showdown before Seattle"; Martínez, "Where Was the Color."

6. Kristine Wong, interviewed by Monica Ghosh, July 28, 2000, https://depts.washington.edu/wtohist/interviews/Wong.pdf; see also Kristyn Joy, "Gender, Immigration, and the WTO," *Network News: National Network for Immigrant and Refugee Rights*, Winter 2000, 12.

7. Martínez, "Where Was the Color"; Anti-Fascist Forum, *My Enemy's Enemy: Essays on Globalization, Fascism and the Struggle against Capitalism* (Montreal: Kersplebedeb, 2003).

8. Lisa Duggan, *The Twilight of Equality? Neoliberalism, Cultural Politics, and the Attack on Democracy* (Boston: Beacon Press, 2003).

9. Joanne Barker, "Territory as Analytic: The Dispossession of Lenapehoking and the Subprime Crisis," *Social Text* 36, no. 2 (June 1, 2018): 19–39, https://doi.org/10.1215/01642472-4362337; Joanne Barker, "The Corporation and the Tribe," *American Indian Quarterly* 39, no. 3 (2015): 243–70.

10. Another kind of color-blind anticorporatism, which I call "global village multiculturalism," is the topic of the following chapter. A range of activists and authors pursued these questions about Seattle in the 1990s and afterward, and their work inspired many of the questions at the center of this essay. In addition to Martínez and Wong, see Anti-Fascist Forum, *My Enemy's Enemy*, and Chip Berlet and Matthew N. Lyons, *Right-Wing Populism in America: Too Close for Comfort* (New York: Guilford Publications, 2018). The Dutch immigrants' rights network De Fabel van de illegaal also published trenchant critiques online in the 1990s. This research follows the work of scholars analyzing race and empire in other global justice protests as well. See Conway, *Edges of Global Justice*; Featherstone, *Solidarity*; Escobar, *Territories of Difference*. Other works on nationalism and race have been influential, including Gilroy, *There Ain't No Black*.

11. "Steelworker Saves Flag at Protest," *The American Legion Magazine*, May 2000, 40.

12. Patti Goldman, interview with the author, June 7, 2018, Seattle, WA.

13. Sarah Adler-Milstein and John M. Kline, *Sewing Hope: How One Factory Challenges the Apparel Industry's Sweatshops* (Berkeley: University of California Press, 2017); Sean D. Ehrlich, *The Politics of Fair Trade: Moving beyond Free Trade and Protection* (New York: Oxford University Press, 2018).

14. Frank, *Buy American*; Ray Kiely, "The Race to the Bottom and International Labor Solidarity," *Review* (Fernand Braudel Center) 26, no. 1 (2003): 67–88. This chapter has partly been inspired by David Roediger's work on "nonracial syndicalism," in which seemingly nonracial worksite unionism could coexist with white supremacy outside of work, in housing, leisure activities, et cetera. See chap. 7 of David R. Roediger, *Working toward Whiteness: How America's Immigrants Became White: The Strange Journey from Ellis Island to the Suburbs* (New York: Basic Books, 2005).

15. For more on dynamics between the Global South and the Global North in global justice contexts, see Brooks and Fox, *Cross-border Dialogues*; Brecher, Costello, and Smith, *Globalization from Below*; Bello, *Brave New Third World?*; Lesley J. Wood, "Bridging the Chasm: The Case of People's Global Action," in Bandy and Smith, *Coalitions across Borders*, 95–117.

16. Jorge G. Castañeda, *Utopia Unarmed: The Latin American Left after the Cold War* (New York: Knopf, 1993).

17. Liberal environmentalists, small farmers, trade unions, consumer groups, and human rights groups were among the most prominent to forge collabora-

tions during the trade negotiations of the late 1980s and early 1990s. Amory Starr, *Naming the Enemy: Anti-corporate Movements Confront Globalization* (London: Zed, 2000). These negotiations were over the GATT and NAFTA. To be clear, Castañeda's proposal was only one during the decade, a period marked by expanding discussions about South-North approaches to opposing neoliberal globalization. See also Kiely, "Race to the Bottom"; Prashad, *Poorer Nations*. The concept of Castañeda's "grand bargain" is also prominent in Brecher, Castello, and Smith, *Globalization from Below*; Brooks and Fox, *Cross-border Dialogues*.

18. Pat Robertson, *The New World Order* (Dallas, TX: Word, 1991).

19. For Pat Buchanan's anti-Semitism in the 1980s and 1990s, see FAIR (Foundation Against Intolerance and Racism), "Pat Buchanan in His Own Words," press release, February 26, 1996, https://fair.org/press-release/pat-buchanan-in-his-own-words/.

20. ABC News, "Transcript of Pat Buchanan's Acceptance Speech," January 6, 2006, https://abcnews.go.com/Politics/story?id=123160&page=1. See also Leonard Zeskind, *Blood and Politics: The History of the White Nationalist Movement from the Margins to the Mainstream* (New York: Farrar Strauss Giroux, 2009), 281.

21. Pat Buchanan, "Time for Economic Nationalism," Pat Buchanan website, *Columns* (blog), June 12, 1995, https://buchanan.org/blog/time-for-economic-nationalism-174. While few right-wing activists actually attended the WTO protests, the far-right Liberty Lobby, the neo-Nazi Matthew Hale, Buchanan, and others praised the WTO protests in their publications. See Mark Rupert, *Ideologies of Globalization: Contending Visions of a New World Order* (London: Routledge, 2000). See also Kay, *NAFTA and the Politics*, and Aaronson, *Taking Trade to the Streets*. It wasn't the first time the US far right had targeted corporate rule either. The Ku Klux Klan in the 1920s and 1930s launched vehement diatribes against the rising "chain stores" of the era: these enterprises were outsiders who threatened the traditional politics of the patriarchal Protestant family and customary white superiority. See Nancy MacLean, *Behind the Mask of Chivalry: The Making of the Second Ku Klux Klan* (New York: Oxford University Press, 1994).

22. During negotiations to include in NAFTA a small amount of US money to support environmental remediation in Mexico, Pat Buchanan asked, "Why should the American people be responsible for cleaning up the pigpen that the Mexicans have made on their side of our common border?" See Timothy Stanley, *The Crusader: The Life and Tumultuous Times of Pat Buchanan* (New York: St. Martin's, 2012).

23. Jim Hightower, interview with the author, February 14, 2013, Providence, RI. For a background on questions of racism and populism, see Joseph Lowndes, "White Populism and the Transformation of the Silent Majority," *The Forum* 14, no. 1 (2016): 25–37; see also Daniel HoSang and Joseph E. Lowndes, *Producers,*

Parasites, Patriots: Race and the New Right-Wing Politics of Precarity (Minneapolis: University of Minnesota Press, 2019), and Kazin, *Populist Persuasion*.

24. Wendell Berry, "Conserving Communities," in Mander and Goldsmith, *Case against the Global Economy*.

25. Movement voices like David Korten and Edward Goldsmith discussed working with the right. (See chapter 6.) Geert Dhondt, interview with the author, August 14, 2018, Philadelphia; Kevin Danaher, Jason Mark, and Arianna Huffington, *Insurrection: Citizen Challenges to Corporate Power* (New York: Routledge, 2003). Korten cast his "people-centered development" as neither "liberal" nor "conservative," as it was based on moving development away from "centralized institutions," including "big government." He claimed that "true populism" was both "liberal and conservative." See David C. Korten, *When Corporations Rule the World* (San Francisco: Kumarian Press, 1996), 9.

26. Mike Dolan, telephone interview with the author, June 17, 2010.

27. Information on the joint meetings comes from "NAFTA Meeting Notes," various dates in 1992, unprocessed records of the IATP, Minneapolis, MN.

28. Ralph Nader, *Unstoppable: The Emerging Left-Right Alliance to Dismantle the Corporate State* (New York: Nation Books, 2014).

29. Mike Dolan, "Mike Dolan: People for Fair Trade/ Network Opposed to WTO," interview by Jeremy Simer, March 3, 2000, WTO History Project, http://depts.washington.edu/wtohist/interviews/Dolan%20-%20Simer.htm. See also Ross Perot, *Save Your Job, Save Our Country: Why NAFTA Must Be Stopped—Now* (New York: Hyperion, 1993).

30. See also Ryan Lizza, "Silent Partner: The Man behind the Anti-Free Trade Revolt," *New Republic*, January 10, 2000, 20–25. As Lizza notes, in 1999 Mike Dolan of Public Citizen drew fire from antiglobalization activists by praising Pat Buchanan's presidential candidacy.

31. Susan Page, "Buchanan Plans to Speak at WTO Protests in D.C.," *USA Today*, April 11, 2000.

32. Patrick J. Buchanan, *A Republic, Not an Empire: Reclaiming America's Destiny* (Washington, DC: Regnery, 1999).

33. Ralph Nader, "Presidential Candidacy Agenda for a New Democracy," Light Party, February 1, 2000, www.lightparty.com/Misc/NaderGreenParty.html.

34. Duggan, *Twilight of Equality?*, 67. See also Leonard Zeskind and Devin Burghart, "Voting along the Racial Faultline: Greens, Browns and the Red, White and Blue," *Searchlight Magazine*, December 2000, 26–27.

35. Anti-Fascist Forum, *My Enemy's Enemy*, 39; Matthew Cooper, "Watching a Gadfly Create a Buzz," *Time*, July 3, 2000.

36. Richard Ellis, *To the Flag: The Unlikely History of the Pledge of Allegiance* (Lawrence: University Press of Kansas, 2005), 276n66.

37. In Seattle, other progressives emphasized US vulnerability. A flier asked, "Do you really want foreign countries competing to serve our school lunches . . .

[or] the purchase of Washington State ferry boats?" People for Fair Trade, "Protest of the Century" flier for Sept. 12 teach-in, Box 1, Folder 2, David E. Ortman papers, University of Washington special collections.

38. Robert Keatley, "Trade Pact Faces Delays, Opposition, Posing Problems for the White House," *Wall Street Journal*, May 20, 1994.

39. Ralph Nader, "Newt Gingrich," Ralph Nader website, November 14, 1994, https://nader.org/1994/11/14/newt-gingrich/.

40. Bob Davis, "Unexpected Obstacles Are Threatening to Delay or Derail Congressional Approval of GATT Pact," *Wall Street Journal*, April 8, 1994. Choate was Ross Perot's coauthor and future vice-presidential candidate.

41. Ralph Nader, "WTO Means Rule by Unaccountable Tribunals," *Wall Street Journal*, August 17, 1994.

42. For background, see Bhushan Bahree, "WTO Tries Again to Create Accord Opening Markets," *Wall Street Journal*, July 18, 1997; Blanca Torres, "Las ONG ambientalistas en las relaciones México-Estados Unidos," *Foro Internacional* 39, no. 4 (1999): 453–78.

43. B. Torres, "ONG ambientalistas," 465.

44. Brooks and Fox, *Cross-border Dialogues*. Nader and Public Citizen generally framed WTO rules about pesticide use in agriculture as a threat to US food consumers, rather than for farmworkers, in the US or abroad. See for instance, Lori Wallach, *The WTO: Five Years of Reasons to Resist Corporate Globalization* (New York: Seven Stories Press, 1999). Jonathan Fox noted the ways both US and Mexican organizations ignored the plights of Mexican and US farmworkers in early anti-NAFTA coalitions. See Jonathan Fox, "Agriculture and the Politics of the North American Trade Debate: A Report from the Trinational Exchange on Agriculture, the Environment, and the Free Trade Agreement, Mexico City, November 14–17, 1991," *LASA Forum* 23, no. 1 (Spring 1992): 3–9.

45. Josée Johnston and Gordon Laxer, "Solidarity in the Age of Globalization: Lessons from the Anti-MAI and Zapatista Struggles," *Theory and Society* 32, no. 1 (2003): 61.

46. Brooks and Fox, *Cross-border Dialogues*, 196–97. Rifts emerged in European-based networks over if and how they should denounce right-wing antiglobalists. See Susan George, "Letter from Susan George to De Fabel van de Illegaal, 99-09-21," September 9, 1999, www.savanne.ch/right-left-materials/george990921.html.

47. For example, see Martin Khor, "Need to Beware of New Issues in WTO (Part II)," David Ortmann papers, Box 1. For some Global South progressives, the emerging dispute settlement mechanisms in the GATT/WTO in the 1990s promised a more democratic process than that which had preceded it—often unilateral trade actions by the US, whose overwhelming market power offered Global South countries little prospect for retaliation. If anything, they claimed

that it was rigged in favor of the US and other economic powers, not the other way around. See Chakravarthi Raghavan, "The World Trade Organization and Its Dispute Settlement System: Tilting the Balance against the South," *Third World Network: Trade and Development Series* 9 (2000), www.twn.my/title/tilting.htm.

48. This is in contrast to ideas of "pooled sovereignty" that allow for decision-making power at multiple levels. Brecher et al. discuss the domestic example of using federal minimum wage laws or environmental regulations to ensure that state- and local-level actors have the health, safety, and well-being to exercise democratic rights. See Brecher, Costello, and Smith, *Globalization from Below*.

49. Perusal of the organizational archives of the Institute for Agriculture and Trade Policy, the National Family Farm Coalition, and Jobs with Justice indicates the wide distribution of Public Citizen publications among other progressive organizations in this period. The same can be said from the collections of Seattle-based "Friends of the Earth" activist David Ortmann. The dolphin case was one of the main cases featured in Public Citizen's anti-GATT material. Robby Stern, a Seattle labor leader, mentioned he had gotten his information from Public Citizen as well. Robby Stern, interview with the author, June 15, 2019, Seattle, WA.

50. This section is inspired by work by Walden Bello and the Third World Network about how Global North stakeholders seeking to "protect standards" can be used to maintain global inequalities. See, for instance, Bello, *Brave New Third World?*

51. Public Citizen paid for expensive full-page advertisements about "Gattzilla" in the early 1990s in the *New York Times* and *Newsweek*.

52. Cecilia Rodriguez, "Save the Dolphins, but Remember Mexican Needs, Too: How Do You Balance Mexican Families' Search for Nutritious, Cheap Food—Such as Tuna—against the Protection of Dolphins?," *Los Angeles Times*, January 13, 1991, sec. Opinion. For a good overview of the North-South dynamics of the tuna-dolphin case and others, see Andrea C. Durbin, "Trade and the Environment: The North-South Divide," *Environment* 37, no. 7 (1995): 37; Carmen G. Gonzalez, "Beyond Eco-Imperialism: An Environmental Justice Critique of Free Trade," *Denver University Law Review* 78, no. 979 (2001): 1007n131.

53. Stephen Dale, *McLuhan's Children: The Greenpeace Message and the Media* (Toronto: Between the Lines, 1996); Durbin, "Trade and the Environment." Note that US unions were historically hesitant about transfers of technology for fear of losing jobs abroad.

54. "The defense of economic interests is disguised by the flag of environmentalism, just as U.S. military intervention is disguised as a democratic crusade," wrote one columnist in the left-wing Mexican daily *La Jornada*. Quoted in Rodriguez, "Save the Dolphins." For collaborations between the US tuna industry and environmentalists, see B. Torres, "ONG ambientalistas," 464. See also "Tuna Boycott Victory," *National Boycott News*, Winter 1992/1993, 25–33.

55. Dale, *McLuhan's Children*, 122–25. For the Mexican government's perspective, see SEMARNAP, *Pesca del atun y proteccion del delfin* (Mexico City: Secretaria de Medio Ambiente, Recursos Naturales y Pesca, 1998). A US trade representative had floated the idea of establishing a convention, like the one on ivory. See Michael Parrish, "Europe Nearer to Dolphin-Safe Tuna: The European Parliament Seeks to Stop Italy's Importation of 'Dirty Tuna' Caught by the Mexican Fishing Fleet," *Los Angeles Times*, November 23, 1991, www.latimes.com/archives/la-xpm-1991-11-23-fi-199-story.html. The stress on multilateral agreements was ultimately affirmed in the "Panama Declaration" of various Latin American and Caribbean countries and a set of US and international environmental organizations, including Greenpeace.

56. Ken Silverstein and Alexander Cockburn, "Tuna, Free Trade and Cocaine," Earth Island Journal 11, no. 3 (Summer 1996), 1, 7. The authors fail to note how US cocaine demand and US international policing priorities pushed transnational cocaine distribution into Mexico in the first place. See also "Dolphin Killers' Ship Rammed," *Earth Island Journal* 6, no. 2 (Spring 1991): 21.

57. Lizza, "Silent Partner." Wallach denied that Public Citizen received funding from Milliken in an interview with *Foreign Policy*. Lori Wallach and Moisés Naím, "The FP Interview: Lori's War," *Foreign Policy*, no. 118 (2000): 29–55, https://doi.org/10.2307/1149669. Public Citizen, to be sure, was a very well-funded organization. Its budget in 1999 was around $11 million, and its Global Trade Watch budget was around $760,000. See Wallach and Naím, "FP Interview."

58. According to the Direct Action Network's framing, Mexico was maintaining its "dolphin-killing" methods and bullying the US with lawsuits and threats. To be clear, the US changed (they did not "eliminate") the law after many years of negotiations.

59. Kristine Wong briefly discusses the nationalistic themes of the Sierra Club's protest presence. See Kristine Wong, "Showdown before Seattle."

60. Mark Engler, "Yes We Can!," *New Internationalist*, November 2, 2002, https://newint.org/features/2002/11/01/labour.

61. As Dana Frank and others have documented, US trade union opposition to imports as a response to trade liberalization had been a regular strategy. See Frank, *Buy American*, and Kay, *NAFTA and the Politics*.

62. Lizza, "Silent Partner."

63. Bob Hasegawa, "WTO Who?" King County Labor Council Newsletter, October 1999, 4, WTO Seattle Collection (Acc. No 5177-003), Box 1, Folder 69 "Pre WTO." For similar example, see Washington State Fair Trade Campaign, "Stop the WTO!" leaflet, March 1999, Box 1, Folder 3, David E. Ortman papers.

64. John Cavanagh, Sarah Anderson, and Hansen-Kuhn Karen, "Trinational Organizing for Just and Sustainable Trade and Development: Some Lessons and Insights," in Brooks and Fox, *Cross-border Dialogues*, 187–210. The authors

noted how the anti-NAFTA coalitions never succeeded in attracting or recruiting activists of color to their efforts (202).

65. Nader, for instance, allowed for important perspectives critical of US unilateralism and power in the 1993 book he edited about globalization. See Ralph Nader et al., *The Case against Free Trade: GATT, NAFTA, and the Globalization of Corporate Power* (San Francisco; Earth Island Press; Berkeley, CA: North Atlantic Books, 1993).

6. INVISIBILIZING IMMIGRATION

1. Brian Derdowski, interview with the author, December 5, 2019, Kirkland, WA. This chapter builds on the work of Margaret Levi and Gillian H. Murphy, "Coalitions of Contention: The Case of the WTO Protests in Seattle," *Political Studies* 54, no. 4 (December 2006): 651–70; and Monica Ghosh, "Inside WTO Dissent: The Experiences of LELO and CCEJ," University of Washington, WTO History Project, March 4, 2001.

2. King County Elections Office, "King County Local Voters Pamphlet," September 14, 1999, https://your.kingcounty.gov/elections/99sep/pamphlet/2012.htm. Derdowski was most concerned about wealthy Californians moving to his region. "Slow-growth" movements seeking to protect nature and tradition often dovetail with protecting white property values. George Lipstiz, *How Racism Takes Place* (Philadelphia: Temple University Press, 2011).

3. Knute Berger, *Pugetopolis: A Mossback Takes on Growth Addicts, Weather Wimps, and the Myth of Seattle Nice* (Seattle, WA: Sasquatch Books, 2009). For the dangers of rhetoric of local community, see L. Fink, "When Community Comes Home"; Benjamin Looker, "Visions of Autonomy: The New Left and the Neighborhood Government Movement of the 1970s," *Journal of Urban History* 38, no. 3 (May 1, 2012): 577–98, https://doi.org/10.1177/0096144211428770.

4. For predictions about NAFTA and migration, see Fox, "Agriculture and the Politics," 4n7. For Mexican perspectives on linking immigration issues to NAFTA negotiations, see Carlos Salinas de Gotarí, *Aliados y adversarios: Historia del TLCAN: 1988–2017* (Mexico City: Debate, 2017); Jorge G. Castañeda and Carlos Heredia, "Another NAFTA: What a Good Agreement Should Offer," in Nader et al., *Case against Free Trade*. For US unions, see Kay, *NAFTA and the Politics*. See chapter 2 and Conclusion. For additional context, see Hanspeter Kriesi, Klaus Armington, and Hannes Siegrist, eds., *Nation and National Identity: The European Experience in Perspective* (West Lafayette, IN: Purdue University Press, 2004).

5. Some analysts had predicted that a deal on the trade of services could allow for Mexico to have some bargaining power against tightening US immigration laws. See Henry R. Nau, "Domestic Trade Politics and the Uruguay Round: An Overview," in *Domestic Trade Politics and the Uruguay Round: An Overview*,

ed. Henry R. Nau (New York: Columbia University Press, 1989), 8–19. The creation of economic refugees in Mexico, and a subsequent surge of migration to the US, were certain ramifications of trade liberalization. Jorge Castañeda and Carlos Heredia argued in 1993 that Mexico should have bargained harder for immigration liberalization policies in NAFTA negotiations. See Castañeda and Heredia, "Another NAFTA."

6. Deborah Orin, "Buchanan Says He'd Wipe the Floor with the Donald," *New York Post*, September 18, 1999, https://nypost.com/1999/09/18/buchanan-says-hed-wipe-the-floor-with-the-donald/.

7. Perot, *Save Your Job*. See chapter 1.

8. Ann E. Kingsolver, *NAFTA Stories: Fears and Hopes in Mexico and the United States* (Boulder, CO: Lynne Rienner, 2001), 59.

9. Caroline Lund, "The Protectionist Trap," *Against the Current*, no. 88 (October 2000), https://againstthecurrent.org/atc088/p1592/. Anti-Mexican sentiments in US unions had been expressed since the beginning of the NAFTA debates. Drawing on the "Buy American" nationalism of the previous two decades, US unionists in some coalitions opposing NAFTA banned foreign cars from their parking lots and criticized Global South immigrants. Rupert, *Ideologies of Globalization*. The AFL-CIO printed placards that said, "Don't send my job to Mexico." See Stanley, *Crusader*.

10. Brooks and Fox, *Cross-border Dialogues*.

11. However, in February 2000 they would change their restrictionist stance. Also, during the 1990s major unions in the federation rejected immigration restriction.

12. "Interview with Presidential Candidate Ralph Nader," *NPR Weekend Edition Saturday*, August 31, 1996; Brandon Bailey, "Nader Crowd Still Keeping Dream Alive; Down in Polls, Nader Draws Support from Disenchanted Liberals," *Wisconsin State Journal*, September 10, 2000. The Dollars and Sense Collective labeled his immigration position in 2000 as "vague." See Dollars and Sense Collective, "Candidates and Consequences," *Dollars and Sense*, no. 232 (November 2000): 14.

13. John Cavanagh, Sarah Anderson, and Hansen-Kuhn Karen, "Trinational Organizing for Just and Sustainable Trade and Development: Some Lessons and Insights," in *Cross-Border Dialogues: U.S.-Mexico Social Movement Networking* (La Jolla, CA: Center for U.S.-Mexican Studies, University of California, San Diego, 2002), 196. For the anti-NAFTA meetings, see "NAFTA Meeting Notes," various dates in 1992, IATP records. The meetings were held at the Capitol Hill Club, alongside the Republican National Committee headquarters. At one meeting, Jim Dorcey from FAIR spoke about their efforts to oppose both immigration and NAFTA on radio talk shows and in print media. See "NAFTA Meeting Notes," October 15, 1992, IATP records. For anti-Mexican banter, see Lizza, "Silent Partner," 24. On Public Citizen funding, see Wallach and Naím, "FP Interview." See also Mi Park, "The Trouble with the Eco-Politics of Localism: Too Close to the Far

Right? Debates on Ecology and Globalization," *Interface: A Journal for and about Social Movements* 5, no. 2 (November 2013): 318–43. See also "Ralph Nader: Conservatively Speaking," interview by Pat Buchanan, *American Conservative*, June 21, 2004, www.theamericanconservative.com/ralph-nader-conservatively-speaking/. Noted anti-immigration leader John Tanton donated $1,500 to his presidential campaign in 2004. See Peter Schrag, *Not Fit for Our Society: Nativism and Immigration* (Berkeley: University of California Press, 2010). In 2004, he called foreign-born professionals working in the US "brain drain specialists" and said Mexico was led by "oligarchs and dictators." See James Ridgeway, "Mondo Washington," *Village Voice*, March 3, 2004, sec. Nation, 26.

14. Some stories professed an ambivalence about immigration. See Art Cullen, "Immigrants, Meatpacking and My Town: I Confess My Confusion," *The Progressive Populist*, April 1997; H. Meadows, "Sierra Debates Immigration and So Should We," *The Progressive Populist*, May 1998. See also Sarah D. Wald, "Visible; Sarah D. Wald, "Visible Farmers/Invisible Workers," *Food, Culture and Society* 14, no. 4 (December 1, 2011): 567–86, https://doi.org/10.2752/1751744 11X13046092851479.

15. For instance, in Mander and Goldsmith, *Case against the Global Economy*, and Wallach, *WTO*. Wallach notes that people will blame immigrants, "greedy farmers or workers," or other scapegoats for "stagnant economic conditions" in the US if a broader anticorporate vision is not popularized (145). The book is dedicated to Mike Dolan. (See chapter 5.) See also Matt Welch, "Nader on Immigration: Friend or Foe?" *Alternet*, October 23, 2000, www.alternet.org/story/9980/nader_on_immigration%3A_friend_or_foe.

16. Thomas Robertson, *The Malthusian Moment: Global Population Growth and the Birth of American Environmentalism* (New Brunswick, NJ: Rutgers University Press, 2012); Jason L. Riley, *Let Them In: The Case for Open Borders* (New York: Gotham, 2008). See Paul Ehrlich, *The Population Bomb* (New York: Ballantine Books, 1968).

17. Riley, *Let Them In*. The switch was likely influenced by threats by the Club's biggest funder, who opposed restriction. See Riley, *Let Them In*. See also Leslie King, "Ideology, Strategy and Conflict in a Social Movement Organization: The Sierra Club Immigration Wars," *Mobilization: An International Quarterly* 13, no. 1 (February 1, 2008): 45–61, https://doi.org/10.17813/maiq.13.1.c7pv26280665g90g.

18. Riley, *Let Them In*. See "Sierra Club Secessionists" chapter in Riley.

19. Heidi Beirich and Edited Mark Potok, *Greenwash: Nativists, Environmentalism and the Hypocrisy of Hate*, ed. Mark Potok, Special Report (Montgomery, AL: Southern Poverty Law Center, 2010), 19, www.splcenter.org/sites/default/files/d6_legacy_files/downloads/publication/Greenwash.pdf. In 2004, Groundswell Sierra developed to oppose anti-immigrant forces, whom they defeated 10 to 1. See also Alexandra Stern, *Eugenic Nation: Faults*

and Frontiers of Better Breeding in Modern America, 2nd ed., American Crossroads 17 (Oakland: University of California Press, 2016); King, "Ideology, Strategy and Conflict"; John Hultgren, *Border Walls Gone Green: Nature and Anti-immigrant Politics in America* (Minneapolis: University of Minnesota Press, 2015).

20. Derek D. Turner, "Are We at War with Nature?," *Environmental Values* 14, no. 1 (2005): 21–36.

21. He also identified as a "bio-centrist."

22. Edward Abbey, "Immigration and Liberal Taboos," in *One Life at a Time, Please* (New York: Henry Holt, n.d.), 41–44; and Edward Abbey, letter to the editor, *Bloomsbury Review* (April–May 1986), as cited in Murray Bookchin, "Yes!—Whither Earth First?," *Green Perspectives*, September 1988, http://dwardmac.pitzer.edu/Anarchist_Archives/bookchin/gp/perspectives10.html. See also Bernhard Forchtner, *The Far Right and the Environment: Politics, Discourse and Communication* (Abingdon: Routledge, 2019); Lisa Park and David Pellow, *The Slums of Aspen: Immigrants vs. the Environment in America's Eden*, Nation of Newcomers: Immigrant History as American History (New York: NYU Press, 2011); M. Park, "Trouble with the Eco-Politics," 26; and Hultgren, *Border Walls Gone Green*. See also Sarah D. Wald, *The Nature of California: Race, Citizenship, and Farming since the Dust Bowl* (Seattle: University of Washington Press, 2016).

23. Murray Bookchin and Dave Foreman, *Defending the Earth: Debate between Murray Bookchin and Dave Foreman*, foreword by David Levine (Montreal: Black Rose Books, 1991).

24. Randy Hayes, telephone interview with the author, April 7, 2022.

25. Gordon and Newfield, *Mapping Multiculturalism*; Lowe, *Immigrant Acts*, 413–23; Jodi Melamed, *Represent and Destroy: Rationalizing Violence in the New Racial Capitalism* (Minneapolis: University of Minnesota Press, 2011). In this section I also draw on the insights of a variety of cultural studies of capitalism and empire. See Iyko Day, *Alien Capital: Asian Racialization and the Logic of Settler Colonial Capitalism* (Durham, NC: Duke University Press, 2016); Ahmed, *On Being Included* (Durham, NC: Duke University Press, 2012); and Shameem Black, "Microloans and Micronarratives: Sentiment for a Small World," *Public Culture* 21, no. 2 (May 1, 2009): 269–92, https://doi.org/10.1215/08992363-2008-029. See also Bonilla-Silva, *Racism without Racists*; Lowe, *Immigrant Acts*; and Charles R. Hale, *Más Que un Indio = More Than an Indian: Racial Ambivalence and Neoliberal Multiculturalism in Guatemala* (Santa Fe, NM: School of American Research Press, 2006).

26. Jeffrey S. Juris, *Insurgent Encounters: Transnational Activism, Ethnography, and the Political* (Durham, NC: Duke University Press, 2013).

27. David Morris, "A Global Village and a Globe of Villages," speech delivered at the Rochester Institute of Technology, April 3, 1997, https://ilsr.org/listen-a-global-village-or-a-globe-of-villages-david-morris-speech-from-1997/; and

David Morris, "Healthy Cities: Self-Reliant Cities," *Health Promotion* 2, no. 2 (1987): 169–76. See also Mander and Goldsmith, *Case against the Global Economy*. This section is heavily indebted to the activist critique of the IFG in Anti-Fascist Forum, *My Enemy's Enemy*.

28. Jerry Mander, interview with the author, January 23, 2019, San Francisco.

29. Andrew C. Revkin, "A Video Challenge to Green Shoppers," *Dot Earth Blog*, November 13, 2007, https://archive.nytimes.com/dotearth.blogs.nytimes.com/2007/11/13/video-challenges-green-shoppers-and-globalization/.

30. Mander, *In the Absence of the Sacred*; Mander and Goldsmith, introduction to Mander and Goldsmith, *Case against the Global Economy*, 21, 15.

31. David Taylor, "Teddy Goldsmith—Obituary," *Green World*, August 21, 2009, https://green-history.uk/people/teddy-goldsmith-obit.

32. Peter Bunyard, "Teddy Goldsmith: A Tribute," *The Ecologist*, September 1, 2009, https://theecologist.org/2009/sep/01/teddy-goldsmith-tribute.

33. Mander and Goldsmith, introduction, 15. See also Edward Goldsmith et al, *Blueprint for Survival* (New York: New American Library, 1974); Edward Goldsmith and International Society for Ecology and Culture, *The Future of Progress: Reflections on Environment and Development* (Dartington: Green Books, 1995); Edward Goldsmith, *The Way: An Ecological World-View* (Athens: University of Georgia Press, 1998).

34. Vine Deloria, *We Talk, You Listen: New Tribes, New Turf* (Lincoln: University of Nebraska Press, 2007); Sandy Marie Anglás Grande, "Beyond the Ecologically Noble Savage: Deconstructing the White Man's Indian," *Environmental Ethics* 21, no. 3 (August 1, 1999): 307–20, https://doi.org/10.5840/enviroethics199921320.

35. Paul Nadasdy, "Transcending the Debate over the Ecologically Noble Indian: Indigenous Peoples and Environmentalism," *Ethnohistory* 52, no. 2 (Spring 2005): 291–331, https://doi.org/10.1215/00141801-52-2-291; Philip Joseph Deloria, *Playing Indian*, Yale Historical Publications (New Haven, CT: Yale University Press, 1998); Paul Heelas, *The New Age Movement: The Celebration of the Self and the Sacralization of Modernity* (Oxford: Blackwell, 1996); Philip Jenkins, *Dream Catchers: How Mainstream America Discovered Native Spirituality* (New York: Oxford University Press, 2006); Macarena Gómez-Barris, *The Extractive Zone: Social Ecologies and Decolonial Perspectives* (Durham, NC: Duke University Press, 2017).

36. Jerry Mander, "Bad Magic: The Failure of Technology: An Interview with Jerry Mander by Catherine Ingram," *The Sun: A Magazine of Ideas*, no. 192 (November 1991), https://ratical.org/ratville/AoS/theSun.html#IV.

37. Mander's romanticism is briefly critiqued in Shari M. Huhndorf, *Going Native: Indians in the American Cultural Imagination* (Ithaca, NY: Cornell University Press, 2001).

38. Martijn van Beek and Fernanda Pirie, *Modern Ladakh: Anthropological Perspectives on Continuity and Change* (Leiden: Brill, 2008), 10–11.

39. The Indigenous were in their "expected" places, and in contrast, migrants were "bodies out of place," no longer distant, distinct, and different. V. Deloria, *We Talk, You Listen;* Grande, "Beyond the Ecologically Noble Savage"; Philip Joseph Deloria, *Indians in Unexpected Places* (Lawrence: University Press of Kansas, 2004); Ahmed, *On Being Included*. As indicated in the neoliberal multicultural politics that CIPO-RFM faced in Mexico (see chapter 4), "eco-Indian" archetypes can reinforce primitivistic stereotypes about Indigenous peoples and have been made to serve as the measuring sticks of authentic Indian-ness, casting people as "ignoble," corrupt, or inauthentic if they fail to live up to the Ecological Indian expectations of settler environmentalists and others. See Audra Simpson, *Mohawk Interruptus: Political Life across the Borders of Settler States* (Durham, NC: Duke University Press, 2014); Gregory D. Smithers, "Beyond the 'Ecological Indian': Environmental Politics and Traditional Ecological Knowledge in Modern North America," *Environmental History* 20, no. 1 (2015): 83–111; and Beth A. Conklin and Laura R. Graham, "The Shifting Middle Ground: Amazonian Indians and Eco-Politics," *American Anthropologist* 97, no. 4 (1995): 695–710, https://doi.org/10.1525/aa.1995.97.4.02a00120. In contrast to this stress on purity, Anishinaabe scholar Gerald Vizenor's work documents the ways mixed-race Native Americans have been seen as ambassadors rather than simply as marginal to the more authentic and "pure" people. See also Scott Richard Lyons, *X-Marks: Native Signatures of Assent* (Minneapolis: University of Minnesota Press, 2010).

40. Conklin and Graham, "Shifting Middle Ground." See 703 for advertising campaign. Hayes authored an essay for Anita Roddick's 2001 book on creating social change; Randy Hayes, "Three Legs Are Better Than Two," in *Take It Personally: How to Make Conscious Choices to Change the World*, ed. Anita Roddick (Berkeley, CA: HarperCollins, 2001), 148–49. See also Beth A. Conklin, "Body Paint, Feathers, and VCRs: Aesthetics and Authenticity in Amazonian Activism," *American Ethnologist* 24, no. 4 (1997): 711–37, https://doi.org/10.1525/ae.1997.24.4.711.

41. Hayes, interview, April 7, 2022.

42. Rainforest Action Network, "Stop the Yanomami Genocide," *Rainforest Action Network Action Alert*, no. 46 (March 1990).

43. Kyra Landzelius, *Native on the Net: Indigenous and Diasporic Peoples in the Virtual Age* (Hoboken, NJ: Routledge, 2004); Maxwell T. Boykoff, Michael K. Goodman, and Adrian McDonald, *Contentious Geographies: Environmental Knowledge, Meaning, Scale* (Abingdon: Taylor and Francis, 2008).

44. Landzelius, *Native on the Net*, 122. Yet RAN in some cases "fixed" the Huaroni and other peoples in space in their representations, taking liberties with how their territories were defined and casting them as more homogenous

than they were. See Boykoff, Goodman, and McDonald, *Contentious Geographies*, 9, 104–9.

45. Lise Fernanda Sedrez, "A Meeting of Minds: Coalitions, Representations and American Non-governmental Organizations in the Brazilian Amazon" (master's thesis, New Jersey Institute of Technology, 1998), 7, 162.

46. Wendell Berry, "Why I Am Not Going to Buy a Computer," in *What Are People For?* (Berkeley, CA: Counterpoint, 1990).

47. Part IV of Mander and Goldsmith, *Case against the Global Economy.*

48. Berry, "Conserving Communities," 410.

49. Berry, "Why I Am Not Going to Buy a Computer." In another essay in the volume Berry defends himself from criticism over his note that his wife types for him. He argues the criticism is driven by misguided notions of feminism that make unfounded assumptions about the division of labor in his household. See "Feminism, the Body, and the Machine," 178–96, See also Wendell Berry, "Caught in the Middle: On Abortion and Homosexuality," *Christian Century,* March 20, 2013, www.christiancentury.org/article/2013-03/caught-middle. Berry was known for his resistance to gay marriage and abortion. For more on Berry's gender conservatism, readers might consult his examination of the sexual harassment claims against Clarence Thomas at his 1991 Supreme Court nomination hearings. Berry situates the moment as reflective of the "disintegration" of community-minded (rural) societies "whose ideal of justice was trust and fairness among people who knew each other." See Wendell Berry, "Sex, Economy, Freedom, and Community," in *Sex, Economy, Freedom, and Community* (New York: Pantheon Books, 1993), 121–22.

50. Wendell Berry, "A Few Words in Favor of Edward Abbey," in *What Are People For?* (Berkeley, CA: Counterpoint, 2018), 39, 40.

51. Berry, "Few Words in Favor," 40.

52. Berry, "Conserving Communities," 411.

53. Berry, "The Joy of Sales Resistance," in *Sex, Economy, Freedom and Community*, xv.

54. Berry, "Conserving Communities," 417.

55. For Berry, "neighborly acts" and a sense of "neighborhood" would power these rural idylls, and his Community Party would galvanize a local economy that would "supply local needs first," and only second export products to "nearby cities." There would be "no institutionalized childcare and no homes for the aged" in these hamlets of collective help. "The community knows and remembers itself by the association of the old and young," so "the old and the young" would "take care of each other." See Berry, "Conserving Communities," 414–15. Berry's celebration of settler agrarian agriculture is accompanied by a general inattention to Native Americans and their conservation and agricultural practices (not to mention their territorial claims). For a critique, see Joseph Wiebe, "Cultural Appropriation in Bioregionalism and the Need for a Decolonial Ethics of Place," *Jour-*

nal of Religious Ethics 49, no. 1 (March 2021): 138–58, https://doi.org/10.1111/jore.1234. Berry writes briefly about Menominee forest conservation in a 1995 essay. While generally complimentary of their efforts, he also concludes that their approach "is not complex enough" for "Kentuckians looking for the pattern of a good local forest economy." See Wendell Berry, "Conserving Forest Communities," in *Another Turn of the Crank* (Berkeley, CA: Counterpoint, 1996), 30–44. Note that Berry wrote a book about anti-Black racism earlier in his career. See Wendell Berry, *The Hidden Wound* (Boston: Houghton Mifflin, 1970).

56. Berry, "Caught in the Middle." Goldsmith spoke, for instance, at the New Right GRECE (Research and Study Group Research and Study Group for European Civilization) conference in 1994. See Tamir Bar-On, *Where Have All the Fascists Gone?* (London: Ashgate, 2007); Tamir Bar-On, *Rethinking the French New Right: Alternatives to Modernity* (London: Routledge, 2013).

57. See Bar-On, *Where Have All the Fascists Gone?* See also George, "Letter from Susan George"; Anti-Fascist Forum, *My Enemy's Enemy*; Angela Y. Davis, "Gender, Class, and Multiculturalism: Rethinking 'Race' Politics," in Gordon and Newfield, *Mapping Multiculturalism*, 40–48. Other works on diversity and multiculturalism include Melamed, Burgett, and Hendler, "Diversity"; Ferguson, *Reorder of Things*; Gordon and Newfield, *Mapping Multiculturalism*; Lowe, *Immigrant Acts*; Coulthard, *Red Skin, White Masks*; Ahmed, *On Being Included*; Gilroy, *There Ain't No Black*.

58. As an armed organization, their physical presence in Seattle would have been difficult. In WTO protests in Cancún in 2003, organizations asked the EZLN to submit a written statement.

59. Goldsmith et al., *Imperiled Planet: Restoring Our Endangered Ecosystems* (Cambridge, MA: MIT Press, 1990). RAN reportedly received $464,080 between 1997 and 2001 in the 1990s from the anti-immigration Foundation for Deep Ecology, which Mander had collaborated with at different moments. M. Park, "Trouble with the Eco-Politics," 26.

60. A. Davis, "Gender, Class, and Multiculturalism."

61. Carol Tice, "Hospitality Industry Gets Ready for Peak," Puget Sound Business Journal, Nov. 15, 1999.

62. For LELO critique, see Joy, "Gender." For Dolan and his coalition, immigrant organizations were generally absent from event schedules and mailing lists in 1999, including a national one with more than 100 organizations. See, for one example, People for Fair Trade/Network Opposed to WTO, "WTO Calendar of Events," October 22, 1999, Michael Woo personal collection. Even if immigration as a topic was obscured, immigrant organizations did attend the protests.

63. Todd Wolfson, *Digital Rebellion: The Birth of the Cyber Left* (Urbana: University of Illinois Press, 2014).

64. Dan Seligman, interview by April Eaton, August 17, 2000, WTO History Project.

65. Scott et al., letter, October 5, 1999, Cindy Domingo collection, University of Washington special collections.

66. Ricardo Ortega, interview with the author, June 15, 2018, Seattle, WA; Cindy Domingo and Juan Bocanegra, interview by Monica Ghosh, Aug. 18, 2000, https://depts.washington.edu/wtohist/interviews/Bocanegra_Domingo.pdf. See also Levi and Murphy, "Coalitions"; and Ghosh, "Inside."

67. With the exception of the IFG's "Voices from the South" event, the majority of the IFG's speakers in Seattle were from the US or Europe. See International Forum on Globalization, "Economic Globalization: The Role of the World Trade Organization Teach-In," media advisory, October 12, 1999, WTO Seattle Collection, University of Washington, https://digitalcollections.lib.washington.edu/digital/collection/wto/id/187/; Ace Saturay, interview by Jeremy Simer of People's Assembly, May 4, 2000, WTO History Project, https://depts.washington.edu/wtohist/interviews/Saturay.pdf.

68. Domingo, interview, June 19, 2017.

69. Ortega, interview, June 15, 2018.

70. Juan José Bocanegra, interview with the author, Jan. 19, 2020, Seattle.

71. Joe Uehlein, interview with the author, May 16, 2016, Tacoma Park, MD.

7. "LOCALIZING" GLOBAL JUSTICE

1. Everything from labor and socialist magazines to anarchist zines and email listservs dedicated their time and space to Seattle and its legacy during the first year of the new millennium. For one example, see the *Monthly Review* (particularly July/August 2000).

2. Jeff Crosby, telephone interview with the author, September 16, 2013.

3. Though I refer to "labor unions" as distinct from "street protesters" in this chapter, that isn't to say that they were always mutually exclusive.

4. Dawn Jenkins, "Grant Proposal (Draft)," October 23, 2000, unprocessed records at the Jobs with Justice national office (hereafter JwJ files). Moen had been in the community since the 1950s. It produced, among other things, specialty parts for toilet repair. See Kristie Daugherty, "Hoov-R-Line Moving to Mexico," *Journal-Enterprise*, May 27, 1999.

5. These sentiments usually failed to acknowledge how the struggle over NAFTA had featured a move by many labor unions to distance themselves from racist scapegoating of "foreign" workers and products and embrace a view targeting corporations as exploiting workers in all countries involved. See Kay, *NAFTA and the Politics*.

6. See chapters 5 and 6 for more on color-blind anticorporatism.

7. Prashad, *Poorer Nations*; Vijay Prashad, *The Darker Nations: A People's History of the Third World*, New Press People's History (New York: New Press,

2007); Nat Weinstein, "AFL-CIO Backs Anti-IMF, World Bank Protest in Washington: 'Dump the Third World Debt,'" *Socialist Action* (blog), April 1, 2000, https://socialistaction.org/2000/04/01/afl-cio-backs-anti-imf-world-bank-protest-in-washington-dump-the-third-world-debt/. For more on the student strike in Mexico, see Gerardo L. Dorantes, *Conflicto y poder en la UNAM: La huelga de 1999* (Mexico City: Universidad Nacional Autónoma de México; Editorial Miguel Ángel Porrúa, 2006.

8. For the United Auto Workers, the United Steel Workers, the IAM, and others, China had been a target before Seattle.

9. Marc Cooper, "Where's Hoffa Driving the Teamsters?," *The Nation*, July 13, 2000, www.thenation.com/article/wheres-hoffa-driving-teamsters/.

10. Kent Wong and Elaine Bernard, "Labor's Mistaken Anti-China Campaign," *New Labor Forum*, Fall/Winter 2000, http://qcpages.qc.cuny.edu/newlaborforum/old/html/7_article2.html.

11. Confidential interview, former Teamsters' staff person. The posters have been catalogued and digitized by the Behring Center at the National Museum of American History; see "No PNTR for China," April 16, 2000, https://americanhistory.si.edu/collections/search/object/nmah_1328505. I have not been able to verify the exact time and place of the photographs displayed. The Teamsters staff person told me they were "stock photos" the union acquired and depict scenes from Chinese history "before the 1980s."

12. Walden Bello and Anuradha Mittal, "Dangerous Liaisons: Progressives, the Right, and the Anti-China Trade Campaign," *Food First Backgrounder* (Institute for Food and Development Policy), April 1, 2000, https://archive.foodfirst.org/publication/dangerous-liaisons-progressives-the-right-and-the-anti-china-trade-campaign/. One banner read, in fact, "No Blank Checks for China's Dictators." (See uncredited cover photo in Bello and Mittal.)

13. John Tarleton, "The IMC Fills a Niche: Protesters Develop Their Own Global News Service," *On the Road with John Tarleton*, October 2000, www.johntarleton.net/imc_feature.html.

14. Tim Waters, telephone interview with the author, January 13, 2012.

15. Robert Weissman from Public Citizen's Washington office played a big role in organizing IMF/World Bank activities. See Robert Weissman, interview with the author, September 18, 2018, Washington, DC. See also Weinstein, "AFL-CIO." Demands for a "social clause" to trade agreements had generated much division between Global North progressives and Global South national representatives and activists in Seattle and before. Global South activists particularly resisted proposals that could level trade sanctions at nations that violated labor standards (inevitably poor countries), rather than tying trade agreements to development assistance for the Global South. See Shareen Hertel, "What Was All the Shouting About? Strategic Bargaining and Protest at the WTO Third Ministerial Meeting," *Human Rights Review* 6, no. 3 (April 2005): 102–18,

https://doi.org/10.1007/BF02862217. For an earlier critique, see Martin Khor, "The WTO and the Battle over Labor Standards," Third World Network, January 13, 1997.

16. Beverly J. Silver and Giovanni Arrighi, "Workers North and South," *Socialist Register* 37 (2001), https://socialistregister.com/index.php/srv/article/view/5755. For Wong and Bernard, the singular and focused attention on China simply outweighed its actual economic presence. See Kent Wong and Bernard, "Labor's Mistaken Anti-China Campaign."

17. Silver and Arrighi, "Workers North and South"; Nita Rudra, *Globalization and the Race to the Bottom in Developing Countries: Who Really Gets Hurt?* (Cambridge: Cambridge University Press, 2008). Rudra argues that the middle classes in poor countries are most negatively affected by trade liberalization, not the poorest.

18. Silver and Arrighi, "Workers North and South." The authors argue that the process of financialization, not "globalization," was the foundation of the contemporary world economic changes.

19. Lee Chang-Geun, "What Has Seattle Left Us With?," Nadir, December 23, 1999, www.nadir.org/nadir/initiativ/agp/free/seattle/picis_seattle.htm.

20. Bello and Mittal, "Dangerous Liaisons."

21. Silver and Arrighi, "Workers North and South." Bello and Mittal, "Dangerous Liaisons." Bello and Mittal criticized how the coalition relied on political dissidents in China (who were denouncing China's human rights abuses) but had no relationships with workers. The AFL-CIO had refused to recognize any Chinese trade union under the rationale that they were simply pawns of the central government. As chapter 1 documents, in Mexico's case the IMF loan conditionalities helped animate and focus the Mexican left's narrative about sovereignty and dependency, and it helped power the unprecedented rise of a left-wing opposition presidential candidate in 1988.

22. Martin Khor, 2000, quoted in Hertel, "What Was All the Shouting About?"

23. Also, trade was already increasing with China. It was already getting its "Most Favored Nation" status approved each year. Kent Wong and Bernard, "Labor's Mistaken Anti-China Campaign." Besides, as one progressive union educator affirmed, "We should engage workers on [sweatshops and prison labor within the US], especially since we might be better able to do more about abuse here than in China." See Michael D. Yates, "Workers of All Countries, Unite," *Monthly Review*, July 1, 2000, https://monthlyreview.org/2000/07/01/workers-of-all-countries-unite/.

24. Bello and Mittal, "Dangerous Liaisons"; Kent Wong and Bernard, "Labor's Mistaken Anti-China Campaign."

25. Bello and Mittal, "Dangerous Liaisons"; Chang-Geun, "What Has Seattle Left Us With?"

26. Silver and Arrighi, "Workers North and South."

27. Bello and Mittal, "Dangerous Liaisons." For other perspectives on Global South alternative plans, see Chang-Geun, "What Has Seattle Left Us With?," and Martin Khor, "WTO and the Battle over Labor Standards," *Third World Network Features*, January 13, 1997. See chapters 1 and 2 for more on UNORCA's rural development plans in Mexico.

28. Yates, "Workers of All Countries, Unite." Note that several high-profile investigations of sweatshops within the US had gained much attention in the mid-1990s (for instance, the investigation of celebrity Kathy Lee Gifford's clothing line).

29. Ray O. Light, "From 'No to WTO' to 'No to China': The US Working Class Takes a Step Backward in Washington, DC," Marxist-Leninist Translations and Reprints, September 2000, www.mltranslations.org/US/ROL/ROLNoChina.htm. Some Marxists declared critiques of globalization to be misguided, since "globalization" was simply the advance of technological and industrial capitalism. They argued that society needed to seek industrial development and eject peasants from their rural holdings and turn them into an urban proletariat, since this was the only path to true world revolution. See Jerry White, "Economic Nationalist Sets the Tone for IMF Protests in Washington," *World Socialist Web Site*, May 3, 2000, www.wsws.org/en/articles/2000/05/wash-m03.html.

30. Kent Wong and Bernard, "Labor's Mistaken Anti-China Campaign"; Light, "From 'No to WTO.'"

31. AFL-CIO, "AFL-CIO: Vigil Sends the Message: No Blank Check for China," ca. mid-2000, http://lobby.la.psu.edu/040_PNTR/Organizational_Statements/AFL-CIO/Vigil.htm.

32. Crosby, telephone interview, September 16, 2013. He said, "I remember the first time I went [to the AFL-CIO] I didn't even know where to go; the first time like six months after Sweeney, it was like I knew half the people, everyone I knew got hired."

33. Or listservs tied to the IndyMedia Center. IMC, which got more than a million hits for its Seattle coverage, set up shop in a small gallery in Northwest Washington, D.C. See Tarleton, "IMC Fills a Niche."

34. AFL-CIO, "AFL-CIO Executive Council Statement: Jobs with Justice Coalition," December 16, 1996, https://aflcio.org/about/leadership/statements/jobs-justice-coalition.

35. Fred Azcarate to staff, February 1, 2001, unprocessed records, JwJ files.

36. Among the latter are its workers' rights boards, coordination of national days of action on a particular theme or campaign, and organizing of the national meeting.

37. Fred Azcarate, telephone interview with the author, July 6, 2010.

38. Nearly half of the members of the national executive board were themselves leaders of local coalitions. In the late 1990s they began mailing to each

local coalition a package of news clippings about other local Jobs with Justice coalitions. They also included updates about nationally coordinated activities and guides about how to initiate campaigns that were gaining ground in other cities (e.g., proposals to increase the minimum wage.) These packets were sizable—and could include as many as thirty items. An example of a campaign discussed was a living wage campaign

39. Staff update, ca. mid-2001, unprocessed records, JwJ files.

40. From June 1999 to November 2000, national Jobs with Justice staff calculated that nearly half of their campaigns featured Jobs with Justice local coalitions helping craft campaign strategy in coalition members' initiatives. Jobs with Justice Planning Committee, "Executive Summary: Evaluating 2000 Program Priorities," December 10, 2000, unprocessed records, JwJ files. Emergent thinking in union-organizing circles has increasingly viewed union members as community members and has challenged the strict delineation between "union" and "community" apparent in 1990s-era union-based coalitions. See Erica Smiley and Sarita Gupta, *The Future We Need: Organizing for a Better Democracy in the Twenty-First Century* (Ithaca, NY: Cornell University Press, 2022); Jane McAlevey, *No Shortcuts: Organizing for Power in the New Gilded Age* (New York: Oxford University Press, 2016); see also Eric D. Larson, "Black Lives Matter and Bridge Building: Labor Education for a 'New Jim Crow' Era," *Labor Studies Journal* 41, no. 1 (March 1, 2016): 36–66, https://doi.org/10.1177/0160449X16638800.

41. During her work for unions, she said she was shocked by the amount of sexual harassment among the organizers, particularly when traveling and staying in hotels. Confidential interview. Understanding the toxic masculinity that permeated so many union staffs and memberships, national organizers helped to create national women's retreats and to advocate for diversity on the executive board. By the late 1990s, the majority of the leadership in local coalitions were white women or people of color. Jobs with Justice executive board, meeting minutes, November 3, 1999, unprocessed records, JwJ files.

42. See chapter 3.

43. Jeff Crosby, "WTO Shutdown: The Kids Are Alright," *Common Dreams*, December 3, 2019.

44. One Jobs with Justice and AFL-CIO activist credited USAS with turning unions' critical attention to sweatshops, and consequently globalization, in the late 1990s. Stewart Acuff, telephone interview with the author, August 11, 2011. For more on USAS, see Liza Featherstone, *Students against Sweatshops* (London: Verso, 2002).

45. Kentucky Jobs with Justice, "The Faces of NAFTA: Kentucky/Mexico Worker Exchange Brings Message of Fair Trade to Kentucky," *Action Lines*, Summer 2002, 1. In these events, both US and Mexican workers criticized "free trade." "Trabajadores de ambos lados de la frontera critican al TLC," *Hoy en las Americas*, June 21, 2002. The delegation was partly funded by the New World

Foundation and was co-organized with Southern Arizona Alliance for Economic Justice. In 2002 this coalition was able to bring two Mexican workers to Kentucky. Other Jobs with Justice groups had organized such worker exchanges in the past, including Massachusetts Jobs with Justice as early as 1994, and Tennessee Industrial Renewal Network (TIRN) in Tennessee.

46. In 2000, in addition to documenting the conditions for Mexican workers at Moen, they built a "Labor in the Pulpits" campaign that recruited workers to testify in churches about the moral need for living wages. They organized press conferences and rallies for nurses trying to form a union through AFSCME.

47. Southern field organizer (Jobs with Justice), report to staff, November 2000, unprocessed records, JwJ files. One USAS activist and later Jobs with Justice staff member recounted how, at least with student activists at her alma mater of Georgetown, unions and students reached an often-unspoken common ground. Students would be sure to make trade and jobs part of their campaigns against sweatshops abroad; unions would be sure that their overtures to USAS would be about global justice, not about blaming foreign countries or imports. Laura McSpedon, telephone interview with the author, November 20, 2022.

48. Dawn Jenkins, meeting notes, ca. late 2000, unprocessed records, JwJ files.

49. Jobs with Justice, "JwJ Returns from Delegation," press release, June 14, 2000, unprocessed records, JwJ files.

50. The other principle being raised in USAS was about leadership—and how immigrant students and immigrant workers could be represented in the organization.

51. Fred Azcarate also mentioned the difference between attacking workers in other countries and defending your job in the US.

52. Azcarate, telephone interview, July 6, 2010.

53. Nancy Haque, telephone interview with the author, July 5, 2009.

54. Azcarate, telephone interview, July 6, 2010.

55. Cassie Waters, telephone interview with the author, November 6, 2011.

56. Jobs with Justice was founded on creating local and national "permanent coalitions," rather than ad hoc alliances to take on single-issue campaigns, since real trust between unions and other stakeholders could only develop over time. The objective was for them to stand up for struggles in which they didn't see a self-interest and to expand how they saw their self-interest over time. Eric D. Larson, *Jobs with Justice: 25 Years, 25 Voices* (Oakland, CA: PM Press, 2013). Azcarate, interview, July 6, 2010. Jobs with Justice's approach was to work with unions or ally organizations on issues where they could find common ground, even if they didn't agree on all issues. McSpedon, telephone interview, November 20, 2022.

57. If it hadn't been for Jobs with Justice, major unions and the AFL-CIO might have skipped A16 altogether. See JoAnn Wypijewski, "A16: Inside/Out-

side Stories," *CounterPunch*, April 15, 2000. For its part, Jobs with Justice avoided the China-bashing activities of April 12. Rachel Miller, one of two National Organizers for United Students Against Sweatshops, told me that she purposely refrained from including the listing of the April 12 Teamsters event in the informational flyer sent out to USAS chapters early in 2000. USAS was an important Jobs with Justice ally, and Miller participated in (and was arrested at) a Jobs with Justice civil disobedience protest supporting Interparking workers. Miller would later become a staff member of Rhode Island Jobs with Justice. Rachel Miller, telephone interview, December 8, 2022.

58. That's not to say that unions, particularly local unions, weren't planning to participate. After our convergence center got raided, the puppet making went over to the SEIU Local 82 building. One current Jobs with Justice staff member recalls that local organizers from the Hotel Employees and Restaurant Employees (HERE) union were active in supporting the A16 protests.

59. Wypijewski, "A16." Azcarate said that "it was a process, [and] because of our close relationships and ties with folks in labor movement, we were much more successful in bridging labor movement interests with the global justice movement interests."

60. Waters, interview, November 6, 2011.

61. Waters, interview, November 6, 2011.

62. Kentucky Jobs with Justice, weekly action schedule, April 2000, unprocessed records, JwJ files.

63. Jobs with Justice, "Immigrant Workers March," press release, April 18, 2000, unprocessed records, JwJ files.

64. See chapter 3 for more.

65. Jobs with Justice, National Meeting schedule, August 2000, unprocessed records, JwJ files.

66. "Organizing for Global Justice," June 1, 2001, unprocessed records, JwJ files.

67. Fernandez, *Policing Dissent*; Amory Starr, Luis Fernandez, and Christian Scholl, *Shutting Down the Streets: Political Violence and Social Control in the Global Era* (New York: New York University Press, 2011); John A. Noakes, Brian V. Klocke, and Patrick F. Gillham, "Whose Streets? Police and Protester Struggles over Space in Washington, DC, 29–30 September 2001," *Policing and Society* 15, no. 3 (2005): 235.

68. McSpedon, telephone interview, November 20, 2022. For a Columbus Day/Indigenous Day protest in Denver, Colorado, in October 2001, a combination of "Gang Squad" police and undercover officers aggressively forced anarchists out of the streets and onto sidewalks despite their small numbers (personal recollection of the author).

69. Mark Tran, "IMF and World Bank Meetings in Jeopardy," *The Guardian*, September 14, 2001, sec. US News, www.theguardian.com/world/2001/sep/14

/september11.usa24. See also Patrick F. Gillham and Bob Edwards, "Legitimacy Management, Preservation of Exchange Relationships, and the Dissolution of the Mobilization for Global Justice Coalition," *Social Problems* 58, no. 3 (2011): 433–60, https://doi.org/10.1525/sp.2011.58.3.433.

70. Rachel Neumann, "Out of Step: Labor and the Global Social Justice Movement," *New Labor Forum*, no. 11 (2002): 38–47. Azcarate, telephone interview with the author, July 3, 2011. The Miami protests were at the summit of the Free Trade Area of the Americas.

71. Mark Engler, "Elbowed Out of Spotlight by 9/11, Anti-globalization Movement Endures," *Foreign Policy in Focus*, September 21, 2011, https://fpif.org/elbowed_out_of_spotlight_by_911_anti-globalization_movement_endures.

8. THE WTO IS BACK

1. Jonathan Watts, "What Drove a Korean Farmer to Kill Himself in Cancún?," *The Guardian*, September 16, 2003, sec. World News, www.theguardian.com/world/2003/sep/16/northkorea.wto.

2. Agriculture and forestry generated income for some, but many Maya indigenous people and other peasants worked in construction or the service economy in the tourist areas of Cancún and Tulum as well. See David Barton Bray et al., "On the Road to Sustainable Forestry," *Cultural Survival Quarterly* 17, no. 1 (April 30, 1993): 38–41.

3. Karen Wright and John Clark, "Terminator Genes," *Discover Magazine*, August 21, 2003, www.discovermagazine.com/the-sciences/terminator-genes. Vandana Shiva's work in the 1990s helped define these forms of genetic science as portending "the second coming of Columbus": that is, she discussed them as a form of bio-colonialism. See Vandana Shiva, *Biopiracy: The Plunder of Nature and Knowledge* (Boston: South End Press, 1997).

4. Alicia Gutiérrez González, *The Protection of Maize under the Mexican Biosafety Law: Environment and Trade* (Göttingen: Universitätsverlag Göttingen, 2010).

5. Vandana Shiva, *Protect or Plunder? Understanding Intellectual Property Rights*, A Global Issues Title (London: Zed Books, 2001), 73–76.

6. Dani Wadada Nabudere and Mapungubwe Institute for Strategic Reflection (MISTRA), *From Agriculture to Agricology: Towards a Glocal Circular Economy* (Johannesburg: Real African Publishers, 2013); Shiva, *Biopiracy*.

7. Quoted in Family Farm Defenders, "What Is Food Sovereignty?," ca. 2003, unprocessed records in the Centro de Estudios para el Cambio en el Campo Mexicano (CECCAM), Mexico City. UNORCA's position on these matters was based on its long-standing view that international commerce, when not properly regulated, constituted a threat to Mexican food stability. Though it had yet to broach

the topic of GMOs in the mid-1990s, its mobilization of food sovereignty and food security was partly premised on how international trade relations could make agriculture even more risky by bringing in dangerous products, insects, and illnesses. UNORCA used both the uncertainties of nature (e.g., drought) and the uncertainties of global politics (e.g., trade wars) as an argument for why agriculture must enjoy a more robust form of national protection.

8. UNORCA and CECCAM, *La guerra por los mercados de alimentos: La Organización Mundial del Comercio (OMC) en la agricultura* (Mexico City: CECCAM; UNORCA, 2003). UNORCA and CECCAM did not discuss the spiritual aspects of agriculture, as Shiva did.

9. In doing so it was likely drawing from the Vía Campesina and Shiva, the latter of whom delivered important speeches in Seattle on the colonialism of the intellectual property regime.

10. UNORCA, "Resolutivos de la Asamblea Nacional de la UNORCA sobre Productos Transgénicos," ca. 2000, unprocessed records in the Centro de Estudios para el Cambio en el Campo Mexicano (CECCAM), Mexico City. Seed use likely dropped because of uncertainties about their health impact and the European Union ban.

11. Shiva, *Biopiracy*. Shiva would soon publish a book that followed up on her 1997 volume. See Shiva, *Protect or Plunder?*

12. UNORCA, "Resolutivos."

13. Mexico signed the Cartagena Protocol on Biosafety to the Convention on Biological Diversity on May 24, 2000.

14. UNORCA et al., "México. Manifiesto de Ciudad Juárez: 'El campo no aguanta más,'" *Tribuna Roja*, no. 90, March 10, 2003, http://prueba.moir.org.co/2004/08/10/mexico-manifiesto-de-ciudad-juarez-el-camp0-no-aguanta-mas/.

15. The WTO wanted to formalize and finalize that initial agreement in Cancún.

16. Mark Halle, "Confidence-Building: A Cure for Post-Seattle Blues?," *BRIDGES Trade News from a Sustainable Development Perspective*, January 2000, www.ictsd.org/bridges-news/bridges/news/confidence-building-a-cure-for-post-seattle-blues.

17. UNORCA and CECCAM, *Guerra por los mercados*, 18–19. The "Development Round" was initiated at the Doha, Qatar, meetings in 2001.

18. For UNORCA's strategy, see UNORCA, "Organización Mundial de Comercio: Agricultura y organización campesina," September 1999, unprocessed records in the Centro de Estudios para el Cambio en el Campo Mexicano (CECCAM), Mexico City. See Vía Campesina, "Que es la soberania alimentaria [sic]," Vía Campesina website, January 15, 2003, https://viacampesina.org/es/que-es-la-soberania-alimentaria/. Proponents of tariff reductions said they would make for lower food costs, but the food crisis of 2008 and other moments show how price volatility has adversely affected the poor.

19. UNORCA, "Propuestas de políticas públicas para el campo mexicano," ca. 1999, unprocessed records in the Centro de Estudios para el Cambio en el Campo Mexicano (CECCAM), Mexico City; Silver and Arrighi, "Workers North and South."

20. In other countries the farmers would protest before a big liberalization deal (like NAFTA; Vía Campesina, "Que es la soberania alimentaria"), but in Mexico corporatism and patron-client politics were so strong that they hamstrung efforts to oppose NAFTA. See Hubert C. de Grammont and Horacio Mackinlay, "Las organizaciones sociales y la transición política en el campo mexicano," in *La construcción de la democracia en el campo latinoamericano*, ed. Hubert C. de Grammont (Buenos Aires: CLACSO, 2006), 58; Victor Suárez, "Por un referente campesino nacional autónomo y de izquierda," *La Jornada del Campo*, September 17, 2011, www.jornada.com.mx/2011/09/17/referente.html.

21. UNORCA et al., "Manifiesto de Ciudad Juárez.'"

22. UNORCA et al., "Manifiesto de Ciudad Juárez.'"

23. They occupied the office of the Secretaria de Agricultura, Ganadería, Desarrollo Rural, Pesca y Alimentación (Ministry of Agriculture, Livestock, Rural Development, Fishing, and Food, or SAGARPA).

24. Los corresponsales and *La Jornada de Oriente*, "Protestas campesinas en 10 entidades," *La Jornada*, January 21, 2003, www.jornada.com.mx/2003/01/21/007n3pol.php?printver = 0.

25. Angelica Enciso, Patricia Muñoz, and Renato Davalos, "Hacia la cumbre de Cancún," *La Jornada*, September 5, 2003, https://media.jornada.com.mx/2003/09/05/021n1eco.php?printver=1&fly=.

26. "Notas rápidas," *Revista Autónomo*, May 2001.

27. For more on the January 31 march, see Miguel Angel Sámano Rentería, "El movimiento ¡El campo no aguanta más! y el Acuerdo Nacional para el Campo: Situación y perspectiva," *El Cotidiano* 19, no. 124 (April 2004): 64–70, www.redalyc.org/pdf/325/32512407.pdf.

28. UNORCA et al, "Manifiesto de Ciudad Juárez." The US was preparing for the Second Gulf War with Iraq at the time.

29. Sámano Rentería, "El movimiento."

30. Olivia Acuña Rodarte and Miguel Meza Castillo, "Espejos de la crisis económica mundial: La crisis alimentaria y las alternativas de los productores de granos básicos en México," *Argumentos* (Mexico City) 23, no. 63 (August 2010): 189–209.

31. UNORCA had recovered from a decline in membership and power in the late 1990s. See Grammont and Mackinlay, "Organizaciones sociales."

32. Ramor Ryan, "The Battle of Cancun—Anatomy of an Unexpected Victory," The Struggle Site, 2004, http://struggle.ws/anarchism/writers/ramor/cancun.html.

33. Bray et al., "On the Road"; Ueli Hostettler, "New Inequalities: Changing Maya Economy and Social Life in Central Quintana Roo, Mexico," *Research in*

Economic Anthropology 22 (2003): 25–59; Dan Klooster, "Campesinos and Mexican Forest Policy during the Twentieth Century," *Latin American Research Review* 38, no. 2 (2003): 94–126.

34. Victoria Santos, interview with the author, August 26, 2018, Felipe Carrillo Puerto (MX). Carreón was briefly detained on an arms charge. Sergio Caballero, "Detienen en QR a lider por supuesta difamacion," *Reforma*, December 16, 1997.

35. Santos, interview, August 26, 2018.

36. Leonor Aída Concha, interview with the author, May 26, 2018, Monterrey (MX). She was coordinator for three years of the Red Latinoamericana. They created REDGE because, in their view, RMALC needed to better consider women's experiences in the global and national economy.

37. Enciso, Muñoz, and Davalos, "Hacia la cumbre de Cancun."

38. Gerónimo Pruij, interview with the author, August 15, 2018, Mexico City; Mark Ritchie, telephone interview with the author, September 24, 2019.

39. "National and Global Call for a United Strategy against the WTO in Cancun," Nadir, ca. 2003, www.nadir.org/nadir/initiativ/agp/free/cancun/strategy_wto.htm.

40. The Alianza Social Continental was a network of organizations that came together after the 2002 World Social Forum to oppose further liberalization of the Americas, particularly in relation to the Free Trade Agreement of the Americas.

41. Concha, interview, May 26, 2018.

42. Geoffrey Pleyers, "El altermundismo en México: Actores, culturas políticas, y prácticas contra el neoliberalismo," in *Los grandes problemas de México*, vol. 6, *Movimientos sociales* (Mexico City: El Colegio de México, 2010), 361–95; Héctor de la Cueva, "La Batalla de Cancún: Balance de una victoria," *OSAL, Observatorio Social de América Latina* 4, no. 11 (August 2003).

43. Gustavo Castro Soto, "Campaña continental contra el ALCA y la Consulta Chiapaneca," *Boletín Chiapas al Día* (CIEPAC), November 15, 2002, www.alainet.org/es/active/2793.

44. UNORCA and CECCAM, *Guerra por los mercados*, 37.

45. Pablo Duarte, interview with the author, August 30, 2018, Mérida (MX).

46. Gustavo Castro Soto, "Desaparezcamos a la OMC," Otros Mundos Chiapas, August 28, 2003, https://otrosmundoschiapas.org/wp-content/uploads/2003/08/DESAPOMC.pdf.

47. One RMALC leader (in personal correspondence) and Victor Suárez, the director of ANEC, told me that the Vía Campesina leadership went on its own and expected everyone else to follow. Suárez noted that the "The Countryside Can't Take It Anymore" had been pushing back against NAFTA for all of 2003. Yet the Vía Campesina decided alone that the main demand had to be "Agriculture out of the WTO" and to have nothing to do with NAFTA.

48. Santos, interview, August 26, 2018.
49. Duarte, interview, August 30, 2018.
50. Santos, interview, August 26, 2018.
51. Rosa Hernández, interview with the author, August 26, 2018; Duarte, interview, August 30, 2018.
52. Pedro Dzib Puc, interview with the author, August 28, 2018; Marcelo Carreón, interview with the author, August 29, 2018; Duarte, interview, August 30, 2018; Victoria Santos, interview, August 26, 2018.
53. Editorial Board, "OMC: La Batalla de Cancún," *Novedades Quintana Roo*, September 8, 2003.
54. Jazmín Ramos, "Salvaguardan policías las plazas comerciales," *Novedades Quintana Roo*, September 8, 2003.
55. "Invierte la comuna $5 mlls. en logística," *Novedades Quintana Roo*, September 8, 2003.
56. Victoria Santos, interview, August 26, 2018.
57. Justo May Correa, "Potencias subsidian su agricultural con mil millones de dólares diarios," *Novedades Quintana Roo*, September 8, 2003.
58. Castro Soto, "Desaparezcamos a la OMC."
59. Eduardo Tamayo, "Cancún: Diferencias de fondo en la OMC," Agencia Latinoamericana de Información, September 10, 2003, www.alai.info/108354-2/.
60. Rosa Herrera, interview with the author, August 26, 2018; Santos, interview, August 26, 2018.
61. "Llega contingente campesino a la ciudad," *Novedades Quintana Roo*, September 8, 2003.
62. Santos, interview, August 26, 2018.
63. Duarte, interview, August 30, 2018.
64. Herrera, interview, August 26, 2018.
65. Jaime Castillo, interview with the author, June 15, 2017.
66. Cueva, "Batalla de Cancún."
67. These statements represented the first time the EZLN had publicly endorsed or participated in what had become known as "global justice" or "anti-globalization" protests and activities, including the World Social Forum. Gomez read statements from Comandanta Esther, Comandanta David, and Subcomandante Marcos. See Baschet, "¿Más allá de la lucha," 35.

9. THE RADICAL ROAD TO CANCÚN

1. This vignette was shared with me by a local resident and CIPO-RFM member in 2010.

2. Many of its organizers in this period were also influenced by Marxism and the politics of the radical local chapter of the National Education Workers' Union (SNTE).

3. Graeber, *Direct Action*; Marilyn DeLaure and Moritz Fink, *Culture Jamming: Activism and the Art of Cultural Resistance* (New York: New York University Press, 2017); Andrew Cornell, *Oppose and Propose: Lessons from Movement for a New Society*, vol. 2, *Anarchist Interventions* (Edinburgh: AK Press, 2011); Bice Maiguashca, "'They're Talkin' bout a Revolution': Feminism, Anarchism and the Politics of Social Change in the Global Justice Movement," *Feminist Review* 106, no. 1 (February 1, 2014): 78–94, https://doi.org/10.1057/fr.2013.36; A. K. Thompson, *Black Bloc, White Riot: Anti-globalization and the Genealogy of Dissent* (Oakland, CA: AK Press, 2003); Francis Dupuis-Déri, *Who's Afraid of the Black Blocs? Anarchy in Action around the World* (Oakland, CA: PM Press, 2014); Wolfson, *Digital Rebellion*; see also Theresa Warburton, *Other Worlds Here: Honoring Native Women's Writing in Contemporary Anarchist Movements* (Evanston, IL: Northwestern University Press, 2021); Peter Marshall, *Demanding the Impossible: A History of Anarchism* (Oakland, CA: PM Press, 2009). Marshall's work, when it mentions Mexico, mostly discusses the Mexican Revolution (1910) and the role of Flores Magón and his PLM party.

4. To be clear, anarchism was much more than that in the Global North in the era, but those are the kinds of anarchism that have been most widely discussed in literature on global justice movements. This chapter draws on Taiaiake Alfred, who wrote that "'globalization' in Indigenous eyes reflects a deepening, hastening, and stretching of an already-existing empire." See Taiaiake Alfred and Jeff Corntassel, "Being Indigenous: Resurgences against Contemporary Colonialism," in *The Movement of Movements. Part 1: What Makes Us Move?* (Oakland, CA: PM Press; New Delhi: OpenWord, 2017), 134. For an excellent study of Oaxacan anarchist youth in the 2006 uprising in the state, see Maurice Rafael Magaña, *Cartographies of Youth Resistance: Hip-Hop, Punk, and Urban Autonomy in Mexico* (Oakland: University of California Press, 2020), https://doi.org/10.1525/9780520975583.

5. Marina Sitrin, *Everyday Revolutions: Horizontalism and Autonomy in Argentina* (London: Zed Books, 2012); Raúl Zibechi, *Dispersing Power: Social Movements as Anti-state Forces* (Oakland, CA: AK Press, 2010).

6. One of these anarchist websites was Ainfos.ca. Indymedia.org was also important. As a graduate student in 2003 I was fortunate enough to visit Klein's film crew and sites during the filming of *The Take* (2004). Groups like the Worcester Global Action Network (tied to the Boston Global Action Network, a global justice group mentioned in chapter 7) helped coordinate tours of Argentine and Brazilian activists These global action networks were formed out of initiatives from the worldwide network called People's Global Action, itself galvanized by the EZLN in Chiapas, Mexico.

7. Klein's documentary *The Take* follows thirty unemployed Argentine auto workers as they attempt to start a cooperative business in their former workplace.

8. Thomas Olesen, *International Zapatismo: The Construction of Solidarity in the Age of Globalization* (London: Zed, 2005).

9. Ricardo Flores Magón, "El pueblo mexicano es apto para el comunismo," *Regeneración*, September 2, 1911; Humberto Escobedo Cetina, "El Magonismo y las elecciones," *Voz Plural: Revista de Información y Analysis de la Sociedad Civil*, June 2000.

10. This new interest in Flores Magón may have started with a seminar and article in 1986 that discussed Flores Magón's collaboration with the Yaqui of the Mexican state of Sonora and the thinker's ideas about Indigenous forms of anarchy. Note that Beas was the founder of UCIZONI, a founding organization of CIPO-RFM (see chapter 4). See Juan Carlos Beas, *Movimiento indígena y Magonismo en México* (Mexico City: Ediciones Antorcha, 1987).

11. Even an experienced reporter who had covered CIPO-RFM from the beginning wondered how the organizations had split so abruptly. See Octavio Velez Ascencio, "Divididos, protestan por separado la alianza magonista y el CIPO," *Las Noticias*, November 19, 2001.

12. Unless mentioned in publicly available sources, all names of CIPO-RFM members and other activists used in this chapter are pseudonyms. Given the high level of repression in Oaxaca, particularly after the 2006 Oaxaca uprising, when these interviews were initiated, I pledged to keep all interview names and personal references confidential. I conducted some of these interviews when I lived for around thirteen months in the CIPO-RFM space in 2006 and 2007. But many were conducted between 2010 and 2012. Of the nine interviewees this chapter cites, five are women and four are men.

13. See chapter 4 for a brief discussion of this language and the era in which it emerged.

14. For more on the political role of these *municipios*, see Jonathan Fox, "Rural Democratization and Decentralization at the State/Society Interface: What Counts as 'Local' Government in the Mexican Countryside?," *Journal of Peasant Studies* 34, nos. 3–4 (2007): 527–59, https://doi.org/10.1080/03066150701802934.

15. CIPO-RFM, "Impacto en comunidades indígenas de CIPO-RFM," ca. 2002, CIPO-RFM library, Santa Lucía de Camino, Oaxaca.

16. CIPO-RFM, "Impacto."

17. "¡Santa Justicia!, detienen a pseudolideres del CIPO," *Antequera*, September 15, 2004.

18. Artemio, CIPO-RFM member, confidential interview.

19. Note that the skull and skeleton are commonly used symbols in Mexico and are associated with the celebration of the Day of the Dead. For a photo of the protest, see Velez Ascencio, "Divididos."

20. CIPO-RFM, "Rostro del CIPO-RFM: Construyendo nuestro camino," flyer, ca. 2001.

21. Artemio, CIPO-RFM member, confidential interview.

22. CIPO-RFM, "¡¡¡Los pobres del mundo no tenemos Navidad!!!," flyer, December 2001.

23. CIPO-RFM's office, in fact, bordered one of these "popular neighborhoods" (*colonias populares*). Many of the residents were Ñuu Savi or Zapotec, and they remembered when the streets had been unmarked, dirt paths that residents, with some city help, had gradually built up. CIPO-RFM's office, which it was granted through a series of *plantones* in Oaxaca City in 2001, is in a more middle-class part of the city near the Municipal Hall of Santa Lucía de Camino, which itself borders Oaxaca City. Santa Lucía de Camino, ironically, is a PRI stronghold.

24. Those in the Fueras Armadas Revolucionarias de Colombia, or FARC.

25. I compiled this information from a variety of confidential interviews with CIPO-RFM members.

26. Pablo, CIPO-RFM member, confidential interview.

27. CIPO-RFM activists had limited access to the internet. By the early 2000s the CIPO-RFM office had one desktop computer with an internet connection. Internet was unavailable in rural areas and indigenous communities.

28. CIPO-RFM, "Enemigos de la injusticia," ca. early 2002, CIPO-RFM library, Santa Lucía de Camino, Oaxaca.

29. The clientelistic strategy of the PRI was always to bind its communities vertically—to a regional leader, who would provide them things in transactional ways—and keep them separated horizontally from other communities. Julián Durazo Herrmann and Julián Durazo Herrmann, "Neo-patrimonialism and Subnational Authoritarianism in Mexico: The Case of Oaxaca," *Journal of Politics in Latin America* 2, no. 2 (August 13, 2010): 85–112; Hernández Díaz, *Reclamos de la identidad*; Recondo, *Política del gatopardo*.

30. CIPO-RFM, "¡La lucha sigue" 2002, and CIPO-RFM, Women's Area, "De la resistencia a la rebeldía," ca. 2003, CIPO-RFM library, Santa Lucía de Camino, Oaxaca. The phrase reportedly originated from a member's declaration at the 2001 Women's Encuentro of CIPO-RFM in Plan de Zaragoza.

31. The late sociologist Jeff Juris was working on a book about some of these anarchist media networks in Mexico. CIPO-RFM's committee produced videos like *Sembrando Esperanza* (2003), later distributed through anarchist and solidarity networks in the US and Europe. The forty-five-minute documentary shared insights and reflections from different CIPO-RFM members and leaders.

32. Mexican president Vicente Fox had been meeting with other regional leaders in hopes of creating such a corridor. Resistance from groups like CIPO-

RFM in Mexico and in Central America ultimately nixed the idea. Guillermo Almeyra, *El Plan Puebla Panamá en el Istmo de Tehuantepec*, Pensamiento propio (Mexico City: Universidad de la Ciudad de México, 2004).

33. Neoliberalism and globalization were often associated, after all, with the production of food, manufactured goods, et cetera.

34. CIPO-RFM, "Como el neoliberalismo afecta a las mujeres," ca. 2001, CIPO-RFM library, Santa Lucía de Camino, Oaxaca, 2, 5.

35. "Ricardo Flores Magón: A 73 años de su muerte, 'Viva tierra y libertad,'" *Fortaleza Libertaria*, November 17, 1995, 10–11.

36. Erick, confidential interview, Oaxaca City.

37. Advertisement on back cover of *Fortaleza Libertaria*, November 17, 1995. See Humberto Escobedo Cetina, *El pensamiento político de Ricardo Flores Magón*, 2nd ed. (Oaxaca: El Autor, 1997); Benjamín Maldonado Alvarado, *La utopía de Ricardo Flores Magón: Revolución, anarquía y comunalidad india* (Oaxaca: Universidad Autónoma "Benito Juárez" de Oaxaca, Secretaría Académica, 1994).

38. *Fuerza Libertaria*, Oaxaca City, January 2000, 15.

39. Chapter 4 discusses the ways these kinds of arrangements can also dovetail with neoliberal kinds of decentralization.

40. CIPO-RFM, "Turismo comunitario" pamphlet, ca. 2002.

41. Jaime Martínez Luna, *Comunalidad y desarrollo*, Cultura indígena (Mexico City: Centro de Apoyo al Movimiento Popular Oaxaqueño, 2003).

42. CIPO-RFM, "12 de Octubre, contra el olvido," October 2002, CIPO-RFM library, Santa Lucía de Camino, Oaxaca.

43. John Zerzan was the most prominent US "anticivilization" anarchist. See John Zerzan, *Future Primitive: And Other Essays*, New Autonomy Series (Brooklyn, NY: Autonomedia; Columbia, MO: Anarchy, a Journal of Desire Armed, 1994); Charles Thorpe and Ian Welsh, "Beyond Primitivism: Towards a Twenty-First Century Anarchist Theory and Praxis for Science and Technology," *Anarchist Studies* 16, no. 1 (March 22, 2008): 48–76.

44. Gerardo, confidential interview, Oaxaca City. For Marxist views of stages of capitalism, see Vladimir I. Lenin, *The Development of Capitalism in Russia; The Process of the Formation of a Home Market for Large-Scale Industry*, 2nd rev. ed. (Moscow: Progress, 1964); and Tom Brass, *Peasants, Populism, and Postmodernism: The Return of the Agrarian Myth*, Library of Peasant Studies 17 (London: F. Cass, 2000). For a critique, see Susan Koshy et al., *Colonial Racial Capitalism* (Durham, NC: Duke University Press, 2022).

45. Maia Ramnath, *Decolonizing Anarchism: An Antiauthoritarian History of India's Liberation Struggle* (Oakland, CA: AK Press, 2012). It can lead to a range of other erroneous understandings, given that anticolonial and decolonial critics have exposed the way the nonmodern is a fundamental part of what gets identified as modern. For anticolonial scholars, for instance, the colonial is the

underside of the modern metropolitan—they can only exist in tandem. See, for instance, Walter Rodney, *How Europe Underdeveloped Africa*, rev. ed. (Washington, DC: Howard University Press, 1981).

46. Richard Stahler-Sholk, "Resisting Neoliberal Homogenization: The Zapatista Autonomy Movement," *Latin American Perspectives* 34, no. 2 (2007): 48–63. Stahler-Sholk provides an important survey of different kinds of autonomy, mostly in Mexico and Central America.

47. The farmers in places like Plan de Zaragoza were not accustomed to drinking coffee. They began to plant it a few generations ago mostly for extra income.

48. Rosa, CIPO-RFM member, confidential interview.

49. The political deployments of Indigenous tradition have been discussed in chapters 4 and 6. Scholars of coloniality and settler colonialism have highlighted the ways colonization and genocide are continuing projects within modernity, rather than exterior to it. Likewise, Indigenous practices are components of Indigenous modernities, rather than merely existing before modernity. See P. Deloria, *Indians in Unexpected Places*; Gerald Robert Vizenor, *Manifest Manners: Narratives on Postindian Survivance* (Lincoln: University of Nebraska Press, 1999); Lyons, *X-Marks*; Walter Mignolo, *The Darker Side of Western Modernity: Global Futures, Decolonial Options*, Latin America Otherwise (Durham: Duke University Press, 2011); Patrick Wolfe, "Settler Colonialism and the Elimination of the Native," *Journal of Genocide Research* 8, no. 4 (December 1, 2006): 387–409, https://doi.org/10.1080/14623520601056240.

50. W. W. Rostow, *The Stages of Economic Growth, a Non-Communist Manifesto* (Cambridge: University Press, 1960). President Carlos Salinas de Gotarí, in particular, justified his support of NAFTA, land privatization, and rescinding the government's responsibility to redistribute land under the aegis of "modernizing" the countryside. See chapters 1 and 2 for more.

51. Cata, CIPO-RFM member, confidential interview.

52. Rosa, CIPO-RFM member, confidential interview.

53. Pablo, CIPO-RFM member, confidential interview.

54. Gustavo, CIPO-RFM member, confidential interview.

55. Ramiro, CIPO-RFM member, confidential interview.

56. Discussion of this is in "CIPO-RFM Women's Area to Fundación Rigoberta Menchú Tum," October 17, 2002, unprocessed records in the CIPO-RFM office, Santa Lucía de Camino, Oaxaca. See also CIPO-RFM, Women's Area, "Vivir para ser libres y luchar para dejar de ser esclavas," November 30, 2002, www.nodo50.org/cipo/documentos/cipo1.htm; CIPO-RFM, Women's Area, "De la resistencia."

57. CIPO-RFM, "Vivir para ser libres," 1.

58. Leonor Aída Concha, interview with the author, May 26, 2018, Monterrey (MX).

59. The women's politics here reflects what R. Aída Hernández has discussed as the gap between Indigenous movements that don't fight sexism and women's movements that reinforce racism and ethnocentrism. See Speed, Hernández Castillo, and Stephen, *Dissident Women*.

60. OIDHO told me they didn't have the resources to do it, which was likely the story for most Oaxaca organizations.

61. They would hand out the *Revolución* newspaper tied to the Revolutionary Communist Party, based in the US.

62. Alfredo, MPR member, confidential interview.

63. The leaders of the education workers' local were much more radical than most unions but still tended to see anarchists as problems in their marches. If the latter would spray-paint graffiti, some union leaders would call them "provocateurs" from the government. Luis, CIPO-RFM member, confidential interview.

64. Alfredo, confidential interview.

65. Daniel, CIPO-RFM member, confidential interview; Andrés, CIPO-RFM member, confidential interview.

66. Iñaki Garcia Garcia, interview with the author, June 2, 2014, Barcelona; Antonia Silva, interview with the author, June 3, 2014, Barcelona.

67. Ángel Bosqued, interview with the author, June 4, 2014, Barcelona.

68. Jorge, confidential interview; Mari, confidential interview; Ana Fernández, telephone interview with the author, May 30, 2014.

69. Josefina, confidential interview.

70. Movimiento Popular Revolucionario, untitled photo of WTO march in Cancún (2003), lent to author by member of the MPR in Oaxaca City.

71. Some of the most significant statements come from the Women's Area; see CIPO-RFM, Women's Area, "De la resistencia" and "Vivir para ser libres"; Josefina, confidential interview; Mari, confidential interview.

72. CIPO-RFM, Women's Area, "Vivir para ser libres"Area and "De la resistencia."

73. Marcelino, confidential interview.

EPILOGUE

1. Bart Ziegler, "How to Start a Garden—with Very Little Effort," *Wall Street Journal*, May 10, 2020, www.wsj.com/articles/how-to-start-a-gardenwith-very-little-effort-11588903200.

2. Jeanette Marantos, "A Happy Little Miracle in Dark Times: The Plant Nursery Business Is Booming," *Los Angeles Times*, March 21, 2020, www.latimes.com/lifestyle/story/2020-03-21/plant-nurseries-are-now-offering-curbside-service-a-resurgence-of-victory-gardens.

3. "Has Covid-19 Killed Globalisation?," *The Economist*, May 14, 2020, www.economist.com/leaders/2020/05/14/has-covid-19-killed-globalisation; "La globalización está muerta," *Ansa Latina*, May 14, 2020, sec. Sociedad, www.ansalatina.com/americalatina/noticia/sociedad/2020/05/14/para-trump-el-virus-mato-a-la-globalizacion_08c46361-0077-42c5-976f-0f1aa5d060ab.html; see also Philippe Legrain, "The Coronavirus Is Killing Globalization as We Know It," *Foreign Policy* (blog), accessed April 20, 2020, https://foreignpolicy.com/2020/03/12/coronavirus-killing-globalization-nationalism-protectionism-trump/. The lack of national emergency supplies led to popular discontent for a variety of world leaders.

4. Michael O'Sullivan, "Globalisation Is Dead and We Need to Invent a New World Order," *The Economist*, accessed May 25, 2020, www.economist.com/open-future/2019/06/28/globalisation-is-dead-and-we-need-to-invent-a-new-world-order.

5. Polls of US Americans have consistently shown a deep discontent with multilateral trade agreements in general. They are generally more popular in Mexico. Note that some critics were noting the slowing of globalization around the time of the 2008 Great Recession. Critics like Walden Bello discussed the phenomenon of "deglobalization" as well. See Walden Bello, *Capitalism's Last Stand? Deglobalization in the Age of Austerity*, 1st ed. (London: NBN International, 2013).

6. In fact, the US and its allies bombed Belgrade in 1999 when it was home to several McDonald's franchises. See Ross Clark, "Russia and the Death of the Golden Arches Theory," *The Spectator*, May 16, 2022, https://www.spectator.co.uk/article/the-death-of-the-golden-arches-theory/. Friedman's theory is from his *The Lexus and the Olive Tree*.

7. "Josh Hawley, "The WTO Should Be Abolished," *New York Times*, accessed May 7, 2020, www.nytimes.com/2020/05/05/opinion/hawley-abolish-wto-china.html.

8. Thomas Gallatin, "Trump Working to Cut China from Supply Chain," *Patriot Post*, May 7, 2020, https://patriotpost.us/articles/70453-trump-working-to-cut-china-from-supply-chain-2020-05-06.

9. Asma Khalid, "Biden and Trump Battle over Who Is 'Weak on China,'" NPR, April 22, 2020, www.npr.org/2020/04/22/840558299/biden-and-trump-battle-over-who-is-weak-on-china; "Trump and Biden Launch Battle over China That Could Define 2020 Election," CNN Politics, April 21, 2020, www.cnn.com/2020/04/21/politics/trump-biden-china-2020/index.html. Voices from the center, predictably, have lumped all the critics together, arguing that the global pandemic has clearly "been a gift to nationalists and protectionists." See Legrain, "Coronavirus Is Killing Globalization."

10. The changes in antiglobalization politics likely reflect the growth of the right but also the limits of the left. Nearly one hundred people attended the main event at Seattle's Town Hall, and the speakers included Nancy Haque, a second-

generation Bangladeshi American and then a Portland Jobs with Justice organizer. Arrested with many others, she penned an important essay about jail solidarity ("I Was Jane Doe #520") in the weeks after the protests. None of the speakers or original leaders of the protests mentioned the rich array of critiques or tensions that emerged out of the protests, including those about race. A few days later I noticed a prominently displayed artifact at the Boston anniversary event: a "No Globalization without Representation" banner with the revolutionary subjects pictured being the English colonists of New England fighting British soldiers in 1776. This banner was criticized by activists of color after Seattle for its tacit acceptance of US nationalism and the mystique of these settler-colonists in US culture. In contrast, the "ShutdownWTO20" website, coordinated by some key Seattle activists in 1999, includes material from a more diverse group about both achievements and problems of the protests. See www.shutdownwto20.org/shutdownwto20.

11. Thompson, *Black Bloc, White Riot*, 130.

12. LELO, the workers of color organization from Seattle (see chapter 6), played important roles in US Social Fora in the 2000s. For more on Miami, see Manuel Pastor and Tony LoPresti, "Bringing Globalization Home," *Colorlines* 7, no. 2 (Summer 2004): 29–32. For more on the US Social Forum, see Marina Karides et al., *The United States Social Forum: Perspectives of a Movement* (Chicago: Changemaker Publications, 2010). Some of the newest work on questions of global justice focus on environmental justice, climate change, and colonialism. See, for instance, Olúfẹ́mi O. Táíwò, *Reconsidering Reparations: Worldmaking in the Case of Climate Crisis*, Philosophy of Race (New York: Oxford University Press, 2022); Wendy Harcourt and Ingrid L. Nelson, *Practising Feminist Political Ecologies: Moving beyond the "Green Economy"* (London: Zed Books, 2015). See also Ashley Dawson et al., eds., "Urban Climate Insurgency," special issue, *Social Text* 40, no. 1 (March 2022).

13. In contrast, note that when UNORCA moved closer to the Mexican presidential administration and its agricultural advisers in the early 1990s, it ended up dividing its organization and failing to achieve the policy changes it had hoped to with its newfound influence.

14. The dangers of green capitalism in the Caribbean and Latin America will be crucial in coming years. See Miguel Ángel Marmolejo Cervantes et al., "Resource Nationalism and Decarbonization," Phenomenal World (blog), July 23, 2022, https://www.phenomenalworld.org/interviews/resource-nationalism/; Rosa Marina Flores Cruz, "El Istmo de Tehuantepec en disputa. El camino de la Asamblea de Pueblos del Istmo (APPIIDDTT) frente al expansionismo de las energías renovables," Revista Mexicana de Estudios de los Movimientos Sociales 4, no. 2 (July 1, 2020): 97–120; Catalina M. de Onís, Energy Islands: Metaphors of Power, Extractivism, and Justice in Puerto Rico (University of California Press, 2021).

15. Arundhati Roy, "Confronting Empire," speech delivered January 27, 2003, in Porto Alegre, Brazil, https://ratical.org/ratville/CAH/AR012703.html.

Bibliography

MANUSCRIPT COLLECTIONS CONSULTED

Industrial Union Department, unprocessed records at George Meany Memorial Archives, Silver Spring, MD
Jim Hightower Papers, Briscoe Center for American History, University of Texas libraries
Jobs with Justice records, Kheel Center for Labor-Management Documentation and Archives, Cornell University Library
SEIU Collection, Walter P. Reuther Archives, Wayne State University, Detroit, MI
Special Collections, University of Washington Libraries, Seattle, WA (Cindy Domingo Papers; David E. Ortman Papers; Jonathan Rosenblum Papers; Robby Stern Papers; Tyree Scott Papers; WTO Seattle Collections)

PERSONAL AND ORGANIZATIONAL FILES CONSULTED

Biblioteca Social Reconstruir (Mexico City)
Center for Study for Change in the Mexican Countryside library (Mexico City)
Libertarian Social Center (Centro Social Libertario) files (Oaxaca City, Oaxaca)
CIPO-RFM Library (Santa Lucía del Camino, Oaxaca)
Institute for Agriculture and Trade Policy (Minneapolis, MN)
National Family Farm Coalition (Washington, D.C.)

Joe Uehlein (Tacoma Park, MD)
Union of Organizations from the Sierra Juárez of Oaxaca (UNOSJO) (Guelatao, Oaxaca)
Rand Wilson (Somerville, MD)
Red de Género y Economía (Mexico City)
Michael Woo (Seattle, WA)

SECONDARY SOURCES

Aaronson, Susan A. *Taking Trade to the Streets: The Lost History of Public Efforts to Shape Globalization*. Ann Arbor: University of Michigan Press, 2001.
Abas, Bryan. "Look for the Union Label: Jobs with Justice Has a Label for One Local AFL-CIO Official: Spy." *Westword*, April 12–18, 1999, 18.
Abbey, Edward. "Immigration and Liberal Taboos." In *One Life at a Time, Please*, 41–44. New York: Henry Holt, n.d.
ABC News. "Transcript of Pat Buchanan's Acceptance Speech." January 6, 2006. https://abcnews.go.com/Politics/story?id=123160&page=1.
Acevedo López, María Guadalupe. *Reestructuración económica y desarrollo en América Latina*. Mexico City: Siglo XXI, 2004.
"Acta de Acuerdos del VII Encuentro Nacional Campesino Celebrado en la Ciudad de Cuetzalan, Puebla, los dias 30 y 31 de Marzo de 1985." In Costa, *UNORCA*, 144–49.
Acuña Rodarte, Olivia, and Miguel Meza Castillo. "Espejos de la crisis económica mundial: La crisis alimentaria y las alternativas de los productores de granos básicos en México." *Argumentos* (Mexico City) 23, no. 63 (August 2010): 189–209.
Adame, Julian Rodríguez, ed. *Por la soberanía alimentaria: Enfoques y perspectivas*. Mexico City: Centro de Estudios Históricos del Agrarismo en México, 1984.
Adler, Paul. *No Globalization without Representation: U.S. Activists and World Inequality*. Philadelphia: University of Pennsylvania Press, 2021.
Adler-Milstein, Sarah, and John M. Kline. *Sewing Hope: How One Factory Challenges the Apparel Industry's Sweatshops*. Berkeley: University of California Press, 2017.
AFL-CIO. "AFL-CIO: Vigil Sends the Message: No Blank Check for China." n.d., ca. mid-2000. Frank Baumgartner, UNC Chapel Hill. Organizational Statements. http://fbaum.unc.edu/lobby/040_PNTR/Organizational_Statements/AFL-CIO/Vigil.htm.
———. "AFL-CIO Executive Council Statement: Jobs with Justice Coalition." December 16, 1996. https://aflcio.org/about/leadership/statements/jobs-justice-coalition.

Ahmed, Sara. *On Being Included: Racism and Diversity in Institutional Life.* Durham, NC: Duke University Press, 2012.

Alexander, M. Jacqui, and Chandra Talpade Mohanty. *Feminist Genealogies, Colonial Legacies, Democratic Futures.* New York: Routledge, 2013.

Alkon, Alison Hope, and Teresa Marie Mares. "Food Sovereignty in US Food Movements: Radical Visions and Neoliberal Constraints." *Agriculture and Human Values* 29, no. 3 (September 1, 2012): 347–59. https://doi.org/10.1007/s10460-012-9356-z.

Alkon, Alison Hope, and Christie Grace McCullen. "Whiteness and Farmers Markets: Performances, Perpetuations . . . Contestations?" *Antipode* 43, no. 4 (September 2011): 937–59. https://doi.org/10.1111/j.1467-8330.2010.00818.x.

Allen, P. "Realizing Justice in Local Food Systems." *Cambridge Journal of Regions, Economy and Society* 3, no. 2 (July 1, 2010): 295–308. https://doi.org/10.1093/cjres/rsq015.

Almeyra, Guillermo. *El Plan Puebla Panamá en el Istmo de Tehuantepec.* Pensamiento propio. Mexico City: Universidad de la Ciudad de México, 2004.

Anaya, Alejandro. *Autonomía indígena, gobernabilidad y legitimidad en México: La legalización de los usos y costumbres electorales en Oaxaca.* Política. Mexico City: Universidad Iberoamericana; Plaza y Valdés, 2006.

Anti-Fascist Forum, ed. *My Enemy's Enemy: Essays on Globalization, Fascism and the Struggle against Capitalism.* Montreal: Kersplebedeb, 2003.

Appadurai, Arjun. "Grassroots Globalization and the Research Imagination." *Public Culture* 12, no. 1 (January 1, 2000): 1–19. https://doi.org/10.1215/08992363-12-1-1.

Aquino Solis, Aristarco. "Las inquietudes en la Sierra Norte no se deben a la rebelión en Chiapas." In *Usos y costumbres, caciquismo, e intolerancia religiosa (entrevistas a dirigentes indios de Oaxaca),* 34–39. Oaxaca City: CAMPO, 1996.

Arrazóla, V. R. "Cuestiona Carrasco que líderes quieran exoneración." *La Jornada,* May 20, 1998.

Ascencio, O. V. "Definirán indígenas acciones vs. 'política represiva' de Zedillo." *Las Noticias,* April 18, 1998.

———. "Ocupa CIPO-RFM juzgados en 6 ciudades; demandan libertad de dirigentes." *Las Noticias,* April 18, 1998.

———. "Siguen mujeres en plantón pues 'no hay respuestas concretas.'" *Las Noticias,* March 12, 1998.

Ashby, Steven K., and C. J. Hawking. *Staley: The Fight for a New American Labor Movement.* Urbana: University of Illinois Press, 2009.

Associated Press. "Reagan Vows to Veto Omnibus Trade Bill." *Idahonian/Daily News,* April 28, 1988, 2a.

Austin, James E., and Gustavo Esteva. "SAM Is Dead—Long Live SAM: Birth, Death and Reincarnation in Mexican Food Policy." *Food Policy* 10, no. 2 (May 1, 1985): 123–36. https://doi.org/10.1016/0306-9192(85)90005-3.

Avendaño, O. R. "Actos violentos en protestas del CIPO." *El Imparcial* (Oaxaca), April 23, 1998.

Bahree, Bhushan. "WTO Tries Again to Create Accord Opening Markets." *Wall Street Journal*, July 18, 1997.

Bandy, Joe, and Jackie Smith, eds. *Coalitions across Borders: Transnational Protest and the Neoliberal Order*. People, Passions, and Power. Lanham, MD: Rowman and Littlefield, 2005.

Barber, Benjamin R. *Jihad vs. McWorld*. New York: Times Books, 1995.

Barker, Joanne. "The Corporation and the Tribe." *American Indian Quarterly* 39, no. 3 (2015): 243–70.

———. *Sovereignty Matters: Locations of Contestation and Possibility in Indigenous Struggles for Self-Determination*. Lincoln: University of Nebraska Press, 2005.

———. "Territory as Analytic: The Dispossession of Lenapehoking and the Subprime Crisis." *Social Text* 36, no. 2 (June 1, 2018): 19–39. https://doi.org/10.1215/01642472-4362337.

Barkin, David, Rosemary L. Batt, and Billie R. DeWalt. *Alimentos vs. forrajes: La sustitución entre granos a escala mundial*. Mexico City: Siglo XXI, 1991.

Barkin, David, and Bianca Suárez san Román. *El fin de la autosuficiencia*. Mexico City: Centro de Ecodesarrollo, 1985.

Bar-On, Tamir. *Rethinking the French New Right: Alternatives to Modernity*. London: Routledge, 2013.

———. *Where Have All the Fascists Gone?* London: Ashgate, 2007.

Bartra, Armando. "Los nuevos campesinos." In *El impacto social de las políticas de ajuste en el campo mexicano*, 169–212. Mexico City: Instituto Latinoamericano de Estudios Transnacionales, 1995.

Baschet, Jérôme. "¿Más allá de la lucha por la humanidad y contra el neoliberalismo?" *Revista Chiapas*, no. 16 (2004). https://chiapas.iiec.unam.mx/No16-PDF/ch16baschet.pdf.

Battista, Andrew. *The Revival of Labor Liberalism*. Urbana: University of Illinois Press, 2008.

Battle in Seattle. Directed by Stuart Townsend. 2007.

Beas, Carlos. "Testimonio: Los retos del movimiento indígena mexicano." *Cuadernos del Sur* 14 (1999): 141–52.

Beas, Juan Carlos. *Movimiento indígena y Magonismo en México*. Mexico City: Ediciones Antorcha, 1987.

Bechtel, Marilyn. "June 11 Rally: 'More Important Than Ever." *People's Daily World*, April 28, 1988, 3a.

Beek, Martijn van, and Fernanda Pirie. *Modern Ladakh: Anthropological Perspectives on Continuity and Change*. Leiden: Brill, 2008.

Beirich, Heidi. *Greenwash: Nativists, Environmentalism and the Hypocrisy of Hate*. Edited by Mark Potok. Special Report. Montgomery, AL: Southern Poverty Law Center, 2010. www.splcenter.org/sites/default/files/d6_legacy _files/downloads/publication/Greenwash.pdf.

Belew, Kathleen. *Bring the War Home: The White Power Movement and Paramilitary America*. Cambridge, MA: Harvard University Press, 2019.

Bello, Walden. *Brave New Third World? Strategies for Survival in the Global Economy*. San Francisco: Institute for Food and Development Policy, 1989.

Bello, Walden, and Anuradha Mittal. "Dangerous Liaisons: Progressives, the Right, and the Anti-China Trade Campaign." *Food First Backgrounder* (Institute for Food and Development Policy) 6, no. 1 (April 1, 2000). https://archive.foodfirst.org/publication/dangerous-liaisons-progressives-the-right-and-the-anti-china-trade-campaign/.

Belluzzi, Michele. "Cultural Protection as a Rationale for Legislation: The French Language Law of 1994 and the European Trend toward Integration in the Face of Increasing U.S. Influence." *Penn State International Law Review* 14, no. 1 (1995): 27.

Beltrán Garcia, H. "Política partidista sobre las manifestaciones de la cultura." *El Imparcial* (Oaxaca), March 11, 1998.

Berger, Knute. *Pugetopolis: A Mossback Takes on Growth Addicts, Weather Wimps, and the Myth of Seattle Nice*. Seattle, WA: Sasquatch Books, 2009.

Berlet, Chip, and Matthew N. Lyons. *Right-Wing Populism in America: Too Close for Comfort*. New York: Guilford Publications, 2018.

Berry, Wendell. "Caught in the Middle: On Abortion and Homosexuality." *Christian Century*, March 20, 2013. www.christiancentury.org/article /2013-03/caught-middle.

———. "Conserving Communities." In *The Case against the Global Economy*, edited by Jerry Mander and Edward Goldsmith, 407–17. San Francisco: Sierra Club Books, 1996.

———. "Conserving Forest Communities." In *Another Turn of the Crank*, 30–44. Berkeley, CA: Counterpoint, 1996.

———. "Feminism, the Body, and the Machine." In *What Are People For?*, 178–96. Berkeley, CA: Counterpoint, 2018.

———. "A Few Words in Favor of Edward Abbey." In *What Are People For?*, 36–47. Berkeley, CA: Counterpoint, 2018.

———. *The Hidden Wound*. Boston: Houghton Mifflin, 1970.

———. "The Joy of Sales Resistance." In *Sex, Economy, Freedom and Community: Eight Essays*, xi–xxii. New York: Pantheon Books, 1992.

———. "Sex, Economy, Freedom, and Community." In *Sex, Economy, Freedom, and Community: Eight Essays*, 117–73. New York: Pantheon Books, 1993.

———. "Why I Am Not Going to Buy a Computer." In *What Are People For?* Berkeley, CA: Counterpoint, 1990.

Birenbaum, David E. "The Omnibus Trade Act of 1988: Trade Law Dialectics." *University of Pennsylvania Journal of International Business Law* 10, no. 4 (1988): 653–61.

Black, Shameem. "Microloans and Micronarratives: Sentiment for a Small World." *Public Culture* 21, no. 2 (May 1, 2009): 269–92. https://doi.org/10.1215/08992363-2008-029.

Blackwell, Maylei. "The Practice of Autonomy in the Age of Neoliberalism: Strategies from Indigenous Women's Organising in Mexico." *Journal of Latin American Studies* 44, no. 4 (2012): 703–32.

Bogues, Anthony. *Black Heretics, Black Prophets: Radical Political Intellectuals*. New York: Routledge, 2015.

Bonilla-Silva, Eduardo. *Racism without Racists: Color-Blind Racism and the Persistence of Racial Inequality in America*. 4th ed. Lanham, MD: Rowman and Littlefield, 2014.

Bookchin, Murray. "Yes!—Whither Earth First?" *Green Perspectives*, September 1988. http://dwardmac.pitzer.edu/Anarchist_Archives/bookchin/gp/perspectives10.html.

Bookchin, Murray, and Dave Foreman. *Defending the Earth: Debate between Murray Bookchin and Dave Foreman*. Foreword by David Levine. Montreal: Black Rose Books, 1991.

Bowen, James D. "Multicultural Market Democracy: Elites and Indigenous Movements in Contemporary Ecuador." *Journal of Latin American Studies* 43, no. 3 (2011): 451–83. https://doi.org/10.1017/S0022216X11000769.

Boykoff, Maxwell T., Michael K. Goodman, and Adrian McDonald. *Contentious Geographies: Environmental Knowledge, Meaning, Scale*. Abingdon: Taylor and Francis, 2008.

Boyte, Harry, Heather Booth, and Steve Max, *Citizen Action and the New American Populism*. Philadelphia: Temple University Press, 1986.

Brass, Tom. *Peasants, Populism, and Postmodernism: The Return of the Agrarian Myth*. Library of Peasant Studies 17. London: F. Cass, 2000.

Bray, David Barton, Marcelo Carreón, Leticia Merino, and Victoria Santos. "On the Road to Sustainable Forestry." *Cultural Survival Quarterly* 17, no. 1 (April 30, 1993): 38–41.

Brecher, Jeremy, John Brown Childs, and Jill Cutler, eds. *Global Visions: Beyond the New World Order*. Boston: South End Press, 1993.

Brecher, Jeremy, Tim Costello, and Brendan Smith. *Globalization from Below: The Power of Solidarity*. Cambridge, MA: South End Press, 2000.

Briggs, Laura. *Reproducing Empire: Race, Sex, Science, and U.S. Imperialism in Puerto Rico*. American Crossroads 11. Berkeley: University of California Press, 2002.

Brooks, David, and Jonathan Fox, eds. *Cross-border Dialogues: U.S.-Mexican Social Movement Networking*. San Diego: Center for U.S.-Mexican Studies, University of California, San Diego, 2002.

———. "Movements across the Border: An Overview." In Brooks and Fox, *Cross-border Dialogues*, 1–69.

Browne, William P. "Challenging Industrialization: The Rekindling of Agrarian Protest in Agriculture, 1977–1987." *Studies in American Political Development* 7, no. 1 (Spring 1993): 1–34.

Buchanan, Patrick J. *A Republic, Not an Empire: Reclaiming America's Destiny*. Washington, DC: Regnery, 1999.

———. "Time for Economic Nationalism." Pat Buchanan website, *Columns* (blog), June 12, 1995. https://buchanan.org/blog/time-for-economic-nationalism-174.

Buhle, Paul. *Taking Care of Business: Samuel Gompers, George Meany, Lane Kirkland, and the Tragedy of American Labor*. New York: Monthly Review Press, 1999.

Bunyard, Peter. "Teddy Goldsmith: A Tribute." *The Ecologist*, September 1, 2009. https://theecologist.org/2009/sep/01/teddy-goldsmith-tribute.

Burguete Cal y Mayor, Aracely, and International Work Group for Indigenous Affairs. *Indigenous Autonomy in Mexico*. Copenhagen: IWGIA, 2000.

"Buy American: Should We Follow That Flag?" *Labor Notes*, Special Section, May 2009, 2.

Caballero, Sergio. "Detienen en QR a lider por supuesta difamacion." *Reforma*. December 16, 1997.

Cárdenas, Cuauhtemoc. "1988 Plataforma Común del Frente Democrático Nacional." Jalapa, Veracruz, January 12, 1988. www.memoriapoliticademexico.org/Textos/7CRumbo/1988-FDN.html.

Carr, Barry, and Martha Tappan. "El Partido Comunista y la movilización agraria en La Laguna, 1920–1940: ¿Una alianza obrero-campesina?" *Revista Mexicana de Sociología* 51, no. 2 (June 1989): 115–49.

Carrasco Altamirano, Diódoro. "Ley de los Derechos de los Pueblos y Comunidades Indígenas del Estado de Oaxaca." Gobierno del Estado de Oaxaca, March 21, 1998. www.diputados.gob.mx/comisiones/asunindi/oaxregla.pdf.

Castañeda, Jorge G. *Utopia Unarmed: The Latin American Left after the Cold War*. New York: Knopf, 1993.

Castañeda, Jorge G., and Carlos Heredia. "Another NAFTA: What a Good Agreement Should Offer." In *The Case against "Free Trade": GATT, NAFTA, and the Globalization of Corporate Power*, by Ralph Nader et al., 78–91. San Francisco: Earth Island Press; Berkeley, CA: North Atlantic Books, 1993.

Castro Soto, Gustavo. "Campaña continental contra el ALCA y la Consulta Chiapaneca." *Boletín Chiapas al Día (CIEPAC)*, November 15, 2002. www.alainet.org/es/active/2793.

———. "Desaparezcamos a la OMC." *Otros Mundos Chiapas*, August 28, 2003. https://otrosmundoschiapas.org/wp-content/uploads/2003/08/DESAPOMC.pdf.

Cavanagh, John, Sarah Anderson, and Karen Hansen-Kuhn. "Trinational Organizing for Just and Sustainable Trade and Development: Some Lessons and Insights." In Brooks and Fox, *Cross-border Dialogues*, 187–210.

Chang-Geun, Lee. "What Has Seattle Left Us With?" Nadir, December 23, 1999. www.nadir.org/nadir/initiativ/agp/free/seattle/picis_seattle.htm.

Charlton, J. D. "Talking Seattle." *Socialist Review* 28, nos. 3–4 (2001): 183.

Chong, Natividad Gutiérrez. *Women, Ethnicity and Nationalisms in Latin America*. New York: Routledge, 2016.

CIPO-RFM, Women's Area. "Vivir para ser libres y luchar para dejar de ser esclavas." November 30, 2002. www.nodo50.org/cipo/documentos/cipo1.htm.

Clark, Ross. "Russia and the Death of the Golden Arches Theory." *The Spectator*, May 16, 2022. www.spectator.co.uk/article/the-death-of-the-golden-arches-theory/.

Coalición de Ejidos de la Costa Grande de Guerrero. "La Coalición de Ejidos de la Costa Grande de Guerrero frente a los nuevos retos del siglo XXI." *La Jornada*, August 10, 1991.

Cockburn, Alexander, and Jeffrey St Clair. *Five Days That Shook the World: The Battle for Seattle and Beyond*. London: Verso, 2000.

Cohen, Larry, and Steve Early. "Defending Workers' Rights in the Global Economy: The CWA Experience." In *Which Direction for Organized Labor?*, edited by Bruce Nissen, 143–64. Philadelphia: Temple University Press, 1999.

———. "Globalization and De-unionization in Telecommunications: Three Case Studies in Resistance." In *Transnational Cooperation among Labor Unions*, edited by Michael Gordon and Lowell Turner, 202–22. Ithaca, NY: Cornell University Press, 2000.

Cohen, Lizabeth. *Making a New Deal: Industrial Workers in Chicago, 1919–1939*. Cambridge: Cambridge University Press, 1990.

Colquitt, Ron. "SCLC President Leads March against IP Lockout." *Mobile Register*, April 11, 1988, b1.

Conklin, Beth A. "Body Paint, Feathers, and VCRs: Aesthetics and Authenticity in Amazonian Activism." *American Ethnologist* 24, no. 4 (1997): 711–37. https://doi.org/10.1525/ae.1997.24.4.711.

Conklin, Beth A., and Laura R. Graham. "The Shifting Middle Ground: Amazonian Indians and Eco-Politics." *American Anthropologist* 97, no. 4 (1995): 695–710. https://doi.org/10.1525/aa.1995.97.4.02a00120.

Conway, Janet M. *Edges of Global Justice: The World Social Forum and Its "Others."* New York: Routledge, 2013.

Cooper, Marc. "Where's Hoffa Driving the Teamsters?" *The Nation*, July 13, 2000. www.thenation.com/article/wheres-hoffa-driving-teamsters/.

Cooper, Matthew. "Watching a Gadfly Create a Buzz." *Time*, July 3, 2000.
Cordtz, Richard. "Concerned about Trade." *SEIU Update* (Public Division) 1, no. 2 (Fall 1987): 23.
Cornell, Andrew. *Oppose and Propose: Lessons from Movement for a New Society*. Vol. 2. *Anarchist Interventions*. Edinburgh: AK Press, 2011.
Correa, Justo May. "Potencias subsidian su agricultural con mil millones de dólares diarios." *Novedades Quintana Roo*, September 8, 2003.
Los corresponsales and *La Jornada de Oriente*. "Protestas campesinas en 10 entidades." *La Jornada*, January 21, 2003. www.jornada.com.mx/2003/01/21/007n3pol.php?printver=0.
Cortázar, Julio. *Fantomas contra los vampiros multinacionales: Una utopía realizable*. Mexico City: Excelsior, 1975.
Costa, Nuria, comp. *UNORCA: Documentos para la historia*. Mexico City: Costa-Amic Editores, 1989.
Coulthard, Glen Sean. *Red Skin, White Masks: Rejecting the Colonial Politics of Recognition*. Indigenous Americas. Minneapolis: University of Minnesota Press, 2014.
Cowie, Jefferson. *Stayin' Alive: The 1970s and the Last Days of the Working Class*. New York: New Press, 2010.
Cowie, Jefferson, and Lauren Boehm. "Dead Man's Town: 'Born in the U.S.A.,' Social History, and Working-Class Identity." *American Quarterly* 58 (June 2006): 353–78.
Crangi, Jerry. "Report from Seattle: How the IA Shut Down the WTO (with a Little Help from Our Friends)." *IATSE District 1 History* (blog), December 1999. http://iatsedistrict1.org/oldhistory/end1999.htm.
Crosby, Jeff. "WTO Shutdown: The Kids Are Alright." *Common Dreams*, December 3, 2019.
Cruz, V. de la, and R. Laura. "La política de la multiculturalidad en México y sus impactos en la movilización indígena." In *Identidades, etnicidad y racismo en América Latina*, edited by FLACSO-SEDE Ecuador. Quito: Congreso Latinoamericano y Caribeño de Ciencias Sociales, FLACSO, 2008.
Cueva, Héctor de la. "La Batalla de Cancún: Balance de una victoria." *OSAL, Observatorio Social de América Latina* 4, no. 11 (August 2003).
CWA. "Union Leaders Kick Off Jobs with Justice Campaign." *CWA News*, June 11, 1987, 6.
Dagnino, Evelina. "Citizenship: A Perverse Confluence." *Development in Practice* 17, nos. 4/5 (2007): 549–56.
Dale, Stephen. *McLuhan's Children: The Greenpeace Message and the Media*. Toronto: Between the Lines, 1996.
Danaher, Kevin, Jason Mark, and Arianna Huffington. *Insurrection: Citizen Challenges to Corporate Power*. New York: Routledge, 2003.

Daugherty, Kristie. "Hoov-R-Line Moving to Mexico." *Journal-Enterprise*, May 27, 1999.

Davies, Thomas. *NGOs: A New History of Transnational Civil Society*. Oxford: Oxford University Press, 2014.

Davis, Angela Y. "Gender, Class, and Multiculturalism: Rethinking 'Race' Politics." In *Mapping Multiculturalism*, edited by Avery Gordon and Christopher Newfield, 40–48. Minneapolis: University of Minnesota Press, 1996.

Davis, Bob. "Unexpected Obstacles Are Threatening to Delay or Derail Congressional Approval of GATT Pact." *Wall Street Journal*, April 8, 1994.

Dawson, Ashley, Marco Armiero, Ethemcan Turhan, and Roberta Biasillo, eds. "Urban Climate Insurgency," special issue, *Social Text* 40, no. 1 (March 2022).

Day, Iyko. *Alien Capital: Asian Racialization and the Logic of Settler Colonial Capitalism*. Durham, NC: Duke University Press, 2016.

DeHart, Monica Christine. *Ethnic Entrepreneurs: Identity and Development Politics in Latin America*. Palo Alto, CA: Stanford University Press, 2010.

de la Madrid Hurtado, Miguel. Introduction to "Summary Description of PRONAL" (October 17, 1983). In chap. 15 of *Food Policy in Mexico: The Search for Self-Sufficiency*, edited by James E. Austin and Gustavo Esteva, 315–42. Ithaca, NY: Cornell University Press, 1987.

DeLaure, Marilyn, and Moritz Fink. *Culture Jamming: Activism and the Art of Cultural Resistance*. New York: New York University Press, 2017.

Dellacioppa, Kara Zugman. *This Bridge Called Zapatismo: Building Alternative Political Cultures in Mexico City, Los Angeles, and Beyond*. Lanham, MD: Lexington Books, 2009.

Della Porta, Donatella, ed. *The Global Justice Movement: Cross-national and Transnational Perspectives*. London: Routledge, 2015.

Della Porta, Donatella, and Sidney G. Tarrow, eds. *Transnational Protest and Global Activism*. People, Passions, and Power. Lanham, MD: Rowman and Littlefield, 2005.

Deloria, Philip Joseph. *Indians in Unexpected Places*. Lawrence: University Press of Kansas, 2004.

———. *Playing Indian*. Yale Historical Publications. New Haven, CT: Yale University Press, 1998.

Deloria, Vine. *We Talk, You Listen: New Tribes, New Turf*. Lincoln: University of Nebraska Press, 2007.

DeLuca, Kevin Michael, and Jennifer Peeples. "From Public Sphere to Public Screen: Democracy, Activism, and the 'Violence' of Seattle." *Critical Studies in Media Communication* 19, no. 2 (June 2002): 125–51. https://doi.org/10.1080/07393180216559.

Denning, Michael. *The Cultural Front: The Laboring of American Culture in the Twentieth-Century*. London: Verso, 1996.

———. *Culture in the Age of Three Worlds*. London: Verso, 2004.
Desai, Manisha. *Subaltern Movements in India: Gendered Geographies of Struggle against Neoliberal Development*. Abingdon, Oxon, New York, NY: Routledge, 2016.
Desmarais, Annette Aurélie. "The International Women's Commission of La Vía Campesina." In *The Women, Gender, and Development Reader*, 2nd ed., edited by Nalini Visvanathan, Lynn Duggan, Nan Wiegersma, and Laurie Nisonoff, 408–13. London: Zed Books, 2011.
———. *La Vía Campesina: La globalización y el poder del campesinado*. Madrid: Editorial Popular, 2007.
Destler, I. M. *American Trade Politics*. 4th ed. Washington, DC: Institute for International Economics, 2005.
Díaz, Floriberto. *Escrito: Comunalidad, energía viva del pensamiento Mixe = Ayuujktsënää'yën—ayuujkwënmää'ny—ayuujk mëk'äjtën*. Compiled by Sofía Robles Hernández and Rafael Cardoso Jiménez. Mexico City: Universidad Nacional Autónoma de México, 2007.
Díaz Ordaz, Gustavo. "Primer informe de gobierno del Presidente Gustavo Díaz Ordaz." *El Día*, September 2, 1965.
Dochuk, Darren. *From Bible Belt to Sunbelt: Plain-Folk Religion, Grassroots Politics, and the Rise of Evangelical Conservatism*. New York: W. W. Norton, 2012.
Dolan, Mike. "Mike Dolan: People for Fair Trade/ Network Opposed to WTO." Interview by Jeremy Simer, March 3, 2000. WTO History Project. http://depts.washington.edu/wtohist/interviews/Dolan%20-%20Simer.htm.
Dollars and Sense Collective. "Candidates and Consequences." *Dollars and Sense*, no. 232 (November 2000): 12–16.
Dorantes, Gerardo L. *Conflicto y poder en la UNAM: La huelga de 1999*. Mexico City: Universidad Nacional Autónoma de México; Editorial Miguel Ángel Porrúa, 2006.
Drainville, André C., and Saskia Sassen. *Contesting Globalization: Space and Place in the World Economy*. London: Taylor and Francis, 2004.
Dudziak, Mary L. *Cold War Civil Rights: Race and the Image of American Democracy*. Princeton, NJ: Princeton University Press, 2000.
Duggan, Lisa. *The Twilight of Equality? Neoliberalism, Cultural Politics, and the Attack on Democracy*. Boston: Beacon Press, 2003.
Dupuis-Déri, Francis. *Who's Afraid of the Black Blocs? Anarchy in Action around the World*. Oakland, CA: PM Press, 2014.
Durazo Herrmann, Julián, and Julián Durazo Herrmann. "Neo-patrimonialism and Subnational Authoritarianism in Mexico: The Case of Oaxaca." *Journal of Politics in Latin America* 2, no. 2 (August 13, 2010): 85–112.
Durbin, Andrea C. "Trade and the Environment: The North-South Divide." *Environment* 37, no. 7 (1995): 16–20, 37.

Edelman, Marc. "Food Sovereignty: Forgotten Genealogies and Future Regulatory Challenges." *Journal of Peasant Studies* 41, no. 6 (November 2, 2014): 959–78. https://doi.org/10.1080/03066150.2013.876998.

———. "Peasant-Farmer Movements, Third World Peoples, and the Seattle Protests against the World Trade Organization, 1999." *Dialectical Anthropology* 33, no. 2 (2009): 109–28.

———. *Peasants against Globalization: Rural Social Movements in Costa Rica.* Stanford, CA: Stanford University Press, 1999.

Editorial Board. "OMC: La Batalla de Cancún." *Novedades Quintana Roo*, September 8, 2003.

Ehrlich, Paul. *The Population Bomb.* New York: Ballantine Books, 1968.

Ehrlich, Sean D. *The Politics of Fair Trade: Moving beyond Free Trade and Protection.* New York: Oxford University Press, 2018.

Ellis, Richard. *To the Flag: The Unlikely History of the Pledge of Allegiance.* Lawrence: University Press of Kansas, 2005.

Enciso, Angelica, Patricia Muñoz, and Renato Davalos. "Hacia la cumbre de Cancun." *La Jornada*, September 5, 2003. https://media.jornada.com.mx/2003/09/05/021n1eco.php?printver=1&fly=.

Engler, Mark. "Elbowed Out of Spotlight by 9/11, Anti-globalization Movement Endures." *Foreign Policy in Focus*, September 21, 2011. https://fpif.org/elbowed_out_of_spotlight_by_911_anti-globalization_movement_endures.

———. "Yes We Can!" *New Internationalist*, November 2, 2002. https://newint.org/features/2002/11/01/labour.

Erickson, Paul D. *Reagan Speaks: The Making of an American Myth.* New York: NYU Press, 1985.

Eschle, Catherine, and Bice Maiguashca. *Making Feminist Sense of the Global Justice Movement.* Lanham, MD: Rowman and Littlefield, 2010.

Escobar, Arturo. *Territories of Difference: Place, Movements, Life, Redes.* Durham, NC: Duke University Press, 2008.

Escobedo Cetina, Humberto. "El Magonismo y las elecciones." *Voz Plural: Revista de Información y Analysis de la Sociedad Civil*, June 2000.

———. *El pensamiento político de Ricardo Flores Magón.* 2nd ed. Oaxaca: El Autor, 1997.

Estes, Nick. *Our History Is the Future: Standing Rock versus the Dakota Access Pipeline, and the Long Tradition of Indigenous Resistance.* London: Verso Books, 2019.

Esteva, Gustavo. "El desastre agrícola: Adiós al México imaginario." *Comercio Exterior* 38, no. 8 (August 1988): 662–72.

Estrada Saavedra, Marco. *La comunidad armada rebelde y el EZLN: Un estudio histórico y sociológico sobre las bases de apoyo zapatistas en las* cañadas tojolabales de la selva lacandona (1930-2005). Mexico City: El Colegio de México, 2016.

Evans, Lane, Tom Harkin, and Jim Hightower. "Renewing, Reclaiming Populism." *Lodi News-Sentinel*, June 6, 1986, 4.

Ezcárraga, D., and G. Pinto. "Desarrollo y retos." *El Imparcial* (Oaxaca), November 16, 1997.

Ezekiel, Judith. *Feminism in the Heartland*. Columbus: Ohio State University Press, 2002.

Faber, Daniel. "Building a Transnational Environmental Justice Movement: Obstacles and Opportunities in the Age of Globalization." In Bandy and Smith, *Coalitions across Borders*, 43-70.

Fabricant, Nicole. *Mobilizing Bolivia's Displaced: Indigenous Politics and the Struggle over Land*. Chapel Hill: University of North Carolina Press, 2012.

Falk, Richard. "Resisting 'Globalisation-from-Above' through 'Globalisation-from-Below.'" *New Political Economy* 2, no. 1 (March 1, 1997): 17-24. https://doi.org/10.1080/13563469708406281.

Fanon, Frantz. *The Wretched of the Earth*. New York: Grove Press, 1968.

Featherstone, David. *Solidarity: Hidden Histories and Geographies of Internationalism*. London: Zed Books, 2012.

Featherstone, Liza. *Students against Sweatshops*. London: Verso, 2002.

Ferguson, Roderick A. *The Reorder of Things: The University and Its Pedagogies of Minority Difference*. Minneapolis: University of Minnesota Press, 2012.

Fernandez, Luis. *Policing Dissent: Social Control and the Anti-globalization Movement*. Critical Issues in Crime and Society. New Brunswick, NJ: Rutgers University Press, 2008.

Fernández Gonzalez, Ramón. "Posibilidades para la producción de alimentos en México." In *Por la soberanía alimentaria: Enfoques y perspectivas*, edited by Julian Rodríguez Adame, 25-37. Mexico City: Centro de Estudios Históricos del Agrarismo en México, 1984.

Fetonte, Danny, and Larry Braden. "Showdown at Nacogdoches: The CWA in Texas." *Labor Research Review* 1, no. 15 (1990): 25-35.

Fink, Deborah. "Reorganizing Inequity: Gender and Structural Transformation in Iowa Meatpacking." In *Unionizing the Jungles: Labor and Community in the Twentieth-Century Meatpacking Industry*, edited by Shelton Stromquist and Marvin Bergman, 218-41. Iowa City: University of Iowa Press, 1997.

Fink, Leon. "When Community Comes Home to Roost: The Southern Milltown as Lost Cause." *Journal of Social History* 40, no. 1 (October 1, 2006): 119-45. https://doi.org/10.1353/jsh.2006.0079.

Fisher, Stephen L. *Fighting Back in Appalachia: Traditions of Resistance and Change*. Philadelphia: Temple University Press, 1993.

Flores Magón, Ricardo. "El pueblo mexicano es apto para el comunismo." *Regeneración*, September 2, 1911.

Flusty, Steven. *De-Coca-Colonization: Making the Globe from the Inside Out.* New York: Routledge, 2004.
Foley, Michael W. "Privatizing the Countryside: The Mexican Peasant Movement and Neoliberal Reform." *Latin American Perspectives* 22, no. 1 (1995): 59–76.
Foley, Neil. *The White Scourge: Mexicans, Blacks, and Poor Whites in Texas Cotton Culture.* Berkeley: University of California Press, 1997.
Forchtner, Bernhard. *The Far Right and the Environment: Politics, Discourse and Communication.* Abingdon: Routledge, 2019.
Fox, Jonathan. "Agriculture and the Politics of the North American Trade Debate: A Report from the Trinational Exchange on Agriculture, the Environment, and the Free Trade Agreement, Mexico City, November 14–17, 1991." *LASA Forum* 23, no. 1 (Spring 1992): 3–9.
———. "Democratic Rural Development: Leadership Accountability in Regional Peasant Organizations, Development and Change." *Development and Change* 23, no. 2 (April 1, 1992): 1–36.
———. "Political Change in Mexico's New Peasant Economy." In *The Politics of Economic Restructuring in Mexico: State-Society Relations and Regime Change in Mexico,* edited by Maria Lorena Cook, Kevin J. Middlebrook, and Juan Molinar Horcasitas, 243–76. San Diego: Center for U.S.-Mexican Studies, University of California, San Diego, 1994.
———. *The Politics of Food in Mexico: State Power and Social Mobilization.* Food Systems and Agrarian Change. Ithaca, NY: Cornell University Press, 1993.
———. "Rural Democratization and Decentralization at the State/Society Interface: What Counts as 'Local' Government in the Mexican Countryside?" *Journal of Peasant Studies* 34, nos. 3–4 (2007): 527–59, https://doi.org/10.1080/03066150701802934.
Fox, Jonathan, and Gustavo Gordillo. "Between State and Market: The Campesinos' Quest for Autonomy." In *Mexico's Alternative Political Futures,* edited by Wayne A. Cornelius, Judith Gentleman, and Peter H. Smith, Monograph Series 30, 131–72. La Jolla: Center for U.S.-Mexican Studies, University of California, San Diego, 1989.
Fox, Jonathan, and Libby Haight, eds. *Subsidizing Inequality: Mexican Corn Policy since NAFTA.* Washington, DC: Woodrow Wilson International Center for Scholars, 2010.
Frank, Dana. *Buy American: The Untold Story of Economic Nationalism.* Boston: Beacon Press, 1999.
Franklin, Stephen. *Three Strikes: Labor's Heartland Losses and What They Mean for Working Americans.* New York: Guilford Press, 2002.
Freeman, Joshua B. *American Empire: The Rise of a Global Power, the Democratic Revolution at Home, 1945–2000.* New York: Viking, 2012.
Friedman, Thomas L. *The Lexus and the Olive Tree.* New York: Farrar, Straus, Giroux, 1999.

Frundt, Henry J. *Trade Conditions and Labor Rights: U.S. Initiatives, Dominican and Central American Responses*. Gainesville: University Press of Florida, 1998.

Gallatin, Thomas. "Trump Working to Cut China from Supply Chain." *Patriot Post*, May 6, 2020. https://patriotpost.us/articles/70453-trump-working-to-cut-china-from-supply-chain-2020-05-06.

Gallegos, Elena, and Arturo García. "Posible cumbre en México sobre la integración de AL." *La Jornada*, September 30, 1990, sec. El País.

Gamboa Ramírez, Ricardo, Antonio García de León, Everardo Escárcega López, Carlota Botey, Enrique Semo, Julio Moguel, and Centro de Estudios Históricos del Agrarismo en México. *Historia de la cuestión agraria mexicana*. Mexico City: Siglo Veintiuno Editores; Centro de Estudios Históricos del Agrarismo en México, 1988.

García, M. "Movilizaciones, anuncian indígenas." *Marca*, January 9, 1998.

García Canclini, Néstor. *Imagined Globalization*. Translated by George Yúdice. Latin America in Translation/En Traducción/Em Tradução. Durham, NC: Duke University Press, 2014.

Gates, Marilyn. *In Default: Peasants, the Debt Crisis, and the Agricultural Challenge in Mexico*. London: Routledge, 1993.

Gauss, Susan M. "The Politics of Economic Nationalism in Postrevolutionary Mexico." *History Compass* 4, no. 3 (2006): 567–77. https://doi.org/10.1111/j.1478-0542.2006.00326.x.

Gautney, Heather. *Democracy, States, and the Struggle for Social Justice*. New York: Routledge, 2009.

George, Susan. "Letter from Susan George to De Fabel van de Illegaal, 99-09-21." Accessed July 6, 2018. www.savanne.ch/right-left-materials/george990921.html.

Gerstle, Gary. *Working Class Americanism: The Politics of Labor in a Textile City, 1914–1960*. Cambridge: Cambridge University Press, 1989.

Getachew, Adom. *Worldmaking after Empire: The Rise and Fall of Self-Determination*. Princeton, NJ: Princeton University Press, 2019.

Ghosh, Monica. "Inside WTO Dissent: The Experiences of LELO and CCEJ." University of Washington, WTO History Project, March 4, 2001.

Gillham, Patrick F., and Bob Edwards. "Legitimacy Management, Preservation of Exchange Relationships, and the Dissolution of the Mobilization for Global Justice Coalition." *Social Problems* 58, no. 3 (2011): 433–60. https://doi.org/10.1525/sp.2011.58.3.433.

Gilroy, Paul. *There Ain't No Black in the Union Jack: The Cultural Politics of Race and Nation*. London: Routledge, 2006.

Glenn, Wayne E. "President Glenn Addresses Jobs with Justice Rally." Speech transcript. *The Paperworker*, November 1987, 21.

"La globalización está muerta." *Ansa Latina*, May 14, 2020, sec. Sociedad. www.ansalatina.com/americalatina/noticia/sociedad/2020/05/14/para-trump-el-virus-mato-a-la-globalizacion_08c46361-0077-42c5-976f-0f1aa5d060ab.html.

Gobierno Constitucional del Estado Libre y Soberano de Oaxaca. *Oaxaca, Plan estatal de desarrollo, 1992–1998*. Oaxaca: El Gobierno, 1993.

Godfrey, Martin, and Steven Langdon. "¿Socios en el desarrollo? La tesis de la transnacionalización en el contexto Keniano." *Estudios Internacionales* 11, no. 44 (December 1978): 45–70.

Goldsmith, Edward. *The Way: An Ecological World-View*. Athens: University of Georgia Press, 1998.

Goldsmith, Edward, Peter Bunyard, Nicholas Hildyard, and Patrick McCully. *Imperiled Planet: Restoring Our Endangered Ecosystems*. Cambridge, MA: MIT Press, 1990.

Goldsmith, Edward, and International Society for Ecology and Culture. *The Future of Progress: Reflections on Environment and Development*. Dartington: Green Books, 1995.

Goldsmith, Edward, et al. *Blueprint for Survival*. New York: New American Library, 1974.

Gómez-Barris, Macarena. *The Extractive Zone: Social Ecologies and Decolonial Perspectives*. Durham, NC: Duke University Press, 2017.

González, Alicia Gutiérrez. *The Protection of Maize under the Mexican Biosafety Law: Environment and Trade*. Göttingen: Universitätsverlag Göttingen, 2010.

Gonzalez, Carmen G. "Beyond Eco-Imperialism: An Environmental Justice Critique of Free Trade." *Denver University Law Review* 78, no. 979 (2001): 985–1016.

González Pérez, Miguel, Aracely Burguete Cal y Mayor, and Pablo Ortiz-T. *La autonomía a debate: Autogobierno indígena y estado plurinacional en América Latina*. Foro. Quito, Ecuador: FLACSO Ecuador; Cooperación Técnica Alemana, GTZ; Ministerio Federal de Cooperación Económica y Desarrollo; IWGIA; CIESAS; UNICH, 2010.

Gordillo, Gustavo. *Campesinos al Asalto del Cielo: Una reforma agraria con autonomía*. Economía y Demografía. Mexico City: Siglo Veintiuno Editores, 1988.

Gordon, Avery, and Christopher Newfield, eds. *Mapping Multiculturalism*. Minneapolis: University of Minnesota Press, 1996.

Graeber, David. *Direct Action: An Ethnography*. Edinburgh: AK Press, 2009.

Grammont, Hubert Carton de. *Neoliberalismo y organización social en el campo mexicano*. Mexico City: Plaza y Valdes, 1996.

Grammont, Hubert Carton de, and Horacio Mackinlay. "Las organizaciones sociales y la transición política en el campo mexicano." In *La construcción de la democracia en el campo latinoamericano*, edited by Hubert C. de Grammont, 23–68. Buenos Aires: CLACSO, 2006.

Granados, H. R. "Nuevas alianzas." *El Extra*, November 20, 1997.

Grande, Sandy Marie Anglás. "Beyond the Ecologically Noble Savage: Deconstructing the White Man's Indian." *Environmental Ethics* 21, no. 3 (August 1, 1999): 307–20. https://doi.org/10.5840/enviroethics199921320.

Grandin, Greg. *Fordlandia: The Rise and Fall of Henry Ford's Forgotten Jungle City*. London: Picador, 2010.

"Grave crisis en el sector agropecuario en AL." *La Jornada*, September 26, 1990, sec. Economía.

Gregory, James N. *American Exodus: The Dust Bowl Migration and Okie Culture in California*. New York: Oxford University Press, 1989.

Grewal, Inderpal. *Transnational America: Feminisms, Diasporas, Neoliberalisms*. Next Wave. Durham, NC: Duke University Press, 2005.

Grubaugh, Stephen, and Scott Sumner. "Monetary Policy and the U.S. Trade Deficit." In *The Reagan Years: The Record in Presidential Leadership*, edited by Joseph Hogan, 237–58. Manchester: Manchester University Press, 1990.

Guerrero Chiprés, Salvador. "Buscará México avanzar hacia una zona de libre comercio en AL." *La Jornada*, September 28, 1990, sec. Economía.

Guthman, Julie. "'If They Only Knew': Color Blindness and Universalism in California Alternative Food Institutions." *Professional Geographer* 60, no. 3 (August 2008): 387–97. https://doi.org/10.1080/00330120802013679.

Hale, Charles R. "Does Multiculturalism Menace? Governance, Cultural Rights and the Politics of Identity in Guatemala." *Journal of Latin American Studies* 34, no. 3 (2002): 485–524.

———. *Más que un Indio = More Than an Indian: Racial Ambivalence and Neoliberal Multiculturalism in Guatemala*. Santa Fe, NM: School of American Research Press, 2006.

Hale, Charles R., and Rosamel Millamán. "Cultural Agency and Political Struggle in the Era of the Indio Permitido." In *Cultural Agency in the Americas*, edited by Doris Summer, 281–304. Durham, NC: Duke University Press, 2006.

Halle, Mark. "Confidence-Building: A Cure for Post-Seattle Blues?" *BRIDGES: Trade News from a Sustainable Development Perspective*, January 2000. www.ictsd.org/bridges-news/bridges/news/confidence-building-a-cure-for-post-seattle-blues.

Harcourt, Wendy, and Ingrid L. Nelson. *Practising Feminist Political Ecologies: Moving beyond the "Green Economy."* London: Zed Books, 2015.

Harvey, Neil. *The Chiapas Rebellion: The Struggle for Land and Democracy*. Durham, NC: Duke University Press, 1998.

———. *The New Agrarian Movement in Mexico, 1979–1990*. University of London, Institute of Latin American Studies, Research Paper 23. London,

1990. https://sas-space.sas.ac.uk/3376/1/B05_-_The_New_Agrarian_Movement_in_Mexico_1979-1990.pdf.

"Has Covid-19 Killed Globalisation?" *The Economist*, May 14, 2020. www.economist.com/leaders/2020/05/14/has-covid-19-killed-globalisation.

Hasegawa, Bob. "WTO Who?" *King County Labor Council Newsletter*, October 1999, 4.

Hawley, Josh. "The WTO Should Be Abolished." *New York Times*, op-ed, May 5, 2020. www.nytimes.com/2020/05/05/opinion/hawley-abolish-wto-china.html.

Hayes, Randy. "Three Legs Are Better Than Two." In *Take It Personally: How to Make Conscious Choices to Change the World*, edited by Anita Roddick, 148–49. Berkeley, CA: HarperCollins, 2001.

Heath, John Richard. "El Programa Nacional de Alimentación y la crisis de alimentos." *Revista Mexicana de Sociología* 47, no. 3 (1985): 115–35. https://doi.org/10.2307/3540495.

Heatherton, Christina. *Arise! Global Radicalism in the Era of the Mexican Revolution*. Oakland: University of California Press, 2022.

Heelas, Paul. *The New Age Movement: The Celebration of the Self and the Sacralization of Modernity*. Oxford: Blackwell, 1996.

Hernández Castillo, Rosalva Aída. *Histories and Stories from Chiapas: Border Identities in Southern Mexico*. Austin: University of Texas Press, 2004.

Hernández Díaz, Jorge, and Victor Leonel Juan Martínez. *Dilemas de la institución municipal: Una incursión en la experiencia oaxaqueña*. Colección Las ciencias sociales. Mexico City: H. Cámara de Diputados, LX Legislatura; Oaxaca: Universidad Autónoma Benito Juárez de Oaxaca; Miguel Angel Porrúa, 2007.

———. *Reclamos de la identidad: La formación de las organizaciones indígenas en Oaxaca*. Oaxaca: Universidad Autónoma Benito Juárez de Oaxaca; Mexico City: Miguel Angel Porrúa, 2001.

Hernández Navarro, Luis. "Doce tesis sober el nuevo liderazgo campesino." In *Autonomía y nuevos sujetos sociales en el desarrollo rural*, by Julio Moguel, Carlota Botey, and Luis Hernández Navarro, 65–104. Mexico City: CEHAM; Siglo Veintiuno Editores, 1992.

Hertel, Shareen. "What Was All the Shouting About? Strategic Bargaining and Protest at the WTO Third Ministerial Meeting." *Human Rights Review* 6, no. 3 (April 2005): 102–18. https://doi.org/10.1007/BF02862217.

Hidalgo Celarié, Nidia, Verónica Vázquez García, and Emma Zapata Martelo. "Experiencias de crédito y ahorro entre mujeres: El caso de la Sociedad de Solidaridad Social (SSS) Susana Sawyer de Álamos, Sonora." In *Antropología de la deuda: Crédito, ahorro, fiado y prestado en las finanzas cotidianas*, edited by Magdalena Villareal, 233–56. Mexico City: Editorial Miguel Ángel Porrúa, 2004.

Hill, Rebecca. *Men, Mobs, and Law: Anti-lynching and Labor Defense in U.S. Radical History*. Durham, NC: Duke University Press, 2008.

Hinrichs, C. Clare. "The Practice and Politics of Food System Localization." In "International Perspectives on Alternative Agro-Food Networks: Quality, Embeddedness, Bio-Politics," edited by David Goodman, special issue, *Journal of Rural Studies* 19, no. 1 (January 1, 2003): 33–45. https://doi.org/10.1016/S0743-0167(02)00040-2.

HoSang, Daniel, and Joseph E. Lowndes. *Producers, Parasites, Patriots: Race and the New Right-Wing Politics of Precarity*. Minneapolis: University of Minnesota Press, 2019.

Hostettler, Ueli. "New Inequalities: Changing Maya Economy and Social Life in Central Quintana Roo, Mexico." *Research in Economic Anthropology* 22 (2003): 25–59.

Huhndorf, Shari M. *Going Native: Indians in the American Cultural Imagination*. Ithaca, NY: Cornell University Press, 2001.

Hultgren, John. *Border Walls Gone Green: Nature and Anti-immigrant Politics in America*. Minneapolis: University of Minnesota Press, 2015.

Hurtado, G. R. "Ninguna petición para expulsar a Ana Bayer." *El Imparcial* (Oaxaca), April 24, 1998.

Instituto Nacional de Estadística, Geografía e Informática. *La mujer en Oaxaca*. Aguascalientes, AGS: INEGI, 1995.

Inter-American Institute for Cooperation on Agriculture. *Plan de acción conjunta para la reactivación agropecuaria en América Latina: El caso de México*. Coronado, Costa Rica: Inter-American Institute for Cooperation on Agriculture, 1989.

International Forum on Globalization. "Economic Globalization: The Role of the World Trade Organization Teach-In." Media advisory, October 12, 1999. WTO Seattle Collection, University of Washington. https://digitalcollections.lib.washington.edu/digital/collection/wto/id/187/.

"La inversión extranjera no menoscaba la soberanía." *La Jornada*, September 30, 1990, sec. Economía.

"Invierte la comuna $5 mlls. en logística." *Novedades Quintana Roo*, September 8, 2003.

Ita, Ana de. "PROCEDE: A Failed Programme to Reduce Poverty and Inequalities in Mexico." WIDER Working Paper, July 2022, United Nations University, World Institute for Development Economics Research.

Jenkins, Philip. *Dream Catchers: How Mainstream America Discovered Native Spirituality*. New York: Oxford University Press, 2006.

Johnson, Oswald. "Omnibus Trade Bill Passed by Congress: Reagan to Measure Stiffening Ability to Retaliate against Unfair Actions Abroad." *Los Angeles Times*, August 4, 1988. http://articles.latimes.com/1988-08-04/news/mn-10208_1_trade-bill.

Johnston, Josée, and Gordon Laxer. "Solidarity in the Age of Globalization: Lessons from the Anti-MAI and Zapatista Struggles." *Theory and Society* 32, no. 1 (2003): 39–91.

Juris, Jeffrey S. *Insurgent Encounters: Transnational Activism, Ethnography, and the Political.* Durham, NC: Duke University Press, 2013.

———. *Networking Futures: The Movements against Corporate Globalization.* Durham, NC: Duke University Press, 2008.

———. "Spaces of Intentionality: Race, Class, and Horizontality at the United States Social Forum." *Mobilization: An International Quarterly* 13, no. 4 (December 1, 2008): 353–72. https://doi.org/10.17813/maiq.13.4.232j1557h7658813.

Kampwirth, Karen. *Gender and Populism in Latin America: Passionate Politics.* Foreword by Kurt Weyland. University Park: Pennsylvania State University Press, 2010.

Kaplan, Amy. *The Anarchy of Empire in the Making of U.S. Culture.* Convergences. Cambridge, MA: Harvard University Press, 2002.

Karides, Marina, Walda Katz-Fishman, R. Brewer, J. Scott, and A. Lovelace. *The United States Social Forum: Perspectives of a Movement.* Chicago: Changemaker Publications, 2010.

Kauanui, J. Kehaulani. *Paradoxes of Hawaiian Sovereignty: Land, Sex, and the Colonial Politics of State Nationalism.* Durham, NC: Duke University Press, 2018.

Kay, Tamara. *NAFTA and the Politics of Labor Transnationalism.* New York: Cambridge University Press, 2011.

Kazin, Michael. *The Populist Persuasion: An American History.* 2nd ed. Ithaca, NY: Cornell University Press, 2017.

Keane, John. *Global Civil Society?* Cambridge: Cambridge University Press, 2003.

Keatley, Robert. "Trade Pact Faces Delays, Opposition, Posing Problems for the White House." *Wall Street Journal,* May 20, 1994.

Kelley, Robin D. G. *Freedom Dreams: The Black Radical Imagination.* Boston: Beacon Press, 2002.

———. *Race Rebels: Culture, Politics, and the Black Working Class.* New York: New York: Free Press, 1994.

Kentucky Jobs with Justice. "The Faces of NAFTA: Kentucky/Mexico Worker Exchange Brings Message of Fair Trade to Kentucky." *Action Lines,* Summer 2002.

Khalid, Asma. "Biden and Trump Battle over Who Is 'Weak on China.'" NPR, April 22, 2020. www.npr.org/2020/04/22/840558299/biden-and-trump-battle-over-who-is-weak-on-china.

Khasnabish, Alex. *Zapatistas: Rebellion from the Grassroots to the Global.* London: Zed Books, 2013.

Khor, Martin. "Free Trade and the Third World." In *The Case against "Free Trade": GATT, NAFTA, and the Globalization of Corporate Power*, edited by Ralph Nader and Lori Wallach, 97–107. San Francisco: Earth Island Press; Berkeley, CA: North Atlantic Books, 1993.

———. "The WTO and the Battle over Labor Standards." Third World Network, January 13, 1997.

Kiely, Ray. "The Race to the Bottom and International Labor Solidarity." *Review (Fernand Braudel Center)* 26, no. 1 (2003): 67–88.

King, Leslie. "Ideology, Strategy and Conflict in a Social Movement Organization: The Sierra Club Immigration Wars." *Mobilization: An International Quarterly* 13, no. 1 (February 1, 2008): 45–61. https://doi.org/10.17813/maiq.13.1.c7pv26280665g90g.

King County Elections Office. "King County Local Voters Pamphlet." September 14, 1999. https://your.kingcounty.gov/elections/99sep/pamphlet/2012.htm.

Kingsolver, Ann E. *NAFTA Stories: Fears and Hopes in Mexico and the United States*. Boulder, CO: Lynne Rienner, 2001.

Klein, Naomi. *No Logo: No Space, No Choice, No Jobs*. New York: Picador, 2000.

———. "Reclaiming the Commons." *New Left Review*, June 2001. https://newleftreview.org/issues/II9/articles/naomi-klein-reclaiming-the-commons.

Klooster, Dan. "Campesinos and Mexican Forest Policy during the Twentieth Century." *Latin American Research Review* 38, no. 2 (2003): 94–126.

Kluver, Randy. "Globalization, Informatization, and Intercultural Communication." *American Communication Journal* 3, no. 3 (2000). http://ac-journal.org/journal/vol3/Iss3/spec1/kluver.htm.

Knight, Alan. "Cardenismo: Juggernaut or Jalopy?" *Journal of Latin American Studies* 26, no. 1 (February 1994): 73–107.

———. "Peasants into Patriots: Thoughts on the Making of the Mexican Nation." *Mexican Studies/Estudios Mexicanos* 10, no. 1 (1994): 135–61. https://doi.org/10.2307/1051969.

Korten, David C. *When Corporations Rule the World*. San Francisco: Kumarian Press, 1996.

Koshy, Susan, Lisa Marie Cacho, Jodi A. Byrd, and Brian Jordan Jefferson. *Colonial Racial Capitalism*. Durham, NC: Duke University Press, 2022.

Kraemer Bayer, Gabriela. *Autonomía indígena: Región Mixe, relaciones de poder y cultura política*. Mexico City: Plaza y Valdés; Consejo Nacional de Ciencia y Tecnología; Universidad Autónoma Chapingo-Dirección de Difusión Cultural, 2003.

Kriesi, Hanspeter, Klaus Armington, and Hannes Siegrist, eds. *Nation and National Identity: The European Experience in Perspective*. West Lafayette, IN: Purdue University Press, 2004.

Krugman, Paul. "Enemies of the WTO." *Slate* magazine, November 24, 1999. https://slate.com/business/1999/11/enemies-of-the-wto.html.

Lajous, Alejandra. *Las razones y las obras: Gobierno de Miguel de La Madrid; Crónica del Sexenio, 1982–1988, sexto año.* Mexico City: Fondo Cultura Económica, 1988.

Landzelius, Kyra. *Native on the Net: Indigenous and Diasporic Peoples in the Virtual Age.* Hoboken, NJ: Routledge, 2004.

Larson, Eric D. "Black Lives Matter and Bridge Building: Labor Education for a 'New Jim Crow' Era." *Labor Studies Journal* 41, no. 1 (March 1, 2016): 36–66. https://doi.org/10.1177/0160449X16638800.

———, ed. *Jobs with Justice: 25 Years, 25 Voices.* Oakland, CA: PM Press, 2013.

Legrain, Philippe. "The Coronavirus Is Killing Globalization as We Know It." *Foreign Policy* (blog), March 12, 2020. https://foreignpolicy.com/2020/03/12/coronavirus-killing-globalization-nationalism-protectionism-trump/.

Lehman, Karen. "Farmer Organizations and Regional Integration in North America." In Brooks and Fox, *Cross-border Dialogues*, 167–79.

Lenin, Vladimir I. *The Development of Capitalism in Russia; the Process of the Formation of a Home Market for Large-Scale Industry.* 2nd rev. ed. Moscow: Progress, 1964.

Levi, Margaret, and Gillian H. Murphy, "Coalitions of Contention: The Case of the WTO Protests in Seattle." *Political Studies* 54, no. 4 (December 2006): 651–70.

Lichtenstein, Nelson, and Elizabeth Tandy Shermer, eds. *The Right and Labor in America: Politics, Ideology, and Imagination.* Philadelphia: University of Pennsylvania Press, 2012.

Light, Ray O. "From 'No to WTO to 'No to China' The US Working Class Takes a Step Backward in Washington, DC." Marxist-Leninist Translations and Reprints, September 2000. www.mltranslations.org/US/ROL/ROLNoChina.htm.

Lipsitz, George. *How Racism Takes Place.* Philadelphia: Temple University Press, 2011.

Lizza, Ryan. "Silent Partner: The Man behind the Anti-Free Trade Revolt." *New Republic*, January 10, 2000, 20–25.

"Llega contingente campesino a la ciudad." *Novedades Quintana Roo*, September 8, 2003.

Lomnitz-Adler, Claudio. *Deep Mexico, Silent Mexico: An Anthropology of Nationalism.* Public Worlds 9. Minneapolis: University of Minnesota Press, 2001.

Looker, Benjamin. "Visions of Autonomy: The New Left and the Neighborhood Government Movement of the 1970s." *Journal of Urban History* 38, no. 3 (May 1, 2012): 577–98. https://doi.org/10.1177/0096144211428770.

López Leyva, Miguel Armando. *La encrucijada: Entre la protesta social y la participación electoral (1988).* Mexico City: Plaza y Valdés, 2007.

López Morales, A. "Sí habrá desarrollo en el istmo, promote José Murat en Juchitán." *Las Noticias*, March 11, 1998.

López y Rivas, Gilberto. *Autonomías: Democracia o contrainsurgencia*. Biblioteca Era. Mexico City: Era, 2004.

Lovera, Sara, and Nellys Palomo. *Las Alzadas*. Mexico City: Comunicación e Información de la Mujer; Convergencia Socialista, 1999.

Lowe, Lisa. *Immigrant Acts: On Asian American Cultural Politics*. Durham, NC: Duke University Press, 1996.

Lowndes, Joseph. "White Populism and the Transformation of the Silent Majority." *The Forum* 14, no. 1 (2016): 25–37.

Luiselli Fernández, Cassio. *Agricultura y alimentación en México: Evolución desempeño y perspectivas*. Mexico City: Siglo XXI Editores, 2019.

Lund, Caroline. "The Protectionist Trap." *Against the Current*, no. 88 (October 2000). https://againstthecurrent.org/atc088/p1592/.

Lyons, Scott Richard. *X-Marks: Native Signatures of Assent*. Minneapolis: University of Minnesota Press, 2010.

MacDonald, Kenneth. "The Morality of Cheese: A Paradox of Defensive Localism in a Transnational Cultural Economy." *Geoforum* 44 (January 31, 2013). https://doi.org/10.1016/j.geoforum.2012.03.011.

MacLean, Nancy. *Behind the Mask of Chivalry: The Making of the Second Ku Klux Klan*. New York: Oxford University Press, 1994.

Maeckelbergh, Marianne. *The Will of the Many: How the Alterglobalisation Movement Is Changing the Face of Democracy*. London: Pluto Press, 2009.

Magaña, Maurice Rafael. *Cartographies of Youth Resistance: Hip-Hop, Punk, and Urban Autonomy in Mexico*. Oakland: University of California Press, 2020. https://doi.org/10.1525/9780520975583.

Mahler, Anne Garland. *From the Tricontinental to the Global South: Race, Radicalism, and Transnational Solidarity*. Durham, NC: Duke University Press, 2018.

Maiguashca, Bice. "'They're Talkin' bout a Revolution': Feminism, Anarchism and the Politics of Social Change in the Global Justice Movement." *Feminist Review* 106, no. 1 (February 1, 2014): 78–94. https://doi.org/10.1057/fr.2013.36.

Maldonado Alvarado, Benjamín. *La utopía de Ricardo Flores Magón: Revolución, anarquía y comunalidad india*. Oaxaca: Universidad Autónoma "Benito Juárez" de Oaxaca, Secretaría Académica, 1994.

Mander, Jerry. "Bad Magic: The Failure of Technology: An Interview with Jerry Mander by Catherine Ingram." *The Sun: A Magazine of Ideas*, no. 192 (November 1991). https://ratical.org/ratville/AoS/theSun.html#IV.

———. *In the Absence of the Sacred: The Failure of Technology and the Survival of the Indian Nations*. San Francisco: Sierra Club Books, 1991.

Mander, Jerry, and Edward Goldsmith, eds. *The Case against the Global Economy: And for a Turn toward the Local.* San Francisco: Sierra Club Books, 1996.
——. Introduction to *The Case against the Global Economy: And for a Turn toward the Local,* edited by Jerry Mander and Edward Goldsmith. San Francisco: Sierra Club Books, 1996.
Marantos, Jeanette. "A Happy Little Miracle in Dark Times: The Plant Nursery Business Is Booming." *Los Angeles Times,* March 21, 2020. www.latimes.com/lifestyle/story/2020-03-21/plant-nurseries-are-now-offering-curbside-service-a-resurgence-of-victory-gardens.
Marshall, Peter. *Demanding the Impossible: A History of Anarchism.* Oakland, CA: PM Press, 2009.
Martínez, Elizabeth "Betita." "Where Was the Color in Seattle? Looking for Reasons Why the Great Battle Was So White." *Colorlines,* March 10, 2000.
Martínez Luna, Jaime. *Comunalidad y desarrollo.* Cultura indígena. Mexico City: Oaxaca: Centro de Apoyo al Movimiento Popular Oaxaqueño, 2003.
Martínez Novo, Carmen. *Who Defines Indigenous? Identities, Development, Intellectuals, and the State in Northern Mexico.* New Brunswick, NJ: Rutgers University Press, 2006.
Mata G., Bernardino. "La autogestión campesina en el desarrollo rural." In *El sector agropecuario en el futuro de la economía mexicana,* edited by Juan Pablo Arroyo Ortiz, 167–83. Mexico City: Fund. Friedrich Naumann, 1991.
Mattiace, Shannan L. *To See with Two Eyes: Peasant Activism and Indian Autonomy in Chiapas, Mexico.* Albuquerque: University of New Mexico Press, 2003.
McAlevey, Jane. *No Shortcuts: Organizing for Power in the New Gilded Age.* New York: Oxford University Press, 2016.
Melamed, Jodi. *Represent and Destroy: Rationalizing Violence in the New Racial Capitalism.* Minneapolis: University of Minnesota Press, 2011.
Melamed, Jodi, Bruce Burgett, and Glenn Hendler. "Diversity." In *Keywords for American Cultural Studies,* 2nd ed., 84–88. New York: New York University Press, 2014.
Mena Munguía, Salvador, and Mario Ramírez Martínez, eds. *Panorama de la agricultura en México.* Guadalajara: Editorial Universitaria and CUCBA, Universidad de Guadalajara, 2014.
Mendoza Zuany, R. G. "Dealing with Diversity in the Construction of Indigenous Autonomy in the Sierra Norte of Oaxaca—Harvard University." *Bulletin of Latin American Research* 27, no. 3 (2008): 351–67.
Meneses, Luis. "Autonomía organizativa y soberanía alimentaria." In *Primer Foro Nacional sobre Reforma Rural en México,* edited by Herminio Baltazar C., 155–61. Mexico City: Universidad Autónoma de Chapingo, 1989.
"México: Erupción sobre elecciones." *Spartacist,* October 1988, Español edition.

Mexico, Poder Ejecutivo Federal. *Plan nacional de desarrollo, 1995–2000: Programa de desarrollo informático.* Mexico City: INEGI, 1996.

Mignolo, Walter. *The Darker Side of Western Modernity: Global Futures, Decolonial Options.* Latin America Otherwise. (Durham, NC: Duke University Press, 2011.

Morales, C. "Generan movilizaciones inestabilidad." *El Imparcial* (Oaxaca), March 14, 1998.

———. "SEGOB investigará a extranjeros." *El Imparcial* (Oaxaca), April 29, 1998.

Moreno, Julio. *Yankee Don't Go Home! Mexican Nationalism, American Business Culture, and the Shaping of Modern Mexico, 1920–1950.* The Luther Hartwell Hodges Series on Business, Society, and the State. Chapel Hill: University of North Carolina Press, 2003.

Moreton, Bethany. *To Serve God and Wal-Mart: The Making of Christian Free Enterprise.* Cambridge, MA: Harvard University Press, 2009.

Morris, David. "A Global Village and a Globe of Villages." Speech delivered at Rochester Institute of Technology, April 3, 1997. Institute for Local Self-Reliance, August 8, 2016. https://ilsr.org/listen-a-global-village-or-a-globe-of-villages-david-morris-speech-from-1997/.

———. "Healthy Cities: Self-Reliant Cities." *Health Promotion* 2, no. 2 (1987): 169–76.

Morris, Stephen D. *Gringolandia: Mexican Identity and Perceptions of the United States.* Latin American Silhouettes. Lanham, MD: Rowman and Littlefield, 2005.

Nabudere, Dani Wadada, and Mapungubwe Institute for Strategic Reflection (MISTRA). *From Agriculture to Agricology: Towards a Glocal Circular Economy.* Johannesburg: Real African Publishers, 2013.

Nadasdy, Paul. "Transcending the Debate over the Ecologically Noble Indian: Indigenous Peoples and Environmentalism." *Ethnohistory* 52, no. 2 (Spring 2005): 291–331. https://doi.org/10.1215/00141801-52-2-291.

Nader, Ralph. "Newt Gingrich." Ralph Nader website, November 14, 1994. https://nader.org/1994/11/14/newt-gingrich/.

———. "Presidential Candidacy Agenda for a New Democracy." Light Party, February 1, 2000. www.lightparty.com/Misc/NaderGreenParty.html.

———. "Ralph Nader: Conservatively Speaking." Interview by Pat Buchanan. *American Conservative*, June 21, 2004, www.theamericanconservative.com/ralph-nader-conservatively-speaking/.

———. *Unstoppable: The Emerging Left-Right Alliance to Dismantle the Corporate State.* New York: Nation Books, 2014.

———. "WTO Means Rule by Unaccountable Tribunals." *Wall Street Journal*, August 17, 1994.

Nader, Ralph, et al. *The Case against "Free Trade": GATT, NAFTA, and the Globalization of Corporate Power.* San Francisco: Earth Island Press; Berkeley, CA: North Atlantic Books, 1993.

"National and Global Call for a United Strategy against the WTO in Cancun." Nadir, ca. 2003. www.nadir.org/nadir/initiativ/agp/free/cancun/strategy_wto.htm.

Naples, Nancy A., and Manisha Desai. *Women's Activism and Globalization: Linking Local Struggles and Global Politics.* New York, NY: Routledge, 2002.

Neumann, Rachel. "Out of Step: Labor and the Global Social Justice Movement." *New Labor Forum*, no. 11 (2002): 38–47.

Nickerson, Michelle. *Mothers of Conservatism: Women and the Postwar Right.* Princeton, NJ: Princeton University Press, 2012.

Nicolaides, Becky M. *My Blue Heaven: Life and Politics in the Working-Class Suburbs of Los Angeles, 1920–1965.* Chicago: University of Chicago Press, 2002.

Noakes, John A., Brian V. Klocke, and Patrick F. Gillham. "Whose Streets? Police and Protester Struggles over Space in Washington, DC, 29–30 September 2001." *Policing and Society* 15, no. 3 (2005): 235.

"Notas rápidas." *Revista Autónomo,* May 2001.

Notimex. "Incluir servicios en la Ronda Uruguay, pedirá México." *La Jornada,* September 23, 1990, sec. Economía.

O'Brien, Jean M. *Firsting and Lasting: Writing Indians out of Existence in New England.* Indigenous Americas. Minneapolis: University of Minnesota Press, 2010.

Ochoa, Enrique. *Feeding Mexico: The Political Uses of Food since 1910.* Wilmington, DE: Rowman and Littlefield, 2000.

Olesen, Thomas. *International Zapatismo: The Construction of Solidarity in the Age of Globalization.* London: Zed, 2005.

Olsson, Tore C. *Agrarian Crossings: Reformers and the Remaking of the US and Mexican Countryside.* Princeton, NJ: Princeton University Press, 2020.

Opel, Andy. "Punishment before Prosecution: Pepper Spray as Postmodern Repression." In Opel and Pompper, *Representing Resistance*, 44–60.

Opel, Andy, and Donnalyn Pompper. "Introduction: An Emerging Paradigm?" In Opel and Pompper, *Representing Resistance*, ix–xvii.

———, eds. *Representing Resistance: Media, Civil Disobedience, and the Global Justice Movement.* Westport, CT: Praeger, 2003.

Orin, Deborah. "Buchanan Says He'd Wipe the Floor with the Donald." *New York Post,* September 18, 1999. https://nypost.com/1999/09/18/buchanan-says-hed-wipe-the-floor-with-the-donald/.

Ortiz, Fernando. *Cuban Counterpoint: Tobacco and Sugar.* Durham, NC: Duke University Press, 1995.

Osorio, L. C. "Anarquía." *El Imparcial* (Oaxaca), April 27, 1998.

Ostendorf, David, and Daniel Levitas, "Education for Empowerment and Social Action in Rural America." *Mid-American Review of Sociology* 12, no. 1 (1987): 55–64.
O'Sullivan, Michael. "Globalisation Is Dead and We Need to Invent a New World Order." Book excerpt and interview by K.N.C. *The Economist*, June 28, 2019. www.economist.com/open-future/2019/06/28/globalisation-is-dead-and-we-need-to-invent-a-new-world-order.
Otero, Gerardo. "The New Agrarian Movement: Self-Managed, Democratic Production." *Latin American Perspectives* 16, no. 4 (1989): 28–59.
Overmyer-Velázquez, Rebecca. *Folkloric Poverty: Neoliberal Multiculturalism in Mexico*. University Park: Pennsylvania State University Press, 2010.
Page, Susan. "Buchanan Plans to Speak at WTO Protests in D.C." *USA Today*, April 11, 2000.
Park, Lisa, and David Pellow. *The Slums of Aspen: Immigrants vs. the Environment in America's Eden*. Nation of Newcomers: Immigrant History as American History. New York: NYU Press, 2011.
Park, Mi. "The Trouble with the Eco-Politics of Localism: Too Close to the Far Right? Debates on Ecology and Globalization." *Interface: A Journal for and about Social Movements* 5, no. 2 (November 2013): 318–43.
Parrish, Michael. "Europe Nearer to Dolphin-Safe Tuna: The European Parliament Seeks to Stop Italy's Importation of 'Dirty Tuna' Caught by the Mexican Fishing Fleet." *Los Angeles Times*, November 23, 1991. www.latimes.com/archives/la-xpm-1991-11-23-fi-199-story.html.
Pastor, Manuel, and Tony LoPresti. "Bringing Globalization Home." *Colorlines* 7, no. 2 (Summer 2004): 29–32.
Peña, Guillermo de la. "Social Citizenship, Ethnic Minority Demands, Human Rights and Neoliberal Paradoxes: A Case Study in Western Mexico." In *Multiculturalism in Latin America: Indigenous Rights, Diversity and Democracy*, edited by Rachel Sieder, 129–56. Institute of Latin American Studies Series. London: Palgrave Macmillan UK, 2002. https://doi.org/10.1057/9781403937827_6.
Pendergrast, T. L., Bobby J. Smith, Jeffrey A. Liebert, and Rachel Bezner Kerr. "Introduction to the Symposium: Rethinking Food System Transformation—Food Sovereignty, Agroecology, Food Justice, Community Action and Scholarship." *Agriculture and Human Values* 36, no. 4 (December 1, 2019): 819–23. https://doi.org/10.1007/s10460-019-09952-z.
Pérez U., Matilde. "Acto de Vía Campesina: Pugnan productores por la soberanía en materia alimentaria." *La Jornada*, April 18, 1996, sec. El País.
Perot, Ross. *Save Your Job, Save Our Country: Why NAFTA Must Be Stopped—Now*. New York: Hyperion, 1993.
Peterson, Patrick. "King March Unlike 60s; Issues Remain." *Sun Herald* (Biloxi, MS), April 10, 1988, b1.

Pierce, Michael. "Orval Faubus and the Rise of Anti-labor Populism in Northwestern Arkansas." In *The Right and Labor in America: Politics, Ideology, Imagination*, edited by Nelson Lichtenstein and Elizabeth Tandy Shermer, 98–113. Philadelphia: University of Pennsylvania Press, 2012.

Pinto, Lucas Henrique. "El surgimiento de la UNORCA y el debate sobre la autonomía campesina: Breve análisis de la trayectoria de construcción del concepto de soberanía alimentaria en México." *Estudios Rurales* 8, no. 14 (2018): 120–52.

Pleyers, Geoffrey. *Alter-Globalization: Becoming Actors in a Global Age*. Cambridge: Polity, 2010.

———. "El altermundismo en México: Actores, culturas políticas, y prácticas contra el neoliberalismo." In *Los grandes problemas de México*, vol. 6, *Movimientos sociales*, 361–95. Mexico City: El Colegio de México, 2010.

Poole, Deborah. "An Image of 'Our Indian': Type Photographs and Racial Sentiments in Oaxaca, 1920–1940." *Hispanic American Historical Review* 84, no. 1 (February 1, 2004): 37–82. https://doi.org/10.1215/00182168-84-1-37.

Popper, Nathaniel. "Working Legacy: Jews and the Labor Movement." *Forward*, April 23, 2009. http://forward.com/articles/105047/new-labor-leaders-take-a-page-from-history/.

Porta, Donatella Della, Massimiliano Andretta, Angel Calle, Helene Combes, Nina Eggert, Marco G. Giugni, Jennifer Hadden, Manuel Jimenez, and Raffaele Marchetti. *Global Justice Movement: Cross-national and Transnational Perspectives*. London: Routledge, 2015.

Porter, Eric. "Affirming and Disaffirming Actions: Re-making Race in the 1970s." In *America in the Seventies*, edited by Beth Bailey and David Farger, 50–74. Lawrence: University Press of Kansas, 2004.

Postero, Nancy Grey. *Now We Are Citizens: Indigenous Politics in Postmulticultural Bolivia*. Stanford, CA: Stanford University Press, 2007.

Postero, Nancy Grey, and Leon Zamosc. *The Struggle for Indigenous Rights in Latin America*. Brighton: Sussex Academic Press, 2004.

Power, Edward. "Labor Chiefs Rally to Urge Rights Bill." *Philadelphia Inquirer*, September 17, 1987, 9b.

Prashad, Vijay. *The Darker Nations: A People's History of the Third World*. New Press People's History. New York: New Press, 2007.

———. *The Poorer Nations: A Possible History of the Global South*. London: Verso Books, 2013.

Pratt, William C. "Using History to Make History? Progressive Farm Organizing during the Farm Revolt of the 1980." *Annals of Iowa* 55, no. 1 (1996): 24–45.

Raghavan, Chakravarthi. "The World Trade Organization and Its Dispute Settlement System: Tilting the Balance against the South." *Third World Network: Trade and Development Series* 9 (2000). www.twn.my/title/tilting.htm.

Rainforest Action Network. "Stop the Yanomami Genocide." *Rainforest Action Network Action Alert*, no. 46 (March 1990).

Ramírez, G. "Emplaza oposición a canjear la intolerancia por acuerdo político." *El Imparcial* (Oaxaca), November 22, 1997.

Ramírez López, Heladio. "El partido y el futuro." *El Imparcial* (Oaxaca), December 2, 1997.

Ramnath, Maia. *Decolonizing Anarchism: An Antiauthoritarian History of India's Liberation Struggle*. Oakland, CA: AK Press, 2012.

Ramos, Jazmín. "Salvaguardan policías las plazas comerciales." *Novedades Quintana Roo*, September 8, 2003.

Recondo, David. *La política del gatopardo: Multiculturalismo y democracia en Oaxaca*. Publicaciones de la Casa Chata. Mexico City: CIESA; CEMCA, 2007.

Rendón, I. "Debe México saldar su deuda con Oaxaca." *Palabra*, November 30, 1998.

Restrepo, Iván. "La alimentación de los mexicanos." *La Jornada*, September 24, 1990, sec. El País.

Revkin, Andrew C. "A Video Challenge to Green Shoppers." *Dot Earth Blog*, November 13, 2007. https://archive.nytimes.com/dotearth.blogs.nytimes.com/2007/11/13/video-challenges-green-shoppers-and-globalization/.

"Ricardo Flores Magón: A 73 años de su muerte. 'Viva tierra y libertad.'" *Fortaleza Libertaria*, November 17, 1995.

Richards, Patricia. "Of Indians and Terrorists: How the State and Local Elites Construct the Mapuche in Neoliberal Multicultural Chile." *Journal of Latin American Studies* 42, no. 1 (2010): 59–90. https://doi.org/10.1017/S0022216X10000052.

Ridgeway, James. "Mondo Washington." *Village Voice*, March 3, 2004, sec. Nation, 26.

Riley, Jason L. *Let Them In: The Case for Open Borders*. New York: Gotham, 2008.

Roberts, Kenneth M. "Neoliberalism and the Transformation of Populism in Latin America: The Peruvian Case." *World Politics* 48, no. 1 (October 1995): 82–116.

Robertson, Pat. *The New World Order*. Dallas, TX: Word, 1991.

Robertson, Thomas. *The Malthusian Moment: Global Population Growth and the Birth of American Environmentalism*. New Brunswick, NJ: Rutgers University Press, 2012.

Robinson, Cedric J. *Black Marxism: The Making of the Black Radical Tradition*. London: Penguin UK, 2021.

Robles, J. H. "Promueven imágen visual en calles de la ciudad." *El Imparcial* (Oaxaca), December 6, 1997.

Rodney, Walter. *How Europe Underdeveloped Africa*. Rev. ed. Washington, DC: Howard University Press, 1981.

Rodriguez, Cecilia. "Save the Dolphins, but Remember Mexican Needs, Too: How Do You Balance Mexican Families' Search for Nutritious, Cheap Food—Such as Tuna—against the Protection of Dolphins?" *Los Angeles Times*, January 13, 1991, sec. Opinion.

Roediger, David R. *Colored White: Transcending the Racial Past*. Berkeley: University of California Press, 2003.

———. *Towards the Abolition of Whiteness: Essays on Race, Politics, and Working Class History*. London: Verso, 1994.

———. *Working toward Whiteness: How America's Immigrants Became White: The Strange Journey from Ellis Island to the Suburbs*. New York: Basic Books, 2005.

Rossinow, Doug. *The Politics of Authenticity: Liberalism, Christianity, and the New Left in America*. New York: Columbia University Press, 1998.

Rostow, W. W. *The Stages of Economic Growth, a Non-Communist Manifesto*. Cambridge: Cambridge University Press, 1960.

Rovira, Guiomar. *Mujeres de maíz: La voz de las indígenas de Chiapas y la rebelión zapatista*. Barcelona: Virus, 1996.

———. *Zapatistas sin fronteras: Las redes de solidaridad con Chiapas y el altermundismo*. Mexico City: Ediciones Era, 2009.

Roy, Arundhati. "Confronting Empire." Speech delivered January 27, 2003, in Porto Alegre, Brazil. https://ratical.org/ratville/CAH/AR012703.html.

Rudra, Nita. *Globalization and the Race to the Bottom in Developing Countries: Who Really Gets Hurt?* Cambridge: Cambridge University Press, 2008.

Rupert, Mark. *Ideologies of Globalization: Contending Visions of a New World Order*. London: Routledge, 2000.

Ryan, Ramor. "The Battle of Cancun—Anatomy of an Unexpected Victory." The Struggle Site, 2004. http://struggle.ws/anarchism/writers/ramor/cancun.html.

Safa Barraza, Alejandra, and Erna Mergruen Rentería. *Las mujeres campesinas se organizan*. Mexico City: UNORCA, 1993.

Said, Edward W. *Culture and Imperialism*. New York: Knopf Doubleday, 2012.

Saldaña-Portillo, María Josefina. *The Revolutionary Imagination in the Americas and the Age of Development*. Latin America Otherwise. Durham, NC: Duke University Press, 2003.

Salinas de Gotarí, Carlos. *Aliados y adversarios: Historia del TLCAN: 1988-2017*. Mexico City: Debate, 2017.

———. *Plan nacional de desarrollo, 1989-1994*. Mexico City: Secretaría de Programación y Presupuesto, 1989.

Salinas de Gotarí, Raúl, ed. *Diconsa en la modernización comercial y la regulación del abasto popular*. Mexico City: Instituto Nacional de Administración Pública, 1988.

Sámano Rentería, Miguel Angel. "El movimiento ¡El campo no aguanta más! y el Acuerdo Nacional para el Campo: Situación y perspectiva." *El Cotidiano* 19, no. 124 (April 2004): 64–70.
Samuel, Howard. "Foreign Investment in the U.S.: A Labor View." *Looking Ahead*, May 1989, 1–5.
"¡Santa Justicia!, detienen a pseudolideres del CIPO." *Antequera*, September 15, 2004.
Santos, Boaventura de Sousa. *Another Production Is Possible: Beyond the Capitalist Canon*. Reinventing Social Emancipation 2. London: Verso, 2006.
———. *The Rise of the Global Left: The World Social Forum and Beyond*. London: Zed Books, 2006.
Saturay, Ace. Interview by Jeremy Simer of People's Assembly, May 4, 2000. WTO History Project, University of Washington. https://depts.washington.edu/wtohist/interviews/Saturay.pdf.
Schrag, Peter. *Not Fit for Our Society: Nativism and Immigration*. Berkeley: University of California Press, 2010.
Sedrez, Lise Fernanda. "A Meeting of Minds: Coalitions, Representations and American Non-governmental Organizations in the Brazilian Amazon." Master's thesis, New Jersey Institute of Technology, 1998.
Self, Robert. *All in the Family: The Realignment of American Democracy since the 1960s*. New York: Hill and Wang, 2012.
SEMARNAP. *Pesca del atun y proteccion del delfin*. Mexico City: Secretaria de Medio Ambiente, Recursos Naturales y Pesca, 1998.
Servin, S. G. "CODEP es una organización fantasma: Diputado Priísta." *Las Noticias*, January 13, 1998.
Shaw, Randy. *Beyond the Fields: Cesar Chavez, the UFW, and the Struggle for Justice in the 21st Century*. Berkeley: University of California Press, 2008.
Shilliam, Robbie. "What about Marcus Garvey? Race and the Transformation of Sovereignty Debate." *Review of International Studies* 32, no. 3 (2006): 379–400.
Shiva, Vandana. *Biopiracy: The Plunder of Nature and Knowledge*. Boston: South End Press, 1997.
———. *Protect or Plunder? Understanding Intellectual Property Rights*. A Global Issues Title. London: Zed Books, 2001.
Sibaja, N. G. "Realizarán indígenas más movilizaciones." *El Imparcial* (Oaxaca), March 12, 1998.
Sierra Camacho, Maria Teresa, Rosalva Aída Hernández Castillo, and Rachel Sieder. *Justicias indígenas y estado violencias contemporáneas*. Mexico City: FLACSO; CIESAS, 2013.
Silver, Beverly J., and Giovanni Arrighi. "Workers North and South." *Socialist Register* 37 (2001). https://socialistregister.com/index.php/srv/article/view/5755.

Silverstein, Ken, and Alexander Cockburn. "Tuna, Free Trade and Cocaine." *Earth Island Journal* 11, no. 3 (Summer 1996), 1, 7.

Simpson, Audra. *Mohawk Interruptus: Political Life across the Borders of Settler States*. Durham, NC: Duke University Press, 2014.

Sitrin, Marina. *Everyday Revolutions: Horizontalism and Autonomy in Argentina*. London: Zed Books, 2012.

Smiley, Erica, and Sarita Gupta. *The Future We Need: Organizing for a Better Democracy in the Twenty-First Century*. Ithaca, NY: Cornell University Press, 2022.

Smith, Jackie. *Social Movements for Global Democracy*. Themes in Global Social Change. Baltimore: Johns Hopkins University Press, 2008.

Smithers, Gregory D. "Beyond the 'Ecological Indian': Environmental Politics and Traditional Ecological Knowledge in Modern North America." *Environmental History* 20, no. 1 (2015): 83–111.

Soler, José. "José Soler: A Life Working at the Intersections of Nationalism, Internationalism, and Working-Class Radicalism. An Interview with Eric Larson." *Radical History Review*, no. 128 (May 2017): 62–76.

Solís M., Leopoldo. *Alternativas para el desarrollo*. Cuadernos de Joaquín Mortiz. Mexico City: Editorial J. M. oOrtiz, 1980.

———. *La realidad económica mexicana: Retrovisión y perspectivas*. El Mundo del hombre. Economía y demografía. Mexico City: Siglo Veintiuno Editores, 1970.

Solnit, Rebecca. *Hope in the Dark: Untold Histories, Wild Possibilities*. 3rd ed. Chicago: Haymarket Books, 2016.

"Southern Pilgrimage for Jobs with Justice." Special issue, *People's Daily World*, April 28, 1988.

Speed, Shannon. *Rights in Rebellion: Indigenous Struggle and Human Rights in Chiapas*. Stanford, CA: Stanford University Press, 2008.

Speed, Shannon, Rosalva Aída Hernández Castillo, and Lynn Stephen. *Dissident Women: Gender and Cultural Politics in Chiapas*. Austin: University of Texas Press, 2006.

St. Clair, Jeffrey. *Five Days That Shook the World*. London: New Left Review, 1999.

Stahler-Sholk, Richard. "Resisting Neoliberal Homogenization: The Zapatista Autonomy Movement." *Latin American Perspectives* 34, no. 2 (2007): 48–63.

Stanley, Timothy. *The Crusader: The Life and Tumultuous Times of Pat Buchanan*. New York: St. Martin's, 2012.

Starr, Amory. *Global Revolt: A Guide to the Movements against Globalization*. London: Zed Books, 2005.

———. "How Can Anti-imperialism Not Be Anti-racist? The North American Anti-globalization Movement." *Journal of World-Systems Research* 10, no. 1 (2004): 119–51. https://doi.org/10.5195/jwsr.2004.308.

———. *Naming the Enemy: Anti-corporate Movements Confront Globalization.* London: Zed, 2000.

Starr, Amory, Luis Fernandez, and Christian Scholl. *Shutting Down the Streets: Political Violence and Social Control in the Global Era.* New York: New York University Press, 2011.

Stephen, Lynn. "The Construction of Indigenous Suspects: Militarization and the Gendered and Ethnic Dynamics of Human Rights Abuses in Southern Mexico." *American Ethnologist* 26, no. 4 (November 1, 1999): 822–42. https://doi.org/10.1525/ae.1999.26.4.822.

———. *Transborder Lives: Indigenous Oaxacans in Mexico, California, and Oregon.* E-Duke Books Scholarly Collection. Durham, NC: Duke University Press, 2007.

———. *We Are the Face of Oaxaca: Testimony and Social Movements.* Durham, NC: Duke University Press, 2013.

———. *Zapata Lives! Histories and Cultural Politics in Southern Mexico.* Berkeley: University of California Press, 2002.

Stern, Alexandra. *Eugenic Nation: Faults and Frontiers of Better Breeding in Modern America.* 2nd edition. American Crossroads 17. Oakland: University of California Press, 2016.

Stockton, William. "Tearing Apart Eastern Airlines." *New York Times*, November 6, 1988, 36.

Striffler, Steve. *Solidarity: Latin America and the US Left in the Era of Human Rights.* Wildcat Series. London: Pluto Press, 2019.

Suárez, B., and F. Pérez-Gil, eds. "La modernización del campo y la alimentación: Un recuento de los últimos años, 1982–1996." In *Sector agropecuario y alternativas comunitarias de seguridad alimentaria y nutrición en México*, edited by L. M. Espinoza. Mexico City: UAM/CECIPROC/INNSZ /Plaza y Valdés, 1999.

Suárez, Victor. "Por un referente campesino nacional autónomo y de izquierda." *La Jornada del Campo*, September 17, 2011. www.jornada.com.mx/2011/09 /17/referente.html.

Sumano, A. G., and J. A. Márquez. "Propone Murat un gobierno que sea incluyente y tolerante." *Las Noticias*, March 10, 1998.

Sunkel, Osvaldo. "Capitalismo transnacional y desintegración nacional en América Latina." *Estudios Internacionales* 4, no. 16 (March 1971): 3–61.

Taiaiake Alfred, and Jeff Corntassel. "Being Indigenous: Resurgences against Contemporary Colonialism." In *The Movement of Movements. Part 1: What Makes Us Move?*, 131–46. Oakland, CA: PM Press; New Delhi: OpenWord, 2017.

Táíwò, Olúfẹ́mi O. *Reconsidering Reparations: Worldmaking in the Case of Climate Crisis.* Philosophy of Race. New York: Oxford University Press, 2022.

Tamayo, Eduardo. "Cancún: Diferencias de fondo en la OMC." Agencia Latinoamericana de Información, September 10, 2003. www.alai.info/108354-2/.

Tarleton, John. "The IMC Fills a Niche: Protesters Develop Their Own Global News Service." *On the Road with John Tarleton*, October 2000. www.johntarleton.net/imc_feature.html.

Taylor, David. "Teddy Goldsmith—Obituary." *Green World*, August 21, 2009. https://green-history.uk/people/teddy-goldsmith-obit.

Tenorio Adame, Antonio. Opening address, February 27, 1984, Mexico City. In *Por la soberanía alimentaria: Enfoques y perspectivas*, edited by Julian Rodríguez Adame, 1–5. Mexico City: Centro de Estudios Históricos del Agrarismo en México, 1984.

Thompson, A. K. *Black Bloc, White Riot: Anti-globalization and the Genealogy of Dissent*. Oakland, CA: AK Press, 2003.

Thornton, Christy. *Revolution in Development: Mexico and the Governance of the Global Economy*. Oakland: University of California Press, 2021.

Thorpe, Charles, and Ian Welsh. "Beyond Primitivism: Towards a Twenty-First Century Anarchist Theory and Praxis for Science and Technology." *Anarchist Studies* 16, no. 1 (March 22, 2008): 48–76.

Tiemeyer, Philip James. *Plane Queer: Labor, Sexuality, and AIDS in the History of Male Flight Attendants*. Berkeley: University of California Press, 2013.

Torres, Andrés, and José Emiliano Velázquez. *The Puerto Rican Movement: Voices from the Diaspora*. Philadelphia: Temple University Press, 1998.

Torres, Blanca. "Las ONG ambientalistas en las relaciones México-Estados Unidos." *Foro Internacional* 39, no. 4 (158) (1999): 453–78.

Torres, Humberto. "No se atiende." *El Imparcial* (Oaxaca), April 28, 1998.

———. "Rechazo a la violencia." *El Imparcial* (Oaxaca), April 28, 1998.

"Trabajadores de ambos lados de la frontera critican al TLC." *Hoy en las Americas*, June 21, 2002.

Tran, Mark. "IMF and World Bank Meetings in Jeopardy." *The Guardian*, September 14, 2001, sec. US News. www.theguardian.com/world/2001/sep/14/september11.usa24.

Trauger, Amy. "Toward a Political Geography of Food Sovereignty: Transforming Territory, Exchange and Power in the Liberal Sovereign State." *Journal of Peasant Studies* 41, no. 6 (November 2, 2014): 1131–52. https://doi.org/10.1080/03066150.2014.937339.

Trejo, Guillermo. *Popular Movements in Autocracies: Religion, Repression, and Indigenous Collective Action in Mexico*. Cambridge Studies in Comparative Politics. New York: Cambridge University Press, 2012.

"Trump and Biden Launch Battle over China That Could Define 2020 Election." CNN Politics, April 21, 2020. www.cnn.com/2020/04/21/politics/trump-biden-china-2020/index.html.

Turner, Derek D. "Are We at War with Nature?" *Environmental Values* 14, no. 1 (2005): 21–36.
United Nations. "World Must Reap Benefits of Globalization without Eroding Cultural Diversity, Republic of Korea Tells Second Committee." Press release, October 22, 1997. https://press.un.org/en/1997/19971022.GAEF2770.html.
UNORCA. "A los campesinos del mundo. A la opinión pública." Ca. 1988. In Costa, *UNORCA*, 349–50.
——. "Convenio de concertación propuesto por UNORCA al gobierno federal." In Costa, *UNORCA*, 101–35.
——. "Manifiesto a la nación." Ca. 1988. In Costa, *UNORCA*, 340–45.
——. "Open Letter to H. Cámara de Diputados and Gabinete Agropecurario." In Costa, *UNORCA*, 356–57.
——. *Una propuesta para el movimiento campesino.* Mexico City: Fundación Friedrich Ebert, Representación en México, 1992.
UNORCA and CECCAM. *La guerra por los mercados de alimentos: La Organización Mundial del Comercio (OMC) en la agricultura.* Mexico City: CECCAM; UNORCA, 2003.
UNORCA et al. "México. Manifiesto de Ciudad Juárez: 'El campo no aguanta más.'" *Tribuna Roja*, no. 90, March 10, 2003. http://prueba.moir.org.co/2004/08/10/mexico-manifiesto-de-ciudad-juarez-el-camp0-no-aguanta-mas/.
UNORCI. "Reglamento de la UNORCI que propone la Unión de Ejidos Lázaro Cárdenas, de Ahuacatlán, Nayarit." In Costa, *UNORCA*, 128–32.
Vacon, Bob. "Thousands Attend Rally to Support Colt Strikers." *Hartford Courant*, September 28, 1987, 1, 9.
Various organizations. "Acuerdos sobre el encuentro sobre crédito y aseguramento y precios de garantía celebrado en el Ejido de Estanzuela de Romero, Municipio de Jerécuaro, Guanajuato, 10 y 11 de Abril de 1983." In Costa, *UNORCA*, 63–82.
Vásquez, M. A. "Marchan 500 de CODECI, por la detención de sus líderes." *Cantera*, April 17, 1998.
Vega, J. "La detención de dirigentes del CIPO-RFM, 'No se va a quedar así.'" *Cantera*, April 24, 1998.
Velasco Cruz, Saúl. *El movimiento indígena y la autonomía en México.* Colección Posgrado 23. Mexico City: Universidad Nacional Autónoma de México, 2003.
Velez Ascencio, Octavio. "Divididos, protestan por separado la alianza magonista el CIPO." *Las Noticias*, November 19, 2001.
Vía Campesina. *Proceedings from the II International Conference of the Vía Campesina, Tlaxcala, Mexico. April 18–21, 1996.* Brussels: NCOS Publications, 1996.

———. "Que es la soberania alimentaria [sic]." Vía Campesina website, January 15, 2003. https://viacampesina.org/es/que-es-la-soberania-alimentaria/.

Vía Campesina and Conferencia Internacional de la Vía Campesina. *La Vía Campesina: Memoria de la II Conferencia Internacional de la Vía Campesina, Tlaxcala, Mexico, 18 al 21 de abril de 1996*. Brussels: Ediciones NCOS, 1996.

"View from Hightower Is That Texas Is Populist State," *Houston Chronicle*, June 8, 1986, 34.

Vizenor, Gerald Robert. *Manifest Manners: Narratives on Postindian Survivance*. Lincoln: University of Nebraska Press, 1999.

Wald, Sarah D. *The Nature of California: Race, Citizenship, and Farming since the Dust Bowl*. Seattle: University of Washington Press, 2016.

———. "Visible Farmers/Invisible Workers." *Food, Culture and Society* 14, no. 4 (December 1, 2011): 567–86. https://doi.org/10.2752/175174411X13046092851479.

Wallach, Lori. *The WTO: Five Years of Reasons to Resist Corporate Globalization*. New York: Seven Stories Press, 1999.

Wallach, Lori, and Moisés Naím. "The FP Interview: Lori's War." *Foreign Policy*, no. 118 (2000): 29–55. https://doi.org/10.2307/1149669.

Warburton, Theresa. *Other Worlds Here: Honoring Native Women's Writing in Contemporary Anarchist Movements*. Evanston, IL: Northwestern University Press, 2021.

Warren, Kay B., and Jean E. Jackson. *Indigenous Movements, Self-Representation, and the State in Latin America*. Austin: University of Texas Press, 2002.

Watts, Jonathan. "What Drove a Korean Farmer to Kill Himself in Cancun?" *The Guardian*, September 16, 2003, sec. World News. www.theguardian.com/world/2003/sep/16/northkorea.wto.

Weinstein, Nat. "AFL-CIO Backs Anti-IMF, World Bank Protest in Washington: 'Dump the Third World Debt.'" *Socialist Action* (blog), April 1, 2000. https://socialistaction.org/2000/04/01/afl-cio-backs-anti-imf-world-bank-protest-in-washington-dump-the-third-world-debt/.

Welch, Andy. "Hightower Present: Save-the-Family-Farm Act Introduced in Congress." *Texas Gazette* (Newsletter of the Texas Department of Agriculture), February 1987, 1.

Welch, Matt. "Nader on Immigration: Friend or Foe?" *Alternet*, October 23, 2000. www.alternet.org/story/9980/nader_on_immigration%3A_friend_or_foe.

West, Cornel. "Populism: A Black Socialist Critique." In *The New Populism: The Politics of Empowerment*, edited by Harry Boyte and Frank Riessman, 207–13. Philadelphia: Temple University Press, 1986.

White, Jerry. "Economic Nationalist Sets the Tone for IMF Protests in Washington." World Socialist Web Site, May 3, 2000. www.wsws.org/en/articles/2000/05/wash-m03.html.

Whyte, Kyle Powys. "Indigenous Food Sovereignty, Renewal, and US Settler Colonialism." In *The Routledge Handbook of Food Ethics*, edited by Mary Rawlinson and Caleb Ward, 354–65. London: Routledge, 2016.

Wiebe, Joseph. "Cultural Appropriation in Bioregionalism and the Need for a Decolonial Ethics of Place." *Journal of Religious Ethics* 49, no. 1 (March 2021): 138–58. https://doi.org/10.1111/jore.1234.

Wiebe, Nettie. "Women of La Via [sic] Campesina: Creating and Occupying the Spaces Which Are Our Right." In *Report: IV Women's Assembly of La Vía Campesina*, 7–11. Harare, Zimbabwe: October 2014. https://viacampesina.org/en/wp-content/uploads/sites/2/2015/06/2015-06-06%20LVC%20women%20articulation%20report%20EN-rev1-c.pdf.

Williams, Gwyn. *Struggles for an Alternative Globalization: An Ethnography of Counterpower in Southern France*. Farnham: Ashgate, 2008.

Wise, Timothy A., Hilda Salazar, and Laura Carlsen, eds. *Confronting Globalization: Economic Integration and Popular Resistance in Mexico*. Bloomfield, CT: Kumarian Press, 2003.

Wolfe, Patrick. "Settler Colonialism and the Elimination of the Native." *Journal of Genocide Research* 8, no. 4 (December 1, 2006): 387–409. https://doi.org/10.1080/14623520601056240.

Wolfson, Todd. *Digital Rebellion: The Birth of the Cyber Left*. Urbana: University of Illinois Press, 2014.

Women of the Popular Indigenous Council of Oaxaca—Ricardo Flores Magón. "Declaración Política de Mujeres," March 9, 1998, Unprocessed records of the Organización India de Derechos Humanos de Oaxaca, Oaxaca City.

Wong, Kent, and Elaine Bernard. "Labor's Mistaken Anti-China Campaign." *New Labor Forum*, Fall/Winter 2000. http://qcpages.qc.cuny.edu/newlaborforum/old/html/7_article2.html.

Wong, Kristine. "The Showdown before Seattle: Race, Class, and the Framing of a Movement." In *The Battle of Seattle: The New Challenge to Capitalist Globalization*, 215–24. New York: Soft Skull Press, 2002.

Wood, Lesley J. "Bridging the Chasm: The Case of People's Global Action." In Bandy and Smith, *Coalitions across Borders*, 95–117.

———. *Direct Action, Deliberation, and Diffusion: Collective Action after the WTO Protests in Seattle*. Cambridge Studies in Contentious Politics. Cambridge: University Press, 2012.

Woodward, C. Vann. *Tom Watson: Agrarian Rebel*. New York: Oxford University Press, 1938.

Wright, Angus Lindsay, and Wendy Wolford. *To Inherit the Earth: The Landless Movement and the Struggle for a New Brazil*. Oakland, CA: Food First Books, 2003.

Wright, Karen, and John Clark. "Terminator Genes." *Discover Magazine*, August 21, 2003. www.discovermagazine.com/the-sciences/terminator-genes.

Wypijewski, JoAnn. "A16: Inside/Outside Stories." *CounterPunch*, April 15, 2000.
Yates, Michael D. "Workers of All Countries, Unite." *Monthly Review*, July 1, 2000. https://monthlyreview.org/2000/07/01/workers-of-all-countries-unite/.
Yuen, Eddie, Daniel Burton-Rose, and George N. Katsiaficas, eds. *The Battle of Seattle: The New Challenge to Capitalist Globalization*. New York: Soft Skull Press, 2001.
Zahavi, Gerald. "Passionate Commitments: Race, Sex, and Communism at Schenectady General Electric, 1932–1954." *Journal of American History* 83, no. 2 (September 1996): 514–48.
Zaretsky, Natasha. *No Direction Home: The American Family and the Fear of National Decline, 1968–1980*. Chapel Hill: University of North Carolina Press, 2007.
Zerzan, John. *Future Primitive: And Other Essays*. New Autonomy Series. Brooklyn, NY: Autonomedia; Columbia, MO: Anarchy, a Journal of Desire Armed, 1994.
Zeskind, Leonard. *Blood and Politics: The History of the White Nationalist Movement from the Margins to the Mainstream*. New York: Farrar Strauss Giroux, 2009.
Zeskind, Leonard, and Devin Burghart. "Voting along the Racial Faultline: Greens, Browns and the Red, White and Blue," *Searchlight Magazine*, December 2000, 26–27.
Zibechi, Raúl. *Dispersing Power: Social Movements as Anti-state Forces*. English ed. Oakland, CA: AK Press, 2010.
Ziegler, Bart. "How to Start a Garden—with Very Little Effort." *Wall Street Journal*, May 10, 2020. www.wsj.com/articles/how-to-start-a-gardenwith-very-little-effort-11588903200.

Index

"A16," 51, 137, 149; "Anti-Capitalist Convergence," 142, 149; arrests, 149; Jobs with Justice national office, 149; Mobilization for Global Justice, 149; "spokescouncil" meetings, 149; unions, 151, 152
Abbey, Edward, 119, 120, 126, 128
acarreado/a, 92. *See also* racism: and stereotypes, Indigenous Mexican
Acuff, Stewart, 152, 264n44
Acteal, Chiapas, 91, 243n72. *See also* Indigenous communities Mexico: repression against; Zapatistas
ACTWU (Amalgamated Clothing and Textile Workers Union), 62, 232n48
AFA-TWU (Association of Flight Attendants—Transport Workers Union), 55, 60, 231n35. *See also* Eastern Airlines strike; sexism: in unions US
affinity group(s), 9, 149, 178, 183. *See also* anarchism, kinds of; "networked" organizational forms
AFL-CIO, 155, 226n2; and China, 138–42, 148, 154, 262n21; critique of neoliberalism, 141; on immigration, 117; and JwJ, 151, 265n57; at Seattle WTO protests, 130
AFSCME (American Federation of State, County, and Municipal Employees), 59, 265n46

agribusiness, 22, 33, 47, 169, 172, 205; and GMOs, 158, 161; vs. small Mexican farmers, 16, 18, 22, 33, 35, 38, 47; and structural adjustment, 137; vs. US "family farmers," 31, 136. *See also ejido(s)*
Amalgamated Clothing and Textile Workers Union. *See* ACTWU
American Federation of State, County, and Municipal Employees. *See* AFSCME
anarchism, kinds of, 4, 11, 178; anarcho-punk, 183, 186; "green anarchy," 188; Mexican Indigenous anarchism (*Magonista*), 4, 11, 165, 177, 178, 192, 200; Western anarchism, 165, 188, 272n4
anti-Asian racism and xenophobia, 63–64, 141. *See also* AFL-CIO: and China
anti-Chinese racism and xenophobia, 3, 11, 64, 138–39, 148, 201, 202; Chin, Vincent, murder, 64, 141
anti-Japanese racism and xenophobia, 64, 102, 141
anti-Mexico racism and xenophobia, 100, 115, 116
antiracism, 188, 203
anti-immigration sentiment. *See* xenophobia
anti-imperialism, 203; Latin American, 24
"Antimodernism," 188, 189
antisemitism, 101

319

INDEX

antiwar movement, 155
apartheid, 68
Aquino Solis, Aristarco, 84, 85
Argentina: financial crisis, 178; in "Group of 20" nations WTO, 174; worker-owned factories, 178
Article 27, Mexican Constitutional, 87
asamblea(s), 180, 186, 189. *See also* CIPO-RFM: organizational structure
Asian Pacific Economic Cooperation, 69
Association of Flight Attendants—Transport Workers Union (AFA-TWU), 55, 60, 231n35. *See also* Eastern Airlines strike; sexism: in unions US
austerity measures, 15; and agribusiness, 137; and job losses, 140; Mexico and IMF, 137
"autonomous" movements in Latin America, 177-79
autonomy: Indigenous demands for, 79; peasant "self-management" (*auto-gestión*), 22; and Zapatista uprising, 79. *See also* Indigenous autonomy
Azcarate, Fred, 148, 150-154. *See also* Jobs with Justice: A16 organizing

Bahr, Morton, 55, 64. *See also* CWA
"Balkanization" of Mexico, 81, 87
Bartolomé, Miguel Alberto, 80. *See also* Oaxaca Indigenous struggles
Battle in Seattle, film, 98
Bayer, Ana, 94, 95.
Beas, Carlos, 94, 95. *See also* UCIZONI
Becker, George, 110, 111. *See also* United Steelworkers
Bello, Walden, 129, 130, 140, 148, 250n50, 262n21
Benton, Sherry, 136, 137, 145-47. *See also* internationalist exchanges: JwJ workers' exchanges
Berry, Wendell, 103, 125-27, 258n49, 258n55
"biopiracy," 161. *See also* Shiva, Vandana
Black community demand for jobs, 58. *See also* Hawkins, Gus
Bogues, Anthony, 6, 210n18
border, US-Mexico: cross-border dialogues, 34, 47, 101, 116, 221n8; policing, 117, 119
Boston Global Action Network (BOGAN), 150
Brazil's Landless Movement, *See* MST
Brecher, Jeremy, 5, 6, 208n12, 250n48

Buchanan, Pat: (anti-Chinese) racism, 138, 139, 247n22; and globalization, 104-108, 111, 113, 247n21; and PNTR, 138; Reform Party, 102, 104, 116, 138; xenophobia, 102, 116. *See also* Nader, Ralph
Bush, George W., 64, 164
"Buy American" campaigns, 63, 65, 66, 100, 145, 148, 253n9

Campo No Aguanta Más, El (The Countryside Can't Take It Anymore), 163, 164, 174
Cancún, Quintana Roo, 156-58
Cancún WTO protests: First Indigenous Women's Summit of the Americas, 190-91; martyrdom, 156-57; repression, 170-73, 194. *See also* Lee Kyung-hae
Cárdenas, Cuauhtémoc, 25, 48
Cargill, 32, 158. *See also* GMOs
Caribbean, 6, 118-19, 157
Carrasco Altamirano, Diódoro: anti-Indigenous racism, 76, 95; and CIPO-RFM, 87, 90, 95; and EZLN, 77, 79, 85; reforms, 76, 78-79, 81-84, 95-96, 239n20, 240n35, 243n61
Carreón, Marcelo, 166, 169-72, 174. *See also* UNORCA
Castañeda, Jorge, 101, 107, 252n5
CECVYM (*Coalición de Ejidos Colectivos Valle del Yaqui and Mayo*), 22, 23
Chávez, César, 68
Chiapas, 23, 45, 77, 80, 91, 121, 192, 210n21
child labor, 99, 100
China: Chinese workers, 139, 140; sanctions, 99; unions preoccupation with, 138-142. *See also* anti-Chinese racism and xenophobia; PNTR
Chin, Vincent, murder of, 64, 141. *See also* anti-Chinese racism and xenophobia
Choate, Pat, 107. *See also* Reform Party
Christian militia movement, 59, 102. *See also* white supremacist right wing
CIPO-RFM: affiliates, 192; cooperatives, 187; EZLN, support of, 74, 77, 85, 86, 91; Indigenous communities, 93, 176, 177, 180, 182, 187; organizational structure, 178, 180, 184, 187; political positions, 86, 178, 179, 188, 189; protests and direct action, 86, 181, 192; repression against, 75, 76, 86, 93, 94; Women's Area, 88, 92, 93, 189-91, 204, 277n71; youth culture, 181-83, 185
Citizen Action, 51, 57, 104

INDEX 321

Citizen Trade Campaign, 105, 106, 108
class. See working class
Clinton, Bill, 102, 138
CNC (*Confederación Nacional Campesina*), 35, 93
CNI (*Congreso Nacional Indígena*), 77, 167
CNMI (*Coordinadora Nacional de Mujeres Indígenas*), 77, 88
Coalición de Ejidos Colectivos Valle del Yaqui and Mayo (Coalition of Ejido Collectives of the Yaqui and Mayo Valleys). See CECVYM
Coalición Obrera, Campesina, Estudiantil del Istmo (Coalition of Workers, Peasants, and Students of the Isthmus). See COCEI
COCEI (*Coalición Obrera, Campesina, Estudiantil del Istmo*), 93
CODECI (*Comité de Defensa Ciudadana y Asistencia a Comunidades Rurales*), 93
CODEP (*Comité de Defensa de los Derechos del Pueblo*), 183
"color-blind anticorporatism": racism and empire as secondary, 99, 114, 120, 131; in white progressive organizations, 10, 105, 112, 129, 130, 199; and xenophobia, 11, 136, 137, 142
Colt Firearms strike, 62, 65
Comité de Defensa Ciudadana y Asistencia a Comunidades Rurales (Committee for Citizen Defense and Assistance to Rural Communities). See CODECI
Comité de Defensa de los Derechos del Pueblo (Committee of Defense of the Rights of the People). See CODEP
Communication Workers of America. See CWA
comunalidad, 84, 187
Confederación General de Trabajadores, Spain (CGT), 192. See also CIPO-RFM: affiliates
Confederación Nacional Campesina (National Peasant Federation). See CNC
Congreso Nacional Indígena (National Indigenous Congress). See CNI
Consejo Indígena Popular de Oaxaca—Ricardo Flores Magón. See CIPO-RFM
Coordinadora Nacional de Mujeres Indígenas (National Coordinating Committee of Indigenous Women). See CNMI
Cordtz, Richard, 66. See also SEIU
corn: genetically modified, 158–61, 190, 194; Mexican, 24, 32, 34, 159, 164, 169, 176, 220n52; US, 69, 100, 158

"corporate robber barons," 52, 53, 55, 57, 61–65
corruption, 88, 89, 182, 242n55.
Covid-19, effect on globalism, 197, 198
CWA (Communication Workers of America), 50, 55, 56, 59, 64, 66, 148, 151. See also Cohen, Larry; Bahr, Morton
Crosby, Jeff, 148. See also CWA
Cruz, Alejandro, 90, 95. See also CIPO-RFM
cyber-activism, 143, 144, 178, 183

Davis, Angela, and critique of liberal multiculturalism, 128
Davis, Russ, 153. See also JwJ: A16 organizing
debt crisis, Latin American, 17, 18, 35
"defensive localism," 15, 16, 25, 28, 46, 52, 59, 213n3
de Ita, Ana, 39, 40. See also UNORCA
de la Madrid, Miguel, 19–21, 23, 24, 215n17
Deloria, Vine, 122, 257n39
Derdowski, Brian, 113, 114, 129
deregulation, 62, 63
"development box," WTO, 162. See also UNORCA
Direct Action Network (DAN), 110, 111, 129. See also RAN
direct action tactics, 88, 181, 204; black bloc, 175; efficacy, 2, 55, 137, 145, 152, 175; in global justice organizing, 5, 7, 51, 90, 98, 119, 120, 149, 151, 178, 203
diversity, deracialized, 126. See also Berry, Wendell; color-blind anticorporatism
Doha, Qatar, 174
Dolan, Mike, 103, 104, 129, 248n30. See also Citizen Trade Campaign
"dolphin safe" tuna, 99, 108, 109, 110
Domingo, Cindy, 130. See also LELO
Duarte, Pablo, 169, 170, 171, 173, 174. See also UNORCA: Yucatán
Dzib Pue, Pedro, 157, 158, 165. See also UNORCA; Cancún WTO protests 2003

Earth First!, 118, 119. See also Foreman, Dave
Earth Island Institute, 98, 108
Eastern Airlines strike, 55, 60, 62, 65, 67
Ejército Popular Revolucionario / Popular Revolutionary Army. See EPR
Ejército Zapatista de Liberación Nacional / Zapatista Army of National Liberation (EZLN). See Zapatistas

ejido(s): as apparatus of control, 21–22; peasant self-determination, 21–22, 47; privatization of, 35–36,37, 224n28; UNORCA's political positions on, 21, 37, 38, 217n30. *See also* UNORCA; Oaxaca: multicultural reforms

"English-only" legislation, 118

environmental justice movements, 120, 203, 279n12

EPR (*Ejército Popular Revolucionario* / Popular Revolutionary Army), 77, 91

Escobedo Cetina, Humberto, 186

Esteva, Gustavo, 84, 241n47

Euro-American civilization, 102, 139. *See also* Buchanan: xenophobia

European New Right movement (ENR), 127

European Union, 3, 115, 172, 201

Evans, Lane, 57. *See also* New Populist Forum

EZLN. *See* Zapatistas

FAIR (Federation for American Immigration Reform), 118, 253n13

Fair Trade Mexico, 167, 168

farmer-labor coalitions, 56, 57, 69

farms: foreclosures, 57, 146; price guarantees, 18; subsidies, 18, 32, 162, 172, 222–23n22, 230n25

feminism, 16, 40, 59, 191, 228n9, 258n49

"50 Years Is Enough!," 150

Fisher, Franz, 172

Fithian, Lisa, 151, 152

"folkloric poverty," 78, 80, 81, 82

Food and Agriculture Organization (UN), 170

food self-sufficiency, 20, 218n37

Foreman, Dave, 118, 119. *See also* Earth First!

Fortaleza Libertaria, zine, 186

Foundation for Deep Ecology, 117, 118, 121, 259n59

Fox, Vicente, 164. *See also* PAN

Free Trade Area of the Americas (FTAA), 155, 164, 172, 186. *See also* Miami 2003 FTAA protests

Frank, Dana, 63, 251n61. *See also* "Buy American" campaigns

Friedman, Thomas, 201

Friedrich Ebert Foundation, Mexico, 27

Garcia, Juan, 205. *See also* JwJ

Gatica, Raúl, 90, 91, 179, 191, 243n72. *See also* CIPO-RFM

GATT (General Agreement on Trade and Tariffs), 18, 26, 100, 108, 249n47

"GATTzilla versus Flipper," 107–109

gender: patriarchal gender roles, 38–42; replicated in social movements, 8, 32, 42, 45, 127, 258n49. *See also* sexism

genetically modified crops. See GMOs

Getachew, Adom, 6

Gifford, Kathie Lee sweatshop controversy, 99, 100, 146. *See also* child labor

Gil, Javier, 37, 38, 222n12. *See also* UNORCA

Gingrich, Newt, 106, 107

global food system. *See* agribusiness

"globalization from below," 4, 204, 208n12

Global North: activism, 10, 73, 74, 124, 139, 154, 261n15; development models, 16, 17, 22, 27, 161–64, 195; multinationals, 117, 139, 140, 164, 188

Global South: activism, 6, 31, 64, 65, 96, 97, 108, 109, 261n15; debt burdens, 2, 3, 16, 109, 137, 139; structural adjustment, 11, 26, 43, 107, 141, 161, 162

Global Trade Watch, 139. *See also* Public Citizen

"global village multiculturalism," 114, 115, 120–22, 200. *See also* color-blind anticorporatism

GMOs: bans, 161; corn, 158, 190; cross pollination, 159; patenting and intellectual property, 156, 159

Goldman, Patti, 99

Goldsmith, Edward: and IFG, 121, 122, 129; on immigration, 122; relationship with Right, 105, 127, 259n56

Gomez, Alberto, 163, 167, 174. *See also* UNORCA

Grassroots Global Justice (GGJ), 203

Greenpeace, 108, 109

Greenpeace Mexico, 109, 110, 190

Green Party, 116, 117, 127; anti-immigrant stance, 127. *See also* Nader, Ralph

"Green Revolution," 26

Greer, Simon, 150–54. *See also* JwJ

"Group of 20" WTO, 174

Guatemala, 78, 79

Guelagetza festival, 81, 240n30

Guerrero, 77, 173

Hale, Charles, 75, 81. *See also* "neoliberal multiculturalism"

Harkin, Tom, 57, 230n25. *See also* New Populist Forum

INDEX   321

Citizen Trade Campaign, 105, 106, 108
class. *See* working class
Clinton, Bill, 102, 138
CNC (*Confederación Nacional Campesina*), 35, 93
CNI (*Congreso Nacional Indígena*), 77, 167
CNMI (*Coordinadora Nacional de Mujeres Indígenas*), 77, 88
Coalición de Ejidos Colectivos Valle del Yaqui and Mayo (Coalition of Ejido Collectives of the Yaqui and Mayo Valleys). *See* CECVYM
Coalición Obrera, Campesina, Estudiantil del Istmo (Coalition of Workers, Peasants, and Students of the Isthmus). *See* COCEI
COCEI (*Coalición Obrera, Campesina, Estudiantil del Istmo*), 93
CODECI (*Comité de Defensa Ciudadana y Asistencia a Comunidades Rurales*), 93
CODEP (*Comité de Defensa de los Derechos del Pueblo*), 183
"color-blind anticorporatism": racism and empire as secondary, 99, 114, 120, 131; in white progressive organizations, 10, 105, 112, 129, 130, 199; and xenophobia, 11, 136, 137, 142
Colt Firearms strike, 62, 65
Comité de Defensa Ciudadana y Asistencia a Comunidades Rurales (Committee for Citizen Defense and Assistance to Rural Communities). *See* CODECI
Comité de Defensa de los Derechos del Pueblo (Committee of Defense of the Rights of the People). *See* CODEP
Communication Workers of America. *See* CWA
comunalidad, 84, 187
Confederación General de Trabajadores, Spain (CGT), 192. *See also* CIPO-RFM: affiliates
Confederación Nacional Campesina (National Peasant Federation). *See* CNC
Congreso Nacional Indígena (National Indigenous Congress). *See* CNI
Consejo Indígena Popular de Oaxaca—Ricardo Flores Magón. *See* CIPO-RFM
Coordinadora Nacional de Mujeres Indígenas (National Coordinating Committee of Indigenous Women). *See* CNMI
Cordtz, Richard, 66. *See also* SEIU
corn: genetically modified, 158–61, 190, 194; Mexican, 24, 32, 34, 159, 164, 169, 176, 220n52; US, 69, 100, 158

"corporate robber barons," 52, 53, 55, 57, 61–65
corruption, 88, 89, 182, 242n55.
Covid-19, effect on globalism, 197, 198
CWA (Communication Workers of America), 50, 55, 56, 59, 64, 66, 148, 151. *See also* Cohen, Larry; Bahr, Morton
Crosby, Jeff, 148. *See also* CWA
Cruz, Alejandro, 90, 95. *See also* CIPO-RFM
cyber-activism, 143, 144, 178, 183

Davis, Angela, and critique of liberal multiculturalism, 128
Davis, Russ, 153. *See also* JwJ: A16 organizing
debt crisis, Latin American, 17, 18, 35
"defensive localism," 15, 16, 25, 28, 46, 52, 59, 213n3
de Ita, Ana, 39, 40. *See also* UNORCA
de la Madrid, Miguel, 19–21, 23, 24, 215n17
Deloria, Vine, 122, 257n39
Derdowski, Brian, 113, 114, 129
deregulation, 62, 63
"development box," WTO, 162. *See also* UNORCA
Direct Action Network (DAN), 110, 111, 129. *See also* RAN
direct action tactics, 88, 181, 204; black bloc, 175; efficacy, 2, 55, 137, 145, 152, 175; in global justice organizing, 5, 7, 51, 90, 98, 119, 120, 149, 151, 178, 203
diversity, deracialized, 126. *See also* Berry, Wendell; color-blind anticorporatism
Doha, Qatar, 174
Dolan, Mike, 103, 104, 129, 248n30. *See also* Citizen Trade Campaign
"dolphin safe" tuna, 99, 108, 109, 110
Domingo, Cindy, 130. *See also* LELO
Duarte, Pablo, 169, 170, 171, 173, 174. *See also* UNORCA: Yucatán
Dzib Pue, Pedro, 157, 158, 165. *See also* UNORCA; Cancún WTO protests 2003

Earth First!, 118, 119. *See also* Foreman, Dave
Earth Island Institute, 98, 108
Eastern Airlines strike, 55, 60, 62, 65, 67
Ejército Popular Revolucionario / Popular Revolutionary Army. *See* EPR
Ejército Zapatista de Liberación Nacional / Zapatista Army of National Liberation (EZLN). *See* Zapatistas

ejido(s): as apparatus of control, 21–22; peasant self-determination, 21–22, 47; privatization of, 35–36,37, 224n28; UNORCA's political positions on, 21, 37, 38, 217n30. *See also* UNORCA; Oaxaca: multicultural reforms
"English-only" legislation, 118
environmental justice movements, 120, 203, 279n12
EPR (*Ejército Popular Revolucionario* / Popular Revolutionary Army), 77, 91
Escobedo Cetina, Humberto, 186
Esteva, Gustavo, 84, 241n47
Euro-American civilization, 102, 139. *See also* Buchanan: xenophobia
European New Right movement (ENR), 127
European Union, 3, 115, 172, 201
Evans, Lane, 57. *See also* New Populist Forum
EZLN. *See* Zapatistas

FAIR (Federation for American Immigration Reform), 118, 253n13
Fair Trade Mexico, 167, 168
farmer-labor coalitions, 56, 57, 69
farms: foreclosures, 57, 146; price guarantees, 18; subsidies, 18, 32, 162, 172, 222–23n22, 230n25
feminism, 16, 40, 59, 191, 228n9, 258n49
"50 Years Is Enough!," 150
Fisher, Franz, 172
Fithian, Lisa, 151, 152
"folkloric poverty," 78, 80, 81, 82
Food and Agriculture Organization (UN), 170
food self-sufficiency, 20, 218n37
Foreman, Dave, 118, 119. *See also* Earth First!
Fortaleza Libertaria, zine, 186
Foundation for Deep Ecology, 117, 118, 121, 259n59
Fox, Vicente, 164. *See also* PAN
Free Trade Area of the Americas (FTAA), 155, 164, 172, 186. *See also* Miami 2003 FTAA protests
Frank, Dana, 63, 251n61. *See also* "Buy American" campaigns
Friedman, Thomas, 201
Friedrich Ebert Foundation, Mexico, 27

Garcia, Juan, 205. *See also* JwJ
Gatica, Raúl, 90, 91, 179, 191, 243n72. *See also* CIPO-RFM

GATT (General Agreement on Trade and Tariffs), 18, 26, 100, 108, 249n47
"GATTzilla versus Flipper," 107–109
gender: patriarchal gender roles, 38–42; replicated in social movements, 8, 32, 42, 45, 127, 258n49. *See also* sexism
genetically modified crops. *See* GMOs
Getachew, Adom, 6
Gifford, Kathie Lee sweatshop controversy, 99, 100, 146. *See also* child labor
Gil, Javier, 37, 38, 222n12. *See also* UNORCA
Gingrich, Newt, 106, 107
global food system. *See* agribusiness
"globalization from below," 4, 204, 208n12
Global North: activism, 10, 73, 74, 124, 139, 154, 261n15; development models, 16, 17, 22, 27, 161–64, 195; multinationals, 117, 139, 140, 164, 188
Global South: activism, 6, 31, 64, 65, 96, 97, 108, 109, 261n15; debt burdens, 2, 3, 16, 109, 137, 139; structural adjustment, 11, 26, 43, 107, 141, 161, 162
Global Trade Watch, 139. *See also* Public Citizen
"global village multiculturalism," 114, 115, 120–22, 200. *See also* color-blind anticorporatism
GMOs: bans, 161; corn, 158, 190; cross pollination, 159; patenting and intellectual property, 156, 159
Goldman, Patti, 99
Goldsmith, Edward: and IFG, 121, 122, 129; on immigration, 122; relationship with Right, 105, 127, 259n56
Gomez, Alberto, 163, 167, 174. *See also* UNORCA
Grassroots Global Justice (GGJ), 203
Greenpeace, 108, 109
Greenpeace Mexico, 109, 110, 190
Green Party, 116, 117, 127; anti-immigrant stance, 127. *See also* Nader, Ralph
"Green Revolution," 26
Greer, Simon, 150–54. *See also* JwJ
"Group of 20" WTO, 174
Guatemala, 78, 79
Guelagetza festival, 81, 240n30
Guerrero, 77, 173

Hale, Charles, 75, 81. *See also* "neoliberal multiculturalism"
Harkin, Tom, 57, 230n25. *See also* New Populist Forum

Hawkins, Gus, 58, 59
Hayes, Randy, 115, 117–19, 124. *See also* RAN
"Heartland feminism," 59
Hightower, Jim, 56, 57, 103; *Progressive Populist* magazine, 103, 117. *See also* New Populist Forum
Hoffa, James, 116, 130, 138
homophobia, 60, 231n35

IAM (International Association of Machinists and Aerospace Workers), 65. *See also* "Martin Luther King, Jr., March for Economic Justice"
IATP (Institute for Agriculture and Trade Policy), 69, 104, 105
identity politics, 5–7, 58, 106, 209n16
IFG (International Forum on Globalization), 104, 122; connection to Deep Ecology, 121; "globe of villages," 121, 123, 127, teach-ins, 120–21, 129.
IMF and World Bank protests April 2000, Washington D.C. *See* A16
IMF and World Bank protests cancelled, 155
immigrant workers' rights, US, 65, 130, 200, 204. *See also* LELO
immigration. *See* xenophobia
immigration and mainstream environmental organizations, 113, 115, 117–20
Imparcial, El (Oaxaca), 90, 94
indigeneity: Indigenous peoples, annihilation of, 16; "indio permitido," 75, 76, 85; "insurrectionary Indian," 75, 85, state-endorsed, 75
Indigenous autonomy, 79, 179, 239n24. *See also* CIPO-RFM; UNORCA
Indigenous communities Mexico: lack of services, 176; repression against, 35, 86, 181; small farmers, 47; stereotypes, 76, 81, 92
Indigenous communities' self-governance: *asamblea* (town assembly), 180; *municipales* (county seats), 180, 181; *usos y costumbres*, 180. See also *sistemas normativos internos*
"Indigenous food sovereignty," 214n5
Indigenous women: autonomy, 84, 88; education and illiteracy, 88; state and economic violence against, 88
"*indio permitido*," 75, 76, 85
Industrial Union Department (IUD), AFL-CIO, 50, 51, 57, 65, 66, 226n2

Institute for Agriculture and Trade Policy. *See* IATP
International Association of Machinists and Aerospace Workers (IAM), 65. *See also* "Martin Luther King, Jr., March for Economic Justice"
International Bridge action, Juárez, 163, 164
International Forum on Globalization. *See* IFG
internationalist exchanges: cross-border collaborations, 101, 205 ; JwJ workers' exchanges (Kentucky-Sonora), 146, 205
internet access, activists. *See* cyber-activism
Interparking Company, 149, 152, 154. *See also* JwJ: A16 organizing
Iowa Farm Unity Coalition, 59

Jackson, Jesse, 148, 230n25
Japan, 64, 101, 102, 233n53
John Birch Society, 102, 104
Jobs with Justice (JwJ): A16 organizing, 142–45, 149–54; and AFL-CIO, 142; Atlanta coalitions, 66–68; Boston JwJ, 143, 150; "corporate greed" mobilizing, 142, 154; diversity of staff and directors, 68, 144; growth, 142, 143, 154; health care reform, 61; immigrant workers campaigns, 65; internal organization, 55, 56, 143; "International Plenary on Global Justice," 154; Kentucky JwJ, 145–48, 265n45; Nacogdoches, 56, 57, 59, 67; Portland (Oregon) JwJ, 143, 150; "Right to Organize," 144; Washington State JwJ, 69, 143
Judd, Ron, 111

Kazin, Michael, 54
King, Jr., Dr. Martin Luther, 66, 67
Klein, Naomi, 74, 178
Korten, David, 129, 248n25. *See also* IFG

Larouche, Lyndon, 59, 102
Lee Kyung-hae, 156, 193
Legacy of Equality, Leadership, and Organizing. *See* LELO
LELO: and WTO organizations, 114, 129; organizing immigrant communities, 114, 129; "Workers' Voices Coalition," 129, 130. *See also* Domingo, Cindy; Scott, Tyree
LIMEDHH (*Liga Mexicano por las Derechos Humanos* / Mexican League for Human Rights), 91, 92

Local 22, *Sindicato Nacional de Trabajadores de la Educación* (SNTE), 77, 182
López Portillo, José, 18
Lorenzo, Frank, 55, 65. *See also* Eastern Airlines strike
"Lost Decade," Latin America, 9, 15

"Made in the USA Foundation," 65
Magonismo, 11, 178, 190, 192, 200
Magón, Ricardo Flores, 179, 186, 273n10
MAI (Multilateral Agreement on Investment), 114
Maldonado, Benjamin, 186
Mander, Jerry, 74, 121–25, 129. *See also* IFG
Martínez, Elizabeth "Betita," 5, 98, 111, 114, 129, 199
"Martin Luther King Jr. March for Economic Justice," 57, 66, 67. *See also* SCLC
Marxist critiques, 4, 16, 141, 183
Meneses, Luis, 21, 23, 24, 26–28, 30, 35, 42–48, 166. *See also* UNORCA
Mergruen, Erna, 39. *See also* UNORCA
mestizo(s), 45, 47, 77, 80, 81
Mexican nationalism, 10, 16, 77, 82, 220n48
Mexican Network in the Face of Free Trade (*Red Mexicana ante Libre Comercio*). *See* RMALC
Mexican Revolution, the, 16, 21, 25, 26, 29, 31, 37, 47–48, 220n48, 224n28
Miami FTAA "Free Trade Area of the Americas" (2003) protests, 155, 203
migration: Indigenous within Mexico, 81, 182; Mexico to US, 181, 203
Milliken, Roger, 104, 105, 106
Mittal, Anuradha, 140, 262n21
Monsanto, 32, 158
MPR (*Movimiento popular revolucionario* / Popular Revolutionary Movement), 188, 191
Mpufane, Glen, 111
MST (Brazil's Landless Movement), 44, 178
multiculturalism. *See* "neoliberal multiculturalism"
Multilateral Agreement on Investment (MAI). *See* MAI
Murat, José, 89. *See also* PRI
mutual aid, 179, 186, 187

NAACP, 67
Nader, Ralph: and Buchanan, 103–106; on immigration, 116, 117, 253n13; protecting US sovereignty, 103, 108–111, 124
Nash, Jock, 104, 105

National Development Plan (de Gotarí). *See Plan Nacional de Desarrollo*
National Education Workers Union (*Sindicato Nacional de Trabajadores de la Educación*). *See* SNTE
National Family Farm Coalition (NFFC), 51, 57
National Rainbow Coalition, 107
National Organization for Women (NOW), 51
"neoliberal multiculturalism" critique of, 75, 76, 78, 85. *See also* Davis, Angela; Hale, Charles
"networked" organizational forms, 9, 35, 51, 55, 70, 129, 143, 183, 184
"New Deal for Indigenous Peoples." See *Nuevo Acuerdo;* Carrasco
New International Economic Order (NIEO), 6
"New Populism," 56
New Populist Forum, 57
"New World Order," 101
NFFC (National Family Farm Coalition), 51, 57
9/11 attacks, 155
"No-Name Group," 105
Norberg-Hodge, Helena, 123.
Noticias, Las (Oaxaca), 91, 93
NOW (National Organization for Women), 51
Nuevo Acuerdo, Oaxaca: critique of, by CIPO–RFM, 85, 87; indigenous groups' participation, 79, 83, 84; indigenous political systems, recognition; 79, 83; privatizes land tenure, 85; and Zapatismo, 85. *See also* Carrasco

Oaxaca: Indigenous struggles, 76, 79, 80, 83–85, 182,184; multicultural reforms, 76–79, 81–85, 89, 94; PRI, 76, 243n61; repression, 80, 90–93, 95, 273n12. *See also* Carrasco; CIPO–RFM; *Nuevo Acuerdo*
Occupy Wall Street, 203
OIDHO (*Organizaciones Indias por los Derechos Humanos en Oaxaca*), 88, 179
Oklahoma City bombing, 102, 104
Organizaciones Indias por los Derechos Humanos en Oaxaca. See OIDHO
Ozer, Kathy, 59

PAN (*Partido Acción Nacional* / National Action Party), 164, 203
peasant-centered food system, 28, 31
peasants Mexico, 18, 20, 21, 24

INDEX 325

Peña Nieto, Enrique, 203, 205
People for Fair Trade/No WTO, 129. *See also* Public Citizen
Perot, Ross, 104
petroleum privatization, Mexico, 18, 25, 203
"plain-folk" evangelicalism, 51, 52, 58, 68, 69, 126
Plan Estatal de Desarrollo, 82, 240n29. *See also* Carrasco
Plan Nacional de Desarrollo (National Development Plant), de Gotarí, 33, 34
Plan Puebla Panama, 185, 192
plantones (occupations), 89, 90–93, 163, 174
PNTR (Permanent Normal Trade Relations), 138, 139. *See also* China
Poole, Deborah, 80, 81
Pope, Carl, 119. *See also* Sierra Club
Popular Indigenous Council of Oaxaca— Ricardo Flores Magón. *See* CIPO-RFM
"popular-Indigenous nation," 87, 88
population and carrying capacity, 119, 120
Prague, Czech Republic ministerial meetings and protests, 152
PRI (*Partido Revolucionario Institucional* / Institutional Revolutionary Party), 19, 25, 35, 48
prison labor, US, 140
PRONAL (*Programa Nacional de Alimentación* / National Food Program), 20
Public Citizen, 69, 105, 106, 139. *See also* Dolan, Mike; Nader, Ralph
punk rock. *See* anarchism, kinds of: anarcho-punk

"race to the bottom" view, 100, 139, 140
racism, 5, 6, 8, 204; and stereotypes, Indigenous Mexican, 92; and US empire as secondary, 99, 112
RAN (Rainforest Action Network), 123, 124, 125. *See also* Hayes, Randy
Ramírez López, Heladio, 89
Ramnath, Maia, 188
Rainforest Action Network. *See* RAN
Reagan, Ronald, 51, 52, 63
"recalcitrant democrats," 75, 85, 86
Red de Genero y Economia. *See* REDGE
REDGE (*Red de Genero y Economia*), 167, 191
Reform Party. *See* Perot, Ross
Regino, Adelfo, 84. *See also* SER–Mixe
repression. *See* Indigenous communities Mexico: repression against

resource extraction, 87, 181
Robles, Sofía, 83. *See also* SER-Mixe
Roman, Nancy, 39, 40, 45, 224n35. *See also* UNORCA
Romero, Martha, 40, 41, 47. *See also* UNORCA
Rural Sustainable Development Law, 46. *See also* Meneses, Luis; UNORCA
Ruta 100, 192

SAGAR (*Secretaría de Agricultura, Ganadería y Desarrollo Rural*—Ministry of Agriculture, Livestock, and Rural Development), 160
Salinas de Gotarí, Carlos, 25, 32, 34, 37, 38, 47, 48, 276n50
Samuel, Howard, 63, 65
San Andrés Accords, 95
Santos, Victoria, 166, 169, 170, 172–74. *See also* UNORCA; Cancún WTO protests
SCLC (Southern Christian Leadership Conference), 51, 66
Scott, Tyree, 129, 130. *See also* LELO
Seattle WTO protests: alliances between progressives and right wing, 98, 105, 112; whiteness, 4–7, 10, 98, 106, 111, 114, 130–131. *See also* Buchanan, Pat; Domingo, Cindy; Martínez, Elizabeth "Betita"; IFG
SEIU (Service Employees International Union), 66, 68
self-determination. *See* Indigenous autonomy
SER–Mixe (*SERvicios del Pueblo Mixe*), 83–85, 87, 89, 183, 185
Service Employees International Union. *See* SEIU
SERvicios del Pueblo Mixe (Services of the Mixe People). *See* SER–Mixe
sexism: rural Mexican, 38, 39; in social movements, 32, 40, 42, 45; in US unions, 60
Shiva, Vandana, 121, 161
Sierra Club: "color blind" approach, 104, 119, 120; and immigration, 117, 118; tuna debates, 108; "Turtles," 98
Sistema Alimentaria Mexicana (Mexican Food System) SAM, 18
sistemas normativos internos, 180, 240n28
SNTE—Local 22, *Sindicato Nacional de Trabajadores de la Educación* (National Education Workers Union), 77, 182
solidarity, labor, 68, 178, 236n71
South Korea, 64, 173

South Korean farmers, 156, 157, 205
Southern Christian Leadership Conference (SCLC), 51, 66
"Southern Strategy," Republicans, 54
social landownership. See *ejido(s)*
Staley lock out, 69
Steelworkers. See United Steelworkers

Taiwan, 64, 136
Taller Universitario de Derechos Humanos (University Workshop on Human Rights) TUDH, 183
"Teamsters and Turtles," 2, 97, 98, 105, 116, 128, 135–40
Tennessee Lesbian and Gay Coalition (TLGC), 53, 60
tequio, 82, 187–89, 240n35
Texas State Employees Union (TSEU), 59
Tlatelolco Plaza massacre, 21
Tlaxcala conference, 31, 42, 43. See also UNORCA, *Vía Campesina*
transgenic corn. See GMOs
transfers of technology, 101, 109, 250n53
Trump, Donald, 1, 3, 102, 135, 201, 202, 204
Trumka, Richard, 62
tuna fishing industry, 108, 109

UAW (United Auto Workers), 59, 62
UCIZONI (*Unión de Comunidades Indígenas de la Zona Norte del Istmo*), 88
Unión de Comunidades Indígenas de la Zona Norte del Istmo (Union of Indigenous Communities in the Northern Zone of the Isthmus). See UCIZONI
Unión de Grupos Ambientalistas de México (Union of Environmental Groups in Mexico) UGAM, 109
Union of Forestry Ejidos of the Mayan Zone, 166
Unión Nacional de Trabajadores (National Union of Workers) UNT, 167
Unión de Organizaciones de la Sierra Juarez de Oaxaca. See UNOSJO
United Auto Workers. See UAW
United Food and Commercial Workers International Union (UFCW), 147
United Mine Workers of America (UMWA), 62, 68
United Paperworkers' International Union (UPIU), 65
United Steelworkers (USW), 110, 139
United Students against Sweatshops (USAS), 70, 146, 147

United We Stand America, 104
UNORCA: *ejidos*, 35–37; gender roles, 32, 42, 45; organizational structure, 35, 36; peasant self-determination, 43; Permanent Agrarian Council (CAP), 37; transnational corporations, 46, 47; Women's Area, 32, 38–42, 45; and Zapatistas, 163, 166
UNOSJO (*Unión de Organizaciones de la Sierra Juarez de Oaxaca*), 85, 87, 89, 95
USA Patriot Act, 155
usos y costumbres, 180, 240n28. See also *sistemas normativos internos*

Vía Campesina, 10, 27, 31, 42–46, 167. See also Tlaxcala meeting

Wallach, Lori, 138. See also Nader, Ralph
Waters, Cassie, 150–53. See also Jobs with Justice
West, Cornel, 59
"white nationalists." See white supremacist right wing
"white breadwinners," 52, 53, 69, 199. See also working class: white
white progressives and right-wing anti-globalization activists, 98, 112
white supremacist right wing, 59, 101
Winpisinger, William, 65. See Colt Firearms strike
working class, 68, 70, 102, 103, 117; class solidarity, 66, 68, 70; of color, 51, 114, 120; and defensive nationalism, 50, 61–63; Mexican, 73, 78, 90; white, 50, 52, 53, 58, 102, 103
World Bank, 56, 109, 137
World Food Organization (WFO), 42
World Social Forum, 155, 203
WTO Cancún 2003 ministerial and protest. See Cancún WTO
WTO Seattle 1999 ministerial and protest. See Seattle WTO protests

xenophobia, 51, 63, 64, 137, 204. See also anti-Asian racism and xenophobia

Zapatista National Liberation Army (EZLN). See Zapatistas
Zapatistas, 43, 73, 84, 85, 166; foreign supporters of, 94; and Indigenous autonomy, 79, 179; and Oaxaca, 179; People's Global Action network, 120; and UNORCA, 174
Zedillo, Ernesto, 81, 82, 87, 95

www.ingramcontent.com/pod-product-compliance
Lightning Source LLC
Chambersburg PA
CBHW021336230426
43666CB00006B/308